THE TOPICAL EXCERPT LIBRARY

CHRISTIANITY

CONSISTING OF

SERMONS, EDITORIALS, ADDRESSES, POEMS,

EXCERPTS FROM MANY SOURCES

WHAT THE GREAT THINKERS OF THIS ERA HAVE
THOUGHT AND SAID ON THIS SUBJECT

COMPILED BY

EUCLID B. ROGERS, D. D.

TWENTY VOLUMES

THE SPRINGFIELD LIBRARY PUBLISHING COMPANY
SPRINGFIELD, ILLINOIS

H. W. ROKKER CO.
PRINTERS, BINDERS AND STEREOTYPERS
SPRINGFIELD, ILLINOIS

COMPILER'S ACKNOWLEDGMENT

For twenty years the compiler has been engaged in the work of the Christian ministry. During that period he has been a constant reader of religious and secular papers, and in a persistent and systematic fashion has clipped and preserved the articles that appealed to him as of marked value. The sources of this compilation, known as "The Topical Excerpt Library"—are many and varied. Acknowledgment is made to The Observer, The Standard, The Congregationalist, The Christian Work and Evangelist, The Freeman, The Presbyterian, Christian World Pulpit, Advance, Commonwealth, Temple Review, Independent, Christian Evangelist, Watchman, Watchword, Epworth Herald, Examiner, Lutheran Observer, Sabbath Reading, Christian Advocate, The Christian, and many others, religious and secular, and it is to these original sources to which all credit for any worth that may attach to and any help that may come from this Library is due.

Special acknowledgment is made to The Brooklyn Daily Eagle and The Outlook for permission to use copyrighted articles.

CHRISTIANITY TRIUMPHANT

I do not respect any proposition merely because it is ancient, or in the mouths of majorities. But I do respect propositions that have seen honest and protracted battle, but not defeat. The test of the soundness of scholarship is that it should contend with scholarship, not once or twice, but century after century, and come out crowned. But the intellectual supremacy of Christianity in the nineteenth century is not a novelty. There are other battle-fields worth visiting by those who walk and meditate, on which Christian trophies stand, more important as marks of the world's agonies and advances than any that ever Greek erected for victory at Salamis or Marathon. I lean on Church history. I go to its battle-fields and lie down on them. They are places of spiritual rest. Gazing on their horizon, I see no narrow prospect, but a breadth of nineteen hundred victorious years. Looking into the sky as I lie there, I hear, sometimes, the anthem: "As it was in the beginning, is now, and ever shall be, world without end." I obtain glimpses of a heaven opened; and behold a white horse, and He that sits on him is called the Word of God, King of kings and Lord of lords. He is clothed in a vesture dipped in blood; but His eyes are as a flame of fire, and on His head are many crowns.—Joseph Cook.

CHRIST'S IDEA OF CHRISTIANITY

BY HENRY WARD BEECHER

"The kingdom of heaven is like a seed; like a mustard seed."—Mark 4:26-33. "It is like leaven."—Mark 13:33-34.

All three parables are vegetable, represent the vegetable kingdom; and they all three illustrate the minuteness of the beginning, the regular stages of the progress, and the reality of the development, though it is not perceptible at first by our ordinary senses. These are the three illustrations that our Savior employs to represent the entrance, progress, and final development of men in the kingdom of God, or the kingdom of heaven—that is to say, in their own religious or moral experience. When you divest it of the parabolical form, and also of the theological and propositional forms through which, in days gone by, it has been trammeled, and come to it as a matter of ordinary experience, it is this, that when a man undertakes to live a Christian life he may begin at the very smallest point, but he has got to go through a regular unfolding, and that regular unfolding at last will bring forth abundant results.

The result, then, of this is, first, that the kingdom of God, or the beginning of a truly religious life in the soul of a man, may be obscure, imperceptible and unconscious. When a man is building a house he can see it as it goes on. That is an outside matter. There is seam after seam, row after row of stone or brick. Gradually the form of the window or the door rises. The second story, the third story, the building up to the roof appears. He can see it day by day. A man goes into his garden and plants, for spring, the early lettuce, or radish, or whatever it may be. He may sit up all night with spectacles and a lantern, but he will not see anything going on; and yet there is something going on which is vitally connected with the whole operation of vegetable development. The seed has not been in the ground an hour before it feels its outward husk swelling by imbibing moisture. It has not been for ten hours in the warm soil before it begins to feel that the material in the seed itself

—1C

is chemically affected, changed. Many a seed has not been twenty-four hours in the ground before there is an impulse in it at one end to thrust down a root, and at the other end to thrust up a plumule or the beginning of a visible stalk; but it makes no noise. It is like Solomon's temple: it is a structure that is built without the sound of a hammer; and whatever it may come to, all the earlier processes of germination and development are invisible and are silent; for if you take it out into the light it will not grow. The seed needs warmth, moisture and luminous darkness—that is to say, considerable darkness, and yet a little invisible light. So it is with the spiritual life.

Then next, the unfolding is gradual in all three of these types that our Savior has given us, as over against the idea of instantaneous conversion, carrying with it a perfected soul, which is directly opposed both to experience and to the teaching of the Savior. The work of God in the human soul is gradual. Thirdly, the work of religion in the human soul is not scattering, accidental, promiscuous, just as it may happen. It has its regular stages, and one will not precede the others except in the order of those stages. First the blade, then the ear, then the kernel in the ear; and you cannot make one of them anticipate the others so that they will not follow in that sequence.

So, although it may be more difficult to observe and register the obscure and not well known stages of development, still, rising out from its conditions of the flesh and working up towards the life in the spirit, it goes through a regular graduation—must, does, always will—though it may not seem to; for as the dough is leavened by the yeast, and no sound is made, no murmuring is heard within, and no sign of swelling is visible without, and it is untraceable, since it is lost, mixed in the flour, so it is in regard to experiences, to hopes and to changes in the human soul.

With this brief analysis, let us proceed to practical cases. First, very much advance is made towards, and, if I might so say, into, the kingdom of heaven, long before it comes to sight, or to one's own consciousness. Men are really entering the kingdom of God, while they suppose themselves to be in the gall of bitterness, and in the bond of iniquity. They are not in the church; they do not participate in any outward exercises of religion; they are not regarded by their friends, by their minister, nor by anybody else, as being real Christians; but the work of Christ in their hearts, the fermentation, is divinely going on, and the stages are distinctly marked, or becoming so.

Thus, when you take a seed, its first germinating is in the dark, out of sight. But in regard to seeds, when they have come to their outward and external forms, they seem to stand still, often a great while, until the root-work is done in them.

Some ten or fifteen years ago, I bought a hundred hickory plants. I put them out in my nursery, and I kept them there three or four years, when it was necessary to take them up for the purpose of using that space for other things. They had not increased at the top, in five years, more than a single inch; they had hardly, I thought, held their own; they were very small. When they had been in my possession perhaps seven or eight years, they were distributed in the place where they were to go. Roots longer than my arm had formed; but the top had grown only a trifle. They seemed to me to have been cast away, and I would have been willing to give the whole of them to anybody who would have taken them. But during all that time they had been going down, down, down; for the hickory always has a tap-root that seeks the center of the earth.

Now as it is in the vegetable kingdom, so it often is in the case of men. All home education that is effectual is a remote preparation for the kingdom of heaven. All ordinary restraints which parents lay upon the passions of their children, upon their appetites, upon their greedy selfishness, all things that tend to ripen them, to shape them, and to bring them away from mere animal tendencies, and give them some degree of kindness, of affection and of regulative life—all these are preliminary stages. They are yeast. They are working. All right knowledge of the truth is an element of the kingdom of heaven in the soul. All conformity to the best things in society morals is also a formative element. The cultivation of sweet dispositions, even if it has not been a conscious election of the highest life, if in part it is ministered to by example, if in part by sympathy, and if in part by the love of praise, is good. The thing itself is good, no matter what watered it. The conformity to sweet dispositions is a direct contribution in a man to the kingdom of God.

These preliminary stages and states are to the Christ-life in the soul very much what the earlier processes of education are to the academic life, to the university life, or to the culture of the philosopher and scholar in his mature years. A child who can only just say its alphabet, certainly is not very literary; and the spelling stage does not foretell for him very great eminence as poet, or orator, or historian; nor does that stage where he can read and understand without spelling; yet every one of those stages is actually part and parcel of that final development which gives a man his reputation as a scholar, although they are humble and very remote root-work.

In every Christian household there is a great deal of root-work going on. If it stops there it is just like the stopping of the plant when the root is beginning to grow. If you cut the top off even with the ground, what is the root worth? Not much of anything now, but it may be worth a great deal by-and-by. It is the indispensable pre-requisite to that plant if it is to be allowed to attain its full growth. Morality is good in every part, but it is not all that you are after. A foundation for a house is good, but if you stop, and do not build on it, what is it good for? It is good for what it foretells. And I suppose the sprout of a seed is good; but how long, if you stop it in the sprout state, will it be before you can get any peaches off from it? Its value is in that which it prophesies, and which you hope. So every form of self-control, whether it be through the law or the family, through a sympathetic bias, through the example of society, or through any other influence whatsoever; anything that tends to inspire a man, to restrain the flesh, to develop the intelligence and to quicken the moral sensibilities, is preliminary work; and it ought to be understood as such. But when you make a discrimination, and say, "This side of that line you are children of the devil, and the other side of that line you are children of God," you convey a great error. You do not find it so in the New Testament. It is not in the spirit and genius of the New Testament to make such distinctions as that. As a substitute for later stages, the preliminary growth is not good for anything; but as a pre-requisite condition, it is good for a great deal.

More than that, conversion is often an imperceptible condition. That is, when a man is converted in the old-fashioned understanding of that word, when he has passed from death to life, when the balance is struck, and it is for purity, for holiness, for obedience to God, for love, he may not know it. There are, I suppose, thousands of persons who are converted, but who don't know it. There are a great many in this congregation who are converted, but who sit here Sabbath after Sabbath wondering whether they ever will be Christians. You are Christians, but you do not recognize your own conditions; for conversion is a voluntary and conscious acceptance of the life, purposes and disposition of Christ. We come to it by imperceptible stages, but we may not recognize when the stages cease. You may have a right to call yourself Christians.

Now let us look at the way in which men come to other things. A man of general education, very fond of the law, reads a book on constitutional law, reads something about practice, and it is his amusement; it is his sense of enrichment of thought. He goes on from one thing to another. He is a merchant, but by-and-by he finds that his merchandise is not profitable; or, it withers to such a degree that he wants to get out of it. He says to himself: "Well, now, I do think I love the law. I will be a lawyer." He is now converted. He is a lawyer. Why? Not merely because he has passed that wall, but because his studies, all the way up, have carried him so far that, if necessary, he could practice, in a common case before a justice of the peace. Even that would make him a lawyer. He has got to get a license; but a license does not make a lawyer. If it did we should often have a great deal better class of lawyers than we do. A license is a mere external requisite of procedure for the protection of the community. There are a multitude of men who know more about commercial law, being merchants, than the judge who sits on the bench, before whom their cases are to come. They are not lawyers in fact, but they have the substance of being a lawyer in them although they have not yet made themselves lawyers.

I knew a young man in Boston, whose father was rich. He had genius particularly in the formative, sculptural art; and his amusement was in making busts and little clay statues. One lucky day the father lost all his property, and the young man was thrown out of business and had to work for his own livelihood. He had already made the busts of friends; and when the motives to indolence were taken away from him, when the golden chair was broken, and he had to get up and go to work, he said to himself, ''What can I do for a living better than this?'' Well, he has come to the artist state already, unconsciously, not expecting to be a professional artist; simply following his taste; but the moment he puts out his sign, showing that he would like to have custom for the sake of self-support, then everybody says, ''He has become an artist.'' He has been an artist a good while; but it is just being developed before the public. The roots of the thing were in him long ago.

It is the same way in regard to statesmen. There are ever so many statesmen who do not go to congress, and ever so many men go there who are not statesmen. Going there does not make a man anything. I know some old New England clergymen, situated in humble parishes, who are never much known except for their prudent counsels in the neighboring churches, who are unheard of outside of their own little county, who read everything, who study the character of every public man and the merit of every great measure that is introduced into the national legislature, and make up their mind about it; and who read the history of like things in other countries.

Where will you find a statesman in public life, or out of it, who was the peer of Dr. Leonard Bacon, of New Haven, who has lately gone from among us? He was one of the noblest of ministers, and also an undeveloped statesman. If he had been elected to congress (as it was proposed to do at one time in the legislature of Connecticut), everybody would have said, ''He is a statesman; he is a senator;'' but he was a senator and a statesman before, only it had not come out and shown itself professionally and avowedly.

Now, there are persons who are brought up in the knowledge of the Lord Jesus Christ, and who are, step by step, brought to the love of Jesus, who would come out strongly if they thought they had any right to do it. There is a style of theology that tells a man, ''You cannot pray until you know how,'' which is like telling a boy, ''You must not swim until you know how to swim.'' It says: ''God abhors the prayer of the wicked; men lost in the fall of Adam all power of will to do anything right; you are not converted, and what are you praying for?'' Sure enough, if that theology is true, a man has got to stand like a toad-stool and wait until something is done to him and for him. He cannot pray under such circumstances. There are multitudes of persons who love the Lord Jesus Christ, but who would not own it, because they have had an idea that this is the technical experience of folks inside the church, or folks that have gone through the peculiar mechanism of an artificially-conceived theological conversion.

They do love Christ, though not with the largeness and liberty that is their privilege. There are multitudes of persons who are living in that charity which is the true test of Christian life; there are multitudes of persons who are living with self-denial, and who are dedicating their life to God, in the service of their fellow-men; there are multitudes of persons who feel the warmth of waves of gratitude to God; and sometimes they cannot relieve the feelings of their heart without giving way to prayer, and even ejaculatory prayer as they walk in the fields and highways; and they are very excellent people. ''I wish they would take a step or two further,'' say men, ''and be converted.'' Bless your heart! they are converted, and are in the kingdom of God! They have not made it apparent; they have not got their licenses to be lawyers; they have not proclaimed themselves artists; but the preliminary stages which qualify them to take a license, or to set up as artists have been performed in them, only they have not had the experience, they think.

You bring a person up in Christian nurture, and in the admonition of the Lord, in the household, and he is gaining more light; he is adapting the light which he has; and he comes into that state of mind in which all he wants in order to realize that he is a Christian is to wake up into consciousness. There are multitudes of men in this house who if they were converted today in a revival of religion, would not be any more Christians than they are now. It is the purpose of their life to live for God and benevolence; but they have had no dramatic action. They have had none of those cataclysms that other men have had, and that are so pleasant for them to talk about afterwards.

Unconscious piety, therefore, is simply this: the being trained from your cradle by your surrounding circumstances into those very moods, and into that very purpose of life which conversion means. It is being inwardly changed, away from animal life toward spiritual life; away from the law óf selfishness toward the law of a true love. The moment a man can have the testimony of himself that that is his purpose, though not his attainment, then he is converted, though he may not know it.

Multitudes of persons are attempting, almost unknown to themselves, to live after the law of the Lord Jesus Christ. They are just like plants. I have accidentally thrown down a plank on a flower-bed; there it has lain for a week; and when I came to lift it up, seeds had come up under it. One had wiggled laterally, and worked its way clear to the edge, to get life, and light, and liberty to grow. I have seen just such Christians, when they got out into the light. They had been growing under incumbrances that made them irregular, crooked, distorted. They might have grown up if you had taken that plank off. I have seen plants come up with a heavy clod, stronger than the seed could turn over. It lifts it up just a little, as though to cry, "Help, help, gardener!" The gardener comes, and with his finger throws the clod off; and up comes the seed after that. It had sprouted already in order to get up to the light, only there was something on it, and it could not help itself.

Multitudes of persons come to their minister and say, "I want you to tell me how to be a Christian." That coming settles the thing. It breaks the unconsciousness. Multitudes of men want to unite with the church; they want to be Christians; they want the Christian life; but they say, "O, those vows; how can I undertake to say that I have a right?" Take them by the arm; bring them into the church, according to the proper methods of church life; and the moment they have joined it by persuasion, by sympathy, by bias, by influence, they feel the difference; and they say, "Why, I am happier! and yet it is something of the same thing that I have been feeling for a good while, only I was under an influence that would not let me take this converted, outwardly-visible step." A little thing, when it comes to the point of departure, will bring a man out of the obscure and the unconscious into the developed and conscious state; for the work is already done, substantially, and the man begins to move off at once in the Christian life.

Then there is more than this. If a man comes into the Christian life from a state of relative unconsciousness of his condition, he will not blaze. Whether or not men come consciously into the state of conversion they will not necessarily blaze. The light that shines brighter and brighter unto the perfect day is rising. There are a great many persons of such a tumultuous temperament that, whichever way they go, in business, pleasure, or anything else, when they go they rush. They never walk. They fly or run. Men, from an enthusiastic mercantile life, from an enthusiastic mechanical life, from enthusiastic circumnavigation as an enterprising man, around the globe, or from an enthusiastic political life, from any ordinary good life, come into an avowed Christian life; and their whole nature is such that if they go at all, they pour out.

When the dew comes down it always comes like dew; and when the gentle rains come they all come like gentle rains; and when tornadoes come they rush and roar, dashing headlong, tempestuous with sheets and oceans of water. That is, in fact, like some men. They never do anything moderately. When a man like that turns and says, "I have been a wicked man; I know it, and I am going to cut the whole thing short and come into the service of the Lord," his being, his imagination, his whole impetuous nature goes in that way. That is his way, and he acts according to his genius and his nature. But another man comes in, a timid, cautious and very conscientious man, and says, "You persuaded me, my dear friend, to come into the church, but I don't see that I am very much different from what I was before I was in the church." He is the same unspeaking, thoughtful, quiet man, and he says, "I have often thought, my dear pastor, that I made a mistake. I don't see that I have the signs and evidences that other men have."

When a man comes into a converted, disclosed religious life, he is going through every one of the Christian graces; he undergoes that same process of development and unfolding which they require. He begins to unfold in the direction of humility. No man ever jumped from the top of pride down to the bottom of humility at one jump, and never will. The change goes on by natural successive stages, one, and another, and another. No man ever came at once from a state of relative indifference to his fellow-men into a state of sensitive perception of their wants and necessities. He unfolds little by little, little by little. If a man has had a preliminary education, he unfolds much more rapidly; but if he has not, then he unfolds slowly.

That is not all. Men unfold according to their nature—a man of a phlegmatic temperment eats slowly, drinks slowly, walks slowly, works slowly, sleeps slowly; and his graces will grow slowly, too. The uniformity and the analogy are carried right through. If a man be lively, quick and nervous, the analogy will run in his religion just as it does in everything else. But still the principle is, first the blade, then the ear, and then the ripe kernel in the ear.

So you will find every conceivable degree in the church. Men are not like plates, in sets. If a plate is broken, you go back to Ovington's and ask him for a plate of this pattern; and it will not do to give you a plate of any other pattern. You have got to have one just like the others, in order to make up the set. Thus people think that Christians are made in sets, and that this Christian doesn't match with the rest in the church. "He has got a different pattern on him," they say. No! no! men are not earthenware or hardware. They are creatures of every conceivable difference—different in genius; different in body; different in appetites; different in proportion of reason, of emotion, of sensibility, or of settled judgment; different in imagination; different in tenderness; different in scope, in rapidity; and every man is converted after his own way and kind. Every flower has its own nature, and grows according to it. Some flowers spread wide on the ground, and blossom; some lift themselves six or seven inches up, and blossom; some climb high, and blossom. I have seen plants like women —beautiful, but held up by a dry stick, around which they have twined. In men, in outward life, there are just as many combinations and variations as you can make permutations in figures or in letters. The glory of Christ's garden is its variety; and that variety runs through moods of quickness or slowness of development. The development is first here, or first there, in all the endless combinations.

"Receive ye one another," saith the Apostle. This man has these gifts; this man that genius, or that method. They are all of grace. It is the one Spirit that worketh all things, and in all. That man may not be a Christian like you, thank God; or he may be, thank God, as the case may be; but a man is to know that whatever he is, he is to bring himself just as he is into the service of the Lord, and under the great law of refusing selfishness. When they begin the Christ-life, some men begin it impetuously, but before they get through they find they have to go stage by stage, stage by stage, until it comes finally to solemn, sober, steady growth and maturity. Another man will come step by step, little by little. The unfolding process goes on with reference to each particular Christian, and goes on with reference to the complex harmony of the whole Christian life and character.

I have made this sermon, not only as unfolding the right way in which a man shall come into the true Christian life, encouraging men to begin, and asking them to join the school of Christ, and to learn of Him, that they may have peace and joy in believing, but also because I think there are multitudes of persons out of the church who belong in it.

Where persons have by the experiences of home education, by the experiences of the providences that have been dealing with them, and by their own reading and meditation, been brought to see the beauty of Christ's nature, to see that His way of life is the right way, and been brought into a desire and into a purpose to live in that way, not as being perfect in it, but simply as having that life planted in them, like a seed waiting to grow under the most favorable circumstances, and to develope—I say all such persons ought to come within the walls of the church, for their own sake; or, if not for their own sake, then for the sake of the church, and for the sake of those outside who follow their example, but are not perhaps as strong as they are.

A man living a Christian life outside of the church is like one of those little patches of cultivation that I see outside of gardens. A plain Irish laborer takes up a little bit of land in the neighborhood where he had his first jobs and where the railway permitted him to plant his little patches of potatoes outside. All the cattle that range in the neighborhood have access to it if they please; he has to defend it in every way. And if it be something besides potatoes—if it be strawberries, he will have more help in picking the strawberries than he will want. Every boy and every neighbor that passes by will wish him good will, and then pluck. When a man is trying to live Christ-like outside the walls of the church, men do not know that he is trying to do it. They think they have a right to pull him this way and to push him that, to tempt him here and to tempt him there; but when they know that he has gone into the school of Christ, they do not want him to play the truant. It does help a man; and, moreover, it is unquestionably in consonance with the wishes of the Lord Jesus Christ that His followers and disciples should dwell together, giving each other all sympathy, and all relative mutual help. Men ought to go into the church of Christ because Christ wants it; because they are better off there; because they are more likely to grow.

CHRISTIANITY TRIUMPHANT

I do not respect any proposition merely because it is ancient, or in the mouths of majorities. But I do respect propositions that have seen honest and protracted battle, but not defeat. The test of the soundness of scholarship is that it should contend with scholarship, not once or twice, but century after century, and come out crowned. But the intellectual supremacy of Christianity in the nineteenth century is not a novelty. There are other battlefields worth visiting by those who walk and meditate, on which Christian trophies stand, more important as marks of the world's agonies and advances, than any that ever Greek erected for victory at Salamis or Marathon. I lean on Church history. I go to its battle-fields and lie down on them. They are places of spiritual rest. Gazing on their horizon, I see no narrow prospect, but a breadth of nineteen hundred victorious years. Looking into the sky as I lie there, I hear, sometimes, the anthem: "As it was in the beginning, is now, and ever shall be, world without end." I obtain glimpses of a heaven opened; and behold a white horse, and He that sits on him is called the Word of God, King of kings and Lord of lords. He is clothed in a vesture dipped in blood; but His eyes are as a flame of fire, and on His head are many crowns.—Joseph Cook.

IS CHRISTIANITY A FAILURE?

BY THE REV. A. F. WINNINGTON-INGRAM, D.D., BISHOP OF LONDON

When I look over this vast city and ask myself what would lead one to conclude that Christianity is a failure, I think I should mention many points like these. Why is it that the labor members, apparently unanimously, in the House of Commons agree to have no religion taught in our schools? I can imagine someone saying, "Is it a fact that, at the end of 1,900 years, this represents the opinion of the working classes of a great so-called Christian country?" That would be the first thing I should name. Then I should point to the great dearth (I will make out the black case first, and then say something against it)—the great dearth there is in all denominations, not only in the Church of England, of a supply of ministers. I suppose if I were to ask any denomination whether there was ever such a lack of ministers as there is today, the reply would be "Never." And people might argue from the fact of this reluctance of young men to live the hard life of a clergyman—a clergyman's life in a poor parish is a hard one and their preference for other and more pleasant duties, proves that religion is a failure in a country where this is the case. Or, again, I might take the argument I have heard over and over again at open-air meetings in Victoria Park and elsewhere about the still existent prevalence of crime and sin in London. "What," it may be said, "has Christianity been at work 1900 years and yet these evils exist! Look at the state of our streets, look at the public houses crowded even on Sunday." I wish they were closed on that day and opened for a less time during the week. "Is this all your Christianity has done?" it may be asked. "Look at the drinking, gambling, immorality and impurity that goes on and is considered sometimes a disgrace by visitors from our distant Colonies, who come to see what the heart of the Empire is, the Empire to which they belong." Or take the mission field. I heard last Sunday one of the most heart-rending stories from the mission field to which I have ever listened. This was at Oxford, where I was presiding over a missionary meeting attended by 500 undergraduates. A missionary from Central Africa pointed out that because he had been left with so few workers, room and opportunity had been left for the erection of a Mohammedan mosque close by the little chapel he had begged the money to build, and had built stone by stone. The crescent was supplanting the cross. This he witnessed with his own eyes. It had come about because this gallant soldier of the cross had been left unsupported in the mission field. And it might be argued that if there is such a slackness about Christianity at home as to leave a man like that despairing over his work in Central Africa, then your Christianity cannot be either good or strong. It could not be strong, as a soldier speaking on the platform, when the Christian depot had thus to surrender. Then people might point, as a reproach to Christianity, to the abject and dire poverty and inequality which existed side by side in London with extreme riches. Taking what may be said on the side of the alleged failure of Christianity, repeating the arguments I have heard set forth with earnestness on secular platforms, we may be bidden to "look at the bitterness which obtains amongst Christians. See a number of Christian bodies at variance with one another, disputing different points often with acrimony, instead of one united, happy, and harmonious Church which Jesus Christ meant, and for which He prayed with His last breath." "And," I have heard it said in the open-air meeting, "when you Christians have agreed as to what you believe, then we will join your number." Lastly, the existence of war might be pointed to after all these centuries of the preaching of the gospel of peace. In spite of the nations of Europe being professedly Christian, they are nearly all armed to the teeth and ready for war, watching each other eagerly lest their neighbor should spring on them. "Can you say," it may be asked, "that your gospel of peace has been a success when this is the case?" Well, I always believe in facing a thing. I don't think there is any good in living in a fool's paradise and pretending that these things are not said about religion. I will now proceed to show you, I hope, that it is the greatest fallacy ever put forth to assert that Christianity is a failure. Let us take the labor party and their resolution to have no religion in the schools. Does that mean that the working classes are un-Christian? Why, my brothers, I have lived amongst them as my constant companions for nine years. I have mixed daily with the working people of East London, and I have heard things said by them against the Church of England

and Nonconformist bodies over and over again, but I have never, except once, heard a word said against Jesus Christ Himself. I believe that by men who never enter a church or chapel there is a reverence for Jesus Christ Himself that is one of the most beautiful hopes of the future. Even in the Socialistic proposals before us, many of which I believe in my heart of hearts are impracticable and would not work, I see the love of Jesus Christ, honor to Him, a desire to be like Him, a feeling that the world today is not conducted on Christian principles. Then as to the dearth of clergymen, let me tell you what I saw at Oxford last Sunday. I preached at St. Matthew's, Oxford, and there were 1,500 undergraduates in the church—1,200 sitting down and 300 standing up. There was not one single sound during the forty minutes I spoke to them, save the sound of my own voice—a most responsive congregation, from many of whom I afterwards received letters. After service at St. Matthew's, 500 of the congregation came to Christ Church Great Hall, where I spoke. I thought they would have enough of me on Sunday, but on Monday night 500 of the undergraduates came again to hear my talk on Christianity. When I left Oxford I said to myself, ''With such a true and deep quickening of spiritual life as I have seen, there is not going to be for many more years an inadequate supply of men for holy orders.'' It was just the same at Yale, in America—the Oxford of the United States. There were 2,000 students to hear me in the morning, and 500 at a voluntary service in the evening. There is amongst that class today an astonishing revival of interest in religion, drawing them towards Jesus Christ, and if we pray and watch you will see from those cultured young men before long a remarkable outcome of ministers of Jesus Christ. What I want to say is this, however. I do not want the ministers of the gospel in our church all drawn from one class. I believe that every man who has got a vocation for holy orders ought to have the way opened to him to become a minister of the gospel of Jesus Christ. In the Church of England her ministers have been drawn too much from one class in the years gone past. My parish priests look round their churches, and if they find among the young men of their congregation those who seem to be really called of God to the ministry, they are told to bring those young men to a council of parish priests and laymen, who select the men they deem fit to be ordained. When I see them and approve them I gather together ten names and, advertising their initials in the public press, I solicit money for their education and training for the ministry, and on every occasion within a week I have had enough money sent me for the purpose. I am encouraged by the feeling that attracted that response.

If Christianity today is a failure, whose fault is it? It is not the fault of Christianity or of Christ. It is the fault of our response to Christ, and we ought to take these criticisms home and say, "Please God, we will roll away that reproach." When the need of the misison field was put before 500 men at Oxford, when volunteers were asked for to go and labor at great personal risk in Central Africa (for two men have died annually since the mission was started fifty years ago), five men offered themselves the next morning.

During our discussions at Bethnalgreen, when it was contended that Christianity was a failure, I remember that one speaker, a working man, got up and said, "I believe myself when I see what human nature is, that Christianity has had the most wonderful success in the world, because the other speakers forget that there is a different set every year, a fresh generation to deal with. It is not the same body of men that Christianity has had to influence for 1900 years, but different sets of men, a new set always springing up. Christianity had to take each generation in hand as it arose, as it took us in hand when we were boys." It is like a schoolmaster with a new set of pupils. You don't pass on characters. It is one of the truths of science that character is not hereditary. The care and teaching has to be commenced afresh with each new generation. When you think what that means and consider the lusts of the flesh and the passions of men, you will regard Christianity as the one success of the world.

As to the poverty and inequality there is in the world, let me say that personally I am perfectly convinced of this: that we must all work towards the equality of opportunity for every son of God in the world; that it is bad and it is wrong, both for the rich and the poor, that there should be this great distinction between the extremely rich and the extremely poor; but I ask this: Who made us find it out? Who is it that has brought the contrast so strongly before us that we cannot help seeing it? What is the secret of the good work done in the foundation of hospitals? Who is behind all the outpouring of the generosity of today? I say, without hesitation, Jesus Christ is. You can trace the progress of Christianity through all Europe by the hospitals you see there, of which for a thousand years the governor was the Bishop of the diocese, because he was the leader of Christianity.

Why is it we feel so acutely today that there are some poor fellows who have no chance in life? It is Christ who taught us that. They used to let the sick slaves die on an island in Rome. In making our land godly our only hope of doing it lies in more Christianity and not less. I have just come from a mission in Canada, and I can only say that from end to end I was received with the most loving welcome by every single denomination on the other side of the Atlantic. I did not detect a single jarring note.

I am determined, God helping me, to have that spirit over here. You cannot, of course, water down your convictions. I am not going to stand up and stultify myself by saying I don't believe in the sacraments, in the creeds, and in the church prayers and I don't believe in the church orders. I should despise myself if I did so, and every Nonconformist would also despise me if I did, because he ought to honor me for standing by the doctrines I hold; but that does not at all prevent me from honoring him in carrying out his work on the lines in which he believes, and there is no reason whatever why we should not do our best for our common faith in sympathy and brotherly love to one another. And we ought to pray that the unity of the Spirit in the bond of peace may be the gift of the Spirit which we have received immediately from Christ.

Then, take war. Well, the existence of war and the possibility of war today is a stain, a stigma upon our Christianity; but, at the same time, we must not be too pessimistic, we must be perfectly fair to all the leading men in Europe today. The Emperor of Russia, the German Emperor, our own King, and on the other side of the Atlantic, President Roosevelt, are all passionately attached to peace, all longing for peace, all desirous of securing peace for the world. I am convinced of that. If that is the case it is owing to Christianity. There would not be a chance of that if Christianity had not been preached and lived for these eighteen hundred years. Go to any unconverted part of Africa, and what do you find? Tribes at war who mean to be at war and

—2C

have no idea of peace. You may have read descriptions of the horrible warfare and bloodshed that prevail among the unconverted heathen, and yet, forsooth, we are asked by some to leave the tribes in their primitive condition unreached by the gospel. I believe that Christianity today is the one success in the world.

Now, I had a friend named Mrs. Bishop, and she was a great traveler. She had traveled in nearly every part of the known world. She was very much consulted by the late Lord Salisbury about matters pertaining to foreign lands. She was prejudiced— she told me herself—against missions, and used to ride twenty miles round to avoid a mission station. How did she end her life? She ended her life by eight years of preaching and speaking from place to place about the Christian faith, which she came to regard as the only hope for the world. I asked her, "What converted you to take such a different line when young and old?" She replied, "Because I have lived in every part of the world, and in every country which has not the Christian faith I find absolute hopelessness and disorder." She was converted by her knowledge of the world to feel that in the Christian faith, adequately conceived and received and lived up to, was the only hope of the world. On the other side of the Atlantic I conversed with the Russian consuls and the Japanese consuls, with the leading men in the United States and with the Governor General of Canada, and what is their hope for every great nation? Their hope is to make them more Christian, to get Christianity more and more into the business life. As I told the business men of Wall street, New York, "stewardship, and not ownership, is the keynote to possessions." I urged them to be more Christian in their transactions, not to take advantage of others. This in London, as well as in New York, afforded the only hope of making a nation happier, more stable, and more useful in the world.

What are you; what is going to be your hope when you come to die? You have got to die. You know your time here is very limited. Now, what is your hope? I tell you frankly I have only one. My hope is in Jesus Christ. I believe myself that He came down from heaven to earth to break down some barrier—how I cannot understand or explain—that I may have forgiveness and acceptance, that I may feel He has taken away my sins by His death and given me the possibility of life because He has redeemed me and saved me in the bright home with God. I should not have known there was such a place if He had not come down from heaven and said, "In My Father's house are many mansions." And if He had not risen again and ascended, I should not have known there was another and a better world at all. Therefore, I say Christ is the one hope for the salvation of my soul and for the life after death. I am here today fighting with my temptations, as you are fighting with yours. I suppose you have a great temptation, you young men, with all your passions strong on you, to let your passions break away and to fling the reins on the neck of your lusts. What is your hope? I tell you thousands have felt your temptations and have overcome them. They have said, "Jesus, help me," and He has helped them over and over again. When millions like yourselves have invoked His help and found it, they cannot be all wrong. They tried Christianity and found it was the one success; in their personal soul they found that Christ helped them. He can break down all evil habit and give you strength to resist temptation. Then I say to you, if all this is true, brothers, what are you going to do today? You have to take your choice between three things: either sitting on the fence and not making up your minds one way or another, which hundreds of our brother men are doing; and I say that in a case like this, "He that is not with Me is against Me." Instead of sitting on the fence and trying to make up your minds as to what Christianity is, God is expecting you to come forth and do some work on earth. There is a battle to fight during your sojourn on earth. Pray every day and work every day. Instead of sitting on the fence wondering whether Christianity is a failure, go and make it a success. When I think over what Christianity really means, discussion about a good man named Jesus Christ Who died on a cross has nothing to say to me at all. There have been plenty of good men who have died for causes in which they believed. But if I believe, as I do with all my soul, that the Spirit of God Himself came down and poured out His life for my salvation, then the old hymn does not exaggerate at all which declares that:

Love so amazing, so divine,
Demands my love, my life, my all.
—Christian World Pulpit.

ART THOU ROCK?

BY THE REV. CHARLES E. JEFFERSON, D.D.

To those who know best the problems of our cities it is becoming increasingly apparent that if the cities of our republic are to be won and held for Christ we must have a higher type of church member than the average Christian now in the field. And from this it must not be inferred that the average city Christian is a heathen man or a publican. He is neither so worldly nor so aristocratic nor so hypocritical as the rural caricaturist often represents him to be. Those who know him best know that he is a social, warm-hearted, honest, sensible man. The worst thing that can be said about him is that he is not strong enough to stand the strain of city life. He is not wicked, but limp. The city like a giant molds him to its will. It pushes the newspaper under his eyes on Sunday morning, and he is not strong enough of will to turn his eyes away. A friend drops in to see him Sunday evening, and he remains away from evening worship. There is a dinner on prayer meeting evening, and his seat is vacant at the prayer meeting.

The average city man is like the proverbial politician—in the hands of his friends. The friends of Christians are their most dangerous foes. It is surprising how sensitive many good people are to social obligations, and how indifferent they are to the obligations of their church. They are punctilious and scrupulous in keeping engagements in society and business, but they have no conscience whatever concerning the duties they owe to their church —and they are not bad people either. They are in many cases lovely people. They are generous, high-minded, chivalric and true, but when it comes to seeing what church membership involves they are near-sighted or blind.

The most sacred covenant any man on earth can make is that which a Christian makes with Christ's church, when he identifies himself with it, and yet people of spotless social reputation and a high sense of honor will trample on their church covenant without a twinge of compunction. They do not do it maliciously, but from weakness and lack of thought. They are caught in the swirl of city life and carried hither and thither by the swift-flowing currents, and before they are aware of it their church life is reduced to a precarious and desultory attendance on divine worship on bright Sunday mornings. Right there lies the secret of the failure of Christianity to master our cities. Church members, with numerous and beautiful exceptions, are not made of the stuff of which heroes are made. They abhor crucifixion. There is a painful lack of the grit which made the Puritans invincible.

We have fallen on easy times. Life is luxurious. Ours is an age of cushions and rose water. But there is arduous work to do. The trumpet has sounded, calling us to battle. Our cities are so many battle fields on which resolute and flint-willed men must wrestle in terrific struggle with the forces of the devil. We have a gospel equal to the world's needs. All we lack is men. Never will Christianity subdue our American cities until there is brought into the field an army of Christians of firmer texture and sterner temper than that possessed by the cohorts now engaged. Some plead for endowments, and others advocate a change of methods, but what we want is men. The members of our churches, as a rule, are altogether too flexible and obliging. They do not know how to strike hard, nor are they willing to stand their ground. There is a widespread fear of being counted narrow, but there is a narrowness which leads to life. "I have a baptism to be baptized with, and how am I straitened until it is accomplished?" So said the broadest man that ever lived. There is a dread of bigotry, but what is bigotry? If placing the kingdom of God first and compelling all things else to bend to it be bigotry, then what the world now needs is bigots. Bigotry is the persecution of others who do not agree with us. The steadfast and stubborn defense of those things which we deem of importance is sweet reasonableness and imperative duty. It is significant that the one thing which Christ first looked for in the men on whose shoulders He wished to roll the world was something which He designated as rock. As soon as a man whose temperament had in it ingredients capable of being fused into granite came under His eye, He gave him a new name— "Rock." Later on when the tides of the world were flowing away from Jesus, this man with the new name stood erect and declared that notwithstanding all learned men were saying one thing, and all the people another, he still was convinced that Jesus was the

Messiah, the Son of the living God. It was then that the Lord declared He would build His church on rock. It is the only rock which can withstand the assaults of the empire of death.

Our cities are crying for rock-Christians. Of gentle Christians and affable Christians and kind-hearted Christians we have abundance. The church today lacks the one quality for which the Lord looks and waits. City Christians should stand like rock amid the seas which surge and roar, and beneath whose billows with alarming frequency honored churches disappear. Like rock they should stand around the Lord's day, beating back the social and industrial forces which are rolling in like a flood. Nothing but rock will save New York and Chicago, Boston and San Francisco from the fate of Sodom and Gomorrah. Like rock church members should resist all invitations of saints and sinners which would lead them away from the duties and the meetings of their church. If Christians are unwilling to fight for the maintenance of Christian institutions and the progress of Christian ideals, who, pray, is going to save the world? The road to victory in these fair, well-spoken days is as of old, by way of the cross. Without sweat and blood and sacrifice and obedience unto death there is no redemption possible for us or our republic. The only Christians who can save our cities from their sins are Christians who have the heroic temper and the undaunted will of Him whom we love to call Rock of Ages.—Independent.

CERTAINTIES IN RELIGION

Are there any certainties in religion? The sectarian strifes in the Christian church have produced a not unreasonable impression that there are none. When, says the skeptic, Christians can agree among themselves as to what they believe, it will be time enough for me to consider the grounds and the value of their belief. But when the Congregational pastor proclaims on one corner as a saving truth what the Roman Catholic priest on the opposite corner denounces as a damnable heresy, when the Unitarian preacher scoffs at as intolerant bigotry dogmas which the Calvinist affirms as fundamental truth, when the Anglican Catholic emphasizes loyalty to a particular church and the Quaker proclaims undying hostility to all forms of ecclesiasticism, the common man has no choice but to shut the door on all this profitless wrangling and devote his attention to practical affairs concerning which something can be known.

There is some justification for this attitude of the skeptic. If the Christians really disbelieved, each the other's creed, the skeptic could hardly be condemned for doubting all of them. If the astronomical experts were evenly divided on the question whether the earth goes round the sun or the sun goes round the earth, non-experts might be excused from forming any definite opinion on the question, as they are now excused from attempting to decide whether the planet Mars is inhabited or not. But in fact there are certain fundamental religious truths on which all Christian believers, Protestant and Roman Catholic, Calvinist and Liberal, churchly and non-churchly, are agreed. They are some fundamental religious convictions which are as surely believed by all Christians as the attraction of gravitation is by all physicists. And into this common inheritance of truth the Christian church has entered by a progress which has been very slow and sometimes accompanied by long delays, but never by retrogression.

In the first century of the Christian era the great majority of mankind were both polytheists and idolaters; that is, they believed that different phenomena had different causes, and that the beings who caused these phenomena were finite beings like themselves, capable of being presented to the eye by symbols if not by actual portraits. Both these beliefs in a world as complex and contradictory as ours were quite natural. There was one peculiar people—the Hebrews—who denied both these assumptions, who affirmed that there was but one great Cause of all phenomena, that this Cause was an intelligent Being, who could only be spiritually interpreted through His likeness to the spirit of man, and that He was too great to be interpreted by either physical symbols or metaphysical definitions. There was no symbol of Him in their temples; there was no definition of Him in their religious books.

This faith in the unity and the indefinableness of God has rooted out the old polytheistic and idolatrous conceptions. The process has been very slow, but it has been very effective. In no Christian church is God represented by a symbol. In a few books of theology there is still some attempt to represent Him by a metaphysical definition, but these attempts are relegated to the schools of theology. That there is one infinite and eternal Creator and Ruler of the universe, not many conflicting rulers, and that He transcends alike all physical symbols and all metaphysical definitions, is the universal belief of the Christian world. It is equally Catholic and Protestant, Orthodox and Liberal, priestly and laic. If the skeptic is really ready to consider any articles of faith upon which all Christians are agreed, here is one article ready for his consideration. Is he really ready to accept this universal belief of all Christians of every school in one wise and beneficent Ruler of the universe, and to conform his life loyally to this Ruler's wise and beneficent laws?

In the first century Jesus of Nazareth was to the great majority of mankind wholly unknown; and the great majority of those to whom He was known regarded Him either with pitying contempt as a fanatic or with indignant aversion as an impostor. Now throughout what we generally call the civilized world He is looked upon almost universally with feelings which vary from a supreme respect to a divine veneration. Catholic and Protestant, Orthodox and Liberal, Anglican and Quaker, agree in looking upon Him as the supremest embodiment in human history of all in man that is most worthy of imitation, and of all in the invisible Ruler of the universe that is most worthy of reverence. It is true that when they attempt to define Him, and particularly when they attempt to explain His relations to the invisible Ruler of the universe, they differ widely. These differences are material. But they are not so material as their agreement. The great, the overwhelming majority of Christians agree in regarding Jesus Christ as the personification in a human life of a God who transcends all our conceptions of personality. But those to whom He is not a Divinity, but only a Humanity, vie with their orthodox contemporaries in the honor which they pay to His name. Ernest Renan bows before Him as a true Son of God; and John Stuart Mill holds Him to be the supremest standard of life and character known to the sons of men. If, then, the skeptic is really ready to give candid consideration to the claims of any article of belief upon which Christians are agreed, here is one for him to weigh well. Is he ready to make the character of Christ the object of his reverence, and the life of Christ the standard by which to measure his own character and conduct? If not, this cannot be because of any division of Christians upon this subject. Whatever may be said of the inconsistencies of their practice, they are not divided in their opinions.

All Christian believers agree also in regarding the teachings of Jesus Christ as affording wise and beneficent principles for the guidance of daily conduct. It is true that few Christians courageously and consistently test their lives by these principles; true, also, that occasionally some literalist will give to some paradox of Jesus Christ a literal interpretation and then criticise it because it is impracticable. But, with few and minor exceptions, the moral teaching of the Christian Church is Christian teaching. Not to push one's way to the front with aggressive ambition, not to sacrifice one's life to the acquisition of things, not to avenge insults and to leave even serious injuries to be corrected and punished by society rather than by personal vengeance, to make doing to others as one would wish to be done by the rule of social and business intercourse, to dare opprobrium and persecution in defending the right, to help the unfortunate, sympathize with the sorrowing, show mercy to the wrong-doer—these and kindred principles of action are inculcated in all Christian literature and by all Christian churches, and are recognized, though unhappily not conformed to, by all Christian disciples. If the skeptic is really ready to consider any article of faith upon which all Christians are agreed, this Christian standard of morality is such an article. Is he really ready to ponder it well, and, if it seems to him just and right, to make it the standard for his own life?

If any reader of this article thinks that we exaggerate the unity of the Christian church, he can test the question by a simple experiment. Cut out for four successive weeks from Monday morning's paper its reports of sermons preached the Sunday before. Cut out from the introduction to these reports all references to the preacher or his church. Then hand the dozen or twenty sermons to a non-theological companion and ask him to designate the denomination of the respective preachers. Some Catholic sermon—Anglican or Romanist—may be disclosed by the preacher's references to the authority of the Church, some Unitarian sermon by its pungent criticism of the orthodox faith; but, with a few such minor exceptions, we venture to prophesy that his companion will hardly be able to make even a shrewd guess as to the denominational origin of the several discourses. Christian teachers are in all essential doctrines as well agreed as the scientists, and better agreed than either the doctors or the statesmen. Christian teachers are as well agreed upon the unity and spirituality of God as are physicists upon the attraction of gravitation; and they are better agreed upon the ethical principles which should govern our social conduct than are the politicians upon the political principles which should govern our political conduct. If differences between the denominations is a good reason for inaction in religion, then the differences between the schools in medicine is a good reason for never calling a doctor, and the differences between political leaders is a good reason for taking no part in the politics of one's country. —The Outlook.

THE ULTIMATE TEST OF CHRISTIANITY

BY THE REV. B. D. THOMAS, D.D.

Christ appears before the world today in the embodied life of His church and His challenge rings out with the confident assurance, "If I do not the works of My Father, believe Me not. But if I do, though ye believe not Me, believe the works." This is the ultimate test of Christianity. If we assume to have the life of God we must prove it by our works. No other evidence will satisfy a skeptical and unbelieving age, a venerable history will not answer the purpose, an orthodox creed will but expose us to contempt. Elegant formality will not add lustre to our character. We shall not command the respect and confidence of the age unless we can appeal to the quality and comprehensiveness of our activities in the interests of our fellow-men. The church of the future must have this distinguishing virtue, whatsoever else she may fail to realize, that she meets the deepest needs of humanity by the potency of her sympathy, as well as by the breadth and grandeur of her plans for its regeneration and uplifting. The question that is rising above all others in these days, in view of the claims of Christianity, is What do ye more than others? If she cannot furnish a satisfactory answer, she will be most assuredly driven from the field. She must prove the divineness of her authority by the superlative splendor of her achievements. It is in vain that she assumes the name of the Crucified if she does not exemplify His spirit. Her sublime pretensions will not save her from extinction if she does not actualize them in the heroism and consecration of her noble deeds.

Now I hold that Christianity with all her imperfections can stand the test. She is not the regnant force she should be in society. She exhibits manifold defects and weaknesses. She might have been more exquisite in her investiture and more queenly in her bearing. Her power and influence should have been a thousand-fold greater; but taking her as she is, her royalty is unquestioned. She stands forth in the midst of this marvelous nineteenth century as its most imperial influence, as its divinest inspiration. I am not oblivious of the fact that there are other religions that sway the lives of millions of the human race; we are willing that they should be judged together, that they should be subjected to the same tests. If the Light of Asia can be shown to diffuse a kindlier illumination than the Sun of Righteousness, then we are prepared to rejoice in his beams. If Confucius or Mahomet can be shown to have achieved grander results than Jesus Christ, then we are prepared to accept the issue. If it can be demonstrated that any form of belief, or any system of ethics or morals, can do more and better for humanity than Christianity, then we are willing that it should be given the place of honor in the estimation and affection of mankind. We want no special pleading or sentimental philosophizing, or specious theorizing; the matter is too solemn. We rest the whole issue on the demonstrative evidence of facts. "If I do not the works of My Father, believe Me not." Our contention is that Christianity can do more for man than any other religion, that it has richer resources, a deeper inspiration, a sumblimer aim than can be found in any other form of belief. We go even further than that, we claim for it the supreme place as God's appointed agency for the subjugation of the world unto Himself. The challenge of Christianity to the unbelief and skepticism of the age is this, "If I do not the works of My Father, believe Me not. But if I do, though ye believe not Me, believe the works."

Let us see how this challenge is sustained. Christianity found the world in spiritual darkness the most profound. In no period of its history, probably, were the nations more corrupt. Power sat enthroned in despotism and blood. The highest culture left the moral nature untouched. Purity was an unknown virtue. Righteousness dared not raise her head amid the universal degradation and degeneracy. The helpless and the weak had no consideration or protection. The indifference to human life was simply frightful. It was the special amusement of the populace to witness shows at which men were compelled to kill one another or to be torn in pieces by wild beasts. The Roman holiday was a carnival of cruelty and licentiousness, all manner of wickedness was practiced in the private life of the whole population without concealment or shame. What was true of the metropolis of ancient heathenism was true also of the provinces. This was the world into which Christianity was introduced well-nigh nineteen centuries ago. Her principles antagonized every form of power. She was without prestige, without distinction save that of infamy, without any of the favoring conditions which are essential to success, and yet, what has she done? Who, uninspired by vision in the gorgeous role of prophecy, could have dreamed of the results of that insignificant and contemptible beginning? Who that stood not at the gates of heaven and heard something of its infinite designs could have divined the possibilities of that religous life which had its birth in a manger and its coronation on a cross, becoming the dominant influence in the civilization of the ages? "Who could have with the loftiest outreach of the imagination anticipated such results as we are privileged to behold?" It has not converted, purified and reformed all men, even in those lands where it has wielded the largest influence, but it has brought uncounted blessings and benefits to millions into whose hearts its saving power has not been received. It has caused flowers to bloom even in the wilderness. It has cleansed and purified the atmosphere of being. It has moved through the ages like a mighty current of regenerative potency. It has caused its gracious beams to play upon the darkness of ignorance, superstition and depravity, until whole peoples have been elevated and refined, even where they have not been converted and saved. The name of the despised Nazarene is already above every other name, and the religious system which He established the most imperial power in the social and intellectual life of the world. There is the fact which commands recognition and acknowledgment. Let the skeptical and unbelieving stand in the presence of its testimony with manly honesty.

It is amazing that there should be men living in the focalized radiance of all this illumination, who take delight in discrediting Christianity. As well might they in the midst of the affluence and fragrance of summer, pour contempt upon the sunlight. What would this land be today—what would any of the more highly favored nations of the earth be, but for the influence which Christianity has exerted upon them? Take away the restraints which she imposes upon evil passions and the incentives with which she stimulates to holy and righteous living. Repeal the laws which she has enacted and lay level with the dust the institutions of beneficence and philanthropy, which she has upreared; quench every ray of light and warmth which she has caused to beam upon human life and you have hurled the foremost nations of the earth back into barbarism and night.

Our contention is that Christianity is divine and that she proves her divinity by her works. Is it an extravagant assumption? Have we claimed for her more than can be substantiated by the most incontrovertible evidence? I maintain that we have not. We need but look at our own immediate surroundings—the liberties we enjoy, the peace and security amid which we live, the tone and quality of the social atmosphere, the blossoming of virtue, beneficience and charity in so many interesting and fascinating forms. Whence their inspiration? They are not the production of the natural affections. Here are the gladdening streams; where is the fountain from which they emanate? Who built these churches and colleges, these hospitals and homes Was it infidelity or was it Christianity? What mighty energy has been at work upon the thought and life of England and America to have accomplished the regenerative and purifying ministry which the past century or two have witnessed? It would be well if the discreditors of Christianity would give themselves to the consideration of these questions. We do not invite them into a realm of theory, but into a realm of facts. "If ye believe not Me, believe the works."

There are those who are willing to admit that Christianity has been a great power in the past, they are not reluctant even to admit that it has been a beneficent power; but they contend that its glory has departed, that it is now little better than a name, other agencies and ministries must be introduced to meet the exigencies of the times. I wonder if these persons have as much as heard of modern missions? I could take them to lands in which during the last half century the hardest, fiercest, rudest heathenism has been subdued. I could show them monsters of cruelty "who could glut themselves upon the flesh of their fellow-men and who would kill innocent human beings to make drinking cups of their skulls, clothed and in their right mind." I could take them to the South Sea where whole tribes of savages have been rescued from their degrading and horrible atrocities and become law-abiding and industrious. I could tell them of the cannibals of the Fiji who "were wont to build the huts of their chiefs upon the bodies of living human beings, who could slay infants and strangle widows without the least compunction and who performed many other deeds that were worthy of being recorded in hell, but are now rejoicing in gospel light and conforming their lives to its precepts.'' I could take them to the New Hebrides, where a few years ago there was not a single Christian and where now there is not a single heathen; or to Madagascar, ''of whose population the French governor told the pioneer missionary that it would be as well for them to try and convert cattle as the Malagassy, and yet today a Christian church stands on the court grounds, and on the coronation table together lie the laws of the land and the Bible.'' Time would fail to enumerate the centers of missionary activity that are in operation in every quarter of the globe. It can be asserted with the utmost assurance that Christianity never exhibited so much aggressive vitality as in the last half century. At the very time when the irreligious and sceptical have been talking most loudly of the decadence of her power, she has been achieving her grandest triumphs. There have been periods of greater religious fervor, but never of greater religious activity. In no single age excepting only the Apostolic have Christian enterprises been pushed forward with greater energy and enthusiasm, or Christian missions commanded a more generous support, or Christian men devoted themselves more unreservedly to the Lord. The old challenge has lost nothing of its pertinency: ''If ye believe not Me, believe the works.''

We have ourselves seen something of the power of Christianity to elevate, sweeten and ennoble human life. We have seen it bringing comfort into hearts that were desolate and hope into souls that were bereft. We have seen triumphs achieved over circumstances that caused us to blush for shame at our own unbelief; we have witnessed the calm, tranquil confidence that is inspired amid trials that would otherwise have been unbearable, and the sweet virtues of love, joy and patience, blossoming amid wintry desolation. We have not been blind to the formality and puerility as well as the miserable inconsistency of much that goes under the Christian name, neither have we been oblivious of those elements of strength and heroism which have come under our notice often in unexpected places. The religion that can do for men and women that we have seen it do for those whom we have known; the religion that can take men out of the lowest depths of depravity and change the actuating principles of their lives, that can take those who were diseased with a worse leprosy than that of Naaman and heal them, that can make sinners saints and blasphemers worshipers; the religion that can develope in the human heart principles that adorn and ennoble character, that can illumine the darkest pathway with a divine effulgence and rob death of its terrors, cannot be other than divine.

THE BEST COMMENTARY

BY HENRY WARD BEECHER

I had a letter from some young person starting out in life, asking, "What is the best commentary I can have on the Bible?" Well, I cannot send them this, because the only commentary of the Bible that is really of much value is a person that is living the Bible; and, really, a Christian is the best commentary on the New Testament that anybody can have. But there are not enough of such commentaries to send out. The edition is small. Organized church life, to a very great extent, is founded in selfishness. There must be a church within the church. Ordinary sects are like light-houses, built of stone, so strong that the thunder of the sea cannot move them,—with no light at the top. That which is the light of the world in the church is not its largeness, nor its services celebrant with pomp and beauty, not its music, not the influences in it that touch the taste or instruct the understanding; it is the Christ-likeness of its individual members.

CHANGELESS CHRISTIANITY

BY THE REV. WILLIAM A. QUAYLE, D.D.

"Jesus Christ, the same yesterday, today and forever."—Hebrews 13:8.

We are dwellers in the morning of the twentieth century, and Jesus was a dweller in the morning of the first century. By His advent He made that morning and by His continuance in life and civilizations and theologies He has created this morning. And the ground into which I wish we might thrust the plowshare of thinking this morning is this: After nineteen centuries incredible for change, absolutely unapproachable for the tumult of ideas, which have both frothed and wrought in that era, how fares it with Christianity? Is Christianity getting flabby? Is Christianity tottering a little? Is Christianity less cohesive a fact this morning than it was in the early morning of its life? Have the two hands of Christianity lost their might? Once, when Christianity was young, it took heathenism by the throat and choked it dead. Once, when Christianity was young, it took enthroned tyranny and dethroned it at a breath. What can Christianity do now? How stands its case after revolutions of thought incredible?

Now the conditions of life have changed utterly in two regards, which I wish to point out at this moment. One is the politico-social regard and one is the intellectual regard.

When Christianity came into the world to do business, politically the earth was a kingdom. It was a bald tyranny. As a matter not of accident but of the encroachment of power the whole earth visible to the eye of history was under the heel of Rome. The Roman Cæsar dictated even the whispers of men's lips. A republic was a vanished dream. The rights of man were not mentioned. Autocracy was tremendously urgent and apparent. That was the political condition in the first century of Christian life and activity. And in the twentieth century kings are largely unseated or the throne has tottered. And politically the world has grown republican. You cannot look the present day politics of the world in the eyes and not know that man seems to have come not only to the ballot but to the sword and wants to elect his own king. The world has grown tired of having a king handed down

—3C

to it, and it wants to have the chance to choose its king because he is brainy and because he has character, and make their own leader. The mood of the present world is therefore republican, and the mood of the era that gave Jesus to the world was, politically, Caesaric.

Now, in the days when Christianity began its house cleaning men were, with great uniformity, ignorant, grossly, palpably, horribly ignorant. To be sure, there were no books. To be sure, printing was not even prophesied of in their dreams. To be sure, what knowledge there was was disseminated by manuscripts slowly and discreetly written by hand. But that is neither here nor there. I do not argue that. I simply note the fact that the era that produced Christianity was the era in which the common man was strangely illiterate. Today the common man has had a schoolmaster and the common man has an open book in his hand and the common man doesn't read his book upside down as the little child does as he leans by his mother's lap and runs over the writing as though he knew the meaning. Today the common man reads the newspapers and feels the pulse of the tide of the world and lives in all the out of doors there is and knows the breath that blows across the world and certifies it is the world's breath. In other words, the world is passing, faster than if the lightnings shod its feet, from the realm of common man ignorance to the realm of common man intelligence. And when Jesus began to do His deeds of marvel the ordinary men were ignorant. Today the ordinary man is a learned man.

The third item of social change to which I refer at this moment is that when Christianity began to keep house the common man didn't count a bit. He was never figured on in their arithmetic. What the average man wanted was never thought about, much less thought out. They killed him, they imprisoned him, they crucified him. They gathered him in job lots, and let the lions of the desert loose at his throat. They turned him in the Coliseum and slew an army for a people's delectation. A King counted. A noble counted. A man—what about him? Ask that in the era that gave Christianity rise. And they would look at you with ridged eyebrows and say: "The common man, who is he? He wasn't around. One man didn't count. They didn't care if his heart broke, or if his hopes were crushed. Who rose in rebellion because a prisoner was shut in a leper's cell to die a thousand deaths? Who cared? They would have told it on the streets, and the Romans would have clanked their shields together and said: "A good joke. A good joke, by faith. A good joke."

Now, if a child cries outside its parents door in the night and some sort of cruel, reprehensible family judgment shuts the door in the child's face, who cares? Why, everybody cares. The preacher would go to the door and pound on the door till his fists bled and say: "Open the door." The lawyer would go to the door and say: "If you don't we will come in, and I will give you what you want." The fellow strolling along the streets smoking his cigar would say: "If you don't open the door I will kick it through." What is doing? Oh, only a little young 'un crying. That is all. It is a child that has a heart. This is the era of sensitiveness to human life. Now, then, I do not mean to argue at this moment, though I think I could, all this revolution of life in politics and in society has been wrought by Christianity.

Now, how does Christianity stand when all its children are grown up folks? Christianity that was good when men were reading their primer book upside down, how does it do now when men are looking the universe in the eyes and reading the literature of the stars and the eloquence of the infinite? That is the first thing I call you to note.

The second series of facts I wish you might notice is that the realm of knowledge has changed so that we are not only in another world, but out of the universe those men knew. In the days of Christianity's novitiate and childhood the theory of the world was the geocentric theory, namely, that the world was the center of all the universe there was; that the sun moved around the earth; that we were the big thing in the universe; that the stars lit their lamps to light us on our way to bed; that the moon smiled to us because we were so comely and so competent, and that theory of the immense importance of the earth by and by gave way. In the year 1543 Kopernic, called Copernicus by most, wrote a little book. And when he was dying the little book just fresh printed was put in his dying hand. And in that little book he propounded the proposition that the earth was not the center of the universe, and that the sun and stars were not tributary to this earth, but that we were tributaries to the sun, and changed the theory of the world from a geocentric to the heliocentric theory. We were the child of the sun. Enough said. No argument is made. You know that now the theory of the earth under which Christianity took its rise is dead. It is deader than the Pharaohs—more dust than the Cæsars. How fares it with Christianity now that the world is no longer the center of the universe, but we are a little by play in a tragedy or comedy? How fares it with Christianity now that the stars are not here to light us, to find the way to bed, but when we are simply a star ourselves that the people well out in the spaces cannot see, even with a telescope? Here we are, a little round world as big as a quarter dollar set in the skies. There is a universe of worlds. How is the world going to stand in the light of Christianity, and Christianity in the light of the world when the earth has lost competency, specific gravity, glory?

Second, the world's age has been pushed back by infinite diameters. In the age when Christianity took its rise the Pentateuch's assertion that the world was made in six days was taken literally. My solemn conviction is that nobody ever ought to write a commentary on the Bible unless he is a poet. Nobody not a poet ever could think of anything right. You have got to have a sky above your head and a million million stars in it before you can understand the gravitation of a particle of dust. And they said six days—Monday, Tuesday, Wednesday, Thursday, Friday and Saturday—the world is made. Now rest. That was the theory of it. What was the trouble with the theory? The trouble with the theory was that the man didn't know that you had to be a poet to guess the riddles of God. My conviction abides that the sublimest chapter, all told, that ever was contrived by the massive intelligence of man is the first chapter of Genesis. I have read every big section of the world's thinking. There are not so many big sections of the world's thinking that the common man cannot read all. And, after having read all the big sections of the world's literature, I say they are all little chapters playing with rattles when compared with the august triumphs of the book that tells of when God did things. When, with only two hands, He went out to make a spacious house, in which eternity could sit down and have room to spare. And when Christianity began keeping house, they thought it was six days. And by and by William Smith came and began to drag out the unwilling story of nature from its unwilling lips, and in a word he found out that geology says the world was not made in six days, nor may be in 60,000,000 years. Nobody knows how long God took at it. God told nobody. He took His time. God is not like a gust of frosty wind upon the frosty sea. God marches across the centuries slowly, slowly. Is He moving whatsoever? Slowly, slowly; and the finger along the dial marches so slowly that you don't know whether it stands still or moves. God Almighty taking time to create His universe.

How fares it with Christianity when its very theory of the ground on which we stand and the dirt on which we build and the air we breathe have been utterly changed?

But when Christianity began to breathe upon the mountains and the valleys of the world it was thought that the universe was stable; and by and by a man by the name of Newton came, a century and a half after Copernicus had gone, and he did what I must solemnly say in reference to and deference to all the big things genius ever accomplished at one time, the most stupendous one thing that has ever been done by the mind of man. He found out that gravitation ruled the world, that the earth and the sun and the moons and the blinking stars were all held by gravitation; that we were a part, we were not all; that we were not one rose blooming in the infinite garden—we belonged to a galaxy. Not only the whole world was a center, but we ourselves, suns and planets, were marching majestically around some other center, though we knew not what, but march, march, across the universe. Gravitation has come and taken its place solidly in the world of thought and cannot be budged. Now, then, how stands it with Christianity with this utter change of astronomical ideas?

But in this time that has intervened between Christianity coming and Christianity staying today the notion of geography has been changed. They thought the world flat. If you walked far enough you could walk off. It was the notion of the drunkard that there must be a termination some place, and when they fell down it was because things quit. And then came a dreamer, a navigator, and then was born a poet, who said this vast thing we will try. They had seen on the moon a photograph of the world, and they had seen when the new moon was shone that its center was hollowed out. And some great dreamers dreamed that that was the world's shape, and if that was the world's shape then the world was a sphere and not a level. And then Columbus said: "Here goes for the try," and the winds blew, and the sails bellied, and the waters called, and the skies changed, and the ship flew on, and by and by they came to shore. And he thought he had half gone across the world. But a man by the name of Magellan came and said: "We will die to try the experiment," and Magellan died on the voyage around the world, but his ship lived to make the circumnavigation, and then they knew that this picture of the world was a good photograph, and the world is round, and a whole half of the earth had been found and the bulk of two Americans that were to hammer at the doors for freedom and a sense of righteousness and civic liberty and the open door for God and a midway station for the gospel in the West. This all today has come. How fares it with Christianity now that its very geography is changed?

Then there came evolution, and it said man came from nothing much, and man has evolved from the insignificant to the significant. And people were troubled, and the man who proposed the theory meant people to be troubled. Some of us have lived and grown through the era of the battles of evolution. So far as evolution stands at this minute it has less proven its case than it had when Darwin left it; less proven its case, but mark, if it has not proven its case still the theory has so strategically impressed the world that scarcely anything figures in the reasoning of men more than the theory of evolution. In other words, here is a tremendous hypothesis, which, as a matter of fact, is a hypothesis, yet has walked into the world's thinkings and reasonings as if proven truth. Now, then, how stands Christianity? If God made the world by a procedure so that life came to its highest from its lowest, how stands Christianity?

When Jesus was here and launched Christinaity on the wide sea of human thinking the Bible, such as they had, namely, the Old Testament, was taken at its face value among those who adhered to it. And in this twentieth century the Bible has been brought to book, and the scholars have said this book was not written by this man, and such a book was not written by such a man, and the inspiration of the scriptures has been denied, and the book has been scoffed at, or the Bible has been made to stand on the defensive, and all sorts of mutilating things have been said in regard to the book, and the theory of verbal inspiration, in my conviction, has been happily wiped from the face of the world. How stands it with Christianity now when its book has been called to book, when this wide utterance that has filled the heavens with 10,000,000 souls has been made to stand and give answer for itself? How stands Christianity now?

How stands Christianity, now that the centuries have gone over its head? How stands Christ now, He of the blooming face and the sky blue eyes? How stands the Christ now that the world that was under His feet has fairly vanished from the thinking of mankind? Why, I think that of all the sultry questions that ever settled down like a thunder-storm atmosphere in the blaze of July days not one is to be compared to that. Can Christianity stay now when everything indigenous to it has gone, when its mountains have changed to valleys, when its sky has been pushed back, when its stars are myths and dreams? Now, how stands Christianity now?

Well, a word with you, beloved? You are here this morning. There is a company of you people in this church. Whose church is this? This is a Christian church. Whose house is this? This is a Christian house. Who paid the bills to build it? Christ's lovers paid the bills to build it. Who pays the bills to keep it open house for sinners and for saints? Answer, Christian hands do. How stands Christianity? I speak to this proposition this morning because I know that sometimes to many hearts there comes sudden fear that wipes out every touch of color from the cheek and makes the heart stagger till it is breathless like a dying soldier, "Can Christianity stand today?" Now we are not here to say whether we can retain an effete thing, nor are we here to hold a myth in our hands like a rose to our nostrils, and see if we can get a breath of perfume. Not that, but the world wants what you men and women and children want—something that will stay when the centuries be bloodless as a corpse, something that when the heavens roll together like a scroll shall shine; something that shall be light in the valley of the shadow of death.

A word with you. Polytheism is dead. Nobody who is in the mood of the century believes in many gods now. The Greek altars, I do not know where they are, and you do not. They are not here. The Roman altars are desolated and dust like the Greek altars. The god Thor and the Norwegian hosts are hammerless, and their hands filled with the breath of winds from the west; that mighty

Thor's hand is dust. There is no hand left. All Europe, whatever its surliness or bestiality, all Europe and America, have not many gods, but one. Polytheism is dead. It cannot stand in the twentieth century. Very well, how stands it with Christianity?

Mohammedanism in the twentieth century cannot keep house. It cannot move west. Nothing that cannot move west can live. The westward march of the world is the life step of the world. Things that cannot get out of the Orient, in life, are bound to die. The only way the Orient can get the second breath is that it quit being the Orient and get to being the Occident. The only way that Japan got the victory in its two hands was by standing and sniffing the west wind of the world and getting the breath of liberty on its cheek, and that revived it, and it gripped the sword, and all its majesty it ever got was by quitting Orient and getting to be Occident. Well, now, Mohammedanism cannot move west. Why not? Because it is fatality. It is fate. It cracks the soul as if it were a nutshell. It does not believe in the freedom of the will. People are creatures, not creators. Very well. You know the twentieth century has outgrown that theory of life. Every free human soul stands sublime and says: "I count." Every man here and every woman here know in their heart they are free. Now Mohammedanism cannot move into the atmosphere of freedom of the human soul because it has an atmosphere and a theology of absolute tyranny.

Well, how fares it with Brahmanism in the twentieth century? Well, Brahmanism is pantheism. Brahmanism holds that the world is everything and we amount to something simply because we are on the world, and the man is a little better than a gnat. And Brahmanism holds that the whole world is divine; that everything is divinity; that a man submerged in weakness is a positive assertion of deity. Men are the effloresence of the dirty world. Now then, that cannot stand in the west, can it? You are on the dirt, but not of it. You walk the ground, but you are not the ground rendered peripatetic. You know in your heart and with your head you know that pantheism is a foolish conviction. How stands it with Christianity in the twentieth century?

Confucianism cannot stand in the twentieth century because Confucianism worships ancestors. Confucianism's face turns backward and not forward. Now, then, no face that turns backward and worships yesterday can live; mark that. No face can simply turn toward effete yesterday and live. You must keep your face toward the forward if life is to sing in your heart and the blood is to bound past your brain. This business of worshiping ancestors is worshiping too little. The ancestors didn't amount to much when they were here and no more now. The worship of folks is clandestine silliness. You cannot make a tomorrow of them. Dead yesterdays make no tomorrows.

Now, men and women, my conviction this morning is this; Nothing—mark, underscore nothing—Christianity stands for has been touched by all the revelations of science and accruing knowledge.

2. Christianity said that man was free, and I myself revert in my thinking to that old saying of great, burly Sam Johnson when Boswell tried to steal a march on him and tried to get him to speak of free will, and big, burly Johnson baffled him and said. "We know we are free, and that is the end of it." Thank God, we know we are free, and that is the end of it. You try to teach a man that we are not free and he is qualified to tell you you are a liar. Why, he knows he is. I stick my hand in a man's pocket and rob him, and then an officer comes to me and says, "You stole something. I say, "I can't help it," and he says, "You are a liar, Mr. Quayle. Come along with me; we have a place for you." I was free. Every man knows he is free. Jesus says that every man is free. Did you hear Jesus invite you to come? He didn't say, "I will push you into the kingdom of God." He said, "Come unto Me." That is freedom of the personality. Is that changed? Thank God, no. The human personality is here, and the free human personality is here; and then out of the free human personality I think it needs no lengthy argument to assert with Christ a divine personality is a necessity. It is unthinkable, scientifically and philosophically unthinkable, that man is bigger than God. Is God out of business in the twentieth century? No. Has science bowed Him out? No. Listen a minute; Lord Kelvin probably is the greatest living scientist. Sir Oliver Lodge is a man who stands well beside him. What did they say a day or two past? They said this, each for himself: "I am compelled to say that, with all the investigations of science up to now, we are no nearer the secret of things than we were." Can you run God out? No,

you cannot run Him out. Can you run Him down? No. Can you put God out of business? No, you cannot put God out of business till you destroy the shop, and if you destroyed the shop He would build another. Why, why,

> Behind the dim unknown
> Standeth God within the shadow.

What does Christianity stand for? For the free human personality. What does Christianity stand for? For the free divine personality. Have the century revolutions changed either? I charge you before Almighty God and the liberty of your own free personality, you of the upward look, and you of the inward hunger, and you who try to fling your wings out into the sky, I charge you to answer, God stands unimperiled in the twentieth century.

What does Christianity stand for further? That sin is here and hurts everybody it touches. Can science get rid of sin? Not at all. Science can take silver and put it in acid and you cannot see the silver. Does it get rid of the silver. Not so fast, friend, not so fast. The silver is all there, but it is changed a little. Every pennyweight of silver is in the acid, and the scientist who knows how can go and hunt the silver up and get it all back. Didn't lose a grain. Because you put a curtain between sin and you that is no sign that you have abolished sin or abandoned it. Christ said sin is here. I want to know how you can deny it, now. If you have ever lived with your own heart you would know that. If you have ever lived with anybody else you would know that. If you ever read history you would know that. If you ever read great poetry you would know that. If you ever read fiction you would know that. If you ever read anything you would know it. Here is sin, and it is very monstrous and it is very terrific. It has assassinated centuries, killed governments, and throttled civilizations. It has led men from the very top of heaven to the very froth and pit of hell. Now, then, Christ talked about sin. Have we got past it? No, not at all. And then Christianity talks about some one that can pardon sin. Oh me, oh me, oh twentieth century, twentieth century. What do you want? And the twentieth century, pale to the lips, says, "I want forgiveness of sins." Well, that is the special glorious privilege of God. Jesus Christ can forgive sins. How do we know He can do it? He does it.

Did I not read you from the book, "Jesus Christ, the same yesterday, today and forever?" Christianity, the same yesterday, today and forever. Ah, twentieth century, nothing Christianity stands for that hasn't kept through. Nothing. Nothing that Christianity promulgated that it doesn't promulgate at this hour. Nothing. Christianity has lived. We know that. Here is a ship frail and beautiful, and it has crossed the seas, and it had its hold filled with gold, and there were so many thousand bars, and the inspector comes down and says, "How much gold have you here? I hold the bill of lading for so much gold." And then they that had the craft in charge produce so much gold, not a bar missing, not a grain gone. O Christianity, thou art the ship. Thou hast sailed across the centuries' seas. O Christianity thou art here. O Christianity, show thy bulk of gold thou hast in thy deep ship hold! And it holds up the free human personality and the free divine personality, and the fact of sin ineradicable by human chemistry and the fact of sin eliminated by divine chemistry! And ah! Christianity, thou hast all! Lost nothing. So, before God and before men, so fares Christianity in the twentieth century. And it will be so when twenty million centuries have passed their shadows across the sun. And it will be here in heaven and it will be here when eternity has been spinning on a million million years. Thank God! O Christ, live forever.—Inter-Ocean.

TWO KEEPS

BY THE REV. A. J. GORDON

Jude 21, 24.

We cannot keep ourselves, and yet we have some part in our own keeping. "Kept by the power of God through faith unto salvation," is the statement in Peter's Epistle. God's power acts through our faith. It does not lay hold of us mechanically or externally, as the vise holds the iron in its grasp. God grasps us through our grasp of Him; He holds us through our hold of Him. His power, in other words, is exercised through our faith. Now we observe that in the Epistle of Jude there are two keepings spoken of. The one exhorts us to keep ourselves; the other commends us to the keeping power of God.

1. "Keep yourselves in the love of God" (v. 21). This is pre-eminently the gospel in distinction from the law. It throws us upon the resources of God's love, instead of enforcing the requirements of our love. The law said, "Thou shalt love the Lord thy God with all thy heart, and with all thy mind, and with all thy strength." Man made an utter failure in attempting to keep this law. So "what the law could not do in that it was weak through the flesh," God sent His own Son to do for us. He revealed the love of God to us. "God so loved the world, that He gave His only begotten Son." "God commendeth His love to us, in that while we were yet sinners Christ died for us." And now we are to accept God's love, and what it has wrought out for us on the cross. The law said, "This do, and thou shalt live;" the gospel says, "Believe, and thou shalt live." And so while before, the law thundered, "Thou shalt love the Lord thy God," grace now says, "We have known and believed the love that God hath for us." And now we are to rest confidingly in God's love, warmed, encompassed, and comforted by it; not by our works trying to win that love, but yielding to that love which has won us. If we have no warmth in our own body, we can go into the sunlight and let that warm us. Oh, believe; leave your own love, which is cold and unsatisfying, and get into the comfort of God's love. Then will you love Him, when you have learned that He has so

loved you. "We love Him because He first loved us." If we can only keep ourselves in His love, then we can exercise a true affection towards Him. Hence, let us remember Christ's last prayer for His disciples: "That the love wherewith Thou hast loved Me may be in them, and I in them"—John 18:26. And the two requisites for keeping ourselves in the love of God are pointed out: "Continue ye in My love. If ye keep My commandments ye shall abide in My love, as I have kept My Father's commandments and abide in His love"—John 15:10. And the other requisite is prayer—"Praying in the Holy Ghost, keep yourselves in the love of God"—Jude 20, 21.

2. "Unto Him that is able to keep you from falling"—Jude 24. "It is a fearful thing to fall into the hands of the living God," says the Scripture. How much more fearful were it to fall out of the hands of a loving God if it were possible. But it is not possible. If we have believed, we have eternal life. And that life can no more perish than God Himself can perish. Therefore the blessed significance of Christ's words, "I give unto them eternal life: and they shall never perish, neither shall any man pluck them out of My hand"—John 10:28. Tauler, the mystic, tells of a poor peasant from whom he gained deep instruction in spiritual things. To his searching question, "But what would you say if God should damn you?" "If God would damn me," said the poor man, "verily, if He would use me so hardly, I have two arms to embrace: the one whereof is deep humility, by which I am united to His humanity; the other is faith and love, by which I would embrace Him in such sort that He should be constrained to descend with me into hell; and I had rather, without comparison, be in hell with God, than without Him in paradise." Oh, bold confession, yet true! Since by the new birth we have been made "partakers of the divine nature," how could we be lost without carrying that nature down into perdition?

Therefore may we boldly say: "Who shall separate us from the love of Christ? Shall tribulation, or distress, or persecution, or famine, or nakedness, or peril, or sword? Nay, in all these things we are more than conquerors through Him that loved us."
—Watchword.

NOT A FAILURE

Christianity we are told has failed. Failed in what? In attempting to give man a knowledge of the true God? In assuming to teach man who he is and what his destiny? No. If in these things it has come short, where shall we go for words of wisdom, words of life and light? Is it then in history that the religion of the Nazarene has failed? How speaks the record? Has it not proved itself the mightiest power on earth? Look at the beginning; a young man crucified—a small company of fishermen, that was about all. When it started on its course through the centuries a little room could hold all its followers. There was nothing in them to recommend it to the favorable notice of the world. They had no churches, no synagogues, no armies. They quickly met with fiercest opposition. Kings and princes set themselves in array against the new religion and laid violent hands on its representatives. "Men clothed in garments smeared with pitch and then lighted up as living torches to add a horrid luster to the festivities of the Roman emperor," illustrate the kind of reception which the early followers of the Nazarene received.

But still Christianity went on round. All grades and classes, monarch and peoples, began to feel its silent, mighty power. Its enemies stood in amazement at its irresistible progress. "We are but of yesterday," said one of the fathers, "and we have filled all that belongs to you, the cities, the fortresses, the free towns, the very camps, the palace, the senate, the forum. We leave to you the temples." But it is not long until the gods are overthrown, and the oracles are dumb.

Need I go on to specify more fully, how Christianity entered the chief cities of the Roman empire, the seats of learning and commerce, the centers of art and trade; how it won to itself the masses, established its name in the proudest capital of the world; how it crossed oceans, traversed lands, and swept from southern shores to northern seas; how it tamed the wild nations of Europe, which even the Cæsars could not vanquish; how it changed the current of the world affairs, broke up the old civilizations of heathenism, and introduced a new development which went on year after year, broadening, deepening; how it was marched through the ages, witness of vast changes, and terrible overthrows, but itself unchanged, unharmed; and how after these centuries of turmoil and upheaval, it lives and is here with us in a power which shakes the world.

All these are facts which the intellectual giants of the earth never can blot from the history of the present and past. Men have had their fits of boasting, but how vain. The noted skeptic, David Hume, predicted that the religion of Christ would soon cease. Voltaire sneered at the cross and boasted that while it took twelve men to plant the gospel in the world, he would show the ages that one man by a single blow could strike it dead. The vulgar Tom Paine wrote his "Age of Reason" to demolish the strongholds of our faith; and Theodore Parker said that he would go through New England, and tear up Christianity by the very roots, and show his generation what a flimsy, weak power was this religion that had dared to show itself in the nineteenth century. But where is Hume and Voltaire and Paine and Parker? Many years already in the grave. And where is the Christianity they thought to strike at a single blow? It is here. Dead? No. It lives fresh and strong as when first it appeared in the towns and cities of the ancient world. Cast your eye over the earth. See what tribes and kingdoms and nations cover its surface.

Christianity is among them all. Follow the sun in his course. There is not a clime on which he throws his light, where the gospel is not heard. Up in ice-bound regions of the north, in the empires of China and Japan, on the strands of India, in the jungles of Africa, among the nations of Europe, on the wide continent of America, in isles of the seas, and at the uttermost parts of the earth, the cross is now being preached. The Christian song swells in the air of every land; the worshipers gather by thousands and millions from hamlet and cot, from mansion and palace, in the assembly of the saints to hear the story of Jesus and Him crucified. Christianity is here. It appears in the better forms of our civilization; in the wisest laws and best governments of the world; in the schools and colleges of the land; and it shows itself in the liberty of conscience that men enjoy and the institutions of civil freedom that are the pride of 60,000,000 on this western continent.

Christianity is here. Who does not feel the presence of its power? If so weak, so foolish, why are its enemies annoyed by its influence? If it has proved a superstition and gone down in disgrace, why so great ado? Why write and talk incessantly about something that has passed into the shades with the Olympian gods? Ah, no. Better say that Hume and Voltaire, and the host of opposers have failed. These have had their day, but Christianity saw them go down into the grave, and in spite of their high boasting, it still lives and makes fresh conquests every year.

After all, who is it that has proved a miserable failure? Julian the apostate, who led forth the legions of Rome to demonstrate the gospel to be false. Porphyry and Celsus, who wrote to demolish the Christian system? Rousseau, and the whole coterie of French infidels who sought to undermine the foundations of God's word? Gibbon, the great historian, who composed his celebrated history of the decline and fall of the Roman empire, in order that he might tear down the superstructure of the Christian faith? The German skeptics who have aimed their heaviest artillery against the cross of Calvary; the free thinkers of the world who have worked to think the gospel out of existence—these one and all have matched themselves against the great Galilean, and have perished. Christianity is still alive, and is abroad among the nations and people like a strong man running the race of victory.

Christianity a failure? When it lives in millions of hearts at present, gives all satisfying peace to the sin-troubled soul, permeates all classes of society, and is going forth as of old, conquering and to conquer. As well might you say that yonder sun is a failure, who has lighted up the globe for thousands of years, and is now shining in the strength of his ancient brilliance. Oh, no, Christianity has not failed. Its trophies are too abundant; its victories too many, and its present power too great. It is marching on. Nothing can stay its progress. Its future is beyond the ingenuity and strength of man or devil to blast.—Theological Monthly.

CHRISTIANITY AS A DELUSION

BY THE REV. DR. T. DE WITT TALMAGE

"He made his arrows bright, he consulted with images, he looked in the liver."—Ezekiel 21:21.

Two modes of divination by which the King of Babylon proposed to find out the will of God. He took a bundle of arrows, put them together, mixed them up, then pulled forth one, and by the inscription on it decided what city he should first assault. Then an animal was slain, and by the lighter or darker color of the liver the brighter or darker prospect of success was inferred. That is the meaning of the text: "He made his arrows bright, he consulted with images, he looked in the liver." Stupid delusion! And yet all the ages have been filled with delusions. It seems as if the world loves to be hoodwinked, the delusion of the text only a specimen of a vast number of deceits practiced upon the human race. In the latter part of last century, Johanna Southcote came forth pretending to have divine power, made prophecies, had chapels built in her honor, and 100,000 disciples came forth to follow her. About five years before the birth of Christ, Appollinius was born and he came forth, and after five years being speechless, according to the tradition, he healed the sick and raised the dead, and preached virtue, and according to the myth, having deceased, was brought to resurrection. The Delphic oracle deceived vast multitudes of people—the Pythoness seated in the temple of Apollo uttering a crazy jargon from which the people guessed their individual or national fortunes or misfortunes. The utterances were of such a nature that you could read them any way you wanted to read them. A general coming forth to battle consulted the Delphic oracle, and he wanted to find out whether he was going to be safe in the battle, or killed in the battle, and the answer came from the Delphic oracle in such words that if you put the comma before the word "never" it means one thing, and if you put the comma after the word "never" it means another thing, just opposite, and the message from the Delphic oracle to the general: "Go forth, return never in battle shalt thou perish." If he was killed, that was according to the Delphic oracle; if he came home safely, that was according to the Delphic oracle.

—4C

So the ancient auguries deceived the people. The priests of those auguries by the flight of birds, or by the intonation of thunder, or by the inside appearance of slain animals, told the fortunes or misfortunes of individuals or nations. The Sibyls deceived the people. The Sibyls were supposed to be inspired women who lived in caves and who wrote the Sibylline books, afterward purchased by Tarquin the Proud. So late as the year 1829, a man arose in New York, pretending to be a divine being, and played his part so well that wealthy merchants became his disciples and threw their fortunes into his discipleship. And so in all ages there have been necromancies, incantations, witchcrafts, sorceries, magical arts, enchantments, divinations and delusions. The one of the text was only a specimen of that which has been transpiring in all ages of the world. None of these delusions accomplished any good. They deceived, they pauperized the people; they were as cruel as they were absurd. They opened no hospitals, they healed no wounds, they wiped away no tears, they emancipated no selfdom.

But there are those who say that all these delusions combined are as nothing compared with the delusion now abroad in the world. the delusion of the Christian religion. That delusion has today 200,000,000 dupes. It proposes to encircle the earth with its girdle. That which has been called a delusion has already overshadowed the Appalachian range on this side of the sea, and it has overshadowed the Balkan and Caucasian ranges on the other side of the sea. It has conquered England and the United States, for they are called Christian nations. This champion delusion, this hoax, this swindle of the ages, as it has been called, has gone forth to conquer the islands of the Pacific and the Malanesia and Micronesia, and Malayan Polynesia have already surrendered to the delusion. Yea, it has conquered the Indian Archipelago, and Borneo, and Sumatra, and Celebes, and Java have fallen under its wiles. In the Fiji Islands, where there are 120,000 people, 102,000 have already become the dupes of this Christian religion, and if things go on as they are now going on, and if the influence of this great hallucination of the ages cannot be stopped, it will swallow the globe.

Supposing, then, that Christianity is the delusion of the centuries, as some have pronounced it, I propose this morning to show you what has been accomplished by this chimera, this fallacy, this hoax, this swindle of the ages.   And in the first place I remark, that this delusion of the Christian religion has made wonderful transformation of human character.   I will go down the aisle of any church in Christendom, and I will find on either side that aisle those who were once profligate, profane, unclean of speech and unclean of action, drunken and lost.   But by the power of this delusion of the Christian religion they have been completely transformed, and now they are kind, and amiable, and genial, and loving, and useful.   Everybody sees the change.   Under the power of this great hallucination they have quit their former associates, and whereas they once found their chief delight among those who gambled and swore and raced horses, now they find their chief joy among those who go to prayer-meetings and churches; so complete is the delusion!   Yea, their own families have noticed it—the wife has noticed it, the children have noticed it.   The money that went for rum now goes for books, and for clothes, and for education. He is a new man.   All who know him say there has been a wonderful change.   What is the cause of this change?   This great hallucination of the Christian religion.   There is as much difference between what he is now and what he once was as between a rose and a nettle, as between a dove and a vulture, as between day and night.

Tremendous delusion!   Admiral Farragut, one of the most admired men of the American navy, early became a victim of this Christian delusion, and seated, not long before his death, at Long Branch, he was giving some friends the account of his early life. He said: "My father went down in behalf of the United States Government to put an end to Aaron Burr's rebellion.   I was a cabin boy, and went along with him.   I could swear like an old salt.   I could gamble in every style of gambling.   I knew all the wickedness there was at that time afloat.   One day my father cleared everybody out of the cabin, except myself, and locked the door.   He said: 'David, what are you going to do?   What are you going to be?'   'Well,' I said, 'father, I am going to follow the sea.'   'Follow the sea! and be a poor, miserable, drunken sailor, kicked and cuffed about the world, and die of a fever in a foreign hospital.'   'Oh! no,' I said, 'father, I will not be that; I will tread the quarterdeck and command as you do.'   'No, David,' my father said, 'No, David; a person that has your principles and your bad habits will never tread the quarterdeck or command.' My father went out and shut the door after him, and I said then, 'I will change; I will never swear again, I will never drink again, I will never gamble again.' And, gentlemen, by the help of God I have kept those three vows to this time. I soon after that became a Christian, and that decided my fate for time and for eternity."

Another captive of this great Christian delusion. There goes Saul of Tarsus on horseback at full gallop. Where is he going? To destroy Christians. He wants no better play spell than to stand and watch the hats and coats of the murderers who are massacring God's children. There goes the same man. This time he is afoot. Where is he going now? Going on the road to Ostea to die for Christ. They tried to whip it out of him, they tried to scare it out of him, they thought they would give him enough of it by putting him into a windowless dungeon, and keeping him on small diet, and denying him a cloak, and condemning him as a criminal, and howling at him through the street; but they could not freeze it out of him, and they could not sweat it out of him, and they could not pound it out of him, so they tried the surgery of the sword, and one Summer day in 66 he was decapitated. Perhaps the mightiest intellect of the 6000 years of the world's existence hoodwinked, cheated, cajoled, duped by the Christian religion. Ah! that is the remarkable thing about this delusion of Christianity—it overpowers the strongest intellects. Gather the critics, secular and religious, of this century together, and put a vote to them as to which is the greatest book ever written, and by large majority they will say "Paradise Lost." Who wrote "Paradise Lost?" One of the fools who believed in this Bible, John Milton. Benjamin Franklin surrendered to this delusion, if you may judge from the letter that he wrote to Thomas Paine, begging him to destroy the "Age of Reason" in manuscript and never let it go into type, and writing afterward, in his old days: "Of this Jesus of Nazareth I have to say that the system of morals He left and the religion He has given us are the best things the world has ever seen, or is likely to see." Patrick Henry, the electric champion of liberty, enslaved by this delusion, so that he says: "The book worth all the other books put together is the Bible." Benjamin Rush, the leading physiologist and anatomist of his day, the great medical scientist—what did he say? "The only true and perfect religion is Christianity.'' Isaac Newton, the leading philosopher of his time—what did he say? That man surrendering to the delusion of the Christian religion crying out: ''The sublimest philosophy on earth is the philosophy of the gospel.'' David Brewster, at the pronunciation of whose name every scientist the world over uncovers his head, David Brewster saying: ''Oh! this religion has been a great light to me—a very great light all my days.'' President Thiers, the great French statesman, acknowledged that he prayed when he said: ''I invoke the Lord God, in Whom I am glad to believe.'' David Livingstone, able to conquer the lion, able to conquer the panther, able to conquer the savage, yet conquered by this delusion, this hallucination, this great swindle of the ages, so when they find him dead they find him on his knees. William E. Gladstone, the strongest intellect in England today, unable to resist this chimera, this fallacy, this delusion of the Christian religion, goes to the house of God every Sabbath, and often, at the invitation of the rector, reads the prayers to the people. Oh! if those mighty intellects are overborne by this delusion, what chance is there for you and for me?

Besides, I have noticed that first-rate infidels cannot be depended on for steadfastness in the proclamation of their sentiments. Goethe, a leading skeptic, was so wrought upon by this Christianity that in a weak moment he cried out: ''My belief in the Bible has saved me in my literary and moral life.'' Rousseau, one of the most eloquent champions of infidelity, spending his whole life warring against Christianity, cries out: ''The majesty of the Scriptures amazes me.'' Altemont, the notorious infidel, one would think he would have been safe against this delusion of the Christian religion. Oh! no. After talking against Christianity all his day, in his last hour he cried out: ''Oh! Thou blasphemed but most indulgent Lord God, hell itself is a refuge if it hide me from Thy frown.'' Voltaire, the most talented infidel the world ever saw, writing 250 publications, and the most of them spiteful against Christianity, himself the most notorious libertine of the century—one would have thought he could have been depended upon for steadfastness in the advocacy of infidelity and in the war against this terrible chimera, this delusion of the gospel. But no; in his last hour he asks for Christian burial, and asks that they give him the Sacrament of the Lord Jesus Christ. Why, you cannot depend upon the first-rate infidels; you cannot depend upon their power to resist this great delusion of Christianity. Thomas Paine, the god of modern skeptics, his birthday celebrated in New York and Boston with great enthusiasm—Thomas Paine, the paragon of Bible-haters—Thomas Paine, about whom his brother infidel, William Carver, wrote in a letter which I have in my house, saying that he drank a quart of rum a day and was too mean and too dishonest to pay for it—Thomas Paine, the adored of modern infidelity—Thomas Paine, who stole another man's wife in England and brought her to this land—Thomas Paine, who was so squalid, and so loathsome, and so drunken, and so profligate, and so beastly in his habits, sometimes picked out of the ditch, sometimes too filthy to be picked out—Thomas Paine, one would have thought that he could have been depended on for steadfastness against this great delusion. But no. In his dying hour he begs the Lord Jesus Christ for mercy. Powerful delusion, all-conquering delusion, earthquaking delusion of the Christian religion!

Yea, it goes on, it is so impertinent and it is so overbearing, this chimera of the gospel, that having conquered the great picture-galleries of the world, the old masters and the young masters, as I showed in a former sermon, it is not satisfied until it has conquered the music of the world. Look over the program of that magnificent musical festival in New York last May and see what were the great performances, and learn that the greatest of all the subjects were religious subjects. What was it on that Friday night when 3000 voices were accompanied with a vast number of instruments? "Israel in Egypt." Yes, Beethoven deluded until he wrote the "High Mass" in D major, and Haydn deluded with this religion until he wrote the "Creation." Handel deluded until he wrote the oratorios of "Jeptha," and "Esther," and "Saul," and "Israel in Egypt," and the "Messiah." That Friday night, 3000 deluded people singing of a delusion to 8000 deluded hearers!

Yes, this chimera of the gospel is not satisfied until it goes on and builds itself into the most permanent architecture; so it seems as if the world is never to get rid of it. What are some of the finest buildings in the world? St. Paul's, St. Peter's, the churches and cathedrals of all Christendom. Yes; this impertinence of the gospel, this vast delusion, is not satisfied until it projects itself, and in one year contributes $6,250,000 to foreign missions, the work of which is to make dunces and fools on the other side of the world—people we have never seen.

Deluded doctors—220 physicians meeting week by week in London, in the Union Medical Prayer Circle, to worship God. Deluded lawyers—Lord Cairns, the highest legal authority in England, the adviser of the throne, spends his vacation in preaching the gospel of Jesus Christ to the poor people of Scotland. Frederick T. Frelinghuysen, the Secretary of the United States, an old-fashioned Evangelical Christian, an elder in the Reformed Church; John Bright, a deluded Quaker; Henry Wilson, the Vice-President of the United States, dying a deluded Methodist or Congregationalist; Earl of Kintore dying a deluded Presbyterian. The cannibals in South Sea, the bushmen of Terra del Fuego, the wild men of Australia, putting down the knives of their cruelty, and clothing themselves in decent apparel—all under the power of this delusion; and Judson, and Doty, and Abeel, and Campbell, and Williams, and the 3000 missionaries of the cross, turning their backs on home and civilization and comfort, and going out amid the equator of heathenism to relieve it, to save it, to help it, toiling until they dropped into their graves, dying with no earthly comfort about them, and going into graves with no appropriate epitaph, when they might have lived in this country, and lived for themselves, and lived luxuriously, and been at last put into brilliant sepulchres. What a delusion!

Yes, this delusion of the Christian religion shows itself in the fact that it goes to those who are in trouble. Now, it is bad enough to cheat a man when he is well and when he is prosperous; but when this religion comes to a man when he is sick, and says: "You will be well again after a while; you're going into a land where there are no coughs, and no pleurisies and no consumptions, and no languishing; take courage and bear up." Yea, this awful chimera of the gospel comes to the poor, and it says to them: "You are on your way to vast estates and to dividends always declarable." This delusion of Christianity comes to the bereft, and it talks of reunion before the throne, and of the cessation of all sorrow. And then, to show that this delusion will stop at absolutely nothing, it goes to the dying-bed and fills the man with anticipations. How much better it would be to have him die without any more hope

than swine and rats and snakes? Shovel him under! That is all.
Nothing more left of him. He will never know anything again.
Shovel him under! The soul is only a superior part of the body
—and when the body disintegrates, the soul disintegrates. Annihilation, vacancy, everlasting blank, obliteration. Why not present all that beautiful doctrine to the dying, instead of coming
with this hoax, this swindle of the Christian religion, and filling
the dying man with anticipations of another life until some in the
last hour have clapped their hands, and some have shouted, and
some have sung, and some have been so overwrought with joy that
they could only look ecstatic? Palace gates opening, they thought;
diamonded coronets flashing, hands beckoning, orchestras sounding. Little children dying, actually believing they saw their departed parents—so that, although the little children had been so
weak they could not turn on their dying pillow, at the last, in a
paroxysm of rapture uncontrollable, they sprang to their feet and
shouted, "Mother, catch me, I am coming!"

And to show the immensity of this delusion, this awful swindle
of the gospel of Jesus Christ, I open a hospital, and I bring into
that hospital the deathbeds of a great many Christian people, and
I take you by the hand this morning and I walk up and down the
wards of that hospital, and I ask a few questions." Dying Stephen,
what have you to say?" "Lord Jesus, receive my spirit." "Dying John Wesley, what have you to say?" "The best of all is,
God is with us." "Dying Edward Payson, what have you to
say?" "I float in a sea of glory." "Dying John Bradford, what
have you to say?" "If there be any way of going to heaven on
horseback, or in a fiery chariot, it is this." "Dying Neander, what
have you to say?" "I am going to sleep now—good night."
"Dying Mrs. Florence Foster, what have you to say?" "A pilgrim in the valley, but the mountain tops are all agleam from
peak to peak." "Dying Alexander Mather, what have you to
say?" "The Lord Who has taken care of me fifty years will not
cast me off now; glory be to God and to the Lamb! Amen, amen,
amen, amen!" "Dying John Powson, after preaching the gospel
so many years, what have you to say?" "My deathbed is a bed
of roses." "Dying Doctor Thomas Scott, what have you to say?"
"This is heaven begun." "Dying soldier in the last war, what
have you to say?" "Boys, I am going to the front." "Dying

telegraph operator on the battlefield of Virginia, what have you to say?'' ''The wires are all laid and the poles are up from Stony Point to headquarters.'' ''Dying Paul, what have you to say?'' ''I am now ready to be offered, and the time of my departure is at hand. I have fought the good fight, I have finished my course, I have kept the faith. Death, where is thy sting? Oh! grave, where is thy victory? Thanks be unto God, who giveth us the victory through our Lord Jesus Christ.''

Oh! my Lord, my God, what a delusion! what a glorious delusion! Submerger me with it; fill my eyes and ears with it; put it under my dying head for a pillow—this delusion—spread it over me for a canopy; put it underneath me for an outspread wing; roll it over me in ocean surges ten thousand fathoms deep. Oh! if infidelity, and if atheism, and if annihilation are a reality, and the Christian religion is a delusion, give me the delusion. The overwhelming conclusion of every man and woman in the house is that Christianity, producing such grand results, cannot be a delusion, a lie, a cheat, a swindle, an hallucination; cannot launch such a glory of the centuries. Your logic and your common sense convince you that a bad cause cannot produce an illustrious result. Out of the womb of such a monster no such an angel can be born. There are many in this house this morning, in the galleries and on the main floor, who began with thinking that the Christian religion was a stupid farce, who have come to the conclusion that it is a reality. Why are you here today? Why did you bow your head in the opening prayer? Why did you bring your family with you? Why, when I tell you of the ending of all trial in the bosom of God, do there stand tears in your eyes—not tears of grief, but tears of joy, such as stand in the eyes of homesick children far away at school when some one talks to them about going home? Why is it that you can be so calmly submissive to the death of your loved one about whose departure you once were so angry and so rebellious? There is something the matter with you. All your friends have found out there is a great change, and if some of you would give your experience you would give it in scholarly style, and others giving your experience would give it in broken style, but the one experience would be just as good as the other. Some of you have read everything. You are scientific and you are scholarly, and yet if I should ask you ''What is the most sensible thing you ever did?'' you would say, ''The most sensible thing I ever did was to give my heart to God.'' But there may be others here who have not had early advantages, and if they were asked to give their experience they might rise and give such testimony as the man gave in a prayer meeting when he said:

''On my way here tonight, I met a man who asked me where I was going. I said, 'I am going to prayer meeting.' He said, 'There are a great many religions, and I think the most of them are delusions; as to the Christian religion, that is only a notion, that is a mere notion, the Christian religion.' I said to him, 'Stranger, you see that tavern over there?' 'Yes,' he said, 'I see it.' 'Do you see me?' 'Yes, of course I see you.' 'Now, the time was when, everybody in this town knows, if I had a quarter of a dollar in my pocket I could not pass that tavern without going and getting a drink; all the people of Jefferson could not keep me out of that place; but God has changed my heart, and the Lord Jesus Christ has destroyed my thirst for strong drink, and there is my whole week's wages, and I have no temptation to go in there. And, stranger, if this is a notion, I want to tell you it is a mighty powerful notion; it is a notion that has put clothes on my children's backs, and it is a notion that has put good food on our table, and it is a notion that has filled my mouth with thanksgiving to God, and, stranger, you had better go along with me; you might get religion, too; lots of people are getting religion now.''

Well, we will soon understand it all. Your life and mine will soon be over. We will soon come to the last bar of the music, to the last act of the tragedy, to the last page of the book—yea, to the last line and to last word, and to you and to me it will either be midnoon or midnight!

UNTURNED CAKES

Hosea 7:8.

"Ephraim is a cake not turned;" that is, overdone on one side, and undone on the other. Excellent and apt symbol of much which we now see all about us!

1. Orthodoxy Without Life.—It is the most serious temptation to which Christians are exposed to substitute creed for conduct.

If one is sensibly weak in his spirituality, he will try to make up for it by redoubled emphasis laid upon his orthodoxy. And there are, alas! too many who are doing just this thing. It is as though a soldier should plant his flag upon a high position, and then go to sleep under its folds, trusting to his standard to win the battle, instead of to his own vigilant and energetic fighting. Creeds are the flags of the church—very necessary as symbols and summaries of faith, but worthless as a substitute for Christian living. Alas for us, therefore, if we are growing more orthodox at the price of growing more and more unspiritual.

A shipmaster, under a fine wind, concluded that he had advanced thirty miles on a certain day. It afterwards appeared that, being in a strong current, he had fallen back thirty miles; that is to say, he had gone forward by the wind and had gone backward by the tide.

When I see a Christian growing more and more zealous for every punctilio of his creed, while he is growing more and more selfish and worldly in his life, I say he is going forward by the wind, and going backward by the tide; when I see a Christian very unctuous in his prayers and exhortations in the church, and very bitter and harsh in his conduct in the family, I say he is going forward by the wind and going backward by the tide; when I hear a Christian defending with all his might the doctrine of the cross and the atonement, and then living such an easy and luxurious life as to remind me constantly of Paul's words, "Of whom I tell you weeping, they are enemies of the cross of Christ, whose God is their belly, who mind earthly things," I say, alas! he is going forward by the wind, but he is going backward by the tide; and when

I hear a Christian avowing and professing constantly that the gospel of Christ is the first and supreme thing in this world, and yet spending a hundred times as much on the luxuries and comforts of life as he does for carrying that gospel to the heathen, I say he is going forward by the wind, but going backward by the tide.

There is a constant need that we re-adjust our conduct to our creeds, not that we should believe less, but that we should live more. To avoid inconsistency, some people contract their belief to the size of the life, as a tailor takes in the seams of a coat which is too large, in order to make it fit the wearer. This is a bad method. Most of the heresies and false doctrines which have sprung up in the church have resulted from the fitting over of theology to conform to a shrunken spirituality.

2. Piety Without Principle.—It is a fearful proof of the deceitfulness of sin, that one may be at the same time very zealous for God and very dishonest towards men, lifting up hands of prayer and exhortation on Sundays and stretching out hands of fraud and peculation on week-days. I say this is a proof of the deceitfulness of sin. It is rather a proof of the deceitfulness of riches. For our Lord, with wonderful wisdom, warns us against "the deceitfulness of riches, which chokes the word and render it unfruitful." And what do you think He means by the expression? Inflated currency, watered stock, bogus bonds, counterfeit money, —are these examples of the "deceitfulness of riches?" Oh, no! This is dishonest riches, which is quite another thing. It is genuine wealth that deceives. It promises supreme happiness in large accumulations, and sets a man to striving with all his might to attain them; and in this striving he is caught in the snares of speculation, or entangled in the wiles of peculation, and suddenly the trap is sprung, and he is plunged into hopeless ruin. The Bible warns him beforehand, "They that will be rich fall into temptation and a snare, and into many foolish and hurtful lusts, which drown men in destruction and perdition. For the love of money is the root of all evil, which, while some coveted after they have erred from the faith, and pierced themselves through with many sorrows." Look at the three or four men who have stood before the public recently pilloried in the infamy of shame and disgrace.

Isn't God's word written above their heads in letters of fire, "They that will be rich fall into temptation and a snare." Look at the homes blasted with indescribable sorrow, and see if God's word is not true. "They pierce themselves through with many sorrows."

Not one of these men intended to steal probably; they only meant to borrow and pay again; to take out for a while and put back again. And so, with their eye upon the shining vision of wealth, they pressed on, and meantime their feet were entangled in the snare, and they were caught. Let us pity and pray for them; but let us also take warning. The standards which Christians are to follow is plainly set forth in the chapter from which I have quoted, "Godliness with contentment is great gain. For we brought nothing into this world, and it is certain we can carry nothing out. And having food and raiment, let us be therewith content." Oh, if Christians would only take heed to these words, and be content with simple food, and plain apparel, and comfortable houses! What a safe path they might pursue! yes, and what temptation they might remove from the path of others!

Defalcations are a symptom as well as a sin. The leprosy has broken out on the face of one or two, and an indignant public cries out, "Unclean, unclean! stand off, stand off!" But the disease is in the veins of society—the malaria of fashion breaking out in the hot fever of haste to be rich. The only way for you to escape that malaria, oh Christian, is to build on higher ground. "For our citizenship is in heaven," says the Scripture. Do you believe it, my brother? Then invest where you live, and lay up treasures in heaven. There is no peril in so doing.

Hear our divine Lord talk to us, "Therefore take no thought, saying, What shall we eat, or what shall we drink, or wherewithal shall we be clothed;' for after all these things do the Gentiles seek?" It is because Christians have been taken up with these things—because they have entered the race of fashion and luxurious living, determined to keep up with the best, that they now see their brother, with hearts no worse than their own, cast down to ruin.

Oh, it has been a time of high exultation among the powers of darkness recently! Three or four prominent church members blacked with state's prison crimes! Ink spots on the face of a negro will excite no comment; but spattered upon the white skin of an Anglo-Saxon, how they will make the every passer-by stop and stare! And Satan doesn't care to blacken one who is black already; but how he exults in defiling a Christian countenance, and in being able to paste this strange label on the character of some prominent church member, "Piety without principle."

3. Morality Without Religion.—It is a saying very hard to be received that morality and holiness are entirely different qualities.

Morality is the religion of the natural man; holiness is the religion of the renewed man. The one grows on the stock of Adam; the other grows on the stock of Christ. Morality, even at its highest pitch, is not holiness; for holiness is something of God, wherever found, like the sunbeams which inhere in the sun and are inseparable from it, even while resting on the earth. Honesty, sobriety, purity,—these are the highest qualities of morality; and noble qualities they are. But love to God, communion with God, consecration to God,—these are the attributes of true religion. Morality says, "Love thy neighbor as thyself." Religion says, "Love thy neighbor better than thyself, and be ready to sacrifice and suffer for his good." Morality says: "Be just; exact no more than is thy due." Religion says, "Be merciful, and forgive thy neighbor his debts if he cannot pay."

Morality says: "Be honest; defraud not the widow and the orphan." But "pure religion," and undefiled before God, is to visit the widow and the fatherless in their affliction.

Let us look to it that our cake is evenly done; that our Orthodoxy has life, as well as soundness; that our piety has principle, honest and square and straightforward, as well as unction; that our morality has holiness as well as uprightness.—Watchword.

CHRISTIANITY A DIVINE FORCE

BY THE REV. DR. P. S. MOXUM

What is Christianity? It has been defined many times, and yet no definition has exhausted it. Christianity is the divine force of truth and love, of thought and life, manifested in and through a divine human personality. It is the divine force by which the perfect individual is to be unfolded, and the perfect society is to be realized. Its typical expressions in human history are the divine Son of Man, and the ideal city of God; the one the type of the individual filled with divinity, the other the type of the society perfected under the law of love.

The two great factors of society, as we know it in the world, are the church and the state. What are these factors? Ideally the church is the whole society exercising the functions of religion, of worship. Ideally the state is the whole society exercising the functions of government, and economic administration. That is the ideal, whatever the real may be. The aim of the church is to become universal by gathering unto itself all humanity, and making itself co-extensive with the race. The aim of the state is to incorporate the whole of humanity in the realization of true freedom, The law of love is the ultimate law of both. They are not two; they are different aspects of the one social entity, which is a redeemed humanity. We cannot be satisfied with anything less in our thought than this ideal. After all, progress in this world is in proportion to our capacity for ideals. Why is Chicago so progressive? Why does it go on with such leaps and bounds? Because men cherish big schemes, because they have large material and commercial ideals, and the very largeness of their conceptions and their aspirations and their ideals, helps them to an achievement far beyond what they otherwise would have attained. The man who has no ideals has forgotten the very pulse-beat of life.

There is an old legend that some Roman soldiers were gathered in a grove shooting at the string that held the feet of a dove to the top of a high pole. The one who cut the string and let the dove free was to receive a prize. An old veteran, with the scars of many battles upon face and breast, stood impatiently waiting his turn.

At last, just as he was gathering up his bow, the one immediately preceding him shot and cut the string, and the white dove sailed away into the blue sky. A momentary look of disappointment swept across the old veteran's face, and then pulling the arrow to the very head, he sent it straight into the zenith; and Jupiter, recognizing the aspirations of the brave old heart, caught the arrow and sent it a flaming meteor across the heavens. Only he who has great ideals will be lifted out of the hum-drum and the prosaic, where life must run on forever a poor material tread-mill.

We must cherish in our religious thinking, and our social thinking, the great ideals. The ideal of the church of Christ is to become co-extensive with humanity. The ideal of the state is to become co-extensive with all people, in the realization of perfect freedom through perfect law. The perfect triumph of Christianity is the realization of the ideal.

Now Christianity has two great ideas or aims. What are these? First, salvation from sin. Second, fulfillment of life. The first has received almost all the emphasis in the past. As you look over the history of the church, the history of Christian work, you will see how, as the rule, men have put emphasis upon the first idea—salvation from sin. Not that they have emphasized it too much, but that that truth has suffered, as all truth suffers, from disproportion. For generations and even centuries in the early history of the church, though not the earliest, the idea that possessed the minds of men who were affected by Christianity was the idea of escape from wrath and penalty, the idea of escape from the flesh which was inherently evil, the idea of escape from the world which was crumbling and was doomed, the idea of escape from self. And so the religious life of men expressed itself in monasticism and other abnormal and morbid ways. That idea ruled human thought for a long time. Then came the idea of salvation through the incorporation of man in the church, the mystical body in which alone was salvation. The individual was lost. The structure, or organic body, the church, became everything. Then came the Reformation, with its rescue of the individual—with its hammers of thought that broke the iron spell and struck off the fetters which held men's minds in bondage. But the Reformation was a revolt, and not a permanent scheme of life. It had great political and industrial consequences, which we are experiencing only in our day, and which we are beginning only now to understand. Now another and stronger tendency is appearing. Individualism, pure and simple, is fatal to true life. It isolates man, it separates him from his fellows and it separates him from his God. It cuts the tie that binds him to the great source of all life, as it cuts the bond that binds him to his fellow-man. Individualism carried to its logical result says, as Cain said, "Am I my brother's keeper?" Man is more than an individual. He is that. He is that marvelous being standing in the midst of this universe who can say, "I," and feel the awful isolation of selfhood, into which no being except the infinite and eternal can ever penetrate. There is a sense in which each soul is as solitary as if it were alone in God's universe. But man is more than an individual. He is a member of an organism. Christianity is the great integrating force, which by the law of love binds men into a common life. Now the church, especially the Protestant church, has emphasized salvation from sin; not too much, perhaps, but it has emphasized it in an individualistic and purely remedial way.

Its mind has been possessed with this aspect of truth. Christianity is more than that. While it includes this idea, it includes also the larger idea and aim of the fulfillment of life. Man is not here simply to be saved from a catastrophe; he is to fulfill a destiny. He is not simply to escape from an emergency, he is to blossom into something great and mighty because God is in him and in the world. He is to attain a vast and high development. The suggestion of this we find so early as in the apostolic epistles. How far Paul's thought reaches. Our philosophy and our theology in their longest flights have not gone so far, in some directions, as have the thoughts of that Jew Paul.

Do you remember when he pictures with one or two swift strokes of his pen the ideal of the individual and the ideal of society in one? He says, "Until we all come unto a perfect man,"—there is the one organism in which all individuals cohere, keeping their individuality yet merged in the common life,—"Until we all come unto a perfect man, unto the measure of the stature of the fullness of Christ." Christ is the type, not of the individual man merely, but of humanity. He is not a man, but he is man,—just as the

—5C

Incarnation itself is a prophecy of the organic life of humanity when God shall become perfectly immanent in his self-conscious creatures.

This development which man is to attain, he cannot attain merely as an individual. It is impossible for man to go alone by himself and grow. He cannot attain unto the largest life by any process that shall take him away from his fellow-men. I cannot live without you; you cannot live without me; for good or ill we are bound to each other, and each individual attains his own largest development, only because he is a part in the one organism in which all are parts. His life finds its fulfillment in the larger life of humanity.

Hence all great progressive and constructive movements in human history are integrating movements. All destructive movements are brief and noisy, as an explosion is noisy. The constructive movements are long continued, and are silent, as the processes of growth are silent. All great progressive and constructive movements in human history are movements toward social development. Today the church, vaguely yielding to the new impulse, growing into a vague consciousness of the larger thought which God is imparting, is coming to the sense of this duty that it must grapple, not with the individual merely, but with society. Education is moving in the same direction. The history of education is the history of an enterprise for the benefit of a class. It was the education of the clergy, and for generations it was only the clergy that were educated. By and by the circle, or the number, of learned professions increased, but they were simply the learned professions, and the phrase lingers to this day as if education were a benefit for a specific order of men. But Christianity conceives of education as for the benefit of man, that is, of humanity. It is the unfolding of life,—not merely a diffusion of knowledges and the acquisition of facts, but the developing and upbuilding of human nature in its capacity to understand God as He speaks in the wonders of His creation, as He speaks in the history of the world, and as He speaks in His Word.

Education and revelation are complementary processes. Let us not be afraid of looking the truth in the face. Education and revelation are almost different phases of one thing. Lessing said a hundred years ago, and like all prophets he was not understood, and some would gladly have burned him, "Die Erzienung ist Offenbarung." "Education is revelation."

What did he mean by that, but that revelation itself necessitates a process of education; that man can receive communications from God only as he develops capacity to receive them; and that only as he attains to breadth of mind and of soul can he receive and understand the thoughts of God. Education is as much a necessity to the growth of religion in its largest sense, is as much a necessity to the reality of religion, as life itself is a necessity. We can make people truly religious only as we make them think.

I say the church has felt the impulse that is moving in humanity today in the line of education, more than perhaps in any other single specific direction. The University Extension movement that has appeared during the last few years, in the educational life of England and America, is a recognition of this truth, that Christianity contemplates, and necessitates, an education for society; that the treasures of knowledge are for all men; that the processes by which men are enlarged are for all men, for all women, for humanity as a whole; that life is seeking fulfillment and enlargement, and that science and art and industry and ethics and philosophy are all the heritage and possession of all the people, and are ministrant to the making of a perfect man. Indeed the deep unrest that prevails in our industrial world, is less the result of the specific causes which men name here and there, than it is of the blind groping passion for life. Men have been shut in and imprisoned, and they are beginning to feel their imprisonment. They are beginning to struggle to escape. They are dimly conscious there is something more and better than they have attained, and they know not exactly what it is. They think sometimes it is more houses and land, and they reach for these, but they will not be satisfied by these. It is more manhood they want. It is greater soul. It is the desire for the fulfillment of life, which works as a passionate yearning in the heart of humanity, and which will not be satisfied until humanity has been filled with the life of God. The enterprise of the modern church must broaden to the breadth of this great idea, the fulfillment of life. The "leaven," and not the life-boat, is the true emblem of its work. We have gone on the principle that salvation was a life-boat expedition in the midst of a wreck, rescuing a soul here and a soul there. Instead of that it is a vital and constructive process which is committed to the church. It is the business of the church of Christ to leaven all humanity with the divine transforming force of truth and love, until humanity shall stand up redeemed, saved, fulfilled, the fit temple and dwelling-place of the eternal God.—Standard.

BY-PRODUCTS OF CHRISTIANITY

BY THE REV. WILLIAM A. QUAYLE, D.D.

"So every good tree bringeth forth good fruit."—Matthew 7:17.

The word by-product does not occur in Samuel Johnson's dictionary of the English language, and my own edition of that classic, bearing date of 1825, does not contain the word. And I am reasonably certain, had anybody on perusal of Samuel Johnson's dictionary said to that big hearted and big brained lexicographer, "Doctor, is the word by-product in your dictionary?" the irascible Dr. Johnson would have turned on him with turbulent speech and would likely have rejoined, "Sir, you are a fool." And yet the word by-product is in Webster's dictionary; and it is a matter of profit and interest to watch the coming of words into a language and to study the wherefores of such inroads. I do not know at what edition of the dictionary this word by-product came to take its place among that goodly company of words which have been deemed fit to wend their way in man's speech down the avenues of England and America forever.

But there the word is. Commerce and manufacture needed it; and commerce and manufacture invented it, and what commerce and manufacture make and need and use will later or sooner come into the dictionary. And so here this word is—a good and sweaty word—all of which words I, for one, love. When a word is sweaty with work, I would kiss it on the lips, whether it be male or female. And with the use, now grown familiar, of this term by-product I think you are acquainted. A product is that for which any given method is primarily used, and a by-product is that which was not first intended, but was something of lesser value or second thought, which by and by came to be a matter of manufacture.

With this discrimination between the meaning of product and by-product, I mean to discuss, as God gives me help, what I term the by-products of Christianity. I know what the product of Christianity is. The eternal product of Christianity is a clean heart, is one man's life made wholesome to God, is the regeneration of one soul with the purpose of the ultimate regeneration of all souls so as to have the world have a clean heart. That is the gospel's primary business. It is the gospel's celestial business. It is that for which Christianity stands, it is that which is Christianity's eternalized glory, and the church is the congregation of such as have conspired with God for a clean heart. And in the mind of the average man the church stands for the product of Christianity, and the average man's mind is usually right. So that the church is the grouping together of people who have learned what the product of Christianity is, and the church stands for the cross on the hill, and the God on the cross, and the new birth, and the living of life by faith and not by sight, and the waking and seeing Him who is in the midst.

That is what the church stands for. But I am not to speak of that entrancing matter this morning, though I love it as I love the breath I breathe, and the sky I live under. I am not speaking of that this morning, though to think of it makes my heart chant, not a requiem, but an epithalamium. But this morning I will speak of the by-products, the secondary outcomes, the things not primarily intended, the shadows of the product of the light of the cross, not the prevailing presence and shadow of the cross. And I am not, this morning, to speak of such by-products as have been mentioned with such keenness of insight and faithfulness of detail embraced in such books as Broce's "Gesta Christi" and Lecky's "History of European Morals." I am to pass these two catalogues of by-products by, and speak of other matters that seem to me to be of sincere value, and, maychance, to which some people have not given sufficient heed.

In other words, these by-products are things which exist by virtue of the product called Christianity. They did not live before the Christ. They do live since the Christ. They are the outcomes of the cleansed heart and regenerated purpose; and, though they be by-products, they are still essential products. Coke and gas are the products of coal. I am told that coal tar is a by-product, but out of coal tar comes perfumes and aniline dyes and the retinue of manufactures which I, being only a novice, know not the names of. Glue is a product, but gum-drops (mirabile dictu) and gelatins are by-products. Coal oil is a product, but the names of the by-products are so multitudinous that only an expert could half name them with even rational correctness. O, beloved, beloved, I am this morning permitted of my God to make a word of observation, and, please God, a word of thanksgiving, for the by-products of Christianity; those things whose largess makes us glad; those things the prevalence of which through our atmosphere makes it worth while to live; those things which make the sky for us and a joy worthier than the singing birds in spring.

The first by-product of Christianity is the essential democracy to which the world marches—I do not say the essential democracy to which the world has marched, but I say the essential democracy to which the world is marching. There never was till Christ came to our town a democracy that was democratic. I am not forgetting. I am not totally unschooled in history. I am not unfamiliar with Greek democracy. I am not unfamiliar with Roman democracy. I am not unfamiliar with the democracy of the Italian cities. I am not unfamiliar with the democracy of Hebrewdom. But, in face of that, what I say at this moment is that until Christ came and died for every one body there was no conception of an accurate, absolute, entire democracy of sentiment. Christ died for units. Christ tasted death for every man . This is the root out of which essential democracy grows. The Greek democracy was a democracy of Athenians; they never guessed that slaves were equal to them. Nobody ever guessed that till the infinite leveling love came from the lips and from the heart of the Son of God. When God's Son unbottled the wine of His life for the redemption of one soul, then only was central democracy, then only was essential democracy, put abroad in the world so that men might breathe it. A democracy with its growing tendency to fairness, a democracy with its growing sense of the capacity of the unit, a democracy with its love for life, however humble, a democracy with its perception that nobody is inconsequential in the earth, a democracy with its further perception that everybody is allconsequential in the earth, a democracy with the perception that one rotten life rots many lives, a democracy with the perception that everybody must be free to the end that anybody must be free; with the sense that everybody has unlimited faculty, with the sense that everybody, whatever his necessity or neighborhood, or condition or penury, or shame or despair, or crushedness—everybody has a right. That is a by-product of Christianity.

I will say this morning, with deference to history and reference to it, that this notion never got into the breath of life until Christ came here; when, that morning on Golgotha's hill, he breathed into the air, and the air, so to say, received the Holy Ghost, that day man was born. Now, I am not unapprised that democracies are dangerous. I am not unapprised that, when you look at a nation 80,000,000 strong and past, you see that the whole is in jeopardy by the whole, and the whole is in jeopardy by the one. It seems a peril such as the world never guessed at, and it is; I don't deny it. When you consider the inroads of men who do not know our government; when you consider the inpourings of populations who come from the worst form of autocracy and penury; when you consider the inroads of these men that come in great flood-tides; when you consider the inroads of Sabbathlessness and riotousness and soberlessness and drunkenness; when you consider that, I don't blame any thoughtful man or thoughtful woman for debating whether or not under conditions like that a government could endure and keep its flag with stars flaunting toward the morning sun and the evening sunset, but I do say that a government on the earth has been constructed, that men dared contrive a government, based on the fact that every man has a heart and every man has a brain, and that every man is competent for patriotism and the glory of great national affairs; that every man has need to put his hand to the pilot wheel of government, and this was a thing so majestical that compared with it the old time republic of Rome and Greece seemed mere pettifoggery.

And when I look at this and remember that this is a by-product of Christianity, every man to stand up and face government, and face learning, and face morals and face God, and be counted—why, when I think of that I turn myself into a Fourth of July celebration and don't stop even at sunset. This is a by-product of Christianity. It came, mark you, only from Him who knew enough about men to know that it was worth while for God to die for the worst of men and the worst of women. Now, I think, and I think you concur with me, that this one by-product was enough to justify Christianity. I have no mood and no time this morning to amplify this matter, only to name it. I want men and women to frankly turn their eyes to the lesser levels of Christianity and to see what wonders grow on the plain below the hill that hath a cross on it and a Christ.

And out of this democracy of life there comes democracy of letters. And to anybody who loves democracy, as I take it for granted all Americans do, the democracy of letters must be an incalculable gladness-making. There are people in this company who can remember when novels were constructed on the theory that you must somewhere or other in the fiction find out that the hero and heroine were not what they looked to be or acted to be, but somewhere or other had "blue blood" in their veins. Do you remember that? I am talking to the men. That was quite a spell ago. Do you remember that? That was the old construction of fiction. Did men count in Homer's "Iliad"? You ought to know that Homer's "Iliad" is not a romance of men, but a romance of rulers. You ought to know that. Are you so far past the insurrections you had with the book as not to know how "The Iliad" does things? "The Iliad" is singing the wrath of Achilles, son of Peleus, or of Ajax, or of Agamemnon, the glory of Hector, the supremacy of aristocracy. That is what "The Iliad" is about. Those days never knew the value or guessed at the value of common men, not once.

And if you read that book you remember that Achilles was made so that his very presence scared armies opposed to him, and they ran away from his shadow. I would like to see anybody now whose shadow is so impressive that a fellow would run away from him. If he had a United States coat on with brass buttons on it, and if he had an American gun, I would like to see the Czar or Emperor come on the field and scare him. What the American would do to him would be to show him a thing. He had better get off the field. That's the English of it, and that's the American of it. Democracy has gotten into life, and democracy has gotten into letters. Do you remember "The Aeneid"—not much about it? It said, "Arms and the man." "Arma virumque tono." Not of the manhood; oh, no. Not the populace of Rome, but one man. Very well. The literature of the world was constructed on the essential supremacy of the few. It was an oligarchy; and "men" are a by-product of Christianity; and modern literature is constructed on the theory of democracy.

Charles Dickens saw—and he was the first English novelist to see it—that folks were of value because they were folks. Thanks be to him, and bless him forever. He was an American born over in England. He was that, an American born over in England, and so it comes to pass that Charles Dickens' books, every one of them, have the ruddy blood of common man in them. "Dombey and Son"—who were they? Tradesmen. And one, a son, a little laddy, born to be snuffed out by the thumb and finger of the grave. "Little Dorrit." Who was she? Oh, nobody. "Little Nell," who was she? Nobody's daughter. Who are those folks that clutter up the road and fill the streets and churn along the way like an army? Answer, "Common folks." And you can't take modern letters and not discover this, that they have been invaded of the soul of democracy. It is man. Who was Mr. Barrie? Ah, Mr. Barrie is a man who saw that the folks over at Thrums counted. That's it. They counted, those Thrums folks. Who is Ian Maclaren? He is a man who went to Drumtochty, and aye, saw folks, saw folks. Who is Robert Burns? A man who thought that a man who was a farmer dared talk in a farmer's speech and dared sing in a farmer's tongue, and the earth listened!

I think this is an invasion not to be measured out save with the inverted bowl of the sky as a cup to hold the juice of this invasion of letters by democracy. This is not lords, not kings, not men born of a hundred kings, but men coming out of the dirt. That's it. That's enough. Robert Browning is an exponent of the exact democracy of God. And if you will read Robert Browning, which some people think they don't know enough to do, or don't want to do—if you will quit that nonsense and take a long, deep drink of him, you will be half drunk. I am sorry for anybody who doesn't read Browning—not to be "Browningesque," not to be "esque" anything. But Browning is a man who saw people counted. And if you will take a retinue of Browning's people, if you will see them marching along, what you will see is that those people are not classified by birth and conditions of ancestry, but by heart and conditions of life. Good; that's better; that's better. That is the invasion of literature by democracy.

You talk about Miss Wilkins—I hope you read her. What did she see? She saw that people counted. You read Annie Trumbull Slosson, read about "Fishin' Jimmy," one of the most elect books that ever dripped from the heart, or "Deacon Phoebe's Selfish Natur'." What you will find is that men count. You read Cable, first book and last, and what you will find is that men count. You read Lowell, though Lowell is less a man poet than a nature poet, and you will find that men count. Why? Because democracy has invaded literature and democracy has invaded life. And, I would say this morning to the glory of the Christ I love, and Whose fame I would in my impoverished fashion sing a little, that it is wonderful how He has changed the literature of the world.

The literature of the world comes to be about men. The old time history was a thing with reference to what kings did and said, and with reference to the battles kings fought, and with reference to the riots that run mad in drunken kings' brains. I call you to witness you can almost drive the kings out of history now and not injure the history a trifle. Green has written "A History of the English People." McMaster has written a history of the people of the United States, and the new interpretation of literature and the new interpretation of history are the new interpretation of the Christ, namely, the democracy of the world. And when I read the books, when I read the fiction and the poetry and the histories, to find that the man who sits on the throne and the woman who sits on the throne are just somebody, then is my heart glad.

Who is Dr. Maclure? Who? Oh, what odds? Who is it? Oh, it is some of us common folks. And the wonder of a woman's heart, if I might mention that sacred matter, every woman's heart is a well so deep that the sky is not so deep, and every woman has the fabric of eternal romance in her soul. Every woman is qualified to love so divinely that God is scared. Love scares intelligent people—it makes unintelligent people giggle—but love is so fabulous. What is the wonder of one good man's life? Oh, it is that he is so big that when he stands straight up his shoulders hit against the rafters of the sky. Very well. And it is in the books, the by-product of Christianity.

Another by-product of Christianity is the modesty of life. Would you care to think of that a moment? The modesty of life. You say that hearts are innately modest. I would love to believe you, but I dare not. The trouble with life is that its tendency is to turn itself out of doors. I have sometimes thought that man was innately modest and woman was innately modest, and then I have read a book like Wack's, "The Congo Free State," and it has revivified all my impressions. Read about the nations of the world that have been out from under the shadow of the hill that hath a cross and a cross with a God on it, and then I have read once more that human life is not to be credited with too much modesty. And Christianity's by-product has been this, to bring humanity in off the street into the house. I think nobody ever in writing the history of the civilizations of the world has been able to measure up to that notion—God's notion—that people are not meant to live in themselves or by themselves, but to live to themselves. Do you know what ails Paris?

You say it drinks absinthe until it is drunk? Oh, no; that is not what ails Paris. Do you know what ails Paris? You say it is lewd. Oh, no. What ails Paris? It lives on the road. Paris takes breakfast on the street. That is not the place to take break- fast, but the place to take breakfast is in your house, in your own dwelling, where wife and children may look into each other's faces while they break bread that comes from the free hand of God. And publicity kills modesty. You cannot live on a boulevard, out on the street, your life with no privacy, and keep your life sanctified. You have got to live indoors somewhere. And the gospel of the Christ taught people that they were sufficient in themselves, for themselves, for service for others. That's it. People thought they were to lean on others or fight against others to live, and Jesus taught the world that people were competent to live lives for them- selves, that they might live for others. We are not to do like those Europeans do who build houses in a park and build a stone wall around the park, and then put broken bottles on the wall. That's what makes me mad when I am in England. I don't like broken bottles any way, nor what they hold, nor while they are on a stone wall. In other words, that a man keeps his premises from the world so that no one could climb over his wall—that is not modesty of life; that is selfishness of life.

But the thing Christ brought into life was the modesty that makes the home a place to garden life. Where is the best place to rear children? Why, at somebody's knees. Where is the best place to rear children? Why, on their knees. Where is the best place to rear children? Why, this side of the world. There is the best place to rear children that are to go to the world out of the house. And the beauty of the city is that at night good folks come home. And at night I love to go down town late just to see everybody on the car. I don't sit down. I hang to the strap. I don't take anybody's seat, but tell my heart "coming home." Many's a time I go on Forty-Seventh street, going to Kedzie, not because I am riotous to spend my hard earned nickel, but because I want to see what is done. And lots of us with our dirty hands and our empty dinner buckets, where are we going? Home, thank God. Going home from where we worked to where we live, thank God. Going away from where our toil was hard to where life grows young. Going away from where we handled mortar and bricks and window casings to where we shall put a circle of a man's dirty arms around a woman's neck, and put a baby on the heart and forget he ever worked, but just had fun here. That's it. And what I am saying is, this is a by-product of Christianity. That is living in one's house. That's going home. This feeling that heaven is only one block off when you have gotten home.

Another by-product of Christianity I name is the moral atmosphere. I would ask you to consider in few terms this: Do you sometimes read Goethe's poems—not his dramas, understand, just his poems—and would you at the same time read Tennyson's poems? I haven't time this morning to discuss them, but I will open pages out. The pages of Goethe are the pages of heathenism come down to date. I read these wicked poems because they are called the bible of the worldly man—namely, the bible of the bad man. I would hate to be the man for whom Goethe's poems were a bible, or even a primer. I think I am decent. But I am saying I read them at the sitting so that I could get the atmosphere. It is first unmoral and then immoral. I will say here this morning, in the presence of people who are familiar with this matter, who know Goethe's poems, there is not one sentiment to inspire life to its better. That is awful. I wouldn't slander even a ghost. I found not one sprig of flower that I would want to perfume life with. It is that old inethical, immoral atmosphere. And in Tennyson it is an atmosphere perfumed with ethicality. In Tennyson you are always in the region of behavior; in Goethe never in the region of behavior. And in Tennyson's poetry you are always on a road that leadeth up to a hill. You can see the top of the hill. It is night, maychance, and you can see the hillside. But there is the road for everybody, and you feel the ethicality of life and the thrill of eternity. Doomed souls feel the hill on which they might have stood. And the by-product of Christianity is to make the Tennysonian atmosphere, to rid us of the Goethe's atmosphere. And God give us the Tennysonian atmosphere. Nothing is so glorious as this, to get a sniff of the right air.

Last week I heard a bluejay talk. Yesterday I heard three of them discuss family matters, and the arbitrament of family affairs, and I kept still. They have plenty of trouble of their own, but I put my book upon my lap and listened for them, and I said, "Oh, you strident voices, you violin strings untuned, you voices that flat and sharp, and don't know which you do—do it once more"—because I felt that I was getting close to the time when I could sniff the air of spring. That is all. Only to get away from the long, dark winter—that old air when morals had no life; that old air when chasteness had no vindicator; when life was "eros," the old time when lewdness and love were twins; the old time when they lashed the horses in the race till the blood dropped; the old time when hearts might be broken and nobody stand a minute to see the precious liquor vanish into the ground; to get from where there is unmoral atmosphere, to where a man's attitude, whether he be on his face or whether he be in the pits of hell chin deep, is that of a man who knows he belongs to the yonder and not to the here. The thrill of immorality is on his face and the rapture of immortality in his heart.

The by-products of the gospel. I see the time is over, but the by-products are not ended. I but say this, that we are much indebted for the things that have come of the Christ. His hands are so full. He giveth us the cross and the heaven open and grave broken through and down. And he giveth life's fair fields and spring time's morning and the fragrance of the coming blossom and the radiancy of the new year and the sense of man as man and the literature of soul as soul and the refreshment of knowing that whatsoever things are pure, whatsoever things are honest, whatsoever things are of good report, we are to know that all such things come from Him Whose we are and Whom we serve.—Inter-Ocean.

RELIGION FOR YOUNG MEN

Lord Bacon said: "Tell me the opinions of the young men of an age, and I will prophesy the future of the land in which they dwell." The poet Goethe echoes the same opinion: "Tell me what a dozen of the brightest young men in the country think, and I will tell you what the history of their country will be." Jesus Christ came to create a new world, and sought to create it by making new men, and therefore, as soon as He had given Himself to His transcendent task in that baptismal act in the river Jordan, He drew young men to Him by the magnetism of His own nature and sympathies, made them the recipients of His spirit, the exponents of His thoughts, the messengers of His redeeming gospel to the world. Nearly all His "elect" workers were young men, and I cannot help thinking that when Jesus saw this reverent and reflective, ardent and Bible-knowing disciple coming into His presence, and listened to his request, "Good Master, what shall I do that I may inherit eternal life?" the thought would flash into His mind, "Is this another impetuous Peter, a loving John, a guileless Nathaniel, or a practical James?" Ever in quest of young men of capacity, grip, energy, and of free and bold spirit, He looked on this young man and loved him, as Eli loved young Samuel, and as Paul loved Timothy.

"Search deep enough into the human and you will always find the divine," says Augustine. The Son of Man sent His plummet far deeper down into the seas of the human soul than any other teacher. He knew what was in man, and detected the divine in its most incipient and elementary forms, and forthwith His heart went out towards it in redeeming helpfulness and grace. Another writer says: "The man whose sympathies go lowest is the man kings have most to fear.'' I will add to this: and the man from whom humanity has most to hope. Such a man is always a gospel. The keys of the future are at his girdle, and the government of men is in his hands. Christ was unspeakably sympathetic with our human nature in all its breadth of interest, depth of woe, and height of possible achievement. Christianity is good news; the best news, indeed, for the aged. It comes to the enfeebled with the promise of undecaying strength, tells the care-burdened of ceaseless joys; and says to the sorrowing in sweetest tones, ''Let not your heart be troubled; believe in God. He cares for you. Your life in its decay and feebleness is dear and precious to Him, and He will preserve it against that day.'' Nor is Christianity other than a gospel for childhood. It says concerning the innocent and artless life of the child, ''Of such is the kingdom of heaven.'' It opens for them a place in the Infinite Love. But believe me, the whole compass and force of Christianity is reserved for youth when it is in the fulness of its power, and gives the best guarantee for scaling the topmost heights of excellency in character and deed. ''I have written unto you, young men, because you are strong.'' It recognizes and exults in the splendid gifts and brilliant opulence of youth. It is perfectly at home with a manhood that will not shrink from the hardest tasks, or slink behind when battle is hottest, but whose unappeasable cry is forward and upward; and ever forward and still upward. Its aims and its capabilities are for making the noblest types of manhood, by the presence and after the pattern of the Manhood of Christ Jesus Himself—Clifford.

ISOLATION BY CONTACT

BY THE REV. WILLIAM A. QUAYLE, D.D.

"I pray not that Thou shouldst take them out of the world, but that Thou shouldst keep them from the evil."—John 17:15.

Jesus is holding family worship. We hear His voice in prayer. These disciples of His, Whom He is accounting to be His father and His mother and His brethren, are here with a bowed heart, and Christ is making prayer for them. If there are better scenes this side of heaven than a family at prayer I do not know what the scene might be. If there is sweeter voice than the voice of prayer I do not know where the voice might be nor what. To tell the truth, anybody praying is worth listening to. I have heard much music first and last, oratories and orchestras, and Niagaras, and the wind booming across gulfs of forests at night, when the storm was high, or when there was battle with ragged waves and ragged rocks—all that music have I heard, but I have heard no music that equaled the human soul at prayer out loud. I have heard little children saying their childish "Now I lay me down to sleep." I have heard grown-up gray-beards pray with trembling voices for the lost daughter or the lost son, "God fetch him back to me!" I have heard penitent sinners pour out tears and words together in a gush of anguish, "Oh, God, forgive me, if You can!" I have heard white-souled folks pray when wings were about to bear them out beyond the sunset and the dark into the daylight and the dawn. But whenever I have heard prayer, then I have stopped my heart to listen to it, because that is the biggest thing any big body or little body has ever done.

Commanding the tempest to be still is not so vast a feat as this that Jesus does when He prays for folks. Whatever your majesties of plan, whatever the statesmanship of your hopes, whatever the widening current of your career, whatever the deepening depth of your design, mark this, soul, that nothing you do or can do or have done is massive and profound like when you walked out toward God and prayed.

Now, prayer is a man or a woman walking out toward God with the understanding that God will walk out toward him. Two

people, from the two rims of the universe, a man and the God.
The man shouldering his way through his clouds and his inclemen-
cies and his mistakes and his apprehensions, but shouldering his
way out toward God, and God running faster than the light toward
him.   Somewhere in the universe two souls, man's soul and God's
soul, meeting—that is prayer.   Now, then, if you know any big
thing like that, what is it?   Empires are grains of dust compared
with that.   History is a flame that is spent compared with that.
All your dreams, though they be fabulous as eternity, are weaker
than a withered dream compared with that.   And Christ is praying.   O heart, stop your loud beating!   O breath, breathe not now!
O pulse, silence, silence!   What is He praying?   And I read you
His prayer, in purpose: ''I pray not that Thou shouldst take them
out of the world, but that Thou should keep them in the world,
from its wickedness.''   And that is what I call this morning isolation by contact; and it is of isolation by contact I design, by God's
grace, to speak.

Now in the conception of Christ, this is a wicked world.   He
never argues it, because He was too smart.   The wise geometer,
namely, the geometer, doesn't attempt to prove axioms.   He assumes axioms.   They are the initial letters of the alphabet of
geometers.   It were a foolish geometer who tried to prove an axiom.
And in Christ's theology and in the theology of people who get
any whither an axiom is that people are bad; that the world is
twisted and askew: that hearts have dregs in them that are bitterer
than gall; that blood is poisoned; that the breath is foul; that
shame clutches at the garment and masters many a life.   And Jesus'
notion of life, therefore, is in the midst of this wicked world to be
clean, in the midst of badness to be good.   He wants to make
people right, which is righteous.   Jesus Christ's business with the
human soul is to make it good.   Jesus Christ is not here to try to
make men rich, though following His plans will make us richer
than we were.   Good people have a fair claim to expect returns
from their efforts of brawn and brain and economy; and the legitimate outcome of a business career of righteousness will be suffi-
ciency and affluence.   But Christ is not here to make people rich
nor to put people in fine houses nor to put people on the boulevard
with the automobile for their vehicle.   That is not Christ's business.   Christ's business is to make people worth being carried by

—6C

any kind of vehicle. Christ's business is to purify character and so justify the career. Jesus' business here is to renovate a world through a renovated individual. Christ's holy vocation and the pouring out of His dynamical forces is systematically and continuously and perpetually to make life good.

Now, then, how is He going to make life good? How is He going to keep life good, and how are you going to make earth a heaven? How are you going to preserve character when once it is renovated? When you make a man's life good, what then shall be done with him? And the theory of the world is, in the usual, isolate him. Do it by segregation. If he was bad, take him away from the foulness, put him over into cleanliness of environment, and thereby preserve a clean soul cleansed. And what I design to enforce, if God will help me, is that that method of keeping apart is not the method of Jesus Christ, and the primary method of this world is keeping clean by keeping apart; and the Jesus method is keeping clean by keeping in.

Now, the business of religion is not to get a man into heaven, though it will do it. It is guaranteed to do it. But the business of religion is not to get a man into heaven; and the business of religion is not to get a man out of the earth, though it can do it. The business of religion is not to ferry souls across the gulf that lies between the here and there, though it will do it. The business of religion is, in the hands and thought of Jesus Christ, the making them good here and to leave them here doing good and to put them out where with clean hands they shall do toil for their living that shall be clean toil. Now I shall say, not criticizing but affirming a truth, that the initial misconception of the Roman Catholic church and the misconception of the Roman Catholic monk is that the business of a man's life is to get away from the world and to save yourself and to pray yourself into paradise. Get yourself at all hazards into heaven. Now, my belief is that if a man stays away and does nothing while he is in the world he is a failure when he gets to heaven. He hasn't anything to show for being here. His hands aren't hard and haven't been hurt, but he hasn't done anything to get them hurt. Life's business is not to go along easily and say I won't be in things and I won't soil my hands, and I won't mix with affairs. Why, truly you can do that, but while doing that you are making a fine character for good-for-nothingness.

A Trappist monk has been in the city, I have read in the paper, and for forty years he hasn't seen the world. Forty years old, and, with deference to him, absolutely a little child. Been staying off somewhere preening himself so as to get his wings ready so as to fly. Why, what is better than that? This is better than that—staying down here familiarizing one's self with the world, getting the world so it can fly; that is better. I will risk any soul getting to heaven all right enough if he stays close to Christ and close to those for whom Christ died, but I insist that it is not worth while taking nothing to heaven. It is not worth taking an imbecile soul to paradise. It is not worth taking an arm up to God and no sheaf under it. "What did you bring?" "Nothing, nothing." "Haven't you been in the world?" "Yes." "Was it a big world?" "I don't know." "Was it a bad world?" "I think so, and I left it." "Is it a bleak world?" "I heard so, and the wind scowled and sconed at the lattice, and I shut the window tight." "Did you see the folks?" "I did not. I was afraid I would get soiled." "Did you shake hands with people?" "No, no; they had dirty hands and were at work." "What did you bring?" "Myself." God will say, "You didn't bring much." Now, listen. Is that worth while? That isn't worth while. That is not God's method. Isolation by segregation?

No. That is the world's method. When there is an infectious disease, we find the diseased person and put him apart. Is it a wise process? It is. Why? Because we don't know any better. Don't know how to do better than that. That is the best method of our present system of medicine, because we don't know how to hinder infection, except by segregation, isolation. But if they knew a better method than that they would use a better method. And our method is isolation. Our method is putting out of touch. Our method is putting the scarlet fever patient and any man with infection, leprosy or otherwise, yonder. Let him be apart, apart. And this is the world's method, and this is doing the level best, but the trouble with isolation by segregation is that it leads to aloftness. Here is a man who has been feted for hundreds of years. His ancestry and his ancestry's ancestry, and back through a hundred generations, have had coats of arms and servants and inalienable estates, and the man has been isolated from people and has been segregated from the world, and the result is that he goes along the world and he thinks he is better than the road. Ah me, the road is always better than we are. You know, when the road lets us walk on it, bless God for such a road. Are we honoring the road to walk on it? Why, no. Is the road honoring us by letting us walk on it? Yes. The trouble with aristocracy of ancestry, therefore, is that it is practicing the worldly wiseness of isolation from contact. It is getting apart from people. It is saying, "I am over here, and if I should get in touch with the scullions of the kitchen I should be blackened with the blackness of the pots. Therefore, I shall stay up here, and keep myself away." Oh, what a poor way to live that is. There is the isolation of the scholar, the man who gets apart immersed in books, and gets to look down on people who do things. And he reads his books and he is conversant with forty languages, and he knows what the Romans thought, and he knows what the Greeks did and said and dreamed to do and thought to do, and didn't do. And he understands how the currents of the world's life run, and can dip his hands down into the pools of history, the bitter waters, and the sweet waters, and he puts them like a dilettante to the lips to taste them, and says these are brackish waters of uncivilization, and these are the sweet waters welling from the mountain springs of what we call civilizations; and he looks down on the people who do things and who carry houses and banks and railroads in their pockets, and he says, "They are in trade." And he is isolating himself from traffic by his scholarship. Is that a big way to live? It is not, it is not, a big way to live. This isolation from the world, this getting apart and watching its thoroughfares, this seeing the world go by and saying, "If you weren't so dirty and big fisted, and if you weren't so occupied in commerce, if so many of you weren't eager to get money, I would go down and mix with you. But as it is, I will stay up here and won't be tramped on and won't be hurt." Certainly, he won't be hurt, but if he stays up there he won't be worth tramping on.

There is a story of Robert Louis Stevenson's. It is called "Will o' the Mill." It has some of those atmospheric touches characteristic of Stevenson at his least or largest. And the water I bring from that mountain spring at this moment is this, that

Will o' the Mill stood on his high mountainside mill home and watched the world go by, watched the drift of people, watched the sometimes three days' march of armies, watched the cavalcades of men at toil—watched, watched, watched, and stood at his door and watched. And as a boy he stood in his door and watched, and as a man he stood in his door and watched, and as age he stood at his door and watched. And far below him somewhere, hid behind the shag of battle smoke, or somewhere hid below the growing cloud of dusty roadways like a storm cloud, and hidden somewhere behind the sinuous windings of the mountainsides and deep precipices, lay the world. And Will o' the Mill died up and aloft and aloof and alone, and death came to him in the dark, between the blinking of the evening star and the winking of the morning star. And he had lived a life of apartness and he had never met the world. This is isolation by segregation; but Jesus stands not for that.

Where are you going? Jesus says, "Right about face." A man is going from the world as fast and far as both feet would bear him, and he called, "Where are you going to?" "Toward goodness." "Right about face," He says. "Goodness is this way. Down where people live and hope and pray and love and don't hope and don't pray. That is the place to get good." How are you going to keep a boy clean? Answer: Wash him up and keep him in a cabinet that is dustproof. He would get out of that. Well, now, won't he break the cabinet? He won't stay in. But that is the boy's fault. I don't speak well of boys' peculiarity that way. How are you going to keep a boy clean. Not that way; that is not the way. But how are you to teach him cleanliness? Say, sonny, go out and work. There is a bar of soap and a little water. When you go out, souse in both and then come out white. That is a better philosophy of life. Here is the world. Is Jesus trying to drive us out of it? Not a minute, thank God. He was the greatest mixer the world ever knew. He liked to be where the calling crowd was. My heart, where is a good place to live? And Jesus says, "Where other people are." Down where they were fishing He stayed around. Bless the man that likes to see other people at work and likes to lend a hand. Down where the toil of the city was on. Down at Capernaum He came and stood at the front door and looked out and then walked out of the front door and walked on. No place is better for the average soul than to be crowded in a crowd. If you all the time are wanting to travel in a private car there is something wrong with you. Why don't you go down on Halsted street about 5 p. m. some time? You would stand on nothing and hold on to not much of anything. But it is fun. Why? Because the empty dinner bucket is there, and the tired man is there, and there has been something doing that day, and the world's commerce has been enriched, and the world has been enriched by these folks. Thank God, this is the place to be. Stand away from the world? Jesus said, "No. Let's go out." And you said, "Where?" And He said, "Where people are. Come on, let's go out,' He said. "Where, O Christ?" you said. "Where people stay. Come, let's go out," He said, "where the masses throng," He said; "out where it is hard work to be good. Come on, let's go out. Come, let's go out where people are bad and ought to be better. Come, come, come." Upon my word, I love this doctrine of Jesus Christ's isolation by contact. Being good not in spite of the world, but by it. Staying with it and keeping clean.

Is it any praise to the snow on the highest mountain that it is always white? No. Why, the dust hasn't spunk enough to get up there. Is it any praise to anybody that he sometimes keeps away from doing the things an honorable life ought to do, thereby keeping unsullied? It is not. Life's business is that it stays where life was and whiten it and be whitened by it. I have noticed that when the sea is at its snarliest and the storm is at its highest, then, the waves break into white foam. When life is full of fury and the perturbations are nigh to despair, Christ said, out of all that grows whiteness. I have seen the plumes of the mad sea waves toss like the rocking white plumes of a knight about to indulge in the luxury of battle. That is nothing but foam out of a sea that was so black that midnight would not seem sullen or dark. And Christ means to make whiteness by the touch of this. Here are politics. What are you doing with it? Standing aloof from it, saying, "I don't like it. I can't tolerate its methods. I don't believe in nose counting and the republic ought to be run on higher methods." Oh, friend, the trouble with you is you are useless. You are useless. You would let the world rot and you would stand off and say, "Too bad, too bad." What is that down there? That is where people are bad. That is where bad voting is; that is where bad people live. What are you going to do with it? Why, fold your arms and stand far off and say, "Let's go over to the lake. The smell is better on the lake. It is a finer flavor on the sea. Let's go there." Jesus said, "What are you doing on the lake?" "Why," you said, "catching the sea breath.' "Oh," He said, "face about. Let's go up to life." How do you like that? It is better. There is something divinely dynamical in that, being good where folks are and being good in the world. Oh, I love that in Jesus. I love that in Jesus. He is not trying to create an isolated icicle. He is trying to create an incandescent heated heart. Where is heartache? Where folks are. Where is heartbreak? Where folks are. Where is heart help? Where folks are. Where shall we bring heart help? Where folks are. And, upon my word of honor as a man, I think it so good to be where life is hardest and where it grits its teeth at its toil, leans over under its burden, and the teeth grind together, and there comes a voice that lends new life, saying: "All lift together!" And the teeth grit, but the load lifts. What is the matter with the shoulders? They ache. What is the matter with the shoulders? They are bleeding. What is the matter with the shoulders? They are sore. What is the matter with the world? It is lifted to where it ought to be—that is all. Now, then, some men want to send the children out and turn every creature out of the house. "Now," they say, "children, go down to Washington park, or to Jackson park, or to Texas. I want to think. Now, children, papa wants to think. Go away off." And then he calls his wife and says: "Don't do anything disastrous to the housekeeping while I am thinking. I am thinking now. Now let everybody be still. I want to think." What is the matter with a fellow's thinker like that, that he wants the isolation of the earth before he can begin to think? What is better than that? I will tell you. It is having a thinker in such shape that if there were all the thunder of all the Waterloo guns around you, you could go on with your business and think your proposition out. Jesus puts life in the masterful system and puts it where it is to master things, not to be mastered by them. "How did you get into heaven?" said Christ. "I dodged up," said the man. "I dodged up." Is life a game of touch and pum-pum-pull-away, and dodging around the runners, and saying, "Can't catch me?" Is life that? It is not that. It is going straight ahead and saying: "You folks can't stop me now, and that is the end of it. Can't stop me now, and that

is the end of it." Death, you can't stop me. Hell, you can't stop
me. The world, you can't stop me. The flesh, you can't stop me.
The devil, you can't stop me. I am on this road, and have got
business here." And you can feel that fellow's tramp across the
road, and when he goes you can look and see his footprints, and
the world follows after him. And he went along, whether things
were pleasant or unpalatable, and went along, whether things
helped or hindered. He said: "Here am I; make way for me."
When he comes hasting up to the kingdom of God, and God looks
at him and says: "You seem to be battered up pretty much."
And he says: "So I am. I didn't like to come up here this way."
And God will say: "You are the kind I want to see come up
here." These poor signs of doing nothing. Oh, me—that is nothing. Does God want that? No. The signs of the world doing
things. Get so dirty in the throng? No. Get so clean in the
throng? Yes.

And the only word to prove to your own satisfaction that this
theory of isolation by contact works, is to say that Jesus did it.
He was not only a spotless Man; but He touched everybody. The
leper and the clown? Oh, yes. And you can read in the book that
tells the strange, sweet story of His strange, divine achievings,
that He touched folks. He touched folks. Didn't put His hands
behind Him and say, "Don't come close now." Ran out their
way and touched them, and was not defiled, but cleansed. Brothers,
sisters, isn't that a good program for a good life? Doesn't that im-
press you as not only being the tramping, tramping of the tramping Christ, but as being the lordly achieving of the lordly achiever,
Christ. Now, I have read a great deal first and last about bacteria;
not that I will tell you what I know, though it wouldn't take me
long. I believe in them. I have had them. I am not the man who
doubts bacteria. But the thing I have noticed in reading about
bacteria is, there are enough bacteria of malignant intent around
to kill us forty times a day, and the only thing that hinders us
mostly from being killed by the bacteria is that most of us have
such a magazine of health that we whip the bacteria out. Now,
I hear persons sometimes saying there are no bacteria. I don't believe with that crowd, no sir. I don't talk with them, because bacteria know better. But having such vigor that you whip your enemies. Very well. What is Christianity? According to Jesus,

health. How much health? Plenty of it. What kind of health? Human and divine health. Where are you going to keep well? Here. What kinds of disease are prevalent here? Plenty of spiritual miasma here? Yes. Weary world? Yes. The weariness and the systematic routine of minor details? Yes. Where are you going to keep spiritual health? And he says, here, here.

And I say at this moment, to the glory of my Christ and to the heartening of your life and mine, that we must stay where people stay, that Christ's doctrine of purity is isolation by contact. Staying here and in the midst of it and by the attrition of it coming out white, white.

Did you notice how the flowers grow through dirt? Did you ever notice a flower coming up? Does it not come up through dirt? Does it put on any vestments to keep the dirt from crowding all around it? It does not. The flower comes up through the dirt, and grows in the dirt, and stays close to the dirt and, amongst the dirt, blooms. Ah me, we are God's flowers; we are meant to be where the dirt is; but we are meant to convert the dirt into bloom and beauty and perfume. What are we here for? To dodge the issue? No. What are we here for? To enjoy the issue? Yes. Keep in the world, impinged on by it, raptured with it, rejoicing for it. And, when you come up the long hill they call Zion's hill, and will come up with a great arm load of immortelles that you grew on the road you traveled—as you come they ask, "What are you sowing, man?" He said, "Flowers." "What for?" "Oh, for fun." "Who will pick them?" "I don't know." "Will anybody pick them?" "I wouldn't wonder." "What if nobody does?" "God will," he says. Sowing flowers. Not looking where he sows them, but going down on the roadways and by the hardest highways, along the loneliest places, up along the weary mountain ways, and when the gleaners of the flowers call to him he looks around and says, "Planting flowers in the world?" Yes. "Didn't get away from it?" No. "Sowed it to beauty?" Yes. Please God, if He will help me, I don't want to get to heaven a nondescript. I don't want to dodge from the lines, not a bit. I want to walk straight along and say, "I own this road. Give me passage. I own this road. Give me passage." Some of these days I want to walk down, and Death will see me and say, "You can't go this road.'' And I will say, ''Old man Death, you have terrified many, but my Christ told me to walk this way, and I am going along this road. Give me passage.'' And he will. And he will.

Isolation by contact. In the world and of it and above it, and wear the world in your heart, and take it up to God, and be able to show a geography of the planet through which you have passed on your heart, where you left it. ''I pray not,'' said the tender voice of Christ. ''I pray not that Thou shouldst take them from the world, but that Thou shouldst keep them from the evil.'' Grate your shoulder up against the world's work. Never mind if the skin comes off and the bone breaks. Get up against the load. You are not to be kept apart from it, but to be kept right in it. Oh Christ, Your voice is like a battle drum, and I heard You speak, and I will answer, ''Here am I.'' Keep me in the world and keep God in me. Pray that, beloved, for Christ's sake—Inter-Ocean.

THE SIMPLER AND GREATER RELIGION

BY PROFESSOR DAVID SWING

''I fear lest your minds might be corrupted from the simplicity and purity that is toward Christ.''—2 Corinthians 11:3.

. Many who live and think in our age are longing for a simpler religion. This desire is heard in sermons, in common conversation, and is seen in the volumes and essays of public men. It may well be a matter of wonder what is meant by a simpler religion. It may be these longing minds are thinking of a more rational Christianity—a form in which reason is more visible than miracle. It may be they are thinking of a life as distinguished from a belief. If we are at some time to have a simple form of Christianity or are to work for such a result we ought to map out our wish and study it, that we may know when it is gratified. Perhaps such a religion has already come. We have all heard of the ''simplicity of Christ.'' What is it? What was it? Will it have any merit and beauty when it shall appear?

Events are defining for us this new term. Each year is pointing out to us that the past Christianity was too complex. It was easily put out of working order. Often machines are made which involve so many movements, so many changes of the direction of power that it is almost impossible for the instrument to do a continuous work for a single day.

Genius has labored long to make a typesetting machine, but the task to be done has been so complex, so full of motions and choices, that the wish of the publishing men has not yet been fully gratified. It was for a long time difficult to make a good watch which besides keeping time perfectly should strike the hour and minute and should continue to work only in one hour until another hour had come. The old, tall, eight-day clock had less difficulty in finding its field of service. A pendulum, a couple of weights, and a few wheels, and all was ready for a performance of duty for a hundred years without any stop for repairs.

In the material pursuits of man it is often necessary to have complex machines, the demand being imperative, but in his spiritual kingdom there is no such inexorable demand. Complexness is never unavoidable. Indeed it is purely gratuitous. There is no more demand for a complex religion than there was for the literary style of the poet Browning. It would have been quite an increase of fame and fortune to that talented man had he possessed a style as clear as that of Shakspeare or Lord Byron. He had noble purposes and great power, but his words always became entangled like a skein of fine silk.

His thoughts were indeed silk, but it was difficult to pull quickly out of the tangle a long needleful of good thread. The greatest of all thoughts can be best expressed in the utmost simplicity because the idea, like a mountain, must stand forth all alone that it may be the better seen. But when a mountain is mingled with a long group and is modified by foothills which reach away in all directions for a half hundred miles there is the most sublime Alp or Appentine injured by a complexity. Christianity is much like an author or a piece of art, it can rise up in its own grandeur and express its divineness or it can be almost hidden and ruined by surroundings in which there are no traces of greatness.

When Pascal lived and created such a sensation in the Romish church of the seventeenth century, his power lay in his ability to raise a laugh over the obscure metaphysical inquiries so dear to that period. Born a geometer and a mathematician, his reason could strip all ideas of their false side, and could detect instantly a piece of bad logic. He loved to ridicule the absurdities of the middle ages and to plead for the simple gospel of the first four centuries. His influence came chiefly from his power to lift up a great idea until by its altitude it made all other ideas contemptible. He turned the morals of the Jesuits into contempt and the name of God into sublimity.

One of the last lessons learned by mankind is this: that simplicity may be power; that it is nearly always the most powerful element in thought and art. The most intricate and senseless of all philosophies are those of the earliest and most ignorant races. The religions of India are unreadable in our age. No modern mind could find the courage to work its way through such wonderful admixtures of fact and invention. Many of the absurd inquiries which attracted the schoolmen and held them captive up to the sixteenth century came into Christianity from the old East. Nearly all of those questions about the size of a spirit, about its ability to travel fast from star to star, its ability to dance on a needle's point came into the Christian period from the heathen world which had flourished long before the birth of Christ. All semi-barbarian races have loved a pomposity of speech and style. As some of the African women in the interior of the Dark Continent wear 100 pounds of iron rings on arms and ankles, assuming that if a ring be an ornament then the more rings the more beautiful the girl who wears them, so in the old theologies the more abundant the notions, the richer the creed. So rich was the Hindoo philosophy at last that it would have filled volumes had the conglomeration ever been fully expressed in writing.

This fondness for entanglement we see in its better days in the Apocalypse of St. John. There is no doubt John was one of the most beautiful characters of all who have lived, but this moral beauty did not save him from being led away by the prevailing charm of excessive figure and of wide labyrinths of thought. In the first chapter of his gospel he exults in the enigma of the Word; and in the Revelation he hands his mind and soul over to the cause of a bottomless mystery and no doubt drank in much sweetness from thoughts which are bitterness to this century. John had in his heart some great poem to be inscribed to Christ, the church and heaven, but the past ages had shaped for him his form of expression, and the result was a poem which, instead of standing sublime and simple like the words of Jesus, lies before the modern world like the wreck of some royal galleon, all marked from sails to anchor with the splendors of the kings of Spain. Over such an ornamental ship the ocean sighs and the suns of summer shine, but the beautiful boat will never sail the sea. So the Apocalypse is a gorgeous barge that will never be under sail again.

Should any one curious over the past and fond of comparisons wish to compare the Jesus and the disciple He loved, he will find much of that difference contained in the mental simplicity of the Master. With Jesus the greater the truth the simpler its expression. As his ideas grew in vastness they diminished in number. As our earth has many little lakes, but only a few oceans, because there is no room for many, so Christ offered only a few truths because each truth had to be thousands of miles in length and breadth. What Christ said is as clear, as rich, as divine today as it was 1800 years ago, whereas much which John wrote is now as faded as the flowers which bloomed around him in Patmos. We see in those two faces the Master and the gentle disciple. John was all the more beloved because he was only the companion planet of the flaming Sun. The central Sun did not need help, it needed only a companion in the realms of space. St. John was this companion, and Christ and he will journey onward forever, hand in hand, the greater and the less.

The many shapes of Christianity having reached this period of reason are compelled to halt for a time. All these modern churches have come through many a tribulation, but, above all, they have come through one long jungle which had thickened ever since the times of the old Aryan tongues. They all halt now because our period asks them what all their enigmas are worth? The age does not seek the money value but the moral value of their stuffs. A priest in a large city is having hymns printed in English to be sung by all his congregation, as hymns are sung here, for, he says, if the English language can speak our wisdom, our wit, our love, our friendship, can it not utter the emotions of our religion? What a sad blunder of society if Cardinal Newman can compose such a hymn as "Lead, Kindly Light," and then must have a little choir sing some Latin words for his congregation, whose hearts and tears are in his English, living thoughts! Often highly educated persons are able to lend their soul to two or three different tongues, but, with the millions on millions of people, there is only one language in and around their spirit. It is the arms, the feet, wings, and senses of their mind. In it is light, out of it all is midnight. In that one language the people live and move and have their being. Coming up to the English tongue the church must throw away its Latin, and talk and sing and pray along with the living heart.

We must throw aside childish affectations and live real lives in a real world. When a Christian church crosses the line and enters Germany it must use the language of Goethe and Schiller; in France it must use the language of Paris; in America it must use the language of Webster and Clay. To use the Latin tongue is only an affectation like that of many of our youth who love nothing unless it lies over the sea. What a wretched blunder had Schiller attempted to write in French, and Ernest Renan attempted to compose his books in German! Dante began his poem with the Latin tongue, but it was too dead a speech for the living Florence. Thus the Latin of the church is only a colossal act in the long history of affectation.

But what the Romanists are guilty of in language the Protestants have been guilty of in their relations to doctrine, for they are attempting to carry onward a bundle of ideas which are fully as dead as the Kings who built the pyramids. Even were they not dead, they are only expressions which pleased generations which are no longer here. There is no public here which cares to discuss the natural inability of the sinner, or the totalness of an infant's guilt, or the inability of a saint to lose his piety, or the worthlessness of morality, or the efforts of Christ in behalf of a few, and that a general and endless punishment of mankind is for the glory of God. There must be a half hundred of ideas which once possessed the power to thrill the public heart, but which now lie dead and friendless. The fashion of this world passeth away. The love of doctrine has declined.

There used to be recognized several kinds of faith. There was a faith in miracles, a faith in the divinity of Christ, a faith which even devils might cherish, and last and best of all came a saving faith. This kind would come only by the intervention of miraculous power. What kind of faith an inquiring soul might have found or might find was exceedingly uncertain. The soul might be mistaken and be like the men, who, in digging a well on their farms, have come upon iron pyrites and have held a feast and invited in all the neighbors to rejoice with them over the discovery of a fabulous vein of gold. It is within living memory that many a young person has longed to have a saving faith, but has been uncertain whether what he had was the purest of gold or only the cheap sulphide of iron. All these old shadings of faith have melted into one—a faith in Jesus Christ as man's beloved friend. If we had asked the poet Cowper whether he had faith in his mother, and whether it was a faith in miracles or in testimony, or a faith which a devil might possess, he would have scorned all our theological chemistry and have said: "I shall love my mother forever." Behold in Cowper's reply the coming simplicity of Christianity! It will rear at last a sentiment which will make earth beautiful and heaven near.

The old theologies were a kind of exhaustive chemical analysis of man as a religious creature; they were a physiology of the religious nerves and tissues,, a microscopic study of the cellular structure as affected by the religious emotions. Among its conclusions one will find the deduction that if a babe should die unbaptized it would be punished in perdition forever by a God of infinite love.

Many centuries were thus dominated by a scientific Christianity. Repentance was analyzed and quite an assortment of repentances were found. There was a repentance without sorrow and one with sorrow, one without reform and one with reform, and then came the chase after that kind which itself needed to be repented of, and then came the search for that sin over which repentance was utterly useless. Equipped with such a scientific religion, the many churches did their work for many centuries. Under it wars, murders, persecutions, and tortures were most common. The spirit of Christ had little to do with the case, because that spirit was not an easy victim to such a theological laboratory. When our vivisectionists cut to pieces a living dog or a living horse they report on the creature's bones and sinews; they never report on the animal's friendship for man.

The vivisectionist sustains no relations to mercy or goodness or justice; his word is made up of weights and measures and times, causes and effects. In Africa, a negro chief having been presented with a rifle by Captain Speke, and seeing no bird or animal upon which to try the instrument, fired at a slave who was at work in a field. The chief went to his palace proud of his gun. What a marvelous combination of lock, stock, and barrel! How bright the iron and steel! how polished and how carved the wood! As for the slave, he lay dying in agony. Such is the science of vivisection—a science of knives and saws, with the human soul and the animal soul left out. It is the African rifle, with the dying slave omitted.

Thus has theology been too scientific. A year or two ago a railway car was thrown over, and a priest who was not hurt in the least, but who was compelled to wade out of deep water and mud came up the bank swearing in an anger and with oaths which consigned to future pain all the railway men who had ever lived in any land. And yet the theology of that priest was a most complete science of salvation. It contained all the dogmas of the church as discovered between St. Augustine and Cardinal Richelieu. Nothing was absent from the theology except religion.

From this elaborate science our age desires to break away and to enjoy more of religion itself. We all perceive that the millions of people do not need the theories of Dr. Briggs or of those who are opposed to that theologian—they need a great, deep friendship with the Man of Galilee, who held in His soul all that is great in human practice or belief. Having had eighteen centuries of analysis of religion how ready the world is for a taste of the good analyzed so long. Newman and Fenelon possessed it; so Calvin and John Knox carried it in their hearts; Paul and Apollos were full of it when the world was young; it sprang up in the soul of John Wesley and came to Whitefield; it inflamed the bosom of Mme. Guion, and away it went to live with the missionaries who traversed these snows in winters long since melted into summers, which also are gone. But if minds so scattered through 2,000 years met in one Christianity then there must be a religion which lies apart from the hundreds of doctrines and which cares for none of them any more than the sea cares for the artists who sit on the sand and attempt to paint its picture. We can imagine the ocean saying to the artist: "Are you trying to make a picture of me? Me? Why, I am 10,000 miles wide, and am not even in your sight! Paint me! Why, I am not here for you to paint. I am washing the shores of England, America, Spain, and France!''

To John Calvin we can imagine Christianity saying: "What! are you delineating me? How can you paint me when I am not in Geneva alone? I was with Magdalen when she prayed; I was with the Joseph who asked to furnish the tomb for my crucified Christ; I was with the mother of Augustine more years than I was with Augustine himself; I was with all the little children which Christ held in His arms; I was with John when he was preaching in the wilderness; I was with the 5,000 once and gave them all the bread of two worlds; I was with the disciples when they sung a hymn, and I was with all the martyrs when they died. Oh, thou citizen of Geneva, thou canst not express me in articles, for I am measureless! I am not a science of plants—not a botany. I am the blossoms themselves—the color and the perfume!''

The Christian religion often seems like that vast structure in Rome to which many architects carried their deepest and most serious genius. Bramante came first. He died, and the great Raphael took his place among the arches and columns. The grave soon called Raphael. Then came Perruzi to stay by the stones for a half of a life time. Angelo then came and gave the great sanctuary twenty-two of his precious circles of the sun. Genius followed genius for 120 years.

In that long procession of Italian summer times these great architects hated each other and quarreled, each with his neighbor. Costelar says that Bramante and Angelo separated by the things of earth are now united in immortality. While the builders were often enemies, the temple grew in its grandeur, because its arches and columns and dome could take no part in the quarrels of daily human life. The great basilica arose each year toward the sky, and each year left the further below, down among the marble chips, the many quarrels of the workmen. It absorbed from the architects their love and their genius, and left all else behind. Thus Christianity can make use of the hearts and powers of genius, but it remands back to oblivion all the discords of fretful minds. It can extract something from a Cardinal Newman, something from John Wesley, something from

—7C

each cathedral and each little chapel in town or field, but in its vast life which is to follow the human race forever it will work its way up toward its God long after we shall have gone away from our quarrelings among the useless chips around the base. It will rise a single shaft sublime but simple.

Christ was so essentially a life that His religion must follow closely the plan of its Founder. There are many intellectual inquiries upon which the church does not know what was or would have been the Nazarene's opinion, but the life of Christ admits of no doubt. The demand of the whole earth is expressed in a few words—a life like that of Jesus. With such a piety before man and in man his present and his eternity will be one wide field of, blessedness.

It must be remembered that a simple Christianity does not mean an unadorned religion. Mount Blanc is simple, but it is wondrously adorned. Coleridge saw it rising majestically "forth from a sea of pines;" he saw on its sides "motionless torrents" and "silent cataracts;" he saw "flowers skirting the edge of eternal frost;" he heard there "a thousand voices praising God." Rising up thus in all the matchless beauty which eternal winter could heap upon its summit, and which eternal spring could weave around its base, yet is that gigantic pile impressive in its central simplicity. It holds no enigmas. It appeals to all the human family and speaks in a language all minds can interpret. So, by a simple Christianity one must not mean a desert. Around a simple creed may be grouped the rich details so much loved by the human heart.

In the simple religion there is a greatness which only the greatest music and eloquence can express. The grander the doctrines of the church the more impressive may be the beauty which they may wear. It was often the misfortune of Europe that it had to place a royal crown upon the forehead of some young idiotic king, or of a royal leader in only the infernal realm of vice. Happy Europe could it have placed its crown jewels upon only those foreheads which were broad with wisdom and power, and white in purity!

Thus has the church often attempted to attach its gorgeous service to a little and false thought. It has waved its silken banners at the burning of a heretic, or has compelled its organ and choir to chant a "Te Deum" over fields soaked with innocent blood. When a simple greatness shall come into the creed, then can a new beauty come into the service of God's house, for since all the arts are only so many languages of the soul they will rise in impressiveness—when at last the soul shall have great truths to follow and express.

Man does not live in a desert. It pleased the Creator to make wondrously beautiful the world of His children. All that these children make and have shall catch something from ornament from the very planet on which they dwell.

When Christianity shall teach its simplest form of doctrine it will still be in the world of music and color, and all sweet and rich beauty. It will ask 10,000 voices to join in its song; it may ask all instruments to accompany the multitude in their hymn; it may invite more flowers to its altars, and then to the material emblems of what the heart loves the simplified church will add a pulpit which can have no themes but great ones, and which can easily find that eloquence which as aroma lies hidden in sandal wood, lies high and deep in the being of God, in the life and deeds of Christ, in the relation of man to man, and in the mysterious flow of our race toward death and the scenes beyond.—Inter-Ocean.

CHRISTIANITY

Christianity is an utterance to man of the divine fullness; and the Bible does not so much declare the human sense of want as it does the divine supply. The difference between the Christian and every other religion is, therefore, infinite—a difference which, however we may account for it, is yet so great and so clear, that while we may properly classify all other religions as expressing, in different forms, the one human yearning and seeking after God, Christianity alone possesses the thought, a thought which penetrates it through and through, of a divine yearning and seeking after man.

The gospel has shown itself fitted to regenerate the world, in illustration of which—since it is well for us to remember the hole whence we were digged—we may cite, in the first place, the experience nearest to ourselves. Our ancestors, but a few centuries ago, were sunk in all the wretchedness and superstition which we now find in the heathen world. For savage ferocity and brutal degradation, they have scarcely been surpassed. The ancient Britons were wild men of the woods, who tattooed themselves, and wore the skins of wild beasts; whose towns were woods surrounded by a mound of earth and a ditch; who offered human sacrifices to their gods; who practiced polygamy; and who, if Cæsar can be trusted, possessed among relations a community of wives. The ancient Scots were cannibals, delighting in the taste of human flesh.

Even as late as the twelfth century, Henry II. of England declared to a Greek emperor, who had asked him of the state of Britain, that Wales was then inhabited by a race of naked warriors. The ancient Saxons indulged in human sacrifices, and selected by lot one-tenth of their captives in war for a bloody offering to their gods. The ancient Gauls hung the skulls of their slain enemies around the necks of their horses, and used them as drinking cups in their feasts. In the family life of these wild savages, the husband possessed the right of life or death over his wife and children. All that we possess of peace and order, of home and family life, all the institutions of society most valuable to us, all purity among us of individual hearts, and all progress toward a better state, is no original inheritance. It comes from no development of native tendencies, but is a fruit borne by a new life with which these ancient savages became enkindled.

The beneficent changes which have occurred in Europe, the beneficent influences which we now enjoy, in distinction from those of our ancestors fifteen centuries ago, I believe no careful student can ascribe to any cause separate from the preaching of the gospel of Christ. The most careful and profound students of history do ascribe them to this. That our present condition, with its incalculable blessings, is no development from original forces in our natural endowment, is still further evident from the fact that the power of the gospel is sufficient to produce the same results among people of the most diverse endowment.

The current skepticism, that Christianity is a Shemitic religion, confined to certain races, to which it properly belongs, while it is only a delusion to suppose that it fits all races, in every stage of their development, is sufficiently answered in the actual facts of the case. Christianity has found its triumphs and shown its fruits in every nation and tribe upon the globe; and its results have been, in every case, the same. Virtue, social order, prosperity, blessedness, the elevation and improvement, in all respects, of the human life, are the uniform and exclusive inheritance of those who receive the gospel.—Seelye's Christian Missions.

CHRISTIANITY AS A MIGHTY GROWTH

As we have come to the close of the nineteenth century, when the changes of the previous centuries are emphasized, it may be predicated that among these changes Christianity makes an exhibit that may well arrest the attention of the thoughtful. We know that doctrine, subsidiary if not fundamental, has changed, and we know, too, that a most significant fact is the infinite capacity which Christianity exhibits of adapting itself to new conditions, and even to assume to itself new and startling accessories. Doubtless the tares have grown plentifully in the Christian church, if not from apostolic times, at least from a very early age, when Greek philosophy produced such a subtle but marked effect upon Christian belief. But it is the peculiar province of Christianity that it can be reformed, revived and largely restated without changing its essential truth. Buddhism, for instance, has indeed been changed. But while it inculcates much beauty of living, it has virtually become an extinct spiritual force. Hinduism is growing, but only as populations grow; it is non-missionary, and like all non-missionary religions, it gives way when brought in contact with Christianity. Then there is Mohammedanism; what religion is more unchangeable?—for the Koran prescribes in minutest detail what the Arabian Prophet would have the Faithful do and believe. But all these and other religions, growing only by accretion as their own populations grow within themselves, are being outclassed by Christianity; especially may we say of Moslemism, with the poet Shelley—

> Now, blazon'd as on heaven's immortal noon,
> The Cross leads generations on.

So it is, while the general tendency of man is to enslave himself to letter and to tradition—for which the Jewish people were so strongly arraigned by Christ—the greatest possible contrast to this tendency is manifested when we regard Christianity. Look at the Roman church of Julius II. and Leo X.; the Eastern church before and after the declared supremacy of the Pope; the Anglican church under the first two Georges, and the Lutheran church of the eighteenth century, and the whole world of Christendom during the Dark Ages—what greater transformations since can be seen anywhere? Then it was the stilled pulse, and decay seemed to have got in, but after all it was only the death that is the prelude to the resurrection. Out of these moribund fragments have sprung new life, not in doctrine, but especially in new spiritual organizations, call them Orders of Dominicans or Franciscans, missionary boards, Christian Endeavorers, as you like, with other organizations for the uplifting of humanity. It is indeed "change" but not "decay" that all around we see. So it is, the warmth of spring and summer follows the cold of winter no more inevitably than a cold Christianity is followed by warmth and a revitalizing process; as a recent writer has said, "A fossilized Christianity in England is met by the faithful fervor, at various times, of a Wycliffe, a Latimer, a George Fox, a Bunyan and a Wesley." The renewal of life even at the most barren period is constant and certain. The spring never quite runs dry; in Florence Savonarola joins ethics to religion, and transforms an entire city and pays the cost with his own life, but now to be glorified as a martyr. In rich, formal Milan St. Carlo Borromeo reveals new depths in the Christian idea of love; the example and memory of St. Vincent de Paul inspires men and women to a love for the suffering which Pliny and Seneca, with all their fine ethical theories, never really felt in their inmost hearts, while in England the Wesleys touch cold hearts with living coals from the altar, and transform a nation. These agencies,—at least their spirit and influence—have penetrated every quarter of the globe, and have been found compatible with all manner of intellectual opinion: here we have one of the most profound and convincing proofs that Christianity is, in the ordering of things, destined to become the religion of mankind. The least of seeds has become a mighty tree, and the birds of the air will lodge in its branches.—Christian Work.

"THE THEOLOGY OF THE LITTLE CHILD"

BY THE REV. FRANK CRANE, D.D.

"And a little Child shall lead them."—Isaiah 11:6.

Men go far to find what is near at hand. They seek happiness in distant lands when that treasure is found only in their own bosoms, if found ever. But, above all things, they search for the solution of the problems of theology in remote and difficult fields, overlooking the real explanation that is before their face day by day. For the explanation of "the ways of God to men" is not to be found in learned books, nor puzzling meditations, nor brain-racking study, but in the little child at home.

Religion presents a strange paradox. It baffles the sages, while it is understood by the ignorant. The savant throws up his hands in despair, exclaiming that the whole matter is "lunar politics," while the peasant draws from the Book of books his richest comfort. Even among great minds testimony conflicts, for while Renan rejects the supernatural, Tennyson clings to it; while Ingersoll rails at Christianity, Lowell and Whittier interweave its lessons into their song.

Turning to Christian believers themselves, we find a diversity that confuses many. Ask a man to join Christ's church, and he replies: "What church? Which one? Shall I unite myself with the Roman Catholics or with the ranks of the Salvation Army? There are many sects. They all disagree. Each contends his own is the true faith. Each contains men of high intellectual ability, many of them wiser than I. When doctors disagree, who shall decide?"

Let us, for a moment, lay aside all questions of church and creed and dogma and get back to the simple question: "What is the religion of Jesus of Nazareth, and how may one grasp it?" And in answer to this let us suggest, first, that no one ever comprehends any subject unless he comes at it in the right way. In other words, the most important thing for us to observe in taking up any matter we wish to understand is the spirit of approach.

No one can hope to become a scientist unless he has the scientific spirit. Could Walt Whitman have become a Huxley or a

Faraday? Could any poet, with eyes for the beautiful only, excel as an observer and classifier of facts and a verifier of theories? On the other hand, could a man with the scientific mind see those subtle verities that the poets deal with? The historian must have the historical spirit. The artist must have the artistic sense. The lawyer is told that he must cultivate what is called "the judicial mind." The musician must have that attitude of soul which puts him in sympathy with the concord of sweet sound. Any book is closed to you unless you put yourself en rapport with the author.

If this be true of these things, how much more is it true of Christianity? How can one expect to understand the Bible unless he brings to it the same attitude of recipiency he must bring to any other book? It is this spirit of approach that the Bible itself insists upon. Paul says that as no man understands the things pertaining to man except one who has the spirit of man, so no one understands the things of God except that one who has the spirit of God. David prayed for God to create in him a right spirit, so that he could teach. Jesus told His disciples that they should know all things concerning the faith when they received the spirit of truth. The Scriptures also allude to those who do not believe as having their eyes blinded and their heart hardened; implying that their incredulity is not due to lack of evidence, but to a condition of their spirit.

What, then, is this spirit which one must have, if he is to understand Jesus? Let us first put away the things which it is not. It is not a spirit of credulity. Blind superstition, accepting as gospel the vehemence of any fakir that happens to exhort us, does not lead to Christian character and the perfect manhood of Jesus. That has been tried, for ages it has been tried, and it has led only to debasement and ignorance.

It is not some strange, supernatural wave of emotion that descends upon a soul from above. To accept this would be to reduce Christianity to hypnotism or clairvoyance. The common-sense of the world refuses to think that one must submit himself to the extravagance which the ranter urges upon us in order to become like Christ. The doorway to the kingdom must be something else than some nervous experience that might be produced by many other causes than the spirit of truth.

Neither, in the third place, is it anything that implies the disannulment of reason. It must be something which, while it may be beyond or beside reason, is yet consistent with reason, something to which reason must give welcome, something that clarifies and ennobles reason.

What is it, then? The answer is that it is the spirit of the little child. The apostle tells us that "we have received the spirit of adoption, whereby we cry, Abba, Father." That is, the Christian feels that he is a member of the Father's family and feels toward Him filial trust. Jesus said that except we be changed so as to become like little children we should in no wise see the kingdom of God. The Bible places so much emphasis upon faith because faith, which would better be called trust, is the attitude of mind which the right child has to a parent. Without faith, therefore, it is impossible to please God, and the just shall live by faith, and we are saved by faith, and so on. All this technical language, not originally technical, but become so by use in ages of theological controversy, means that it is only by getting toward God the child's attitude toward its parent that we come at the secret of the kingdom. The faith that saves is not the assent given by the intellect but it is the confidence bestowed by the heart.

This is a most distinctive feature of Christ's teaching. When He teaches us to pray He says, "Our Father." He insistently uses the term "Father" in alluding to God. He takes up the children in His arms and calls those who are like them the greatest in the kingdom of heaven. He rejoices in spirit and exclaims: "I thank Thee, O, Father, that Thou hast hid these things from the wise and prudent and revealed them unto babes!" He exhorts us to right lives by giving us the motive that we may be "the children of our Father which is in heaven." He encourages us to pray always and not to faint by reminding us that none of us, if asked for bread by our child, would give him a stone, or, if asked for a fish, would give a serpent. In His most famous parable He illustrates the relation of God toward a wayward soul by a prodigal son. Calling Himself the Son of God he sweeps His arm outward toward the crowd of common people and cries: "Behold My mother and My brethren!" If God clothe the grass of the field, He says, and care for the lily, how much more shall the Heavenly Father care for

His own children! Thus the whole tenor of Jesus' teaching is the childhood of man and the fatherhood of God.

Let us now apply this key to some of the mysteries that bar us from faith and cause us such misery and uncertainty of spirit, and see how easily the child spirit will make things plain. Not that purely speculative inquiries will be answered; we will get no more information about the locality of heaven, or the duration of hell, or the nature of the Trinity, or the mode of baptism, than we had before. It was not the purpose of Jesus to add to our store of speculative knowledge; He came to tell us the things we need to know in order to get into a right relation toward God and toward our fellowmen. But while the child spirit will not increase our store of intellectual concepts, it will give us a most helpful insight into our real difficulties that might interfere with our trust in God and with the development of character.

For instance, it is a very actual perplexity to many of us how God can love us so tenderly as the Scriptures say He loves us and yet allow or cause us to suffer affliction. "If He loves me," says the grief-burdened mother, "how is it possible that He can take my child away from me?" She asks this question, bending over a little coffin, and such an inquiry cannot be lightly dealt with. A merchant wants to know how a loving God can allow his store to burn just at a critical time when it ruins him. The crippled, the blind, the deaf, the stricken of men, put the same question. Now remember the child, your child. Has it not often occurred in your family that certain arrangements which you thought necessary were considered by the child most cruel and unjust? You perhaps tried to explain to him and he could not see it. At last you fell back on the statement that while the child could not comprehend the wisdom of your acts now, yet he would see it all when he grew a little older. It stands the same with God and the soul. This whole earthly life is but a childhood, a brief fragment of years, compared with the eternity we have to live. "What I do," said Jesus, "thou knowest not now; thou shalt know hereafter." Tears may fall, hearts may break, disaster may come, but if we are God's children some day all will be made plain. You will look back upon your present grief in the days to come above, just as you now look back upon the denials of your childhood, and say that these things, after all, are the best that could have happened.

Then there is the old puzzle of prayer. How often do we pray and receive not what we want? And why should we pray at all when God already knows what we need? But how is it with your own child? Do you not deny him many more requests than you grant? Does he not run to you with innumerable demands which you are compelled lovingly to refuse? And would you, for that reason, think that he ought never to come to you again with his simple wants? To determine the efficacy of prayer by any enumeration of the number of petitions granted and the number denied, or by any other so-called "tests," shows a misapprehension of the whole matter. The object of prayer is not to get what we wish, but to live in communion with God. I remember that on one occasion my little boy, about five years old, wanted very much to play with my razor. It was a pretty toy to a child. I had to take it away from him. He cried lustily. He could see no reason why he was not fully competent to play with it, and I could not make him look at the matter from my standpoint. And how many of our importunities to God are exactly parallel to this!

We can now see, too, how a man is to come into communion with God. What shall I do to be saved? How shall I approach God to receive forgiveness for my sins? To get the answer to this ask yourself how you would expect your child to return to you after he had wandered away. Would you insist upon certain rites and ceremonies he was to observe? Would you require that he indulge in prescribed manner and number of genuflections? Not at all. All you would want him to do would be to return to you and say honestly and sincerely, "My father, I have done wrong. I have been a fool. I am sorry for it. I want your love and your forgiveness." That would be enough and more than enough. How many of you, indeed, would give all you have in the world if your wayward boy would return and say this to you? And will your heavenly Father ask more than you would ask? Is He not as good a father as you are? Go home to your closet and get upon your knees and just say to Him: "O, my Father, I am sorry that I have done that which displeased Thee. Forgive me. Take me unto Thy love and forgiveness. I want Thy love more than I value any evil thing." That is the child's way to God, and there is no better.

Even so it is with death. Men fear death as children fear the **dark.** How can a man have assurance that all is well when the cold damps of the awful sea of shadows are blowing into his face? On one occasion my little boy was made to sleep in a room alone, away from his mother and myself. We thought he was old enough to learn to sleep by himself. He was quite brave about it and consented readily when I told him it was the manly thing to do. That is, he was brave enough until the light was put out. We listened awhile, for he was in the next room to us. Pretty soon we heard him call faintly: "Papa!" I arose and went to him. "What is it, my boy?" I said. "Do you want anything? Are you afraid?" "No," he answered, "I don't want anything special. I'm not afraid. I just want you to sit here a minute and hold my hand." I sat on the side of the bed and took his hand in mine. In a few minutes he was asleep.

And what are you, my friends, and I, but "infants crying in the night, and with no language but a cry?" When the darkness of death comes there is but one thing that can assure us. It is to reach up the hand and feel that it clasps the hand of the Father. Death is as natural as life. It is as natural as sleep or night. But in that hour we can have no knowledge; we can only have faith. If all your life you walk hand in hand with the Father He will not desert you then.

THE SECRET OF CHRISTIANITY

BY THE REV. DR. LYMAN ABBOTT

"Unto you is born, this day, in the city of David, a Savior, which is Christ the Lord."—Luke 2:11.

In the Anglo-Saxon version of the New Testament the word "Savior" is rendered for the Anglo-Saxon word "helper." You know also that the word "Christ" is not a proper name, but a title equivalent to "The Messiah"—the Lord.

Every great movement has at the heart of it some secret, which if we can discover it, will disclose to us the secret of that great movement. What is the secret at the heart of Christianity, which has made it the great power that it is? In asking you to consider this question you will understand, of course, that I am not undertaking in half an hour to answer the entire question; I am only going to try in that half hour to indicate the essence of Christianity —the secret of its vitality. The Jewish people were in more than one sense "a peculiar people." Among other things in this: That their faces were turned toward the future. All other nations look backward for their golden age, but these "peculiar people" looked forward for theirs. They believed that a time was coming when there would be peace instead of war and for themselves prosperity instead of universal poverty. They believed that this great time would come through their own nation and that Jerusalem would become the holy city and the mistress of the world. And their prophets even pointed forward to this divine consolation, and they indicated that it would come through some deliverer. Sometimes they regarded the nation itself as that deliverer; sometimes a succession of prophets; sometimes a single prophet; sometimes a single man, as a king or prince, as a teacher, as a priest, as a "Man of Sorrows, and acquainted with grief." However different or incongruous or inconsistent these prophecies might be, they pointed the minds of the people forward to a great delivery and deliverer. So the shepherds perfectly well understood the angels when they said: "The Deliverer has come; the Helper is here. You will find Him cradled in the manger." When Jesus began His ministry His first sermon, of which we have a record, was preached in the synagogue at Nazareth. He went into the synagogue, a roll was open before Him and He read one of the prophecies of the great Deliverer Who was coming and then said: "This day is this Scripture fulfilled in your ears. I have come. I am that Deliverer." Having begun His ministry in this way, He went out to be a helper and fed the hungry, taught the ignorant and healed the sick and dispensed the gospel of hope. Once John the Baptist, perplexed to know if this was the Messiah, for things went on much the same and no great thing seemed to be accomplished, sent Him a message saying: "Art Thou the Messiah?" and Christ said to the messengers, "Wait here, see what you will see, and then go and tell your master." They waited and saw, and then Christ told them: "Go your way and tell John what things ye have seen and heard; how that the blind see, the lame walk, the lepers are cleansed, the deaf hear, the dead are raised, to the poor the gospel is preached."

No man can undertake to help his fellowmen really sincerely, on a large scale, without coming in contact with men who do not want the help, those who are making something out of the misfortunes of their fellowmen. Christ came in contact with such, and they leagued themselves together to destroy Him. He was arrested and brought before the Jewish tribunal and asked, "Are You the Messiah?" And under a solemn oath He said, "I am." Pilate said, "Are You a king?" He said, "I am." To both the Jewish tribunal and the Roman He said, "I am," and for that He was condemned to die, and for it He died. When He died the hopes of His disciples dissipated. They said, "We thought He was to be the great Deliverer, but evidently He was not." Rumors of His ascension began to circulate and, little by little, they became convinced, and then they said, "Ah, He is the Deliverer, after all." If you will turn to the book of Acts and read one of the sermons there you will see that was the burden of all the apostolic ministry. No new theology, ethic or law. Their messages were all the same: "The Deliverer is come; He is here; the deliverance has begun."

In the first century rule was by absolute despotism. Gradually government has been transformed, until now it is completely established and there is no government in Europe west of Russia that does not at least recognize the fact that government is not for the government, but for the governed. All industry was servile. Half the Roman population were slaves and the other half were on the edge of famine and only kept alive by the largess of others. Wherever Christianity has gone the chain has dropped from the slave and labor has been emancipated. There were no schools in Rome and none among the Jews, except those connected with the synagogue, but wherever Christianity has gone it has established schools and wealth has been diffused among the people. This is called an age of concentrated wealth. That is not so. There never was an age, and that is especially true of America, when wealth was more distributed. There are charities everywhere. The church has also changed the conception of punishment, so that punishment has become reformatory. The object of the old pagan religion was not to help man; it was to appease the wrath of God or to purchase the favor of a corruptible God. Christianity has altered all that with various degrees of success. The church of Christ is engaged in the work of lifting the burdens of men, in inspiring them with courage and nobler purposes. Christianity is not a mere sum of doctrines, a new method of worship or a new law of morals. It is a great historical movement.

Flowing down through the centuries with ever widening and deepening current, blessing every land it has touched and carrying with it some measure of helpfulness, Christianity has done, through the centuries, what Christ did in those four short years—it has helped the helpless, fed the hungry, taught the ignorant, given courage to the despairing and brought glad tidings to the poor. The secret of Christianity, then, is helpfulness. This it is that distinguishes the theology of the Christian religion from the theology of all other religions. It is a new doctrine respecting God —not absolutely so, but still new contrasted with the teaching of other religions. Everywhere on the globe men believe in the aid of God and in the power of God. The distinction between the Jewish religion and Paganism was not that one called God Jehovah and the other Baal. It was that one worshiped justice and the other power. The message of the Pagan religion was of an omnipotent power back of the affairs of nature and life. The message of Judaism was that God is a righteous God and demands righteousness of His children. Still we need to understand that God expects righteousness from us, and nothing less will satisfy

Him. In later Judaism there came the greater message. No longer God as a powerful, just God, but God as a God who will help you to be righteous. The message of the later prophet was mercy. Mercy, go back to Homer, Confucius, Seneca, Marcus Aurelius; do not find it there? No. Some time ago I made that statement and a professor said to me: "Are you quite sure of that?" I said: "I am not sure, but you are a student of the Orient and I wish you would look it up and tell me if I am wrong." Three weeks after I received a letter, saying: "The only revelation of the mercy of God in the old Hindoo religion is this: 'O, Veruna, are thou not also merciful?' Put that alongside "what can separate man from the love of God." The distinct characteristic of Christianity is this mercifulness of God. Today in my country home they are suffering from drought, and yet, if I were to go on the hillside and run a tube down a little way into the ground, I should strike a spring full of water. So God is full of mercy. This is the revelation of the New Testament; and whatever your troubles, sorrows, sins, you can go to Him and find His loving kindness and tender mercy. You don't find that in any other religion.

A man falls into a pit and cannot get out. Presently Confucius comes along and says: "My dear fellow, I am sorry you have fallen down there. If you could only get out Confucius would show you how to walk so that you would keep out." Then a Brahmin sees him, and says: "I am sorry, but there is no help for you; you never can get out. The only chance for you is to fall into an eternal sleep and forget your misery." Next comes a Mohammedan, who says: "I am so sorry to see you there, but Allah is just, and you deserve it. He is not merciful, and you will never get out." Last comes a Christian, who says: "I myself have been down there. I tumbled down there once. I know just how you can get out." And he gets a rope and pulls the man out of the hole and puts his feet upon a rock. That is the difference between the Christian and Pagan religions. The Christian religion is the only religion in the world that offers to help men out of the burden of their sins and the consequences of their misery. But, O! the pity of it, men don't want it. Napoleon said: "Scratch a Russian, and you will find a Tartar." Scratch a Christian and you will find a Pagan. It seems to me that Chris-

—8C

tian congregations are full of Paganism. I receive letters every week from men and women who never yet have learned that if they have made a blunder or committed a sin, and perhaps involved others in peril because of their mistake, God can take care of it all and they can trust Him to help, if only they will turn from their evil ways.

Helpfulness is the secret of Christian theology. So it is the secret of our Christian ritual. It is at the heart of all worship. We come to church, not driven by fear or compelled by custom, and not by conviction. Why? Not to be entertained by an amusing lecture. Then, why? At the heart of it all it is this: Some sense of the truth of that message that God is love and that, somehow or other, we are dependent on His love and have had something from His love, and we want to give Him something in return. I do not say that is true of all, but still if it were not for the sense of the love of God and the desire to be thankful the church would close their doors and the chimes cease to ring. What is the Roman Catholic service? First confession and then absolution. The same thing of the Episcopal service, and of the Congregational. We don't go into the confessional; we don't stand up as a priest pronounces an absolution, but D. L. Moody as truly preached absolution as any Catholic priest or Episcopalian rector. If you want to know what men believe, don't go to the creeds or catechism. Go to the hymn books. They express our faith and real experience; they are our creed, sung over and over and over again. And what does the hymn book say?

"Love divine, all love excelling." "Thanks be to God Who giveth us the victory."

Imagine, this Sabbath morning, a citizen of Mars coming down and entering different churches. He would go into a Catholic church and see the altar and the candles and the robed priest and the incense, and he would say: "What are you doing here?" The answer would be: "We are here to worship the Lamb Who hath redeemed us." In the Episcopal church he would see no candles and incense, and would again ask the question. The answer would be: "We have come to praise the Lord Christ Who hath redeemed us." In the Congregational, Baptist or Presbyterian church he would see no altar or candles or vested priests. "What are you doing here?" he asks and the reply is: "We have come here to sing the praise of the Man of God Who hath redeemed us.'' And in the Quaker meeting house he would see no choir or preacher or service and hear no singing, but they would all be sitting still doing nothing—absolutely nothing. And their reply to the same question would be: ''We are giving our praise to Christ, Who hath redeemed us by His blood. We cannot find any utterance which will express our gratitude and we are simply speaking in the silence of our hearts.'' He would go back and say: ''They were all drawn together by a sense of God's love that had given His Son for their redemption. It is the love of God that makes us one, and only that. I was once in a Catholic church in Paris and after watching the service for a time I walked around behind the altar and found there a service of deaf and dumb people. The service was the same at heart; the love of God inspiring the thanks of men.

I remember an old English divine beginning his sermon: I can do all things—and then saying: ''That I deny. But let us see, what is this: 'through Him that strengthened me.' Ah, that is another thing; that I can do.'' It was a quaint way of putting it, but it made the text stick in my mind, and I have never forgotten it. This is the secret of the power of Christianity. You will find men say: ''Thou shalt love the Lord, thy God with all thy strength,'' is the summary of Christianity. That is a mistake. Christ gave that as the summary of the Jewish law. When asked, ''What is the chief end of the Jewish law?'' He said, ''Thou shalt love the Lord thy God. * * * and thy neighbor as thyself;'' but when He was about to die He left as a legacy to His disciples, this: ''A new commandment give I unto you; that ye love one another as I have loved you.'' How did He love us? He laid down His life for us. That is Christianity. Judaism is justice; Christianity is sacrifice. What makes a Christian nation? Not a creed written in a constitution, not an established church, an organ or music. What will make America a Christian nation? We have about us dependent and inferior races. Loving our neighbor and the Filipino and the negro and making them men— nothing else will make us a Christian nation. And what makes a Christian church? Not fine windows and music, but making the world wiser and better. What would Christ do for your employes and servants? Helpfulness and service is Christianity; the heart and the center and circumference of it. All Christian theology is summed up in "God so loved the world that He gave His only begotten Son," and all Christian ritual in the Psalm: "Blessing and honor and glory and power to Him that sitteth upon the throne and that hath redeemed us." All Christian power is summed up in: "I can do all things through Him that strengthened me;" and all Christian duty is summed up in the one law, "Love one another as I have loved you."—Brooklyn Daily Eagle.

WHAT IS CHRISTIANITY?

BY THE REV. DR. JOHN WATSON

It is to believe that at the heart of things is a Power with a mind and a will, from Whom everything has come, and by Whom everything is sustained; Who is immanent in the universe, and specially inhabits the human soul; Who is directing everything to moral ends, and Whose character can be summed up in love. That Jesus Christ came from God and is in a sense peculiar to Him the Son of God, that He has declared the character of God to the human race, has broken the power of sin, and is the point of union between God and man.

It is to fight the lower self at the base of our nature, to give the supreme place to the soul, to carry the cross of Christ in daily life, and to keep His commandment of love, to forget one's self, and to think of others, to serve instead of ruling, to give instead of taking, to suffer instead of resisting.

It is to hope that in the long battle between right and wrong, right will conquer, that the things apparently evil are making for good, that the agony of suffering will end in the blessing of holiness, that God is working everything up into something better in this world and that which is to come, and that humanity will one day be raised to the perfection of Christ.

Faith, Hope and Charity:—without the faith there can neither be the charity, nor the hope; without the charity the faith is not living; without the hope the charity is not crowned. The charity proves the faith and creates the hope—the greatest of these is charity. He who loves is therefore most surely a Christian—The Congregationalist.

THE CHRISTIANITY OF CHRIST

BY THE REV. DR. MADISON C. PETERS

"Now if any man have not the spirit of Christ, he is none of His."—Romans 8:9.

Christ must be known as Savior before we can follow Him as Exemplar. Where there is justification sanctification accompanies it. Wherever there is a change of state there must be a change of character. The atonement, the at-one-ment that saves is at-one-ness with Christ. Salvation consists not merely in saving from sin, but the curing of sin and the perfecting of the nature. There is a difference between believing in Christianity and believing on Christ. It is not the sight of a man's arm stretched out of the water that will save him from drowning, but the taking hold of it.

In a certain formal sense the baptized man is a Christian, just as foreigners who have been naturalized are American before the law. But the mere act of naturalization will not make any man a good American. There is a vast difference between naturalizing a man and nationalizing him. He is an American, no matter where born, who has an American heart, and he is a Christian who has the spirit of Christ, and not he who makes more noise in the world about his orthodoxy than the Master ever did. I believe in the importance of professing faith in Christ as the foundation of the sinner's hope in the prescribed way, but grander than that is a life all animated and all-pervaded with the spirit of Him who "went about doing good." The great end for which Christ came into the world was to die for sin, to make an atonement. But suppose that after His death and resurrection Christ had not ascended to heaven, what would have been His mission? Not to die for sin —that was over—but to make the world wiser, happier and holier. His mission would have been simply a life of doing good. Christians are to carry out Christ's purpose. The same authority which binds us to honesty in the commandment, "Thou shalt not steal," equally binds us to beneficence in the commandment, "Do good unto all men." Many a man looks at his correct life and exclaims, "I have done no man, woman or child any harm." But you must not only "cease to do evil," you must "learn to do well." From the moment that you become a Christian you must become useful and unselfish. Christ's entire life was a beautiful embodiment of that "love which seeketh not her own." The Christian is to show forth Christ in His life, to manifest Christ's spirit. He served others, so must we. He was compassionate and infinitely tender. So must we be. His loving deeds must find a transcript in our lives. The divine Savior gathered His expiring breath to plead for His foes. We must repeat in our lives something of His forgiveness and forbearance. Christ was prayerful. So must we be. Without prayer our religious life will fade as a flower on which no sun shines. Christ's "meat and drink was to do the will of Him who sent Him." We must make our heavenly Father's business the business of life. Our Christianity must not be a secondary thing; our gifts must be the choicest. Our noblest ministrations must be for Him. Do something for somebody before you die. Your joy in heaven will be to know that you have been Christ in the world to somebody, that you have been like Him, and that you have done His work by helping somebody up and on. Bring some message of help to the lowly, some word of encouragement to the disappointed, and thus you will make your life comfortable, your death happy, your funeral one at which tears will be shed, your account glorious, and your eternity blessed.

WHAT CHRISTIANITY IS

BY THE REV. NEWELL DWIGHT HILLIS, D.D.

Christianity is not the Book—that describes Christian life; Christianity is not a creed—that analyzes the Christian life; Christianity is not a sacrament—that promotes the Christian life. Christianity is not the Sermon on the Mount—that is the architect's plan, of which the Christian is the cathedral. Christianity is a vital force, the living Christ within the living soul, building a ripe character. In the school room you have a map of Maine and Florida, but the real thing is the forests of Maine and the orange groves of the South. Handel wrote his musical score, but when that score is translated through the cornet and the violins and the 'cello and the flute and 100 other stringed instruments, and 1000 voices unite, then the score of Handel becomes the music that he describes. In the Kensington Museum in London are the cartoons of Raphael. These are charcoal sketches, the outlines of Raphael's great masterpieces. From them, as models and skeletons, he painted his angels and seraphs and the Madonna and Child. And the Sermon on the Mount is an outline sketch of the Christian. It is a verbal description of what Christ was and what His disciples are to be. It is Christ's ideal of the Christian. It is His sketch of what He wants you to become. And you are to translate it into pure thoughts, into holy deeds, into stern resolves, until your intellect is clear and your will strong and iron in its firmness, and your character as white as a cloud and firm as a mountain.

Oh, for a church made up of such Christians? Oh, for a time when these ideals of perfect manhood shall prevail! The power of the church is only incidentally in the pulpit. It becomes omnipotent through men who incarnate ideal sermons. The living church is the one in which these living ideals are transforming men. Fortunately, multitudes are being transformed, and these transformations are the most glorious events in life. It is given to the clod to climb to the grass. It is given to a rose bough to burst into bloom, it is given to a cloud storm to hold the rainbow; to the night is given a star. But the most wondrous thing in creation is the soul, carried up to beauty of character, made wise by the truth, made pure and sweet by Christ's love, made righteous and holy by God's cleansing grace. In Stratford, lovers of Shakspeare have planted in his garden only those flowers that are mentioned in the poet's plays. There you will find eglantine, the rosemary, the woodbine, the modest pansy, the sweetbriar, all the humble flowers. And Christ hath His garden, and the flowers that bloom in it are the fruits of His spirit; hate is not there, envy and strife, and vulgarity and covetousness are expelled, as men expel the burr, the thistle and noxious night-shade, but love and joy and peace are there, blooming as sweetly as flowers whose roots are in heaven, but whose bloom and sweetness and perfume are the glory of our earth.

WHY WE BELIEVE IN CHRISTIANITY

BY THE REV. C. L. PALMER

W. W. McLane says that ''Christianity, considered as a system of religion, consists of three things, namely, the revelation of the character, love and will of God; the redemption of men from the penalty and power of sin; and the regeneration of men by which they are brought into vital correspondence with God and into the fulfillment of the conditions of eternal life. Revelation, Redemption and Regeneration are the essential elements of Christianity. That these three things are claimed by Christianity and for it cannot be questioned. All that is preparatory in the Old Testament, and all that is promised in the New Testament, fall under these heads.''

It is in this religion, which is so aptly defined in the foregoing paragraph, that all grades of intelligence and social standing have had implicit confidence from the opening of the Christian era until the present. It is needless to remark that for such there must be more than one substantial reason, else numberless human beings would not have followed its teachings and relied upon its salvation. It is quite within our province to ask, Why do we believe in Christianity?

I. Because of its source. We can say of our religion what we believe can be said of no other, that it has come from God through Jesus Christ. He is the Author and Finisher of our faith, the brightness of the Father's glory, the Captain of Salvation, the Deliverer, the Friend of sinners, the great Shepherd of the sheep, the Head of the church and the Alpha and Omega. He is designated with these heaven-given titles because of His attitude toward the plan of salvation, which He perfected with His blood. Many of the most important doctrines of Christianity are either clearly implied or plainly taught in the Old Testament Scriptures, but their full meaning was concealed from human view because the great expositor had not come to clarify the truth as it is in Him. But as the life of the incarnate Son of God was being lived in Palestine, the veil was drawn, and the significance of the lamb of the altar more fully realized. It is on account of the person and teachings of Christ that He becomes worthy of the title of Creator of Christianity.

II. Because of its code, which is the Word of God. Every system of religion has its book which is considered as inspired and therefore invested with authority. Many of these, however, are merely compilations, and while they contain a certain proportion of sound doctrine are fraught with serious error. As Christians we think that no book can compare with our Bible, and so doing we only demonstrate an inevitable conclusion. For there is no acumen which can array sufficient evidence against it to destroy our confidence in the Book divine that stands unmoved in the face of the most violent adversary.

III. Because of its advocates. It is an axiom in the commercial world that a valuable article of merchandise enlists the best men as agents. This identical principle is evident in Christianity, for its intrinsic worth has been appreciated by an inexhaustible array of the greatest minds and finest spirits. The catalogue commences with the Lord Jesus Christ, Who came to bring life and immortality to light. Associated with Him were twelve devoted men who are not to be classed among the least in the kingdom of heaven. Leaving Biblical days and tracing the progress of that faith of which Jesus is the author, we find no want of devoted followers who continued loyal to the end of their days on earth, and are now enjoying the blessed state of the saved. Our churches contain the germ of Christian civilization. The ministry has no cause to be ashamed of its quality, while the missionaries demonstrate their consecration by their self-denial. Thank God that all the true children of God belong to this class.

IV. Because of its mission. And what is the mission of Christianity? The mission of Christianity is to save from sin, which involves more than can be described. I make no apology for giving the following familiar illustration, for it is an example of the spirit and purpose of our religion: "A man had fallen into a deep, dark pit, and lay in its miry bottom groaning and utterly unable to move. Confucius walked by, approached the edge of the pit, and said, 'Poor fellow, I am sorry for you; why were you so unwise as to fall in? Let me give you some advice: if you ever get out, do not fall in again.' The man replied that he could not extricate himself. That is Confucianism. A Buddhist priest next came along, and seeing the man said, "I am very much pained to see you there; I think that if you could climb up part way, that I could reach down and save you.' But the man in the pit was entirely helpless and unable to rise. That is Buddhism. Next the Savior came by, and hearing his cry went to the edge of the pit, stretched down, laid hold of the man and brought him safely to the top, and said, 'Go and sin no more.' That is Christianity. We believe in it not alone for what it is, but for what it does."

V. Because of its requirements. While there is no system of religion capable of raising men to so high a moral character, there is no system which imposes conditions so perfectly just. The minute and complex demands of Judaism have been superseded by the simple requirements of the gospel. Faith is one condition. "Believe on the Lord Jesus Christ, and thou shalt be saved." "He that believeth and is baptized shall be saved." "Whosoever believeth on Him shall not perish, but have everlasting life." It is a condition of mercy, for all may comply with it, from the most humble to the most exalted. Stress is also placed upon a life which corresponds with the profession of the lips. It is not Christian to pretend to be a follower of Christ under certain circumstances, and to evince a worldly disposition when absent from religious conditions. That is hypocritical. Of it there is too much.

VI. Because of its conflicts. It is perfectly reasonable to assert that no institution has had as many and as varied battles to fight as this our faith. Not all the armies of earth have stood face to face with such enmity and hatred. Even its founder was despised and rejected by men. While he was yet a little child Herod issued an edict that all children under the age of three years should be murdered in order to prevent the coming of One who should dethrone him. The life of Christ was one of continual opposition, and the prediction made by Him that His apostles and followers should be subjected to persecution has been fulfilled to the letter. Since the ascension of Christ the conflict has continued to rage, and it will until the Lord shall come again.

VII. Because of its victories. The conquest of territory, the development of philanthropy, are not worthy of comparison with the effect that the gospel has had on human hearts. Christians are a miracle of grace. No empire can glory in such victories as the recreation of souls. It has conquered the hearts of infidels, and made them loyal to Christ. It has converted those who hold false doctrine to itself. It has given comfort to the distressed. It has taken the place of pain and sorrow. It has taken the lowest of men and made them examples for us to follow.

VIII. Because of its future. As Christians we have nothing to fear. Christianity can encounter no greater enemies than it has already conquered. The forces which command the future are already marshaled, and shall yet be centralized, unified and victorious. The creed of Christianity has known 1800 years of conflict, but not one defeat.'' So it will continue to spread from one quarter to another until all shall have heard of Christ, the Lord, and it will ever continue to be the only faith which culminates in the Christian's rest.—Christian work.

CHRISTIANITY AND MONEY

BY THE REV. A. C. DIXON, D.D.

Abraham, the friend of God, was rich. Job, the warrior of God against the wiles of Satan, was rich, and both were good men. Moses the law giver and leader was poor. His parents were slaves, and doubtless worked in the brick kilns of Egypt. Moses deliberately chose poverty, esteeming the reproach of Christ greater riches than the treasures of Egypt. Elijah and the prophets were poor men.

If we turn to the New Testament we find that Christ chose poverty rather than wealth. He had not where to lay His head, and lived uopn the charity of others. Peter and Paul were poor. On the other hand, Joseph of Aramathea, and Barnabas were rich men. Joseph used his wealth in giving Christ decent burial, and Barnabas in a time of emergency supplied the needs of the early church. The Apostle John was evidently a man of means, and at the request of Christ he took Mary to his own home. These facts recall the Scripture, "The Lord maketh poor and maketh rich." Poverty and wealth are the gifts of His love. If poverty be better for us than riches, He will give poverty. If riches be better than poverty, He will give riches. We conclude, therefore, that both poverty and wealth may be tokens of God's favor. And in the church there is a place for both. "The rich and the poor meet together; the Lord is the Maker of them all."

When Money is an Enemy.—When it is an obstacle to salvation. Jesus said, "It is easier for a camel to go through the eye of a needle, than for a rich man to enter the kingdom of heaven." We try to tone this down by making the eye of the needle mean a little gate outside the great gate in the wall of Jerusalem. The camel, in order to pass through that, must kneel and have his burden removed. But we cannot help wondering why a camel should ever want to go through that little gate when the big gate was open. Whatever else it may mean, the word translated needle here does mean the little instrument used by a woman in sewing, and Jesus therefore means to say that it is absolutely impossible for a man who trusts in his riches to be saved. In the parable of the sower "the cares of this world and the deceitfulness of riches" choke the word. When wealth deceives its owner into believing that he is heaven's special favorite, and because he has ability to make money he will therefore go to heaven, it is his greatest enemy. And even when men do not depend upon their wealth for salvation, they may allow the cares which it produces to choke the word, and make it untruthful.

The love of money is a root of all evil, which, while some coveted after, they have erred from the faith, and pierced themselves through with many sorrows. "But thou, O man of God, flee these things......fight the good fight of faith." There is not an evil in the world of which the love of money may not be the root. Take the Standard Dictionary and beginning at A and ending at Z mark every word that means something bad, and you will find that under some circumstances the love of money may be the root of that evil. Out of this root grow malice, envy, hatred, murder, lust, divorce, alienation of friends, war—indeed everything that curses humanity.

But money itself is not a root of evil, but the love of it. Now let the flashlight of God's truth in upon our souls. Let each one ask the question, Do I love money? Do I find myself gloating upon it? Pleased in laying it up, delighting to fondle it, pained at parting with it? These things are the signs of love. Is money the supreme motive in my life? If so, I have within my soul the root out of which every evil may grow. That root needs only the genial atmosphere and favorable surroundings to grow any sin. And if the flashlight of God's truth should reveal a love of money in our hearts, we may take it for granted that we are covetous, and we need to crucify this sin of sins. It is idolatry, and is classed with fornication and uncleanness. It pollutes the soul, defiles our whole being, makes us filthy before God. It would snatch the scepter from the hands of God, steal His crown, and usurp His throne. No wonder the man of God is commanded to flee these things, and is exhorted in this connection to fight sometimes the good fight of faith, for the battle against the love of money is the most terrific that any soul has to wage.

It is well for us preachers to remember that these words were written to a pastor, and, whether we are willing to admit it or not, the love of money is one of the greatest evils we have to contend with, "Which, while some coveted after, they erred from the faith." We are tempted to preach so as to please our rich hearers. We may want their influence and covet their money. We are tempted to learn what they believe, and preach to suit them. We become thus puppies rather than prophets. Many of the heresies which emanate from the pulpit may be traced to the rich pewholder. He gives the pastor to understand what he wants proclaimed from the pulpit, and the pastor is obedient. Such a pastor we need to pity more than to blame, for sooner or later he will be pierced through with many sorrows. His own soul will wither, and his own church will go to pieces, and as iniquities go in groups he will doubtless fall into other sins.

Christianity is the friend of the helpless. It raises its voice against monopolies that grind the poor. "He that oppresseth the poor to increase his riches　*　*　*　shall surely come to want." Proverbs 22:16. The prophet Isaiah strikes the keynote of Christianity on this subject when he says, "Woe unto them that join house to house, that lay field to field, till there is no place, that they may be placed alone in the midst of the earth!" We are to bear and not to increase each other's burdens, and the man or company of men who, by means of their money, combine for the destruction of competition and the increase of prices thus oppress the poor, are the enemies of God and man.

Herein lies one of the greatest economic dangers of the day. Time was when individuals competed with individuals in business, then came the partnership where two or three men joined interests for the cheapening of production, or the enlargement of their sales. Soon the corporation took the place of partnership. In the partnership business the law dealt primarily with the partners, and each one was held responsible for the debts of the concern, but this responsibility has been largely evaded through the corporation. The law now deals with the money rather than with the men, and hence corporations are looked upon as soulless.

But the latest phase of business is the corporation of corporations known as the "Trust," and the temptation of these corporations of corporations is to become monopolies. To oppose the corporation, that is the union of men and money for the carrying forward of great enterprises, is folly supreme. To destroy such corporations would be to destroy our railroads, and steamship lines, and every great enterprise that demands large capital. But while we admit the right of men to combine for the furtherance of their business, we deny their right to monopolize. We also deny the right of the millionaire and the great corporation by cut-throat competition to destroy his weaker rival. A man is doing a small business and supporting his family; a great store is opened within a block, and the millionaire owner of that store, learning the wares in which this man deals, begins to sell those articles at less than cost, losing money as he can afford until the poor merchant is driven out of business, and his wife and children made to suffer. Now the law should deal with this millionaire merchant as a conspirator, and make him suffer for his crime.

A man in Pennsylvania had built up a business which brought him an income of $25,000 a year. At his death the widow continued the business. The agent of that great corporation offered to buy her business for $75,000. She, of course, refused because her income of $25,000 capitalized at five per cent would be half a million, and yet this great corporation succeeded in getting her business into its clutches. Through its influence the railroads refused to carry the produce of this widow, and as a result her business fell to pieces. The agent of the corporation then offered $65,000 and she was compelled to take it. Now the law should deal with the responsible parties in this corporation as with thieves and robbers. A trust that seeks to drive everyone else in the same business from the face of the earth is an outlaw, an octopus, a demon, whose presence should not be tolerated. Such a Trust should be taken in hand by the government, and its affairs managed under governmental control. Indeed, the more thought I give to the subject the more I am convinced that all monopolies, whether of water, mail, light, travel by steam or trolley, should be under the management of the government and administered in the interests of all the people.

There are, of course, objections to this, but the objections to it are not so numerous and strong as the objections to monopolies, run in the interest of individuals or corporations. A corner is a temporary monopoly. Some man has bought up all the wheat in the world, and he demands his own price for it. A trust which has become a monopoly is a permanent corner. What one sharper in business has done for a day or two a combination of men are doing every day. If the corner in the necessities of life is an iniquity, the monopolistic trust is a greater iniquity, in so far as all days exceed one day. When money is thus used to oppress the poor it is a gigantic enemy of Christianity.

We have in the 5th chapter of James the portrait of men who thus oppress the poor, and they need to hear the ringing exhortation of the inspired Word. "Go to now, ye rich men, weep and howl for your miseries that shall come upon you. Your riches are corrupted, and your garments are moth eaten. Your gold and silver is cankered, and the rust of them shall be a witness against you, and shall eat your flesh as it were fire. Ye have heaped treasure together for the last days. Behold the hire of the laborers who have reaped down your fields, which is of you kept back by fraud, crieth; and the cries of them which have reaped are entered into the ears of the Lord of Sabaoth." God will avenge the wrongs that are done to the poor where by withholding their wages, or increasing the prices of the necessaries of life, their wages will not purchase enough for their support. Silver and gold thus accumulated is a canker that eats into the soul. The rust does not gather upon the money but upon the man who piles up the money. It shall eat their flesh as it were fire. Read the biographies of men who have thus amassed fortunes, and you will find that miseries came upon them which were enough to make them weep and howl. One of them who gathered millions through a corner in wheat died some time ago in a junk shop miserably poor as he had been miserably rich, and he is but a sample of many.

"They that will be rich fall into temptation and a snare, and into many foolish and hurtful lusts which drown men in destruction and perdition." The wild race after wealth is today drowning men by the thousand in destruction and perdition. They are enticed into the snare of wanting to get money without the long toilsome process of labor, and they fall into the temptation of taking from the bank where they are employed that they may speculate, expecting, it may be, to return what they have taken, and the result is the penitentiary.

"Charge them that are rich that they do good." If they will manage their money it will be a useful servant, but if they allow their money to manage them, it becomes a cruel master. The early apostles put their money into the hands of the Holy Spirit to be used as He might direct. The Holy Spirit used some of this money in supplying the needs of the poor Christians, and left some of it in the hands of the apostles, for we find that they possessed money after distribution had been made to the needy. But the spirit was not confined to the use of money. Peter said, "Silver and gold have I none, but such as I have give I unto thee." Peter had something more important than silver and gold. He would have been poor indeed with millions, if he could not by word or touch heal the men at the gate. The church is not dependent upon the money for success, though it can use money to the glory of God. On one occasion a sorcerer offered to pay money for power, and Peter replied, "Thy money perish with thee." Power in the church of God cannot be purchased with money; it can come only through faith and character. Master your money that it may serve your God, but if it masters you and makes you its servant, a slave on a Southern plantation was a free man compared with you. Agassiz said, "I am offered $500 a night to lecture, but I have not time to make money." General Gordon refused hundreds of thousands of dollars offered to him by the Chinese government. Some people cannot understand the motives of Agassiz and Gordon. Agassiz was so busy searching for the secrets of nature that he did not have time to make money. Gordon was so busy with the affairs of war and state that he had no time to take care of money. Both had enough money, because their lives were so full of other things.

Christianity gives a motive for the making and use of money. In Ephesians 4:28: "Let him labor, working with his hands the thing which is good, that he may have to give to him that needeth." The world says, Make money that you may make more money. Make money that you may have power that comes of wealth. Make money that you may enjoy the pleasures that riches bring. But Christ says, Make money that you may have to give. "It is more blessed to give than to receive." Not a few preachers, I believe, have deliberately chosen, like their Master, to be poor, that by preaching the gospel they may make others rich. We may be excused for magnifying our calling, for we believe it is the highest

—9C

on earth, but next to preaching the gospel I envy the position of the man who has talent for making money honestly, and then enjoys the pleasure of giving it, that it may work for God and humanity. I know of one wealthy Christian who supports sixty young preachers in college every year. He cannot preach himself, but he is equipping others that they may preach the gospel he believes and loves. Money which is very perishable may be transmuted into character which is immortal. By giving to missions, to education, to the support of the gospel we may lay up treasures in heaven which neither moth nor rust doth corrupt. Jesus said, make yourselves friends of the mammon of unrighteousness, that when you fail they may receive you into everlasting habitations. By means of money fill heaven with redeemed saints who will welcome you when you enter the gates.—Commonwealth.

THE INFLUENCE OF THE STUDY OF OTHER RELIGIONS ON CHRISTIAN THEOLOGY

BY A. M. FAIRBAIRN, D.D., LL.D.,

Principal of Mansfield College, Oxford

In beginning the discussion of the subject which has been allotted to me, this preliminary remark may be allowed: So much depends on the intellectual attitude of the student, both toward religions and theology, that the term Study ought to be qualified by "Scientific." The Scientific Study of religions will be at once critical and comparative—i. e., will scrupulously sift out the true from the false, and carefully appraise and compare only what criticism has made sure of. A study of religions which is intended only to be an apology for our own will educate no theologian, conserve and enlarge no theology. The student who goes to other faiths simply to find out what is evil in them in order that he may compare it with the idealized good he professes to find in his own, will come back worse than empty handed, with gifts that soil rather than cleanse the mind of the bringer. This is not to be construed as applying to the formal or official Christian apologist; it may apply to him, but it has a much wider application. We have but to see it practiced on our own religion to discover its futility. To find all the scandalous tales of the Old Testament from Cain onward through Noah and his sons, Lot and his daughters, David and his adulteries, Solomon and his wives, the spoiling of the Egyptians and the massacre of the Canaanites, to the apostasy of Peter and the betrayal by Judas, set out as characteristic of Christianity over against an ideal Hinduism, abstracted from the Vedanta and the Bhagavad-gita, without any reference to the religion of the temple and the street, of the festival and the fair, of the ascetic and the social life—is to learn a lesson in the rudiments of the justice which the spokesman of one religion owes to the ideas and the histories, the men and the institutions, of every other. The man whose eyes are not open to the best in other faiths will be blind to the real good in his own, and be quite incapable of enlarging and clarifying what he has received by what he has discovered.

The most general effect which the comparative study of religion tends to have on theology is in broadening, and, as it were, humanizing the thought on which theology builds. Our apologetic has been too critical and defensive, and has suffered from the want of positive and constructive ideas. It has on the speculative side tended to make itself the opponent of the scientific interpretation of nature, fearing now the atoms and the architectonic forces of the physicist, now the epochs of the geologist, and now the biologist's mutation and evolution of species; and, on the historical side, it has been ineffectively suspicious of the criticism which has freely handled now documents, now events and now men dear to the religious imagination. But the study of religions places us as regards both of these tendencies in a higher and more advantageous position. On the speculative side it makes man rather than nature the ultimate problem of thought. Its constructive ideas may here be said to be two: (1) Nature is not the interpretation of man, but man of nature. There is no problem nature raises which he does not raise, and in addition one, which underlies all others. How did thought come to be? Without thought there were no man, and without it there were no nature; it is the essence of his being, and holds within it the key to the whole mysterious system to which he belongs. And (2) man is the interpreter of religion, but religion is the interpretation of man. He is never without it, and everywhere it is the measure of his progress, the standard of his civilization. We do not think of arguing in the old way, there are no tribes without the idea of God, for God is an elastic idea and it is easy for men so to define it as to exclude whole peoples from the ranks of its possessors; but we do not argue, we affirm as a simple matter-of-fact, which no competent anthropologist will now dispute, there are no tribes without religious ideas and customs. They do not grow into them, they do not grow out of them, but the tribe, the ideas, the society, and the customs grow together in indissoluble unity. So integral are the ideas that man does not become man or realize society and civilization, law and order, without them; and so powerful are they that they govern his progress and determine the kind of culture, the quality of the character he realizes. And so the speculative falls over into the historical problem; to study the religions is to read the process by which society has been formed, states have risen, and man in the course of his historical existence has constituted a unity and an order by reaching out toward some invisible and ideal end. But history cannot be so conceived and man remain an isolated unit; he must stand related to some cause that works through him and that achieves by means of him its order and its aims. Thus out of the study of religion comes a philosophy of man which relates him as though to an eternal Thinker, and as a living will to a larger Will whose organ and minister he is. From this point of view theology can enter on a richer inheritance than ever it knew in its palmiest days, and become the philosophy of all the philosophies, the science which holds within it the reason of all the sciences. If only it can prove itself an heir worthy of this splendid inheritance, it will prove itself, as the solvent of our most mysterious mysteries, the master of man's reason, commanding it by the only authority it can obey without losing dignity or suffering depravation, the authority of the truth.

Of course, as a comparative science the study of religions may fulfill a more direct and immediate apologetic purpose; it may become a finger-post indicating the religion which experience has proved to be in structure and ideal the highest. The thing the study makes evident at the outset is the necessity of religion to man; it does not lie in his choice to be without it; it holds him in spite of himself. He may divert himself by thinking that when he has denied one religion he has denied all; but as a simple matter-of-fact his very denial undergoes a sort of apotheosis, and comes out a form of worship, a belief according to which he must try to order his life. But when we pass from the freak of the individual to the law which fulfills itself in history, what do we find? That a tribe or people or society is as its religion is, that the higher its ethical ideal and the stronger and purer the authority by which it is enforced, then the greater the place the people will fill, the nobler the part it will play in history. And what does this principle not only allow, but require from the comparative study of religions? An indication of the highest and of the qualities and characteristics by virtue of which it stands where it does. What may be accomplished let an older and more rigorous science tell. Comparative anatomy examines, brings together, and classifies the multitudinous organisms that make up the wondrous world of life; and with what result to man? Has it not placed him first in the order of sentient beings, most beautiful and perfect of living organisms? And may it not well be the last result of comparative study in our field to prove the religion of Christ the apex of the world's religions, the end to which all the others have pointed, the perfect type into which the virtues and truths scattered through all the rest have been gathered, yet only to be harmonized, sublimed, transfigured by a light all its own, the true divine reason which everywhere works in obedience to divine love? And so it is possible that this study may yet become the basis of a new Analogy, more comprehensive, more appropriate to these days than Butler's. He assumed premises that the skeptical thought of his own century conceded, but the skeptical thought of our century denies. Its method, too, hardly satisfies the more critical spirits of today. We do not make our belief more credible by loading another belief with incredibilities. We may simply persuade to the renunciation of both. Two darks do not make a bright. It is not good to relieve Christianity by deepening the shadow on the face of nature till both stand, as it were, under a common eclipse; it were better to burnish and brighten the light in the heart, and on the face of revealed religion till its sunshine penetrates all nature, and her very shadows become radiant with the silver that sweeps above and behind the cloud. And if comparative study can be used to show that the highest religion is the most credible, a glorious center in which all excellencies have converged, and where have been combined and harmonized the truths man as a religious being most needs and best loves; and if, binding the comparative to the philosophical question, we can show how that religion as native and necessary to man has an indefeasible right to be, that that right is most absolute in the perfect religion, which as such at once explains and supersedes all imperfect religions, may we not have an apology, the very apology our generation needs, for religion in general and the religion of Christ in particular?

The study of religions has also enlarged the conception of religion, and made evident the unity of its several parts. It has made it impossible to think of theology in isolation from worship and polity, institutions and conduct. The thought of a religion is as much expressed in the behavior as in the speech of its votaries, as much in the customs it sanctions, the laws it enacts, the ritual it observes, the practices it follows, and the social or class distinctions it approves and maintains, as in the creed it subscribes, or in the confession of faith it makes. In no way may we so utterly misinterpret a religion as by confining our studies to its systems of theology or its higher philosophies. The thought that organizes the life is what we have most need to reach and to understand. Now, this enormously widens the range and enhances the worth of theology. It means that with a church or people as with a man, as the heart thinks, so the character and the conduct are. Hence the function of theology becomes the highest possible; it is not the mere exposition or vindication of a creed, it is the creation of a vital religion, the codification, as it were, of the ultimate law of life, individual and collective. And this enlarged idea of its function gives a heightened value to its several parts as well as a sure measure of proportion of balance. We look at each doctrine in relation to the whole of thought and action, and see the idea or question of the hour, not through the hour, but through its bearing on the complex organism which the present is building up for the benefit or injury of the future. A little bit of autobiography may illustrate what I mean. There is no question that so moves and agitates the churches today as the priesthood of the minister, and we have had it discussed under almost every possible relation, historical, literary, theological, ecclesiastical. But years before I had occasion to study the priesthood in the Anglican or the Roman church I had tried to understand its rise, its character and action in the religion and history of India. I had there endeavored as an earnest but I hope dispassionate and critical student of religions to read the forces which had governed the destinies of a people, organized its society, determined the forms of its worship and the modes of its thought, and had regulated the evolution of its ethics and its conduct, and it seemed to me as if the most potent of those forces was the sacerdotal and sacrosanct claim embodied in the Brahman family. To have seen what the priesthood had done in one country and for one religion was to have one's eyes opened to it in other lands and religions, to be compelled to study both its generic and its specific qualities, to analyze its roots and reasons, its effects on character, on society, on thought and conduct wherever it rose to power. And it was from the priesthood of India that I came to the priesthoods of Europe, and came not with a fixed judgment as to their identity in tendency and idea—that would have been the act of a fanatic or a partisan, not of a student and inquirer—but with a standpoint from which to view them, a method of research as to their rise, and growth, their history and claims, and a habit of analysis which forced one to examine their antecedents, their consequences, and their action on church and state, on Christian thought and institutions, on conduct and worship, personal and collective. This is an illustration, given not for the purpose of fixing a fictitious value to a personal opinion, which in itself may be worthless enough, but only to indicate that the study of religions, by compelling the student first to look at the parts through the whole, gives to each part some of the significance and dignity of the whole, and then to conceive each as a living member of a living organism, and not as a mere isolated dead atom, a doctrine to be logically defined or exegetically proved, but not to be reached as a real factor to the life it helped to create and qualify.

But it is in the interpretation of the highest religious beliefs that the most decisive influence has been exercised. There is a remarkable difference between an idea regarded as a religious belief and as an intellectual conception. This difference relates not so much to the greater note of conviction which marks the religious belief as to the greater reality which belongs to it and the immediacy with which it bears on life. Religion in dealing with its beliefs has an audacity and a vigor of logic quite unknown to philosophy, and this is the more emphasized by its logic being expressed even more in conduct and character, in action and institutions, than in dialectic. Now, it is in its ultimate ideas that the constituent and differentiating elements in a religion are to be found, and by the comparison of these we may discover and determine the qualities that give to our beliefs their highest intellectual value and religious force. The action of our study may in this region be represented by the cardinal ideas of Christian theology: Man, God, the Godhead, the Incarnation and the Atonement.

1. In studying the religious man, who is their subject and vehicle, assumes a new significance. We gain a new idea of the unity of the race, of the solidarity or reciprocal responsibility of its members, the being of each for the other and all for the whole. Neither in any single science nor in the collective sciences can we get as sure or as deep an insight either into the homogeneity of

the families of man or into the unity of their history. The first impression here of the inquirer is as to the bewildering diversities of religious belief and custom; the last conviction of the thinker is the similarity or even identity of underlying idea and impulse, notwithstanding the infinite variety of form and expression. Now, this has come to fortify theology in one of its weakest places, and to make it sagacious where it was wont to be neither sane nor wise. The doctrine of original sin has during most of this century been slowly dying, partly because of the irrational and impossible forms in which it has been stated, and partly because there was wanting a solid intellectual basis on which it could be built up. But this basis is precisely the thing the study of religions is promising to supply. It is bringing us back with opener eyes to the Pauline conception of the ethnical and the ethical, the spiritual and the intellectual unity of man. It is showing us how he has in his religious development passed through certain stages, used certain forms, followed a given order, how his mind has been under what Paul would have termed a law, has conformed to it and obeyed it. We may conceive fear and ignorance as potent factors of religious ideas. Observances may explain the organization of worship and society through the customs of totem and taboo, may dwell on the influence which dreams and sleep and death have had on beliefs and ceremonies, but what we mean in all this is that the noblest impulses and loves of the human soul have had to struggle upward to the light through the superincumbent strata of the most ignoble terrors, barbarous ways and childlike passions. We have here, then, the material and means for reconstructing a dissolved yet cardinal doctrine: A development which has been so marvelously uniform, not in time, but in process and in order, supplies us with a conception of man's organic unity, of the moral quality of his nature and state, of the law or laws that govern his growth, the flesh that ever lusteth against the spirit and the spirit that ever warreth against the flesh, of the connection and coherence of his present with all his past, and of each unit with its parent and coexistent units—such as a theologian who is capable of taking occasion by the hand may yet build into a doctrine of man that shall eclipse the feats of our most valiant systematizers and restore even in an age of criticism theology to more than her ancient power.

2. What constitutes a religion is a man's belief in a God or in gods; what differentiates religions is the sort of God the man believes in. No religion can civilize unless it be moral, and the kind and quality of its morality will depend on the character of its God. But without Monotheism we can have neither an ethical deity nor an ethical religion; for wherever gods are a multitude you can have no sovereign law, only the passions, lusts, rivalries, crimes, which are born from the strife of jealous and colliding wills. And the one God must be personal and concrete, not neuter and abstract. We live in a day when Pantheism has made a peculiarly impressive appeal to the imagination of the poet and the reason of the man of science; and has appeared as a sublimer and more reasonable belief than Monotheism. But this is an opinion which the history of religions refuses to justify. Hinduism is here signally significant. It shows us as an historical matter-of-fact how Pantheism has been used to vindicate the most extravagant Polytheism and the grossest and most debased cults. It can make a deity out of a man or a monkey, a snake or a tree; it can find a reason for the apotheosis of the most elemental of passions and the most rigorous of virtues, for the worship of the hideous and fierce Kali as for the practice of the severest austerities. And in all this its logical consistency is complete, for it has no ideal save the deification of the actual, and its ultimate truth is the right of what is to be. But Monotheism cannot admit a multitude of unethical deities and the legitimacy of their worship, nor can it justify an actual which is in conflict with its ideal of truth and justice—*i. e.*, the moral character of God. Hence it has within and behind it a force which seeks to compel the actual to become as the ideal, and so it must operate forever as a factor of moral amelioration and progress. On this ground the doctrine of the divine unity assumes a new significance for theology, because it defines the highest function of religion, and stands in a more satisfactory relation to thought. It appears as the basis of our whole view of life, makes it rational in its source, moral in its nature and issue, immortal in its potency and promise. It ceases to be a personal opinion and becomes a judgment of history. The thought that starts with it and builds on it feels that what lies behind it is not simply an inspired text, but a divine reason unfolded and verified by the collective life of man.

3. But we must find a higher category for the divine than unity and personality. It is indeed a mistake to think that the process which simplifies the conception of God makes Him more credible and intelligible, for the more easily He can be packed within a logical formula the more He becomes a mere physical unit or metaphysical abstraction. And here we may find Mohammed as significant as we have already found the Hindu. Islam believes in the unity of God with a transcendent force and fury of conviction, but it is in a physical rather than ethical unity, God conceived as will rather than as light, life and love. He is an Arab chief magnified into the Omnipotent, irresistible, pitiless to foes, indulgent to friends. This idea determines the character, the worship, the politics, the history, and the fortunes of Islam. It knows conquest and submission, but not redemption and obedience, knows victory and despotism, but not grace and freedom. But to Christianity the ethical qualities are all in all to deity; he is not so much power as reason and righteousness, truth and love. But the peculiarity of these attributes is that they cannot live in solitude; society is necessary to their being. Power may make a solitude into a world which will may govern, but love can be only where life is, for we cannot conceive a God who is essentially love as eternally alone. Love is as impossible where there is no object as where there is no subject. Egotism does not cease to be self-centered by becoming infinite; an eternal eternally absorbed in self could have nothing to spare either for the making or the remaking of a world. If, then, we are to avoid the frigid almighty will of Islam we must not fear so to conceive the divine unity as to find within it an ethical manifold, the distinctions and differences which turn deity from an inflexible will or contemplate intellect into the home of grace and truth, the affections and virtues which unfold into a living world. To save ourselves from intellectual difficulties by surrendering those ethical qualities which are the very God of God, were the last unwisdom; and Islam has come to save us from it, and teach us to affirm that society is of the essence of God, that we have the more ethical religion because we have the only ethical deity, a Godhead whose beatitude is the unity of righteousness, truth and love.

4. But the person and priesthood of the Redeemer have received another and higher significance from the study of religions.

On this point one illustration must suffice. In old discussions on the atonement much, indeed too much, was made of the universality of sacrifical rite, for such rites are by no means universal, and their real import was, as a rule, overlooked. For they do not represent the highest, but rather the coarsest and most depraved acts and elements in religion. Man shows his intrinsic baseness nowhere so much as in his efforts to propitiate deity; in the things he offers and seeks, in his mode of offering and his manner of expecting, there is expressed a notion of God and what pleases Him which turns Him into something less and worse than a vindictive man. If there is any one lesson more than another which the religions teach us, it is this: Leave man with something to do to propitiate God and he will devise rites and follow practices which will at once lower God in the eye of reason, deprave his own conscience, undignify his own nature, and transform the main instrument of his elevation into the main agent of his deterioration and decay. This is no rash generalization; it is simple, stern, indubitable fact. The rites of appeasement or propitiation are in all religions the focus of the forces that materialize and deprave. But how does this affect Christian theology? It brings out the contrast of its one sacrifice to all sacrifices. God takes it out of the hands of man and offers it Himself. Its qualities are all ethical, for they are all of Him. And He offers it once for all; it can never be repeated, man can never share it, it stands in its divine solitude an object of faith, capable of acceptance, incapable of repetition. And so there is satisfied man's deep need of reconciliation with God, while he is saved from the evils incident to buying the reconciliation on his own terms and in his own way. To have made evident the gain to religion by the abolition through the God's own act and his Son's obedience of all propitiatory rites and sacrifices may be classed as the last and most noble achievement of our comparative study.—Independent.

THE CHRISTIAN'S POSSESSIONS

BY THE REV. DR. JOHN F. CARSON

"All things are yours; whether Paul, or Apollos, or Cephas, or the world, or life, or death, or things present, or things to come; all are yours; and ye are Christ's; and Christ is God's."—1 Corinthians 3:21-23.

In these verses Paul furnishes us with an inventory of the Christian's possessions. It is well for us now and then as Christians to "take account of stock," to find out what we are worth, to examine our inheritance and note the things that we possess which we would not have if we were not Christians. The things named by the apostle in his inventory are such as are common to all men and may be possessed by all. But possession, after all, is a matter of appreciation. Some men never possess their possessions. Only the men whose lives are in touch and harmony with God really possess the things which Paul names as belonging distinctively to the Christian. It is a broad, measureless, rich inheritance which God has provided for them that love Him. That is not the general conception of the Christian life. Most people fancy that the Christian life is a narrow, cramped life, "an apprenticeship," as Amiel puts it, "to a progressive renunciation." Far from it. The Christian life is a consistent acquisition. It often involves self-denial, but every act of renunciation is followed by the acquisition of a more precious treasure and blessing.

In his inventory of the Christian's possessions, Paul names, first, the ministry. "All things are yours; whether Paul or Apollos, or Cephas." Some one suggests that Paul enters the cheapest article on the list first. That may be so, but the suggestion is hardly in the line of Paul's purpose in this Scripture. His aim was to persuade the Christians of Corinth not to think lightly or cheaply of any of their religious teachers. There was a division among the Christians of Corinth over their ministers. Some said, "I am of Paul." His sound doctrine, strong reasoning, invincible logic appealed to them and they magnified his type. Others said, "I am of Apollos." He was an orator. He indulged rhetoric. He flung fine sentences. He had the ability to cast his opinions in phrases that had flesh enough to catch the imagination. He carried his audience heavenward on the wings of his eloquence. Some in Corinth magnified his type. Still another class said: "I am of Cephas." He was an impulsive, emotional preacher. His pathos touched and thrilled the heart and some magnified his type. Each adhered to his own chosen type and rejected the other. Paul condemned this attitude. He told the Christians at Corinth that all the teachers were theirs—the philosophic Paul, the oratorical Apollos, the emotional Cephas. All types belong to the Christian. The men who can lead us into wider fields of thought, the men who can give beautiful expression to the aspirations of mind and heart, the men who can sound the depths of feeling—all are yours, for all are necessary in order to express the totality of truth.

There is such a thing as absolute truth. It is not found, perhaps is not findable, by any one type of searchers after truth. Men search in the line of their own mental and moral tendency. For any one to ignore or set himself against any teacher is for him to refuse to look upon the whole of things and truth and that makes men blind partisans in politics, hateful pessimists in society, prejudiced bigots in religion. Every heresy or half truth arises from the tendency to look at a part, and not at the whole, and to exaggerate that part at the expense of the whole. Each has a part of the truth. The type of preacher or teacher who appeals to us has a part of truth. But the part we have is not enough, for it is not the whole. We need all types of teachers in order that we may know the whole truth, that we may see life in its completeness. All teachers are ours. We have a property right in them. We are to get light and leading from them all. It is a weakness to see value only in one aspect of truth and listen to only one form of teaching. Every teacher who declares what he believes and lives on has something to teach us and we impoverish ourselves by neglecting his teaching. In building up ourselves in the most holy truth we must take the best from every teacher. Yonder great structure in Rome furnishes me with an illustration. It is the product of the genius of many architects. Bramante came first. When he died the great Raphael took his place among the arches and columns. But the grave soon claimed Raphael. Then came Peruzzi, who spent half a lifetime with the stones. After Peruzzi came Angelo, who gave twenty-two years of his life to the great sanctuary. Genius followed genius for 120 years. These great artists quarreled and the workmen quarreled with one another, but the temple grew to its grandeur. As the basilica rose each year toward the sky it left further below, down among the marble chips, the many quarrels of the workmen. It took from each artist his love and genius and left all else behind. This is what must be done in the upbuilding of individual life and of the race in truth and righteousness—we must take from every teacher the message of his heart and genius and leave all differences below among the wastes of life. All are ours. We are to get truth from Calvin and Arminius, from Whitfield and Wesley, from Edwards and Channing, from Spurgeon and Newman, from Moody and Martineau. If we are after truth in its fullness and completeness, we will listen to all teachers, to Paul and Apollos and Cephas, for all are ours.

The second item which Paul names in his inventory of the Christian's possessions is the material universe. "All things are yours—the world," that is the physical universe, all created things and forces. On the mountain top the devil pointed Jesus to "all the kingdoms of the world, and the glory of them," and said, "all these things will I give Thee, if Thou wilt fall down and worship me." And the devil repeats that promise to all the sons of men and none know its falseness better than those who have yielded to his suggestion. The kingdoms of the world and their glory do not belong to the devil. They are not his to give away. Who owns the world? The possession is in dispute. I asked a lawyer last evening, What is the first thing you do when the ownership of a property is in dispute? and he told me that he first searched the title. Let us do that. Let us trace the title back from year to year, from century to century, and we will find that the title is vested in God Himself. I read, "The earth is the Lord's and the fulness thereof." And in the last deed that was executed I read that the Father made His Son head over all things. In not one word in all the divine document is there an intimation that this world was ever given to Satan. Hell was made for the devil and his angels. He is an intruder in the world, and there is a great warfare going on to drive him out of the world which he has entered and into which he has brought disgrace and death. This is our Father's world, and we are to win it back from the darkness and despair and death into which Satan has led it. The world is yours, yours to redeem, yours to enjoy, yours to control.

In non-Christian countries and times the world was man's master. The forces of nature were regarded as divine, and men worshiped the sun, the sea, the sky, the stars. They felt themselves inferior to the world. The world was not theirs, they were the world's. From this slavery to the world Christianity has redeemed men. "You are not the world's," is Christianity's message to man, "the world is yours." Christianity teaches that the divinity is in man, not in matter. It declares that there is an element in man that is not in the universe, an element that makes man superior to the universe and compels it to do his bidding.

The world realizes itself fully only in the Christian. None possess the world as Christians do. It has been under Christian influences that alchemy has changed into chemistry and astrology into astronomy, that vague and visionary speculations have passed into definite and demonstrated science. The telescope, the microscope, the spectroscope claim the wide universe and they are the products of Christian civilization. Science did not find a home where Buddhism or Confucianism or Mohammedanism reign. Science found her home in the heart of Christendom, that is, the progressive science that we know today, the science that has revealed the secrets of nature and that has made the forces of nature the servants of men. The place and prominence of science in the life of today reinforce the message of Paul to the Christian, the world is yours.

The world is yours not only to know and to understand, but to use. God made the world for man, not man for the world. He rules it for man and just as man enters into harmony with His rulership does the world minister to him. The world and all its resources and forces are most at the service of man in Christian countries. This is not an accident. Those who seek for first the kingdom of God and His righteousness have all things added. Those who are most loyal to Jesus Christ will most inherit the world.

The world is yours, not only to understand and to use, but yours to enjoy. It is not the man who bows down and worships the material universe who most delights in its beauty and rejoices in its power, but it is the man who worships the God who is above the material universe and rejoices in it as the work of His hand. The world is yours. It is a sanctuary whose great symbols are sacraments. The world is yours. It is a storehouse whose mighty forces are for your use. The world is yours. It is a temple whose superb beauty is for your delight. The world is yours, yours to enjoy, yours to use, yours to bless and make more beautiful.

The third item that Paul names in his inventory of the Christian's possessions is that which pertains to the inner consciousness. "All things are yours—life." You are more than life, because you are conscious of life. The life of which you are conscious is yours. All that the term life means, of consciousness, energy, growth, love, joy, hope—all are yours. Life is yours as a Christian because your identity with Christ gives your life a spiritual purpose and destiny. Life without the spiritual motive and end is emptiness and nothing at the core. Without the spiritual the whole system of things in this world is baffling and pathetically incomplete, unsatisfying and disappointing. Men without the spiritual vision have found it so and have said so. John Stuart Mill says of his father, James Mill: "He thought human life a poor thing at the best." Miss Martineau wrote: "I never loved life and would any day of my life have rather departed than stayed." "The world's winter is going," wrote George Eliot, "but my everlasting winter has set in." But life is quite another thing to the man of spiritual vision. It has interest and purpose and meaning and moves to splendid results.

Paul names death as the fourth item in his inventory of the Christian's possessions. "All things are yours—death." At first notice the mention of death in this connection "sounds like a false note in the apostle's triumphal strain." But on second thought we realized that Paul did not make a mistake when he placed death on the list of the Christian's possessions. Death is ours as the ministry is ours, as the world and life are ours. Death is not the master of the Christian, but his servant. Death takes us away from good things of this life, its fellowships, its employments, its joys, but it takes us to the good things of the life after this, its fellowships, its employments, its joys. Death is ours because Christ has taken away the sting of death. It is sin that makes men fear death, that makes death man's enemy. If there had been no sin there would have been no death. Because of sin death is a fact of our life. But Christ has removed the guilt and the power

—10C

of sin.   He has given to all who trust Him the sense of forgiveness and peace.   Death is no longer an avenging Nemesis.   It is the Father's messenger, robed in black, calling us home to Himself.

Present things constitute the fifth item in Paul's inventory of the Christian's possessions. "All things are yours; things present." It is the common notion that things to come belong to the Christian, but it is not so generally believed that things present are his. My brethren, whatever be our inheritance hereafter the things of the present belong to us if we are Christ's. Things present—literature, art, music, science, commerce—name the good things of the present and tell me if they are not in the possession of Christians? Our best literature is Christian. Colet, Bacon, Coleridge, great Shakspeare's self, Milton, "God-gifted organ voice of England;" Coleridge, Wordsworth, Tennyson, the Brownings, Hawthorne, Whittier, Lowell—at whose breasts were these nursed? So in art. Raphael, Leonardo, Murillo, were Christtions. So in music, to name the masters is to name Christians. So of science, the master men—Galileo, Kepler, Newton, Herschel, Owen, Farraday, Agassiz, Dana, Dawson, Lord Kervin—are Christians. Would you mention commerce? Who can rival the Christian in the business world? Commerce did not develop into power in China, or Turkey, or Africa, but in Christendom. Things present are yours. Every bright and healthful pleasure, all intellectual feasts, all magic books are yours. It was faith, Christian faith, that inspired Beethoven and Mozart; that created the soul of Shakspeare and Tennyson; that put the brush into the hand of Turner and Tissot. Things present are yours.

Paul names the future as the last item in his inventory of the Christian's possessions. "All things are yours; things to come." This is the last and the best. "Things to come." The Christian is the possessor, or may be, of everything that belongs to time and he is the heir of everything that belongs to eternity. "Things to come." How much is wrapped up in these three short words "things to come." In Christ we are heirs of the future. Heaven and all that it means—freedom from sin and sorrow, not a sinful act, not a pain, not a tear, not a sigh. "Things to come." Fellowship with those whom we have loved and lost awhile. Listen, all ye whose hearts are buried in yonder graves at Greenwood and Evergreens and Cypress Hills, at West Laurel Hill and Woodlawn.

Do not sit longer among the tombs. Your loved ones are not there. They are home, and by and by, when your day's work is done, you will be with them. And best of all, you and they will be with Jesus forever more. I want to see Jesus. I want to fall down at His feet and look up into His blessed face and listen to His gracious words. "Things to come." Eternity is yours. We are not going down to loss and waste, we are going up to gain and realization, we are not going to surrender and defeat, we are going to victory and coronation. Things to come are ours. Are there palms and crowns and thrones? Is there a music that ear hath not heard and a glory that heart hath not conceived? Then all these are yours.

There is only one thing in the whole passage which Paul says is not ours. "All things are yours; whether Paul, or Apollos, or Cephas, or the world, or life, or death, or things present, or things to come; all are yours." Only one thing is not yours—"ye are Christ's." I am glad of it. We are not our own. We belong to Him and because we are His we are joint heirs with Him of all His possessions. Without Him nothing is ours, however for a time things may seem to be ours. United with Him all things are ours, for as one of the old Puritans says, "If you marry the heir you will have all." "My beloved is mine and I am His."

> I pray Thee, Savior, keep me in Thy love
> Until death's holy sleep shall me remove
> To that fair realm where sin and sorrow o'er,
> Thou and Thine own are one for evermore.
> —Brooklyn Daily Eagle.

IS THE OLD GOSPEL WORN OUT?

BY DR. JOHN RHEY THOMPSON

"But though we, or an angel from heaven, preach any other gospel unto you than that we have preached unto you, let him be accursed."—Galatians 1:8.

There be those among us today who take open issue with Paul precisely at this point. If we are to believe these prophets of ill-omen we must expect another gospel. Christianity, they tell us, has run its utmost bound, and is now fast emptying itself of vital force. It is aged and outworn; it is feeble and decrepit; it lags superfluous on the world's great stage; the pathetic hour of its dissolution is near at hand. As the Mosaic succeeded the patriarchal phase of religious evolution, as Christianity itself displaced Judaism, so now some fresh form of religion must succeed to Christianity. In the past, this religion did a good work, a necessary work, a great work, a work without which the human race could not have reached its present high planes of living and thinking, and we ought not to be rude to it now in the time of its weakness, senility and decay. Let us turn our faces away from it, but let us do it reverently. Once it was lusty and vigorous with life; now it is palsied with age. The gloomy portents of death multiply; let us turn away quietly and leave it alone. It is with such high sounding phrases, such lofty and patronizing airs, that we are being assured of the impending final collapse of the religion of Christ.

This, then, is the great question we are to study today. Are there signs of the fatal decrepitude of the gospel? Is Christianity dying? It is my purpose to dispute the soundness of this bold assumption. Rather, it is my purpose to state and defend the proposition that the gospel which Paul declared to the gentile peoples, the religion which we now know as Christianity, is, in its nature and contents, forever incapable of essential diminution or final exhaustion; that it is the final, permanent, absolute form of religion for man ;and that it possesses in ample, copious and inexhaustible supply all the elements of universal and perpetual youth and vigor.

Let us clear the ground, for it is necessary that you should clearly understand what I do not undertake or attempt to do. For example, I do not undertake the defense of all the varied interpretations of Christianity. In undertaking to show the essential truth of astronomy, it is not necessary that a man be charged with the defense of all the various theories concerning the heavenly bodies which from time to time have been put forth and labeled astronomy. I do not undertake the defense of all the instruments which Christianity employs, or has employed, such as the pulpit, the Bible, the Sunday, the sacraments, the Sunday schools and the like. I by no means assume the defense of all the acts and forms of the various ecclesiastical organizations called churches, which have tried to embody to men the genius of the gospel. I make no effort to reconcile and harmonize the clashing and contradictory formulas and systems which have been put forth by honest men in the sacred name of Christianity. Suppose I raise the question, 'Is popular education declining in America?' What would be involved? Under this form of statement, what, in all candor and firmness, could be required of me? It could not be exacted of me that I should defend all the various theories of popular education which have been in vogue here, or that I should vindicate all the various systems for the training of teachers, or that I should convincingly demonstrate the practical wisdom of all the methods and instruments employed by American educators in training the popular mind. The proposition would strike deeper than all these things. Do parents show less or more eagerness than formerly in the education of their children? Do fewer or more children, in proportion to the population, attend the various schools of the land? Are the people of America less willing than formerly to expend their money in support of efficient schools? What are the practical results? Do the young people and children who attend the public schools of America know less or more? Are they better equipped in knowledge and actual mental discipline than the children of former generations? It is by asking and answering questions like these that we would be able fairly to determine whether popular education was declining in America. I undertake a similar task as regards Christianity. Is the religion of Jesus Christ a distinctly diminishing force in the lives of men?

First—Christianity grounds itself in the actual conditions of human life; it finds the unanswerable reason or occasion for its being in certain plain, obvious, undisputed facts of organic human nature. Did you ever stop to consider why men have religions at all? What is the reason or occasion for their being? Is there any stern, imperious need in the facts of human life for their existence? I will name two or three classes or groups of facts which are universally predicable of man and of human life. The first body or group of facts to which I allude is denoted by such words as intelligence, reason, free will, responsibility. The second group of facts might be expressed by the words transgression, willfulness, guilt, penitence and the like. Still another body or class of facts entering into man's life suggest themselves when we use the words struggle, weakness, pain, sorrow, pugnaciousness, mortality. If you will reflect for a moment, you will see that but for these and similar classes of facts in man's life, there would be little need or occasion for religion in any of its offices. If we were not intelligent beings, we could receive no instruction and would be in need of none. If we were self-moved automata, and not free to choose our courses, we could not be accountable for our actions, the doctrine of responsibility at once disappears. We do transgress laws which are for our good, and the feeling of guilt invariably follows every act of willful transgression. If we were not the subjects of weakness and sorrow, there would be no need for comfort. If our present lives were not fugitive, perishing, like the flower of the field, vanishing like the vapor, we would not be yearning after another life, fine, strong, secure, beyond the reach of time and chance and change. Are these alleged facts actual facts? That is, are these facts, facts? Are they real or simulated? Are they the results of the over-refinements of an artificial civilization? Are they fanciful, fictitious, the products of diseased states of the body or mind? Who has shown these facts to be false? Who has shown that they have no basis in reality? No mathematical facts, no chemical facts, no material facts, no facts of any sort soever are or can be more real than these facts. They are not the invention of cunning priests in ages of ignorance. They are the great, broad, obvious actual facts of human nature and human life.

Second—If Christianity is becoming devitalized, if it is dying out it must appear in the gradual undermining, the slow weakening, the growing unreasonableness of those great truths by which it has its life. There are certain vital or necessary organs in the human body. They are the organs by means of which we have our physical lives and without which we could not live. I may lose a finger and yet live. I may lose the whole hand and survive. I may even have my arm amputated at the elbow or shoulder and not lose my life. But if my heart or my lungs or any other vital organ should be taken from me I would at once die. A man is dying when any one of his vital or necessary organs is giving out, decaying. There are certain truths which are vital, essential to Christianity. They are the truths in which it has its life and without which it can have no proper life. What, now, are some of these vital, necessary truths of the gospel? The primal one, of course, the one that by implication contains all the rest, is the great and sublime truth of God—His existence, His presence, His providence, His character, His absolute immanence in all things, His absolute lordship over all things. There is the truth of revelation, or that it has pleased God to make known His will by various communications to men, other than what is disclosed in the material framework of the universe and the reason and experience of mankind. There is the truth of inspiration, or that the spirit of man is permeable and inspirable by the spirit of God, and that the spirit of man has been so permeated and inspired, being thus made the vehicle of authoritative divine communications.

At the very heart of Christianity is the truth of incarnation, that at the fitting time it pleased the Infinite to humble Himself to a participation of the life of man; to limit Himself by human conditions, to manifest Himself through the medium of the flesh, to make His life real and comprehensible to men by living among them, subject to similar conditions. The gospel proclaims the gracious possibility of spiritual rescue and cleansing, the fact of spiritual regeneration, the mingling of God's Spirit with the human spirit, so that a new spiritual life is initiated, nourished and supplied by God Himself. There is the wonderful and precious disclosure in the gospel of our eternal life, beginning here, to be continued, carried on, and perfected, amid far other conditions, in a state of being vastly superior to anything of which we can now form any conception. These, then, are some of the vital truths of our holy faith, viz., God, revelation, inspiration, redemption, incarnation, sacrifice, regeneration, sanctification, eternal life. It is in these truths that the gospel has its life. Have they been undermined? Have they been weakened or emasculated? Where does the man live who has pushed God out of His universe? I have very recently been reading John Fiske's "Idea of God." Now, if there be any man in America who is entirely familiar with the very latest verifications and results of true science, that man is John Fiske. And what is his conclusion? It is, in substance, that every advance in human knowledge is but the addition of so much evidence in favor of the sublimest of all truths, that "the infinite and eternal Power that is manifested in every pulsation of the universe is none other than the living God."

As I grow older, the boundaries of human knowledge widen so before my eager eyes that at times I am fairly oppressed with a sense of my ignorance; but I can at least say, in all sincerity and humility, that I have been a diligent reader and seeker after truth for twenty-five years and I know of no man, I have read no book, I know of no facts which to the slightest degree weakens the hold of the great truths of the gospel on my reason and my heart. Has it been lucidly demonstrated that these great truths are no longer worthy of rational belief?. If so, who has made this demonstration? What is the title of his book? Where does this man live? He certainly thus far has succeeded in escaping the public notice, for a larger number of clear-headed, big-hearted men and women give credence to these Christian truths today than have accepted them at any former period of religious history. While these truths remain unshaken, impregnable by all assault, so long, I repeat, as they are able to commend themselves as living truths to the minds and hearts of the strongest men and women in the world, it is idle to talk of the decay of Christianity. Whatever else may be said of it, with such strong, solid, indestructible foundations, it is at least a living religion!

Third—Christianity undertakes the lofty and difficult task of regulating and inspiring human conduct. In all systems of ethics, in all schemes of human conduct, two great ideas appear. There is, first, the moral standard, or rule of conduct, the measure or gauge by which our actions are to be governed; and, second, the moral impulse, or motive, the energy by which we are impelled to make our conduct square with our knowledge. What we are to do, and how we are to do it, are the two practical questions in the noble science of right living. If it can be shown that the moral standards of Christianity are arbitrary and irrational; if it can be shown that they are crude, unfit, ill-adapted to men; if it can be shown that they are partial, mechanical, cruel; that they are local, limited, insufficient; if these things can be shown, then a fatal impeachment of Christian ethics has taken place.

What, now, is the acknowledged moral standard of Christianity? Let its divine Founder answer this question. "Thou shalt love the Lord thy God with all thy heart, and mind, and soul, and strength, and thou shalt love thy neighbor as thyself. On these two commandments hang all the law and the prophets." And what is the nature or genius of this moral rule? How may these comprehensive precepts or commandments be described? They are positive, not negative; they are spiritual, not arbitrary; they are reasonable, not mechanical; they are universal, not local; they are ample, expansive, incapable of exhaustion. A mechanical religion may, for example, exact of its votaries that they shall pray five times every day, with the face turned in a given direction, the body in a certain posture. It is easy to conceive of how a day might come in which the devotee should find need for other, and many other, prayers than those prescribed in the formal ritual. Such a religion would be not only formal and mechanical, but it would be insufficient. Contrast with this the moral rule of Christianity, in which the emphasis is placed, not on the number of prayers, not on the posture of body or the direction of the face, but on the spirit of prayer, and how manifest at once is its vast superiority. The moral rule of such a religion knows no limitations of climate, color, condition, culture, age. It is at once simple and rational, and universally applicable. In the frozen Arctic seas, in the torrid tropics, and in the temperate zones, in city and country, in knowledge and ignorance, in wealth and in poverty, in health and in sickness, wherever we may be, whatever our lot, we can understand and practice that sum of human duty which consists of fervent love to God, our Father, and man, our brother.

Is it possible for us, is it possible for any man, to conceive of a loftier, a more engaging, a more perfect model or moral standard for human conduct than is furnished for us, and for all men, in the life and character of Jesus Christ? Is there any limit to it? Who has found any defect in it? Where is the least flaw? What lynx eye has discovered His fault? Who has measured up to it? Who has exhausted the moral energy and impulse supplied by the divine and moving drama of His life and death? Has anybody filled up and overpassed the goodness of which He is the one perfect exemplar in the world's entire history? Where is the man to be found who, having perfectly copied the spirit and example of Jesus Christ, yet declares himself unsatisfied? The elements of love, service, sacrifice, as incarnate in Jesus Chrst—where, I say, are the men who, having surpassed these, long for other and higher spiritual food? Thus we see that when the most searching tests are applied, Christianity does not fail as the regulator and inspirer of human conduct, nor is there the slightest evidence that the spiritual growth of men will ever go beyond the perfect moral rule declared and exemplified by our divine Redeemer.

Fourth—The strongest possible argument against the assumption that Christianity is dying is furnished by the methods and mental attitude of infidelity itself. How can I bear more effectual or convincing testimony to the substantial wisdom, ingenuity and sagacity of my opponent, rival or competitor than by subsequently quietly adopting his plans, his tactics, his weapons? If beaten in a canvass for Congress here in New York, I remove to North Dakota, there secure another nomination and at once adopt the plans, methods and tactics of my successful competitor here, am I not giving his methods and plan of campaign my highest personal indorsement? This is precisely what infidelity has done and is now doing. It has stolen from Christianity the words, the phrases, the very ideas, with which it now seeks to wage its warfare. For example, it talks loudly of large mindedness, breadth, toleration, liberality. "We want no narrow church religion. We want a religion for humanity," say these loud and boastful declaimers. Have they forgotten that it was just because of His breadth and liberality that Jesus was at first opposed and persecuted? The first Gentile infidels ridiculed the very idea of a universal religion. "What," they said, "the same religion for the Gaul and the Scythian and the Parthian, the Greek and the Roman?" The idea was preposterous, and they scouted it. The different people must have their different gods, and be religious according to their own climate and ethnic genius; but the dream of a religion for humanity was to them an idle dream.

CHRISTIANITY AND LOVE

BY BISHOP E. G. ANDREWS

"Now the end of the commandment is charity out of a pure heart, and of a good conscience, and of faith unfeigned."—1 Timothy 1:5.

Every careful reader of the English Bible takes knowledge of the fact that the English language, like every other living language, is in process of change. He knows the significance of words, as well as their form, and occasionally their order changes. He reads, for instance, in the Psalms: "My heart is fixed, O God, my heart is fixed," and he remembers that the word "fixed" at the time our version was made had the meaning, which we still retain in our colloquial speech, "to be fixed up," and so he reads: "My heart is prepared, oh God, my heart is prepared." He reads in the Epistle to the Thessalonians that they which are alive at the second coming of Christ shall not prevent them that are asleep, and he remembers that the word "prevent" originally meant to precede simply, and came to have its present meaning because he that precedes another is likely to get in the way of that one and obstruct another who follows, so he reads that at the second coming of Christ they that are alive shall not precede, or shall not have the advantage over them that sleep in Christ, for both alike shall be called to meet their Lord in the air.

So in this text we have the word "charity," a word which today signifies either almsgiving or kindly judgment of others, but in the time of our version it had the meaning to which the new revisers have returned, viz., "love,' 'or "benevolence," and in this passage we read this statement: The aim of the commandment is benevolence, good will, effective love, even as we speak of the love of man to God, then also to His fellow men.

Another Bible criticism is worth our while. The word "commandment," like the word "law," may have either a narrow or a broad significance. The narrow significance of that is "particular precept" attended by "particular sanction." A broader meaning is that of a "holy ordained institution and system," and that broader meaning evidently should be here used because of the context. We come then to the entire statement: "The end, or aim, of the whole Christian institution is love out of a pure heart, and of a good conscience, and of faith unfeigned."

It originated in a heart of boundless love toward man in an act of love unparalleled we may suppose in all ages of eternity—even the gift of God's only Son. All its precepts turn in this direction. Church organizations and ministrations of every kind, if they be rightly directed, have simply this purpose to discharge the human soul of that selfishness that belongs to it by nature, and to enter into all the love of God.

Now all familiar with the New Testament know that this is no solitary utterance—it is but one of many broad and comprehensive statements. One came to the Master saying: "Which is the first and great commandment?" And He answered: "Thou shalt love the Lord thy God with all thy heart, and with all thy soul, and with all thy mind, and with all thy strength; this is the first commandment, and the second is like unto it: Thou shalt love thy neighbor as thyself. On these two commandments hang all the law and the prophets." In another passage St. Paul tells us that "Love is the fulfilling of the law." If there be any other commandment, it is briefly comprehended in this saying: "Thou shalt love thy neighbor as thyself." St. James calls this the "royal law." St. Paul tells us: "Above all things, have fervent charity one toward another." And St. John, in a memorable passage, in one of his epistles, tells us that "God is Love, and he that dwelleth in love dwelleth in God and God in him."

Christ told the story of a man who went down from Jerusalem to Jericho and fell among robbers, as one may nowadays do on that road. They robbed him, stripped him of his raiment, wounded him, and left him half dead. Then came one of the chief representatives of the current religion, a priest, and passed by on the other side. Then there came down a subordinate representative of the current religion, a Levite, and looked and passed by on the other side. Then came a heretic in religion, an alien in race, and looking upon the wounded man, he was moved with compassion and dismounted, and bound up his wounds, set the wounded man on his own beast, brought him to an inn and took care of him for the night and paid the charges, leaving money for additional charges, saying to the innkeeper: "If it costs more I will repay when I come again." And that alien in race, that heretic in religion, the Lord Jesus presents before us as the one great example of our practical religion.

Perhaps some one will say, however: Is love such a peculiarity that it does not exist where there is no Christianity? That it does not exist with those who reject Christianity? Is it not a common experience in human life? To which question we say yes, unquestionably. Love is the common heritage of human life. It belongs to human nature to love as it does to think. It is part of our constitutional endowment. It is the bond of society. It is the point at which Christianity meets the human soul. It is indeed the one thing which binds us to the eternal God. So that in all climes and all ages men have known what it is to love. The very Egyptians, who could ruthlessly put to death the first born of Israel, knew what it was to wail through all their habitations when their own first born lay dead.

Now be pleased to notice two facts in this natural love. In the first place, much of it is simply instinctive, a divine implantation for high purposes, but because not founded in moral reason, divine reason, therefore without moral worth. It is but part of that endowment of human nature by which the propagation and the education of the race is made possible, but it does not imply of necessity any high moral quality. The bear will rush on the point of the spear in the defense of its cubs. The wildcat will die for its young. The eagle, with unwearied patience, will teach the young eaglet to fly. Will you, therefore, say: "Behold, what paragons of moral excellence?" Would you not say of them if they lacked parental and filial love: "Behold what monsters?"

In the second place, this natural love is marked by great limitations in its extent. It is laid upon one's family and one's friends, upon one's neighbors and country, upon those who are of the same race, or it may be of the same religious faith, or of the same political persuasion, and it is hemmed in by these limitations. How many a man goes to the market place and to the exchange with perfect indifference to the prosperity and happiness of his fellow man and wrestles with them in business to return to his home to lavish gladly upon his family all his ill-gotten gains.

There are many generous men in all our communities, but they may be also men desirous of having their generosity duly acknowledged and trumpeted abroad throughout the world, and if they fail of that acknowledgment, somehow their charity seems to sour upon them, and they feel that they are not recognized as they expected to be. Benedict Arnold was an eminently brave and skillful soldier, and so far as we know a true patriot, but he was a spendthrift, and when Congress censured him in various ways he at length became Benedict Arnold the traitor. The truth is that it is very easy to overload all the joists and timbers of our soul with these defects, and we may notice in passing that a great deal that passes for charity is oftentimes a thin veneer over unmeasured masses of selfishness, and we may further notice that sometimes we have credited ourselves with very great tenderness and good will toward men, because, for instance, we wept over the griefs and woes of the heroes and heroines of fiction, and yet find ourselves (such is the inertia of our nature) never so much as lifting up our hands to relieve the unutterable woes that crowd in human souls all around us.

Another defect of the natural love is that it is simply an unrighteous love; I mean it lacks the quality of righteousness in that it is a mere kindly affection and desire to do kind things to those who are objects of our love, while at the same time there is no recognition of that foundation which upholds the whole process of human life, that fundamental truth which only can confer any large and permanent well being.

Finally, this natural love is oftentimes ungodly. That is to say, it is the recognition in man (the children of God) of this or that scintillation of the infinite goodness, while it withholds from Him Who gathers unto Himself all conceivable excellences, all truth, patience, generosity, tenderness, temperance, long suffering, all purity—while it withholds from Him the heart's true loyalty.

So that this native or natural love of which we speak is indeed oftentimes a very faint reflection and image of that perfect love toward which Christianity calls us. And so we turn back to the text, and hear the words that St. Paul said: "The aim of the commandment, the whole aim of the Christian institution, is love out of a pure heart, and out of a good conscience and out of faith unfeigned.

First—In this matter of Christianity we have to do with such divine forces in their operation upon human nature as yield hopes of even this great result. It is not that we expect ourselves to attain any such goodness, but is it not possible that He Who made this thing we call the human soul with all its varied powers of observation, reason, imagination, fancy and memory, conscience and will, He Who made this strange, subtle, intangible thing we call the human soul, may not He remake the soul, enter into its profoundest depths, so reconstruct, reorder and inspire it that it may shine in all the likeness of God? Is it not said, "He will do for us far more exceedingly than we can ask or think?" And that is the warrant in this Christian church, and in all these Christian churches for the high aspiration toward which Christianity points us.

And the other thing to be said is this, that however true it is that most of us who profess and call ourselves Christians, come far, very far, short of this high ideal of character; however true it is that with many of us our Christianity is simply, as it were, an attempt to secure self-wellbeing in the long reaching future—alas! that it is such a narrow form of Christianity as that—however true that may be, nevertheless I take it for granted that perhaps every one present has during some time in his experience come in contact with some soul, has become intimate perhaps with some life, upon whom the divine truth, the divine providence and the divine inspiration has so operated in transforming power that the soul seems to have entered into the very fellowship of God, even has become radiant with divine life, the features have been chiseled by the soul within, the eye has looked tenderly out toward all men whom it has met, and now and then the very habitation and habit of such a person becomes unspeakably endearing, because of this dwelling of the Lord Christ within.

Second—The aim of Christianity is love not only out of a pure heart, but also out of a good conscience. That is to say, its aim is not a mere sentimental overflow of tears and pity; it shall be a living and mighty engine within, under the guidance of God, as to method, and as to measures, of a widely instructed moral sense. Christianity is something beside mere happiness. It aims at the great soul of life under the guidance and shaping of an instructed moral nature.

And finally the love at which Christianity aims is a love out of faith unfeigned. Let me put it concretely:

Shut your Bibles. Lay them aside, let the dust cover them. It is all a myth. There is no truth in it. There is no divine and eternal Father, pitying all His human children and longing to help them. That is imaginary. The heavens never opened that the Son of God might come down and throw his arms around human nature, and lift men up out of their sin and sorrow, Godward and heavenward. That is only a vain myth, and Christmastime and Eastertime are commemorative of purely imaginary events. There is no divine Spirit, descending and touching the human soul. Prayer is an impertinence and folly. Providence. There is no providence. The world is really but a great machine, revolving and revolving. There is no hereafter. Write as the French did over the gateways of their cemeteries a century ago or more; write, 'Death and eternal sleep.'' No God, no Christ, no Holy Spirit, no prayer, no providence, no judgment, no heaven, no hell, no faith. Then look out! Look out! at first for August and September massacres, and the streets of Paris running with blood. Look out for utter selfishness everywhere. ''Let us eat, drink and be merry for tomorrow we die.'' The insect that lives a brief moment in the sunshine has as much reason for divine charity as man who lives his season a little longer, but dies likewise. No faith.

Let faith return. Bring back your Bible. Behold one living and eternal God. He is love, and He has loved this poor world so that He has effected redemption for mankind and lifted them across the heavens. Has thrown His arms around man, in order that He might lift him up by His Holy Spirit. Prayer, so that the broken-hearted and the sufferer and desolate may go apart from the eyes of man and pour out their hearts to God, Whose ear can catch their faintest sigh, and Whose eye beholds the falling tear. Providence. No sparrow falls to the ground without His knowledge, and the very hairs of your head are numbered. Death; transformation. Life here; introduction to the life eternal. Let these truths enter and live within human souls, and somehow the human race has become transformed by these facts. I cannot meet a man, woman or child, but at once I know there is one whom God loves. Why should not I love that one? And so it comes to pass that wherever Christianity is there is still love where it was not.

Two inferences are interesting. There may seem to you to be various defects in the historical parts of the Bible, but if you will only tell me where there is a system whose breath is love, whose inspiration is love, which makes this earth a paradise and a very heaven of love. If you tell me where that comes from I am sure I shall know how God comes down to our world in the gospel of Jesus Christ.

Second. How much Christianity have you? Not how much religion. The Brahmin, the Mohammedan have religion; that is common in all nations, but how much Christianity have you? There is one answer. So much Christianity as we have self-forgetfulness, self-sacrifice, charity; so much and no more. May God help us. There is infinite resources for us. Let us look to heaven, and let us look to earth, and do the little things at hand in order that when the opportunity may come we may nourish within ourselves the victorious forces of helpfulness until at length, if it please God, we shall be like our Lord Jesus Christ, Who has the very fullness of love toward man.—Brooklyn Daily Eagle.

UNDER THE INFLUENCE OF MODERN MOVEMENTS OF THOUGHT

Christianity is becoming a new thing, precisely as, with the advance of science, our age-old world is becoming to us a new thing. We are bound to believe in Christianity, but our question today, repeated with a new eagerness, is "What is Christianity?" The twentieth century stands before this immense phenomenon, pondering chiefly two things—the challenge offered here to its intellect, and second, the challenge offered to its morality. As an existing world-force the New Testament religion is with us, fully in evidence, a fact which none may question. But it is also an assertion, a doctrine, and the point is "How do we stand to that?" "The New Testament 'miracles,' " cries the modern man, "are incredible. Its ethics are impossible." The whole question is here. Let is consider it a little.

Christianity, to begin with, strikes hard upon our intellect with its element of the extraordinary, of the abnormal. Assuredly the gospel is charged with this element. However far we carry our criticism of the documents—if, for instance, with Pfleiderer and Harnack, we regard the opening chapters of Matthew and Luke as a late addition to the original tradition; if, as to the Resurrection, we, with Sabatier, take Paul's statements as supplying the clue to what actually happened; if, with many modern scientists, we consider the healings wrought by Jesus as resolvable into cure by suggestion, by the power of a supreme mind and volition over certain bodily states—even at this lowest estimate of the facts, we are, in the gospel story, in contact with a phenomenon, a power, a Presence unique in history. We have only to note in the way in which the New Testament writers speak of Christ, their whole attitude towards Him, and to ask ourselves how the state of mind came about which caused such expressions to rush to their lips, to realize that we have here the beginning of a new spiritual era, introduced, as all new eras are, by a new force and quality of Being. Modern philosophy talks of the "Super-man." It is a belated expression. The "Super-man" has been with us these two millenniums in the person of Christ.

It is to us odd in the extreme that men should, at this time of day, be raising objections to the doctrine of the abnormal, or, if you will, of the supernatural. As a matter of fact, man cannot get away from the supernatural, do what he will. It is part and parcel of himself, of his history, of his world. We may build it out from our immediate prospect, keeping our eye fixed on our garden plot, on our bit of business, of politics, of this and that secular interest. But we have only to lift our eyes to the heavens on a clear night to see how impossible is the attempt. In a moment we recognize that this is infinity, and that we who gaze are indissolubly and mystically related to it. The commonest man of us, to use Emerson's phrase, must hitch his wagon to a star. And the cosmic story all through has been of the supernatural; of happenings, that is, which have transcended the previously existing natural. When the first beginnings of life showed, in a hitherto dead world; when, out of mere animalhood, rose the phenomenon of man with his mind and soul, we see traced here the line of that incessant upward movement, each step above the natural that had gone before; of that slow but constant disclosure of new phases of the Infinite Life, of which the appearance of Christ, of His person, teaching, and work, were a sequence not less logical than wondrous. When we call Christianity supernatural, it is in fact to ally it with the entire planetary process, so far as we have yet gone. That the invisible Power should, after ages of firemists, of cataclysms, of prehistoric monsters, have exhibited Himself in man, was in itself evidence and prophecy that He would later disclose Himself in the super-man. Paul's word about the first and second Adam is evolution pure and simple.

But the Christian ethic? Much modern criticism rests its main arguments here. Its impressiveness lays in the contrast drawn between the ideals of the Sermon on the Mount and the ideals of the modern world. "We do not really believe the gospel, because we do not believe in humility, in turning the other cheek, in self-renunciation, in inward purity. On the contrary, we believe in worldly position and success, in paying out our adversary, inostentation, in young fellows 'sowing their wild oats.' and so on. The world today, in fact, finds the Galilean morality an impracticable dream." So says many a critic.

There is, of course, nothing new in this criticism. The difficulty it opens has been before men through all the Christian ages. In view of the present discussion one may reread with interest that letter of Augustine to Marcelline in which he urges that "those precepts as to turning the other cheek and not resisting evil relate to the inward disposition of the heart rather than to the outward conduct," and where he goes on to argue that severity to criminals may be the truest mercy, and that a just war may be waged in conformity with Christian benevolence. But we have lights on this subject which were not open to Augustine. For one thing, New Testament criticism, as handled by scholars such as Wendt, Harnack and Wernle, has given a recognition never before accorded to one peculiarity of the ethical method of Jesus. He constantly enforced His ideal by a most daring use of hyperbole. That it was meant as hyperbole was contained in the expressions themselves. No man, for instance, could by any possibility have the promised hundred-fold of mothers.

That is one point, but it is not the really important one. The complaint today is that the doctrine, when all reservations are taken, is fundamentally impracticable and has always been so. It offers the transcendental to a world which is severely practical. Suppose we grant this, where does it bring us? Some of us find here one of the greatest reasons for our belief. The gospel ethic is abnormal just as its facts are abnormal, and for the same reason. It is a moral heaven, infinitely above us, but which always inspires us. Imagine a New Testament with an *a la mode* guide to conduct, a kind of glorified "Lord Chesterfield's Letters to His Son!" Do we want an ethic on a level with modern practice? What an ennobling production? The miracle of the New Testament teaching is that while it fits no age it has uplifted them all. The Spencerian evolutionist, John Fiske, declared that the Galilean teaching is a prophecy of what is assuredly to be realized in the later stages of the human evolution. Man in relation to it is like an asymptote to a curve, ever approaching, yet never reaching. But the effort to reach is his daily salvation. In his march onward man gazes ever on this vision of perfection hung high above him, feeling instinctively that in this impossible lies, nevertheless, his destiny and his bliss.

Do we believe? Yes, assuredly, in a gospel that has been everything to us, and will be yet more. It is a prophecy that is only beginning to be accomplished. Christianity, as Vinet has so finely said, is "the eternal youth of the human race." Its present and future fortunes may be summed up in the great words of Schleiermacher: "For why should it be overthrown? The living spirit of it indeed, slumbers oft and long. It withdraws itself into a torpid state, into the dead shell of the letter. But it ever awakes again as soon as the season in the spiritual world is favorable for its renewal, and sets its sap in motion."—Freeman.

THE FERTILIZING RIVER

BY THE REV. W. M. TAYLOR, D.D.

"And everything shall live, whither the river cometh."—Ezekiel 47:9.

The vision to the description of which these words belong is one of the most striking of those which were vouchsafed to the captive seer by the river of Chebar. It was designed to represent the nature, origin, progress and results of the gospel; and thus regarded, it suggests many important matters for consideration. Thus, it is a vision of waters, and that symbolizes the fertilizing, as well as purifying, influence which the religion of Christ has everywhere exerted. Then, it is a vision of waters issuing from the temple of God; and that reminds us that the gospel is no mere human expedient, but is indeed the revelation of God's mercy to mankind. Farther, it is a vision of waters flowing out from under the altar of the house of God; and we have thereby recalled to our remembrance the truth that men are redeemed and regenerated only through their acceptance of that deliverance which Christ wrought out for them by the sacrifice of Himself on their behalf. Once more, this is a vision of waters gradually rising. They grew deeper the longer they flowed. First they were to the ankles; then to the knees; then to the loins; then "waters to swim in, a river that could not be passed over." Now, that illustrates the progress of the gospel over the world. It was not to take sudden and immediate possession of the earth, but rather to flow over it as the tide flows over the shore. That is a view of the case which may relieve the depression that weighs down our hearts when we think of the (comparatively speaking) tardy advancement which the gospel has as yet made among men. One wave bears but a small proportion to the full tide, and for any thing we know, the past eighteen centuries may be no more than so many separate waves in that steadily-rising tide which is yet to cover the earth, for "a day is to the Lord as a thousand years, and a thousand years as one day." In any case, if at the present moment the waters be even "to the ankles," that, especially when taken in connection with the cumulative force of other proofs, is an assurance that the time is coming when there shall be "waters to swim in—a great river that cannot be passed over."

Such are some of the leading features of this vision, with the instructions which they analogically convey to us concerning the gospel of Christ. But without dwelling longer on them now, let me proceed to my special theme, which I may announce as the influence of Christianity on human institutions and occupations, or the indirect effects of the gospel on the relationships and pursuits of men.

1. Take it in the first place in its bearing on men's social condition. And here I go at once to the household. The family is the center of human society. We cannot look upon mankind as merely a multitude of units. Not one of us stands completely by himself, for each one of us is born into a little circle already existing. As Maurice has said, "Our relation to father and mother is the primary fact of our existence, so that we can contemplate no facts apart from that." The family is the earliest school at which we are placed; and the lessons which we receive in the household, the examples which are there set before us, above all, perhaps, the influences to which we are there subjected and by which we are unconsciously affected, have more to do with our after history as individuals, and with the future character of the community to which we belong, than we can possibly estimate. "Home is the head of the river," and an influence, whether blessed or pernicious, exerted there, will effect all its after course.

Now, it is capable of the clearest proof that Christianity is the only thing that has given purity and loveliness to the household. Indeed, in its true ideal, the family may have said to have been virtually the creation of Christianity, for in Rome, which was the heir of the civilization of the ages, and in which it is commonly conceded that men had attained the highest degree of refinement which has been reached without revelation, there was little home-life worthy of the name. This being the case, we need not wonder at the state of things that existed, and does not yet largely exist, in heathen lands. Wherever the gospel has not gone, woman has been degraded into a slave, and ground down beneath the galling tyranny of her husband. Then as to the little children, who shall tell us how many holocausts of victims infanticide has burned upon its altars? While as regards the aged, it would be impossible to reckon the number of them who have been left to starve in the desert, or to perish by the river side.

I may be told, indeed, that such things as these are not quite unknown among ourselves. I may be reminded of the brutality of drunken husbands, and the cold-heartedness of children to their parents, of which we have the records occasionally in our public prints. But the cases are not parallel. That which is the rule in Pagan lands is the exception here. That which among the heathen is nothing accounted of, is here viewed with abhorrence and regarded as a crime.

Now, how shall we account for the difference? Simply by the influence of the gospel of Christ. The Lord Jesus has revolutionized, if not created family life. He gave sanctity to the marriage tie by re-enacting the primal law, that one man should be the husband of one wife. He restored woman to her true position as the help-meet and companion of her husband. He took the little children in His arms and blessed them—for that touching scene in the gospel narrative is only a type of the work in which He is still engaged wheresoever His message of love is proclaimed. By His tender care for His venerable mother in the very climax and crisis of His own agony, He gave a sacredness to old age which has gathered to it ever since the reverence, the affection, and the benevolence of men.

But not to dwell longer on the domestic influence of Christianity, let me direct attention for a moment to the effect which the religion of Jesus has had in promoting kindness between man and man. Nothing strikes the student of ancient history more painfully than the indifference to human life which seems to have prevailed in all Pagan lands. The pages of classical authors are continually stained by the record of some deed of cruelty. But lest I should be suspected of exaggerating this evil in order to make out a better case, let me give you one or two quotations from one who will not be charged with speaking under any particular prejudice upon the subject. In his introduction to his little volume on the Commentaries of Julius Cæsar, Anthony Trollope has said: "The cruelties of Marius as an old man and of Augustus as a young one were so astounding as, even at this distance, to horrify the reader, though he remember that Christianity had not yet softened men's hearts. Marcus, the old man, almost swam in the blood of his enemies, as did also his rival Sulla; but the young Octavius, he whom the gods favored so long as the almost divine Augustus, cemented his throne with the blood of his friends." Again he says: "That which will most strike the ordinary English reader in the narrative of Cæsar is the cruelty of the Romans—cruelty of which Cæsar himself is guilty to a frightful extent, and of which he never expresses horror." Once more, after giving an account of the deaths, mostly by violence, of the greater number of those whose names are mentioned in Cæsar's writings, he goes on to say: "The bloody catalogue is so complete, so nearly comprises all whose names are mentioned, that it strikes the reader with almost a comic horror. But when we come to the slaughter of whole towns; to the devastation of country, effected purposely that men and women might starve; to the abandonment of the old, the young, and the tender, that they might perish on the hill-sides; to the mutilation of crowds of men; to the burning of cities told us in a passing word, to the drowning of many thousands—mentioned as we should mention the destruction of a brood of rats— the comedy is all over, and the heart becomes sick. Then it is we remember that the coming of Christ had changed all things, and that men now—though terrible things have been done since Christ came to us—are not as men were in the days of Cæsar." To this terrible passage nothing needs to be added. I may only remind you that in ancient Rome, while there were many buildings where murder was perpetrated to give zest to the sports of a holiday, there was not a single edifice devoted to such benevolence as those to which our modern hospitals are consecrated. What a contrast is here presented between that picture of Gerome, which portrays the gladiatorial fight in the crowded amphitheatre, and that other, by an English artist, which depicts the nurse in the hospital of Scutari! In the former, you have in the sickening foreground the two combatants. One has overcome the other, and with his uplifted sword is waiting for directions. The wounded slave has turned his eye, with agonizing earnestness, upon the Emperor, pleading for his life, and even his conqueror seems almost to join in his mute appeal. But the vestal virgins, each with her thumb turned downward, are voting for his destruction, and he on whose nod a human destiny is at the moment hanging has so little concern upon the matter that his whole attention seems to be given to the fresh fig that he is eating; while on the benches round and round, the multitudes are enjoying the spectacle as the great feature of their holiday festivities.

And now look on this other scene. A hospital ward, with sick and wounded men, lying on comfortable couches; a clock upon the wall whose fingers point to an hour past midnight: and in the forefront a gentle woman, with a lamp in her hand, passing from bed to bed, all unconscious that the rough soldier behind her has risen on his elbow to kiss her shadow on the wall as she goes by. Let that stand for a specimen of holiest benevolence! Now what has made the difference between these two? I answer, the life, death, resurrection, and influence of Him who said: "He that will be greatest among you, let him be your servant, even as the Son of Man came not to be ministered unto but to minister, and to give His life a ransom for many." Thus on the banks of the river of Christianity domestic happiness and practical benevolence do flourish in vigorous and attractive life; and if we wish to make other nations sharers with us in the priceless blessings, we must send them that gospel out of which among us they have sprung.

2. But look, in the second place, at the influence of the gospel upon civil liberty. It has been alleged that the Bible is the enemy of freedom, but they who so speak "know neither what they say, nor whereof they affirm." They reason from the abnormal state of things which existed when the priesthood of an apostate church rode roughshod over the liberties of men, but they are willfully blind to the condition of affairs in the world at the present time. Take the map of the globe and ask what those countries are which have the fullest measure of civil and religious freedom, and you will find that they are those in which the gospel

of Christ is most widely known, most generally believed, and most commonly obeyed. The Bible indeed contains no treatise on civil government, but its principles lay the ax to the root of every form of despotism. Jesus has taught us not only to assert freedom of conscience for ourselves, but to respect and defend its exercise by others. He has commanded us to "honor all men," because they wear that nature which He consecrated by His incarnation; and wherever the mystery of His cross is even dimly understood, men are disposed, while receiving its salvation, to sacrifice themselves for others' good. Hence the whole spirit of Christianity stimulates men to look not only on their own things, but also on the things of others; and that is the disposition out of which true liberty is born. See how all this is established by the history of the Protestant Reformation. Wherever in the sixteenth century the gospel found a foot-hold in Europe, it cleared forthwith for liberty also a place of asylum, which, by-and-by, became the headquarters of propagandist activity in its behalf. The name of Geneva is as prominent in the history of the progress of European liberty as it is in that of religious reformation; while, on the other hand, the nations which in those days stamped out the incipient workings of spiritual reform, are those whose histories since that time have been darkest with despotism, or reddest with the blood of cease- lessly recurring revolutions. John Milton was right when he said of the authors of the New Testament, that they were

> "Men Divinely taught, and better teaching
> The solid rules of civil government,
> In their majestic, unaffected style
> Than all the orators of Greece and Rome,
> In them is plainest taught, and easiest learnt.
> What makes a nation happy, and keeps it so;
> What ruins kingdoms and lays cities flat."

3. But look, in the third place, at the department of litera- ture, and you will see how, when the river of the gospel has flowed into a nation, it has quickened that also into richer growth. Take here the stories which have been garnered up in our own mother tongue, and when you come to look into the subject you will be surprised to discover how much the Word of God has had to do with the character and quality of English literature. Up till the time when John Wycliffe sent his "poor priests" up and down

England with his version of portions of the Scriptures in the vulgar tongue, there could not be said to be any English literature, and there was hardly any English language. Just at the very time Wycliffe was engaged in his great work, now precisely 500 years ago, Geoffrey Chaucer was writing those "Canterbury Tales" which have charmed so many generations of readers, and which bear on them certain indications that their author had come under the widening and ennobling influence of the truth which the parson of Lutterworth proclaimed. Nor was this in itself unlikely, for both of these men were proteges of him whom we know in another connection as "Old John of Gaunt of time-honored Lancaster." In any case these two between them laid the foundation of our language and literature; but as from the nature of the case the Bible went into more homes and hearts than Chaucer reached, we must attribute to Wycliffe the principal share in that literary revival which the succeeding centuries witnessed in the mother country. Nay, it is somewhat remarkable that just as Chaucer's poems were contemporaneous with Wycliffe's Bible, so the age of the Reformation under Henry, Edward, and Elizabeth, the day that is of Tyndale's, Matthews', Coverdale's, and the Genevan Bibles, has always been regarded as the palmiest time of English literature; while again, the age which saw Wordsworth, Coleridge, Scott, Southey, and that whole band which made the early part of this century so renowned, was the successor and inheritor of that in which Wesley, Whitefield, and their fellow-evangelists had carried religious revival over England and America. In more recent days Macaulay came out of the Clapham sect; Carlyle learned his volcanic earnestness in the most intensely spiritual of the Scottish denominations; and Tennyson has but sung to his matchless music the truths which his friend Maurice and he have learned together from the Word of God as interpreted by their age. Read over again that paper of rare wisdom and still rarer wit, in the "Eclipse of Faith," entitled "The Blank Bible," and you will be astonished at the extent to which, as there indicated, the influence of the Bible has gone into our literature. Avowedly religious writers, of course, have been indebted to it for their all; but even those who have had no directly spiritual aim have been largely beholden to its quickening power. Take from Shakspeare those passages of his writings which have been suggested or colored by the Word of God, and you rob him of some of the greenest leaves in his laurel crown. But for the Bible, the "Paradise Lost" of Milton might have been little better than an echo of Homer, and the "Paradise Regained" would have remained among "things unattempted yet in prose or rhyme." But for it where would have been the "Pilgrim" of John Bunyan, the "Task" of William Cowper, and the finest passages of Wordsworth's "Excursion"? Without it we might have had the passionate and misanthropic shriekings of Byron, but we could not have had the sweet music of his Hebrew melodies. Without it we might have had some of the songs of Burns, and perhaps, also, some of his patriotic odes, but the world would never have seen his "Cotter's Saturday Night." Without it we might have had the weird mysticism of Poe, but we could not have possessed some of the matchless lyrics of Whittier and Longfellow. But what need I say more? Take the Bible out of our literature, and you not only rob it of its glory, but you destroy it altogether; for if in the years of the past it has seemed to be like a tree bringing forth its fruit in its season, and having leaves for the healing of the nation, the reason has been because it has been planted on the bank of that mystic river which the prophet saw, and because it drew from that its vital nourishment. Now what the gospel has done for the literature of our mother tongue, it will do for that of every land to which it is sent. Livingstone's venerable father-in-law once said: "When Livingstone was led into the unknown regions of Africa, he had a future before him of which they had often spoken together. They had frequently talked with each other, when they imagined they could see vessels sailing on those magnificent lakes, and cities with churches rising on their shores." So I think our missionary brethren, when they see what the translation of the Bible has done for our language, may comfort themselves with the assurance that, as the centuries roll on, there shall spring up out of the work they have accomplished, literatures which shall do as much for other nations as that of our tongue has done for those to whom it is vernacular. Unnoticed, and, to a large extent, unknown, they are laboring now; and when they return to the churches by which they were sent out, there be those among us who sneeringly say: "It is only a missionary." But the day is coming when their names shall be mentioned by the people at the birth of whose literature they have presided, as we now name Tyndale and Wycliffe, as men the latchets of whose shoes we are not worthy to stoop down and unloose.

4. Look, now, in the fourth place, at the influence of Christianity upon science. It may seem a bold thing for me to attract attention to this aspect of the subject. I may be reminded of some utterances of physical philosophers, which virtually accuse the Christian religion of arresting the progress of science, and which have exalted Mohammedanism, so far as science is concerned, above the gospel. But I would remind these friends that there is a wide difference between the syllabus and the New Testament, and I insist that the two shall not be confounded. I claim that here, as in other things, the religion of the Bible shall be tested, not by the utterance of individual men, or by the decrees of Popes or councils, but by its own book, and by its tendency and influence, wherever it has been permitted freely to develop itself. Now look around you, and tell me, where in the present day the physical sciences have made the greatest progress? Has it not been in those countries in which Protestant Christianity has taken the strongest hold? And am I not entitled to ask: Is this by accident? Nay, when I find that in other departments Christianity has had a quickening influence, am I not warranted to conclude that the intellectual activity which it fosters, and the spirit of inquiry which it evokes, have told also on science, and so have contributed to the production of its present excellence? Then, so far as the contrast with Mohammedanism is concerned, I may surely point to the fact that science is today, in Protestant lands, far ahead of what it is in Moslem countries. How comes it, then, that Islamism did not keep its pre-eminence, if ever it had it? The answer is easy. In past ages it was contending with a system of Christianity which was virtually idolatry and polytheism, and so its faith in one living God gave a vigor to the thinking of its disciples which could not be imparted by the mummeries mediæval Romanism. But now Christianity stands not upon the church, but upon the Book. Its watchword is: "Prove all things; hold fast that which is good;" and so, wherever the New Testament goes, it provokes inquiry, strengthens intellect, encourages independence, while, at the same time, it imparts to the universe a sacred interest, as the work of Him Who is "our Father." Christianity has reared the platform

on which all scientific associations stand today, and the very liberty which men of science have to utter unpopular opinions—shall I say even heretical opinions?—has been won for them by Christian men. Had all the martyrs of Christianity, and especially of Protestantism, been as weak-spirited as Galileo, we might all have still been groaning under the intolerance of the Inquisition. But in standing up for liberty of conscience and of opinion for themselves, the witnesses for religious truth have won also for science the right to hold and teach its own deductions and beliefs. Now, that is indispensable to its advancement, if not even to its existence; and so when you examine it thoroughly, you will be constrained to admit that this mystic river has fertilized the roots of science also, and though for the moment there may seem to be a misunderstanding between some Christians and some men of science, for which, as it seems to me, both parties are to be blamed, yet the two departments never can really inspire each other, and the advancement of the one will invariably be accompanied by the progress of the other. Nor could we have a finer illustration of that fact than in the services which our foreign missionaries have rendered to the science of our times. Their labors in ethnology, geography, philology, botany, zoology, and even astronomy, have called forth the thanks of men of the highest eminence in all these departments. Indeed, every mission-station is in a sense also a scientific observatory, and the records there kept are pre-eminently valuable, for those who make them are educated men, trained to habits of exactness, and interested in everything that will help on the work to which they have given their lives. Their science is a part of their religion, and so, as one of the incidental advantages of our missionary enterprise, we are laying annually at the feet of philosophers a store of facts which are of unspeakable value to them in their work. And this is only as it ought to be, for the gospel teaches men to follow truth at all hazard; and every new triumph of science will in the end give a new impulse to spiritual religion.—The Pulpit.

THE TWENTIETH CENTURY RELIGION

BY EDWARD EVERETT HALE

It is thirty years ago that in an address before a thousand people in Providence, Dr. Robinson, then president of Brown University, said that it seemed certain that no religious organization then existing would exist in the same form at the end of one hundred years. The bold prophecy challenged attention then, perhaps it gave birth to more discussion than Dr. Robinson foresaw. Thoughtful and judicious people who had something of the spirit of prophecy, as he had, were confident of its truth.

A generation of men has passed, and it is even more certain than it was then that before the year 1971 every form of religious administration will be changed which existed in the year 1871. People who have a thoroughgoing idea of what is meant by the word religion, will say that religion itself is unchangeable, and is the same yesterday, today and forever. They will say that ecclesiastical traditions change, that theological definitions change, that the relations of church administration to civil administration change, but that religon is always the same. On the other hand, to the majority of English-speaking people the word religion means a series of external forms or methods—of conventionalisms which can be studied separately, as a man may study chemistry, or hydrodynamics, or the Latin language.

There is nothing infrequent in such use of one word to express two very different realities. Thus we may say that a message came "as quick as the post," meaning to speak of great swiftness. In the next minute we say "a man stood as still as a post," meaning to describe absolute fixity. Precisely so, men may speak of the absolute relation between God and man, and say that they are speaking of religon. Another set of men at the same moment may be speaking of the shape of the vane on a steeple, or on the place of the burial of a dead body, or on the color of the dress of a priest, or of the attitude to be assumed in prayer, and will say that they are discussing matters of religion.

Such utter contrasts of meaning in the central word must be borne in mind in all that anybody says of the religion of the twentieth century. So radical is the distinction, indeed, that there has been danger, at times, that the word religion would die out. But on the whole it has reasserted itself, and is probably used more thoughtfully now than it was fifty or a hundred years ago.

It is, perhaps, worth observing that as long ago as Cicero's time he gives two etymologies of the word radically and essentially different from each other. Once it is said to come from "religare," to bind again and again, to continue an ancient obligation. Or, it is said to come from "religere," to make a new choice, "to get the best," as the fine American proverb says, to profit by the constant advance of human intelligence. It is a little pathetic to see and to say that Cicero himself was quite indifferent as to these two etymologies. For him, religion was simply a matter of the augurs, as shoemaking was of the shoemakers, or sculpture was of the sculptors. It was no affair of his. You paid your money and you can have it as you choose, camelopard or elephant.

This is the more pathetic because such is exactly the attitude toward religion of a great many people today, an attitude encouraged, indeed, by most people who call themselves priests.

As early in 1804, when my father graduated at Williams College, he said in his commencement part that the Roman Catholic church was at an end. He said, with the proud conceit of a young man of twenty years, "Infidelity has put an end to Catholicism, and now we may trust Christianity to put an end to infidelity." It was a brave bit of prophecy for a youngster on the frontier of New England. At the end of a century its fulfillment and its non-fulfillment stand contrasted; its measure of truth and its measure of error. It proved convenient not long after for Napoleon to lift the Pope upon his throne again. But I think nobody pretends that the See of Rome, or the accidental candidate who may be crowned by any conclave of cardinals, will have much to do with the larger affairs of the world on the birthday of the third millennium.

1. Simplicity of administration, simplicity of statement, simplicity of profession—simplicity will be a characteristic of the religon of the year 2001. Think how people even laugh now about the old controversies; words or ideas for which brave men died, or thought they died, are pushed on one side or thrown overboard, as

a seaman might throw overboard the rag with which he had scrubbed the deck. It is true, alas! that even in the last generation of men the inquiries for truth have been expected, once and again, to justify themselves before conclaves, councils, conferences or conventions, which, in the small use of the word, called themselves "religious" assemblies, and claimed peculiar power. But the days of such nonsense are numbered! Real religion is so asserting itself that no condemnation of genuine inquiry after truth will be possible after another generation has gone by.

2. As essential to this simplicity of religion there will be a gradual reduction of the pretenses of priests. More ministers perhaps—no priests. In fact, the century may see almost an annihilation of ecclesiastical orders. The absurd pretense that a child of God needs any Lord Chamberlain to introduce him to his Father is in fact dying away now and will be quite done with before another hundred years have gone by.

3. The great contribution which the nineteenth century has made to the working religion of the world is in the world's sense of the "Real Presence." These words now mean not the occasional presence of God in a wafer, but the permanent presence of God in all Life.

> "That not a breath of Life can be,
> O Fount of Being, save from thee."

To take Dr. Stebbin's words, men have learned to spell nature with a large N. To take Jeremy Taylor's words, it is God who warms us when the sun shines. To take Robert Stevenson's, it is God who packs away in the coal mine the heat of the sun whose rays, though 1,000,000 years old, ripen the corn of the year 1900. Such prophets as Channing, Emerson and Martineau, such poets as Bryant, Sterling and Tennyson, such observers as Darwin, Mivart and Carpenter, make the Real Presence a certainty to all sorts and conditons of men and women. The century which is equipped with such faith will not falter in its use of omnipotence. It will not be afraid of the word Pantheism. It will not be satisfied with paddling in the froth of the ocean. It will make resolute and long steps forward in its determintaion that God's will shall be done on earth as it shall be done in heaven; that it is done with the same majesty, the same strength, and the same certainty.

—12C

The astronomers have given us a convenient parable in their suggestion as to the processes of the life of the planet Mars. From the white snow crests of the polar region of Mars there stretch out into what would have been arid tropics those lines of irrigating canals which are marked by belts of green as summer suns renew their life. And we are told that it is possible that the people of Mars are so unanimous in living all for each and each for all that by their work—in harmony like the harmony of the planets and stars of heaven—they work with their God in compelling the Arctic to water the Tropic, in alluring the sun to give their daily bread to all the men and women on their planet. This suggestion may be true or not, but as a parable it will show what this world of ours might do if men and women in the Arctic or in the Tropic zone, instead of marching and counter-marching, in place of volleys and charges without jealousies of race, without personal intrigue, were combined in one determined project to feed starving India, to convert the waste Saharas, to plant seeds of human society where are now desolate prairies, and to give chances for joy and health and strength to the starving pigmies of the wynds and crypts of cities.

Such union of all for each—such readiness of each to live for all, is one of the dominant features of the religion of the twentieth century.

Simplicity, a present God, the kingdom of heaven at hand, indifference as to traditional methods and a constant decline of ecclesiastical authority—these are the characteristics of absolute religion, the religion of the Golden Rule, the religion of the twentieth century—Christian Work.

THE SURVIVAL OF THE UNFIT

BY JOHN G. OSBORNE

The Christian system abounds in paradoxes. Or, in perhaps better words, at many points its principles contradict the world's maxims. Examples are familiar, and we have here a test. Any worldly policy or maxim that does not measure up to the essential standards of Christianity must be regarded with suspicion, if not with positive disfavor.

In these days we hear much of the survival of the fittest. Starting with certain well-known natural phenomena, it has come to be generally accepted as a scientific principle. We need only to remind ourselves that the last word of science may not yet have been spoken, and that possibly other explanations may appear. And the law supposed to be true in nature is held true also in society, in morals, in economics, in mentalities, even in religion. Unconsciously perhaps, but not less surely, we are building on this foundation the entire structure of our civilization.

Consider a moment. In all human activities only the greatest achievements are worthy of note. Only the millionaire gets his name in the papers as a successful man of business; only the most expert organizer becomes a "captain of industry;" only the shrewdest of politicians are in charge of the Ship of State; only the most accomplished shine in social functions. In education only the cleverest brain, like the most avoirdupois in football, wins a point in the game. Only the most eloquent preachers secure the fat salaries and the long list of titles. And whichever way we turn, from pulpit and platform, in the press, at the school and the university, on the athletic field, in the counting room, the factory and the party caucus, before every boy and girl in the land is rung with endless variations, but all pitched in the same key that old Pagan proverb, *"Aut Caesar, aut nullus."*

Occasionally, in deed, one hears of modest, half-hearted exhortation to a different course. But such falls upon dead ears. These exhorters have little faith in their own doctrines. They are mostly those that content themselves with small things because larger ones are beyond their reach. Examples of genuine self-abnegation are conspicuously rare in these days, and exhortations that are not reinforced by the daily life may as well remain unspoken.

Simply from a humanitarian standpoint it would seem about time to call a halt. Thus far, perhaps, the prizes have been comparatively numerous, and a reasonable hope of success added the most powerful incentive to effort. But, with the rapidly increasing army of competitors, and the close and still closer organization of society, and the accumulating concentration of wealth and power and influence in few and comparatively fewer and still fewer hands, the time has arrived when the distribution of prizes in this grand lottery will be increasingly unequal, and for every one that wins, thousands and tens of thousands must miserably fail.

And what of those that fail? Only this: that as the aspiration was high, the effort strenuous, the hope buoyant, the prize most brilliant, so is the defeat most crushing, the despair the deepest, the ruin most irretrievable. It is a most solemn question for the leaders of thought in our day to answer. What is to be the fate of this defeated multitude? How can society absorb this mass of industrial and mental and moral wreckage? And upon whom rests the responsibility?

If we turn now to the Christian system we find in it a radically different principle. The Master said of Himself, "I came not to call the righteous, but sinners." Not to the proud Pharisee, or to the learned and self-satisfied priest; not to the haughty Herod or the patrician Pilate, but to the malefactor on the cross came those wonderful words, "Today thou shalt be with Me in Paradise." Even Lazarus from the gate of Dives was carried by angels into Abraham's bosom. It is the glory of the Christian system, that which forever separates it from every human creed or philosophy, that it seeks out and saves the lowest and the vilest, the most unworthy, and exalts them to places of honor and privilege at the right hand of the Father; that it takes no account of worldly distinctions or possibilities; that it rewards the smallest service, and crowns all alike with the same richest blessing, even immortality. Why do we not, as disciples of this simple and beautiful faith, seek much more earnestly to make it a practical reality in our daily lives, in our communities, in our churches, in social relations, in business, in industry, in government? If we cannot all at once hope to turn the tide of civilization into this better channel, we can at least correct the current of our own thoughts, and throw the inspiration of our example and the power of our personality into this divine work—the redemption of the unfit, and thus do our humble part toward restoring to shipwrecked humanity the long-lost image of the Creator.—Christian Work.

VISIBLE CONNECTION

"I don't say that a man's got to put through or even help put through every reform movement he talks loud about," remarked Mr. Reynolds, in a mildly judicial manner. "There's a good many diff'rent brands o' reform, and pretty near all of 'em are kind of appealing to a man that reads and observes and thinks. If a man thinks, he talks; and some of the goings on on this little ball o' ours have got to be talked about. That's the only way to put a stop to 'em or to help 'em along. Human needs must be cried up by the human voice."

"True," assented the audience of one.

"What I contend," continued Mr. Reynolds, "is that there ought to be some kind o' visible connection between the thing a man cries up and himself. He don't need to 'lustrate in his person all he's howling for, but the beginnin's must be there or folks wont' take stock in it. I don't know but what something that came under my observation will make that clear to ye."

Mr. Reynolds' audience preserved the silence of good-fellowship, and he went on:

"Las' spring, long 'bout April, a stranger came into Job S. Chandler's liv'ry stable, where a number of us thinking men were setting. He was a nice-appearing chap, well-dressed and real good-spoken.

"He had hair restorer to sell, and he set out what 'twould do in A1 style. I never heard any drummer that could touch him for language. Most of us were a leetle mite bald on top and knew it—being married men—and he had us fingering our heads in no time, and I don't mind owning up that I saw myself as I looked forty-two years ago, when I went courting.

" 'Well,' says he, when he saw he'd got us up to the sticking point, 'there ain't any manner of doubt in my mind but what I've struck a class of American citizens that know a good thing when they see it.'

"He smiled and sat down on the thill of one o' Job's buggies. I s'pose he'd got kinder het up talking. 'Tany rate, he took off his hat to mop his forehead—"

"Well?" questioned the audience, filling Mr. Reynolds' pause as he intended it to be filled.

"His head was as bare an' shiny as a peeled onion," Mr. Reynolds readily responded.

"That hair restorer might have been all he claimed it was. It might ha' been just the thing for our heads. I don't say it wasn't. But after we saw his head it would have been against common sense to take stock in him or his stuff. You see what I've been driving at, don't ye?"

"Perfectly," replied the audience, politely and candidly.

CHRISTIAN CONFLICT

Our Savior declared that He came not to send peace but a sword. In the beatitudes He also said: "Blessed are the peacemakers, for they shall be called the children of God." The religion of Jesus Christ is many-sided. It is aggressive as well as peaceful. We find that men hardly ever express in single utterances the average of their nature. Elijah was a brave, heroic spirit, yet he fled from the cruelty of a wicked queen, and in despondency asked to die. John, the type of loveliness in fiery zeal, invoked consuming wrath on the Samaritans. Our Savior, in the hour of physical weakness, asked that the cup of suffering might pass from Him, but instantly added, "Thy will be done." The utterance of Christ that He came not to send peace but a sword, seems to be in conflict with the peace which passeth all understanding which He brings to every true believer. But there is no contradiction or lack of harmony. We must look at the many-sidedness of Christ's life and character to see it in its beauty, completeness and perfectness. So in the religion of Jesus Christ. There is diversity of plan, principles, and operation in it, and yet perfect unity and completeness. There must be diversity in order to have real unity. When we view a beautiful marble statue moving round on a pivot, we must not look on one side of it, but upon all sides as it moves round, to get the complete conception of the artist's thought and purpose in the statue. So we must look upon Christianity, in its diversity of thought, plan, purpose and operation to see its symmetry and perfectness as a system of salvation and soul culture.

Sin in its nature and work requires conflict. Christianity is its foe. Christ and Christianity, such are their nature and purpose, they must and ever will be antagonistic to Satan and sin. Sin is a fixed and unyielding power. It is not a tender plant which a worm may gnaw away and destroy in a night. It is a tree whose roots are deep and firm. It is old and tough and cannot be broken down like a young and tender twig. The ax has to be laid at the roots. Its universal grip, its tenacious principles, gray-haired customs, its deep-rooted prejudices, its intolerant bigotries, its long-loved gratifications are known and felt in every land, among all peoples and in all ages. Its power is legion. We have only to attack it and we shall not fail to see the power and magnitude of the conflict. Let the religion of Jesus Christ with its purity, righteousness, and cleansing power come in contact with the impurity, unrighteousness, pet sins and meanness of men and, what a conflict is aroused! Let Christ and Christianity come in conflict with the selfishness, ambition, greed, gain, purposes and power of corporations, trusts, and unions of whatever name, and what a fierce fight wages! Attack any of the great Pagan religions, Buddism or Islamism with their millions of adherents, and what a war is inaugurated! Every true reform is a conflict of right with wrong, truth with error, liberty with slavish thraldom, human elevation with human degradation. There can be no true peace until the battle is over and victory won for the right. This conflict is a personal one, a continuous warfare. The Christian has to war with sin, the flesh and the devil. It is a fight with foes without and foes within. As internal or civil wars are the most bitter and intense, so the Christian's fight with the lust, pride, wicked thoughts, aims, desires and purposes within. The fiercest and bloodiest wars which have cursed the earth, and at the same time purified and elevated the race, have been the conflicts between religious principles, between truth and error, right and wrong. The conflict will go on, quietly or fiercely until the kingdoms of this world become the kingdoms of Christ, until the principles, the love and spirit of Christ shall reign and rule in the world. The Christian's personal warfare with Satan and sin will not cease until the earth life is swallowed up in the heavenly.

We are not to wage this conflict alone. Christ our Savior is our Captain. God, the Son, the Holy Spirit, and all the divine forces are in the fight. In fact, every Christian is a soldier in God's army. Christianity has had to gain its ground inch by inch, yet what inroads upon the enemy she has made, what grand victories won! Christ and the apostles stood alone. The Savior and leader died, and the apostles stood alone. At Pentecost the followers of Christ numbered but a few hundred. The founder of Christianity died not a sceptered King grasping as Charlemagne, the symbol of royalty, but upon the shameful cross, amid the jeers and taunts of Jews and Romans. Christianity had no army, no protection from law, no nationality, no literature, no churches, no strong foothold. But what a change in the eighteen centuries! The gospel is in every land and on every isle of the sea. Pagan superstition, life and nationality are giving way to a Christian civilization. Christianity gives foundation and character to law, purifies and elevates literature, directs commerce, controls art and science, ever lifting the human race in scale of being and activity. Christian nations dominate the world. The religion of Jesus Christ makes the purest, the most beautiful, most intelligent and refined homes, the best society, the best schools, the highest manhood, the loveliest womanhood, the truest and most exalted nationality. Man is lifted up by grace from the degradation, mire and scum of sin, his feet put on a rock, given a right mind, a new song in his mouth, a right trend in life. No man an heir of woe, but of eternal life and heaven; with a new heart, a changed will, he goes on from grace unto grace, victory unto victory, until he shall wear a crown. Such is the triumph of the Christian conflict in the past, in the present, and shall be in the future. It develops spiritual strength and power, and makes of men the giant oaks and towering pines in social, intellectual, business and national life. It unfolds the highest soul beauty which ever molds and manifests itself in the physical life. Hawthorne has somewhere said that the human face is never so beautiful as when the soul has passed through some great conflict. The lovliest flowers of grace come from this conflict. Beautiful flowers grow on icebergs, and some of the most delicate and fragrant come from Alpine heights and snows. Man is made for spiritual character and beauty. He needs therefore the stern discipline of conflict. The young man meets it as he opens the door of his father's house and looks out on life. The sound of battle is heard. Will he triumph? Only as he fights the good fight of faith through Christ. The eagle is not made for the valleys and the shadows. His beak and talons, his eye and wing speak of an upward reach and a lofty sphere. So with us; our attributes, the image we bear, speak of the life and destiny we should have. We are to live in the sunlight of God, and dwell in the realm of faith and love. Through strenuous endeavor, by patient suffering, not by peace but by a sword, are our victories to be won. It is by the way of the cross we are to win and wear the crown. As fellow workers with God, Christ, and the Holy Spirit we are in the conflict. The world is to be evangelized by the unity of divine and human effort. It may take centuries to accomplish it. But the promise is that every knee shall bow to Christ and every nation shall be a part and factor of His kingdom. May it be ours in the heavenly throng when the battle is over, and the grand triumph gained, to sing the anthems of praise to Him who won the glorious victory.

HOW TO BECOME A CHRISTIAN

BY THE REV. JOHN RHEY THOMPSON

"And the disciples were called Christians first at Antioch."—Acts 11:26.

Antioch, in Syria, the third metropolis of the classic world, was founded about 300 years B. C. by Seleucus Nicator, one of the Greek kings of Syria. It is situated at the point of junction between the mountain chains of Lebanon and Taurus. Its site was at once commanding and beautiful. It was built on the northern slope of Mt. Silpins, while at its feet rolled the broad, navigable, famous Orontes River. The soft breezes of the great sea, distant but sixteen miles, gave its inhabitants health and coolness. Richly adorned by the lavish genius of ancient art, the residence of the profuse Greek kings of Syria; inferior in grandeur and in influence only to Alexandria and Rome; a vast city of over 500,000 inhabitants it well deserved its title of 'Queen of the East,' the third city of the Pagan world. No city, after Jerusalem, is as intensely and vitally connected with the early history of apostolic Christianity as Antioch. The Christians who were driven from the city of Jerusalem after the martyrdom of the first martyr, Stephen, were scattered as far abroad as this city of Antioch, and here they preached the gospel. Here the first Gentile church in the world was founded; here the disciples of Jesus Christ were first called by the ever memorable, undying name of Christians; here the Apostle Paul first exercised any systematic ministerial work—it was in fact his first charge where he was the junior preacher under Barnabas; here he started forth on his first missionary journey; here also he began and ended his second great missionary journey. It was to Antioch that the first Judaizers came from the city of Jerusalem to disturb the peace of the infant church and to vex the righteous soul of the great apostle of a universal and spiritual faith.

"And the disciples were called Christians first in Antioch." I have selected this particular text of scripture tonight that I may speak to you as to how men become Christians. Or, in other words, what it is to be a Christian; and by what process or methods or modes men and women enter upon the Christian life.

The word Christian particularly signifies a follower of Christ. When I say an Aristotelian, I mean one who is a follower of Aristotle, as he was himself a disciple of Plato. When I speak of a man as a Platonist, I mean one who has accepted the philosophical ideas of Plato and so far as Plato lays down any moral rules for conduct it is implied that he would accept them as governing his conduct. Following Christ means the same thing; that we believe the things that Christ has told us to believe and that we will do, or are doing, the things He told us to do. Plainer than this I could not make it, even if I had eternity in which to explain it. Following Christ now necessarily means something different from what it meant in the days of His own ministry. When He called Simon and Andrew to leave their nets and ships and follow Him they saw a man standing on the beach of the Lake of Galilee and they heard a voice and they left their ships and their nets and they followed an actual, living man. So did James and John and the sons of Zebedee, when He called them; so did Matthew, sitting at the receipt of custom in the city of Carpernaum, leave all, rise up and follow Him when He called him to be a disciple. Now-a-days there is no voice, except the voice of the representative of Christ, a man who is an agent, a messenger, an ambassador. But Jesus Christ Himself we do not see. When men are called to be Christians in this modern time they are to endue them with a Christian disposition and they are to accept Christian beliefs. The elements of a Christian dispositon we need not mistake, unless we are careless or insincere; for the summary of what constitutes a Christian disposition Jesus Himself gave us. Supreme love to God and unselfish love to our brother man is the comprehensive summary of what is meant by a Christian disposition. One that is either in germ form or in a state of continual development. Those glorious fruits of the spirit which Paul enumerates in the fifth chapter of the epistle to the Galatians, when first cultivated or developed, produce a Christian disposition leading to Christian conduct which, by successive acts confirms and establishes Christian character. Now, when men are urged to follow Christ now-a-days these same men, who are presumably honest and sincere and candid about it, say: "Why, these qualities and this disposition you put emphasis upon and that you say are necessary in Christian life and character, no man can instantly produce them by the effort of his own will and yet you tell us we are to make instant choice of the Christian life." Now, this objection is partially true. No man can in one single, bold, magnificent stroke make a Christian out of himself.

The word "disciple" in the text will help us greatly at this point. The etymological meaning of the word "disciple" is a learner, a pupil, a beginner, a student, a scholar; and I might read it and say: And the students, the pupils, the beginners, were called disciples first in Antioch. Its meaning is perfectly clear, then, and I cannot better illustrate it than by following its etymological suggestions. How does an ignorant man, who has been awakened to a sense of the disadvantages and penalties of ignorance, secure the intellectual training such as we call education? For there is no distinction between education in moral and spiritual elements and education in intellectual elements. Now, how would a man proceed who has been convicted of a realizing sense of his ignorance? First of all, there is the distinct purpose or choice on his part that this state or condition of ignorance shall be displaced or followed by a state or condition of knowledge. Nothing can be done until there comes into his mind the clear determination that he will be a student, a pupil, a scholar, a learner. This is the first step—a very important step—the fixed, resolute choice and determination to be a scholar. Then, second, in the case of such a man, there is renunciation, a separation, an abandonment, on his part, of all alien courses, companionships, associations, habits—everything that will interfere with his purpose to become a scholar or a student. For example, if he has been a member of some gay and perfectly harmless, in a moral sense, social circle or set, and finds nevertheless that he cannot live the social life of enjoyment and festivity that he has heretofore enjoyed, and execute his purpose to become a scholar, there is the necessary abandonment and separation of the man from this social circle; he renounces, or gives up, all alien associations and habits and courses and conduct. In the third place, there is the adoption on his part of all friendly and helpful and congenial agencies and instrumentalities. As, for example, the man I am speaking of has been the subject of a spiritual awakening. There are books; he reads them. If necessary, he will hire tutors, or, if he cannot have tutors or teachers, he will go to some school, or, if he cannot go to a school, he will become a member of some intellectual society or association, where he will have intellectual incentives to execute his purpose. In the first place, there will be the continued, patient, never tiring—yes, the continued untiring use of all means, tools and agencies, whether books or teachers or laboratories or museums or what not—that will help him to bring his impatient and restless and truant faculties into obedience to his will. Now, this is the way in which a man who has been awakened to a sense of ignorance proceeds to become educated.

It is precisely the way in which a man becomes a Christian. I do not mean it is greatly like it; it is precisely like it. There is no mystery about becoming a Christian. There is no magic about it; no legerdemain about it; no slight-of-hand about following Christ or becoming a Christian. It is a sane thing and a rational thing and a wholesome thing and a philosophical thing. It is as much sane and rational for the spiritual development as the like process is for the lower form of intellectual development.

Now, can man become a mature or perfect Christian at once —instantly? The man who made the objection was right so far. No man can instantly become a mature Christian; but a man can instantly resolve to become a Christian. A man can instantly begin to be a Christian, and a man will never be a Christian who does not instantly begin. There comes a time when he makes the choice of or rejects the Christ as Master of his life forever. Then comes, in natural order, the renunciation, the giving up evil ways, of corrupt and demoralizing ways, all known evil practices or sinful habits. If a man has detected in himself a tendency to insincerity, to exaggeration in speech or even invention; that is, if a man finds, with a little encouragement, he would make a first class Ananias, the only way to put truth in the place of falsehood is for that man to watch himself at precisely those points. If a man is given to his cups and has become a drunkard, how can he spend his evenings in company with men who drink and expect to be sober? This work is absolutely necessary at this point. There is no compromise between good and evil, right and wrong, sin and holiness. In the Christian life no man can be a Christian and allow sin in his lfe, heart or character. The Christian is arrayed against it, with his hand uplifted to fight it all the time. It is a state of war between the Christian and every form and degree of evil.

I meet a man on Broadway, at the corner of Pearl street, and in conversation he tells me he is on his way to the Fifth Avenue Hotel; he is going there right off. But his face is turned toward the Battery; yet he tells me he is going to the Fifth Avenue Hotel. I will tell you one thing; until he faces about, until he turns square round, he will never get to the Fifth Avenue Hotel, unless he goes right round the world. Face about he must; there is no other way for a man who faces the Battery at the corner of Pearl street to get to that hotel but to turn round. That is all, but it is everything to a man who wants to get to the Fifth Avenue Hotel. It means he will get there; but if he faces the Battery he will never get there of his own volition unless he goes around the world.

Then comes the positive part, the gradual but entire putting on of Jesus Christ. I need not tell you how much is involved here. Much more than I could describe in all my ministry until it comes to an end. How to learn to love God? You go about it in the most natural way in the world. I pronounce these words. "Aristides the Just." What does that mean to at least many of you? Practically nothing. If, however, I tell you that this title of the Just was given to a Greek citizen of Athens, a wealthy man, because of his scrupulous care always to be just under all circumstances, notwithstanding great and sore and seductive temptations to be unjust; that in the presence of battle and after battle with all the spoils of the enemy in his hands nothing was so remarkable about him as his constant justice, so that finally the leader of the opposite faction in the city, Thermistocles, persuaded the people that Aristides, in consequence of his justice, was obtaining an overwhelming influence in the city, and therefore ought, for the future good of the city, to be banished; and they proceeded to take a vote

and did banish him because he was so just that he was gathering
to himself a preponderating influence. When they took the vote
one ignorant fellow, who could not write, came to Aristides himself with the shell and asked Aristides, whom he did not know,
to write his own name on the shell. "Why," said the statesman to
the fellow, "what wrong has Aristides ever done you?" "Oh," said
the fellow, "none at all; but it irritates me to hear everybody
calling him Aristides the Just. Let him be put beyond
the walls and then we won't hear of it any more."
And so Aristides took the shell and wrote the fellow's name. Need
I tell you that twice in great crises he returned, notwithstanding
his exile, to save his country? I might go on, but don't you begin
to warm up to Aristides the Just now? You feel at least some
degree of admiration at last, don't you? But a few moments ago,
however, you had never heard of him. What he did was a matter
of indifference. Now you become interested. You might study
him until you became enthusiastic. I have learned to admire Aristides since I found what kind of a man he was. And so by finding
out what God is, what relations He sustains to man, how tender He
is in His relationship, how He conducts Himself toward men in
their penitent relations to Him, you learn to love God by exactly
the same process, namely, by finding out about God and in no magical sort of a way. And so it is: step by step, day by day, all
gracious qualities and divine dispositions are to be obtained by
spiritual development and culture. Place yourself under certain
influences, surround yourself by such associations as will tend to
evolve a lofty Christian character and that Christian character will
surely come.

The best way and the quickest way to get rid of evil is to put
good in its place. "Be not overcome of evil, but overcome evil with
good," Paul wrote to the disciples at Rome. Here is a farmer
greatly troubled about a field overgrown with dockweeds and
Canada thistles. There are two conceivable ways of his getting
the mastery of these weeds—these noxious growths. One is to go
round with a scythe and cut them up close down to the ground,
and then, when he has done that, to take a hoe and go tramping
over that field from time to time watching where they spring up
and when he finds one springing up he can go at it with his hoe

and throw it away. I suppose after a while he would get rid of the weeds, but it would be slow process. The correct way would be for him to get a sub soil plow, a real good one, turn that plow into the field, plow up the dockweeds and thistles, when they will decay and become an admirable fertilizer in time. And then either sow the field with oats or plant it in corn and after a year or two put it in wheat; and, I tell you, the dockweeds and Canada thistles will all be gone and he will have corn or oats in place of them; and that is better than to go round with a hoe cutting out a single weed at a time. Instead of evil put good in its place: "Be not overcome of evil, but overcome evil with good."

Now, some man will say to me—and I dare not close without talking to him for a moment—some man will say, "Why, you have never once, since your sermon began, referred to the Holy Spirit. You have excluded from your Christian life the Holy Spirit." I have done no such thing. Far from it, and very far from it. I have assumed the existence and personality of the power of the Holy Spirit from the time I spoke the first word. Conscientiously and deliberately have I assumed the office of the Holy Spirit. A farmer standing by a fine field in early May says to his neighbor: "I tell you, I raised magnificent crops on this field last year." Does he mean by that to ignore or exclude the sun and its life and heat? Does he mean that here was no rain? Does he mean, when he says, "I raised magnificent crops last year," that there was no sunlight fell on them; that he was not dependent on that great luminary for the light and heat—not dependent on the clouds for the rain? No. He meant all the while that the sun shone and the rains fell. Exclude the Holy Spirit! Why, I have assumed His existence all the while. When I talk about man being good; when I talk about the fruits of the Spirit; of a Christian disposition I as much assume the Holy Spirit as the farmer does the sun, for we can neither think a good thought, nor perform a good act, nor pray a good prayer, nor lead a good life without the Holy Spirit than the farmer can raise anything without the benign influences of nature. But as God gives the sunlight and the rain freely to all men so He will give the Holy Spirit to all men who want to live a Christian life.

Are you a Christian? Will you become a Christian? You never can become one until you begin, and every such beginning is necessarily instantaneous—immediate, because it is the effort of the will and it is caused by the will's putting forth of its sovereign power. Will you become a Christian? You cannot become a perfect Christian at once. Begin to be a perfect Christian.—Brooklyn Daily Eagle.

BROTHERHOOD IN CHRIST

BY THE REV. ST. CLAIR HESTER

"I beseech thee for Onesimus, that thou shouldst receive him, not as a servant but above a servant, a brother beloved."—Philemon 10, 15, 16.

The cases are not numerous of an appreciative employer and genuine friend sending a fugitive slave back to his legal owner. Few have the slaves been who once having tasted the sweets of freedom in a distant city were willing to return to servitude. No less rare have been the masters who, after regaining possession of their human property, gladly presented the creature with liberty.

Imagine a red hot Abolitionist of Boston in the year 1859, after harboring a fugitive negro from the South, and becoming attached to him, resolving, on account of delicate regard for his owner's legal right, to send Uncle Tom back to Dixie, thus putting him again under the control of a white hot slave dealer of Charleston, S. C., for example. Imagine Uncle Tom, who had stolen enough of his master's money to pay his way to Boston, yielding a ready consent to the plan. And then imagine the Charleston owner welcoming his returned runaway as a friend and brother and declaring him to be henceforth a free man. I say imagine these things, because in all probability they never did happen and never could have happened. And yet, remarkable as it is, almost this identical situation is brought before us by the short epistle of twenty-five verses from which the text is taken. Paul the Apostle is the kind friend who desired and needed the services of a companion. Onesimus is the slave dispatched with a letter. Philemon is the well to do citizen and slave owner of Collose. How is such kind consideration for the rights of others, such rare sympathy and kindness and forebearance to be accounted for?

—13C

What is the cause of such behavior, all the more to be wondered at because of the time and circumstances? The explanation
is obvious and easy. Evidently there is something in common between these men of a nature very different from the forces that
repel men from each other and embitter and enrage them. Clearly it is at variance with the social creeds and exclusive cults of their
own and preceding ages. A change has been wrought in their nature. In spite of difference in position, fortune and education,
they have discovered a bond of equality existing between them.
They are drawn together in a unity of the same spirit. The explanation is that the love of Jesus has shined within their souls and
quickened into action every virtue that slept there and broadened
and deepened and sweetened their whole nature. It was brotherly
love, the specious seed implanted and developed and exemplified
by Jesus of Nazareth that prompted the apostle to send and Onesimus to go and Philemon to receive in kindness and good will. The
leaven of His teaching is thus showing its effect in widely separated
portions of the mass of humanity. And it is destined to work wonders as the ages roll along. In the minds of those who have seen
His light there has grown the conviction that beneath all external
condition, however diverse, there is a touch of nature, a common
dependence, a common salvation, that makes the whole world akin,
that makes all mankind one. This idea of unity did not originate
with the Greeks, though the most cultured of ancient peoples, nor
with the Jews, though the most religious of ancient peoples. Salvation was not of the Jews, but for the Jews exclusively.

This was the fixed limit until one day a multitude sat about
a Jew of Nazareth and some one said, "Behold Thy mother and Thy
brethren without seek for Thee." And He answered, asking, "Who
is My Mother or My brethren?" And looking around upon them
which sat about Him He said, "Behold My mother and My brethren.
For whosoever shall do the will of God, the same is My brother and
My sister and mother." A wholly new conception, a wholly new tie
of relationship. They who do the will of God are brothers beloved.
What a definiton of brotherhood for men to read, mark, learn and
inwardly digest. This novel idea seized upon men's minds and
built up within them a consciousness of fellowship. It is repeated
and illustrated and emphasized in a hundred ways by His disciples

and followers. The outgrowth and upgrowths from this planting have been continuous and manifold and cover the earth today with beneficence and charity. To it are attributable many of the greatest achievements in history, many of the noblest movements for human betterment, many of the beautiful lives that together form a heavenly halo about the church of God. Emancipation in England, emancipation in America, emancipation in Russia, follow as natural results of the Christian culture of brotherhood. It has been conserved and passed on and applied by organized Christianity—the church—for 1900 years.

The love of brother does not stop at freeing his body. It also endeavors to protect him from harm. In the fulfillment of such a purpose it is worthy of a great Christian nation—it is to the honor of the statesmen who move in it that there shall be some restraint upon the traffic of unscrupulous traders, especially in intoxicants and harmful drugs, with savage and half civilized tribes. It would be the height of brutal inconsistency to free the slave at home and suffer the trade in human flesh abroad and then permit brewers and rum-sellers, in their greed for gain, to exterminate wild and nomad races by means of their liquid death. We who are strong should bear with and guard against and if possible cure the infirmities of the weak. This is of the very essence of brotherhood. It applies not merely to our conduct toward the aborigines of Africa and the Southern and Eastern seas, but also to the ignorant, the degenerate and the irresponsibles at home. For their sakes we must grapple with and cast out the great curse of modern times—rum. We must dam up vice and lessen temptation. Again, brotherly love does not stop with freeing men's bodies or protecting them against harmful persons and things. It seeks to enter their hearts, to enshrine itself within their affections and purify them, to quicken conscience, to influence their thinking, to form habits and fashion character, to set up an ideal of perfection within. Its final step is to open up and re-establish broken communication between the soul of man and its divine Creator and source, through communion with Jesus Christ.

Now, while all may be one in Christ as a matter of fact, all are not. Why? Some are ignorant and do not know Him. Some have degenerated and departed from Him. Some choose to ignore

Him and pass Him by on the other side. One in skeleton, in flesh and blood, all human creatures may be, but physical resemblances do not make men brothers beloved or brethren in Christ. Only they who do the Father's will are or can be at unity with Him and with one another. Know the truth, see and yet see not, do not the Father's will, and you thereby choose to be none of His, and reject the sacred ties of brotherhood.

The new era upon which we have entered is rich with promise of a higher and a general cultivation of fraternal relations. The great truth, the solidarity of the race, established by science, has locked arms with the greater truth, upheld by Christianity, that all men were meant to be brothers beloved in Jesus Christ. A new science, sociology, has appeared in response to the growing interest in human well being. Men of every nation and condition are active in the ranks of socialists. Social questions are most popular. Social problems, such as vast accumulations of capital, the relations of employer and employe, the enormous growth of cities, the submerged tenth, housing the poor, compulsory education, are receiving careful consideraton on the part of statesmen, philanthropists, legislators, and even the ordinary voter. The philosophers, too, have contributed to the popular subject. Auguste Comte introduced the term altruism, and Herbert Spencer, following his lead, has endeavored to show that egotism, self-regarding, and, altruism, other regarding, exhaust the range of human motives. Christianity takes issue with them and holds that besides the good of self and the good of others, there is another and more powerful incentive to virtue and that is the will of God. Do this and you make self good and your neighbor happy. Fail to do it and the tie of brotherhood is broken.

Society is divided up into so-called unions. Their object is to get trade, to raise and steady wages, to prevent competition, to promote sociability and friendship and mutual advantages. But in some way or another the majority of them fail of their purpose. Their oneness is in name only. There is no harmony of feeling, no reciprocal affection, no genuine and lasting accord for the highest good of all concerned. The reason is this, men do not recognize, or they refuse to believe that there can be no lasting real, soul-satisfying union without Christ. He is and must be the center, the base, the starting point. His are the hands that gather up the many separate lines of interest and desire and aspiration and endeavor and weld them into one mighty mutual cord of sympathy, love and trust. Other foundation can no man lay than is laid already in Jesus Christ.

In enumerating the forces that make for consciousness of fellowship, that build up and strengthen brotherly love in the hearts and minds of men, first of all because most important of all, the church, organized Christianity, must be given the precedence. Another force is emigration, the shifting of people from one land to another, who form new ties and at the same time retain old ones. When friction of trade and clash of commercial interests generate heat and lead to alarming talk of conflict between powers, such as England, Germany and America, for example, the bosoms of those who have loved ones in both the old land and the new are torn with anxiety and indecision and dread, and the happy result is that strong and urgent advocates of peace are in harmonious action at the two storm centers. The barriers of ultra-patriotism and prejudicial nationalism are thus being gradually beaten down. The intermarrying of royal families may be mentioned as a means of promoting brotherly love among the nations. The rulers of Europe are all more or less related. The late Queen Victoria, by virtue of her large and powerful family connection, was known to have been instrumental in discouraging all movements or measures that tended toward war. Again and again the idea of a strong young man fighting his grandmother would have seemed laughable, if it had not been so serious. Remember, too, that most wars, until recently, have been the results of personal enmities and spites between monarchs. To place the principals and instigators of strife under the restraints of family ties would seem a happy way of preventing international conflicts.

Interpenetration of culture, socialization of literature, the sharing of all men in the achievements and productions of the genius of the few must be included in any list of fraternal forces. National, political and sectional lines are no longer drawn in scholarship, in discovery, in invention, in research. The knowledge of a Darwin, a Pasteur, an Edison, may be had by any one for the asking. The world spirit of fraternity is supreme in literature and subordinates, assimilates and utilizes every vital racial and national element for universal human and humane ends. A recent illustration of this is the organization and union at a meeting in Paris of eighteen learned societies, representing almost every nation of Christendom.

Other formative influences of brotherhood are the numerous and easy facilities of travel and communication. The hermit kingdoms have been explored and described and mapped and aborigines no longer fall on their knees at the sight of white men and worship them as superior beings. Acquaintance begets friendship and friendship may ripen into love.

Add to the forces already mentioned humanitarian, philanthropic and charitable enterprises and institutions, as homes for soldiers and sailors, for the aged, the blind, the cripple, asylums, hospitals, nurseries, sanitariums, their name, their work is legion, administering to almost every form of suffering and needs. Manifold are the manifestations of the Christ spirit doing good with all men. Multiform are the agencies that teach the Master's golden rule.

Missions deserve a place and distinction apart from all other things that quicken and cultivate brotherly love in the souls of men. The final commands of the Christ and the first study of those joined to Him and initiated into His earthly kingdom was to "Go ye into all the world, preach, teach, baptize, announce the glad tidings." By virtue of this standing order to His church and His followers the missionary par excellence, in spite of all the carping and criticism of prime ministers, politicians, land grabbers and trade promoters, remains the servant with highest credentials and in his work for human brotherhood, approaches nearest to the ideals of the Lord.

Paul the Apostle, Onesimus the slave, Philemon the owner, stand before the world and the Christians of all ages as worthy examples of brothers beloved. A union such as theirs will endure and satisfy the desire that dwells in the hearts of men for sociability, for sympathy and mutual help. Its cementing bond was not gain, not advantage, not promotion, not entertainment or intellectual development, but Jesus Christ. May we ourselves and all God's children on earth come and be drawn into an inseparable oneness with Christ.

THE LIFE OF THE CHRISTIAN

BY THE REV. G. CAMPBELL MORGAN, D.D.

"The disciples were called Christians first in Antioch."—Acts 11:26.

"With but little persuasion thou wouldest fain make me a Christian." —Acts 26:28.

"If a man suffer as a Christian, let him not be ashamed; but let him glorify God in this name."—1 Peter 4:16.

These are the only occasions of the occurrence of this word Christian in the New Testament. Seeing that it has come to be so universally used, it is interesting thus to go back to the beginnings, and consider what it meant in those early days. This may help us in the understanding of its true significance.

From the first instance it is evident that it was a term applied to the disciples of Jesus by the outsiders. This is in itself a suggestive fact. The first and simplest meaning of the word is, a follower of Christ. Thus the supreme impression made upon the men of Antioch by the little band of disciples was that of their allegiance to Christ. It was of Him they spoke, His commandments they obeyed, and His spirit they manifested. So constantly was this true that the men of Antioch said, "These people are Christions, the whole truth about them is told when this is said, as to religion and morals and business and everything else. They are people of one idea, and that is Christ. They are Christians."

In the second instance the word is part of the supercilious question of a king who is impressed with the aggressive spirit of Paul. This is also interesting, as revealing the spirit of these earliest Christians. They were not merely followers of Christ themselves, but they were anxious to bring all with whom they came into contact into the same relationship to Christ. Even Agrippa, amusing himself for an odd hour by hearing one of these Christians talk, was impressed most of all with the prisoner's desire to secure the submission of the king to Christ.

The third and last instance is the only one in which the word is used by a Christian. Peter recognizes that this name applied to persons makes them at once liable to suffering, and then he urges those to whom he writes not to be ashamed of any such reproach. Rather let the name be accepted, and let those who hear it be worthy of it, "Let him glorify God in this name."

These instances account for the name and suggest certain facts concerning those who bear it. External manifestations of speech and conduct and habit gave rise to the name. The three facts suggested are those of discipleship, propagandism and suffering. A Christian was a Christ soul, whose business was that of bringing other into like relationship, and who rejoiced to be able to suffer in comradeship with the Lord.

These, however, are but the statements of the outward and evident facts. What lay behind these? How are we to account for this whole-hearted loyalty to Christ in personal life, in service, in suffering? The answer to these questions brings us face to face with the deeper meaning of the name Christian. Here, as in other cases, Christianity has taken hold of a word and expanded and glorified it. A Christian is so in the sense in which the men meant who first used the word, but the reason of that is that he is a Christian in a deeper and more wonderful sense. They of Antioch saw the fruitage of life and said, "It is Christian," and they were right; but that was due to the fact that out of sight and in the deeper and hidden life these men were Christians. The root of life was Christian, therefore the blossom and fruit were Christian also.

The hidden fact was that of the presence of the Christ in the inner life of these people by the new birth. They had received Christ by believing on Him, and in the inner shrine of their lives He loved and reigned by the Holy Spirit's administration. This could have but one result—that of the outworking in character and conduct of the character and conduct of Christ. His spirit and love were reproduced in them, and the enterprises of His heart became the business of their lives; and the world's misunderstanding of Him resulted in reproach for them, and in that reproach they rejoiced, as it gave evidence of their approximation to Him in outward manifestation.

A Christian, then, is one in whom Christ is formed by the miracle of regeneraton, and through whom Christ is manifested before the eyes of the world, and with whom Christ co-operates in the work of saving men, and to whom Christ grants a fellowship in His suffering.

The nature of Christian life is Christ's life taking hold upon all the inner life of man, changing, dominating, impulsing; and Christ's life blossoming in character and bearing fruit in conduct.

Neither of these aspects of Christian life must be forgotten. The holding of the doctrine of regeneration never saved a man or made him a Christian. Neither can a man become a Christian by endeavoring to reproduce the Christly character and conduct. As well try to grow tulips without bulbs, or, on the other hand, without placing the bulbs in the conditions of soil which bring forth life. As is the root to the fruit so is the new life to the new character and conduct. A root treasured as a root and never planted is utterly valueless, so also is a doctrine of new birth, held in the realm of intellect and never buried in the heart and will.

Yet these facts are related as cause and effect. Let a man yield himself to Christ, and straightway the waiting Christ takes possession and that man becomes a Christian in the hidden center of his being. Now let him yield day by day and hour by hour to the new promptings and desires created by the indwelling Christ, and he shall become to the utmost reach of the circumference of his life a Christian. This outward fact men will see, and so know of the inward.

Never try to begin to be a Christian at the circumference of things. Be a Christian by letting Christ have possession of the center.

THE CHIEF ASSET OF CHRISTIANITY

BY BISHOP E. R. HENDRIX, D.D., LL.D.

"His chief asset was himself." Such was the tribute paid to an eminently useful man who did not lack what men are pleased to call "the sinews of war." It was the man behind the money that counted. The wisdom and grace to use resources are more important than the resources themselves. It is that undefinable thing that Bradstreet takes into account in rating men. It is not simply what a man has that counts, but what a man is. It is his character, his sense of honor, his unswerving integrity no less than his business sagacity and his accumulations which make up his standing and establish his credit. Hence the double rating of what a man is no less than of what he has. It would be a lamentable rating when what a man has is his chief asset rather than what he is. Men are last weighed in God's scales as they are first weighed when they come into the world—naked. What a man weighs when by himself, without any of the mere belongings which count for so much in society, that the man is. That is the asset that passes current in both worlds. It is the true coin and currency of the realm. That realm is the kingdom of God, on earth and in heaven.

If Russia needs to examine her "war chest" before she attempts her most daring feats of diplomacy, that what she plans in the council she may exploit in the field, no less should Christendom carefully examine her assets in all thoughts about the means and methods of Christian progress. Having undertaken to build a tower will she be able to finish it? It is not so much a question of material as it is of labor. Men are more than mortar. It is not even a question of muscle and skill, but of character and co-operation. Iron and steel have their breaking point, and granite its crushing point, but man is spiritual and has no breaking point when strengthened with might in the inner man. God's granite and porphyry and marble, whether for His temple on earth or in heaven, are men. "To him that overcometh will I give to be a pillar in the temple of my God and he shall go no more out." The dome of heaven rests on redeemed men, on men as Christ makes and strengthens them.

It is not strange that before Christ even attempted to extend His kingdom after His ascension He bade his disciples wait until they were endued with power which would enable them to be witnesses. This was what was meant when it was said of our Lord that "when He ascended up on high He gave gifts to men, some apostles, some prophets, some pastors and teachers, for the perfecting of the saints, for the work of the ministry, for the edifying of the body of Christ till we all come in the unity of the faith, and of the knowledge of the Son of God, unto a perfect man, unto the measure of the stature of the fullness of Christ." The finished product of Christianity is men, men who have received power to become sons of God. All Christian progress leads to this. The chief means of bringing this about was first of all the Son of Man, and last of all the men whom He could recreate in Christ Jesus unto good works. The marred and defaced coin has at best an undefinable value until it is reminted and bears not only the image and superscription of the king, but even his rating. What men are worth depends entirely on that rating of the King. Shall we take men at their own rating of themselves or at our Lord's rating? The pessimism of the agnostic sees nothing ahead of men but despair and extinction, preceded by endless conflicts between labor and capital, between poverty and prodigality. All of man's boasted greatness is vanity when separated from Christ. The true achievements of the race are by its Head. "Now we see not all things put under Him, but we see Jesus." That sight saves us from despair. What Jesus was He helps us to be, and what Jesus did He helps us to do. The chief asset of Christianity is both personal and real, and real because personal. And yet it is not lands and bonds as men count them, but as God reckons them. Our Lord is most concerned for men great enough to administer upon lands and to know how to use bonds. Therefore the promise: "Ask of Me and I shall give thee the heathen for thine inheritance and the uttermost parts of the earth for thy possession." The sword is to him who can wield it. The kingdom of heaven must be within if it ever takes on organic form without. True Christian progress is within. Heaven and earth shall pass away, but the sons of God endure forever. What makes Christlike men is the true means of Christian progress. Such men are the chief asset of Christianity.

Money is pulseless. It is a weight rather than wings. It may sink men when the purpose of the giver may be to save them. To give all one's goods to feed the poor may not only profit him nothing, but may profit them nothing permanently. Never was poverty so persistent as when men and women flocked to the monastery gate for bread. Man becomes a parasite when he ceases to labor for his daily bread. Words are lifeless though they be spoken with the tongues of men and of angels. Humanity has been exhorted enough by persuasive words to have been transformed long ago into saints. Only love is warm, living, eternal. Only love can save. There must be a transfusion of blood to save the race. Men willing to die for their kind as did the Lord are worth more than all the resources of wealth and eloquence. This explained Brainerd's success among the Indians, as he declared: "I thought of nothing else. I cared for nothing else but their conversion. I dreamed of it in the night, and lived for it in the day." Such a man vitalizes everything that he says or does. It was what he was that gave value and life to what he did. In our search for means let us not forget men. Men are means and more than all other means. Men are methods, too, for nothing is so creative as love. What overcomes inertia, whether due to indifference or helplessness, is the true condition of progress. Love alone can do that, the love of God shed abroad in the heart by the Holy Ghost that is given unto us. It is not natural, instinctive sympathy that makes man's needs the measure of effort, and man's appreciation its reward, but love that is born of Christ's love and that never faileth, "despairing of no man," as the Revised Version puts it. *Nil desperandum* becomes thus the motto of Christ's workers. (Luke 6:35.)

There is a remnant of Paganism in our worship still and will be so long as we keep thinking simply of getting to heaven and escaping hell. Only selfishness can make these the chief aims of living. We may count our works as the Buddhist counts his beads and so reckon our assets in things. God is concerned about what we are as that alone can give value to what we do. "I never knew you" may be Christ's response to those who reckoned their works and even catalogued them as making sure of a ready entrance into heaven. Love was wanting in everything that was done and all was valueless. The key to heaven is not in our hand.

It is in ourselves. Our own moral progress is the true measure of Christian progress. What God has done in us shows what He may do with us. It is how God has enriched our lives that determines how much He can enrich other lives through us. Therefore let us think less of doing and more of being, less of what God can do through us than of what God is to us. It was only because Paul felt in Him the power of an endless life and ever sought to count all things but loss for the excellency of the knowledge of Jesus Christ his Lord that he was able to do all things through Christ that strengthened him. Paul was the chief asset of the Apostolic church, as Luther was of the sixteenth century and Wesley of the eighteenth.—Christian Work.

THE CHRISTIAN'S WARFARE

BY DR. DEAN RICHMOND BOBBITT

God has made the world, and He has made man, to subdue and conquer the world. It is His way, and, though often mysterious, must be the right way, the best way, the only way. Let us be at rest, then, about the fact of battle, the universality of struggle, the appointment each one of us has to conflict. What then? Ah, it is for us, then, closely to attend to the inferences and consequences of this great premise, this fact, this method, this way of battle. Note that even war has its laws. If we see struggle everywhere, we also see victors and vanquished, those who survive and those who go down. The great law of "survival of the fittest" is true in all realness, as it is true in nature, among animals, beasts, insects, birds and butterflies. Darwin's law is the law also of the Bible, of life, of society. The weak go to the wall; the strong live, crowned as victors. But beyond Darwin's natural law of the survival of the fittest there is the great question of what is the fittest. The fittest, as God tells us in thousands of cases, is not those who cry "a tooth for a tooth and an eye for an eye." There are factors greater, more far reaching, more powerful than brute force. Listen to one who summons us for life's battle in its larger, better meaning: St. Paul suggests putting on the breastplate of faith.

What does that mean? Not faith in an Alexander, or Cæsar, or Charlemagne, or Napoleon, or Wellington, or a Washington or Grant, but faith in One who is a still greater captain, in a still greater battle than battle heard in the clash of steel or seen in the gleam of bayonet or thundered in the crash of warrior with warrior, or in the shock of passion; faith in a good spiritual leader; faith in One Who fought life's battle and won it. And this breastplate, which quenches all the fiery darts of evil, is not only of faith, but of love. How strange that sounds, love in battle, love in contest! Yes, that is a greater power than passion, love of God, love of man, love for the Christ. And there is another piece of armor, viz., hope. The hope of salvation—life's battle is often without that; men struggle in despair, they fight on without hope. They see no light ahead, there seems no dawn for their night. But not so with the one having faith in God, through Christ. Above all noises of battle, above all clash of conflict, above shock and crash and fierce contentions, above suffering, sorrow, trouble, stands One Who puts on a helmet, the hope of salvation, covering us with the very omnipotence of His power, as victors now, as victors forever.

THE TURNING MOVEMENT IN CHRISTIAN ARGUMENT

Our fathers used to discuss with great relish and confidence what they called the evidences of Christianity. Laymen and students alike felt a deep concern in the arguments for the inspiration of the Bible, and the existence of God, and the immortality of the soul. The air was sometimes thick with the lively controversies which raged between the opposing hosts. In one age it was deists, in another it was secularists, in another it was agnostics who brought their battle cries and their weapons against the servants of Jehovah. Today who are they who rage and imagine a vain thing against the life of faith? Whoever they be, let us know them and their methods of attack, and the artillery with which the church shall break them in pieces.

We must always begin by recalling the fact that Christianity is not a religion which we are proposing to create. It is here. It is fast becoming the one universally accepted religion of the race, heir of all the truth and discoverer of all the error and evil in all other religions. It is here at the center of human history. It is an actually working historical force and the cause of all that is best and noblest in human experience. To find it mixed with evil is just to say that it is working in and through our sinful nature. What needs scientific explanation is not the sins of Christian men and Christian communities—that is easily explained— but the deflections from sin, the elevations above self, the visions of the divine truth and righteousness, the felt love of God, the felt strength of the Holy Spirit, the felt joy and peace of pardon and cleansing. It is as much the task of science to explain these as to explain the unfolding of a flower or the downfall of an empire. But it is irrelevant to this work to argue on abstract grounds against the existence of God, or against our knowledge of Him, or against immortality. Most defenders of Christianity have formed the fatal habit of arguing as if they were creating a new religion, instead of simply explaining the historical reality and glorious nature of that which has been, as religion, present to all human experience, and as Christianity, present to and productive of the best of human history. They have not realized that Christianity, if it is true, is absolutely true. If its claims are real they are of supreme authority over every human being. Hence Christianity is not the creature of a philosophy or a movement of science; it cannot depend for its existence upon the changeful moods of man's mind. It belongs to the very structure of things. It is as necessary to man as the law of gravitation to the solar system. It is as necessary as language and food and sleep. To see that once is to see the whole of human history, and to esteem all arguing for and against the Christian faith, in a new light.

People sometimes feel as if they could believe more easily if they had lived in the first century, if they could have seen the new day dawn, the rosy light on the hilltops kindling the plains with the love of God and the darkest valleys with His mercy. But it is the first century that we live in. This is the first Christian century in India and China, in Africa and Fiji. Some one has said that every human being does in a real sense begin history over again. Change the environment of the child from a palace to a bandit's hut or a wolf's lair and what kind of adult have you? Many men around us have lived through heathenism in practice and faith. For them it is the Christ of the first century who is revealed as Savior and King, and indwelling Spirit.

People sometimes feel as if they could believe the Bible if they knew exactly how and when and by whom its books were written. Even the most conservative enemies of higher criticism invent the vague pictures of "original autographs" to comfort their faith. But after all the Bible is an existent, working fact. It is organically related today no less than at first to the very being of the church. It began to come into existence with the church and today the church lives with it—the Word of God—in its very heart. And it is the Bible which works now the will of God and the salvation of man that must be explained.

Now these are facts. No argument can disprove them. What is open to the opponent of faith is only one thing—not to prove that God does not exist, or that Christ does not live today, or that man is not to live forever. No logic can ever be constructed to prove these negatives. He can only prove that Christianity is a force destined to wane and vanish by proving positively and finally that certain known and actual causes, other than the revelation of God and the resurrection of Christ, produced all that faith, all that goodness, all that human comfort, all those visions of the true and the lovely and the pure. But when we know those causes they will surely excite in us a wonder and a praise and astonish us with a glory which at present we find only in God and His Christ.—American Weekly.

WHO IS ENTITLED TO THE NAME CHRISTIAN?

It is said that a certain man upon being asked "Are you a Christian?" answered, "Of course I am. Do you take me for a heathen?" This man did not profess to be a disciple of Jesus Christ, but he was a citizen of a Christian commonwealth, believed in the general trustworthiness of the biographies of Jesus and conformed more or less perfectly to the laws of life laid down by the Founder of our religion. Was he entitled to the name Christian?

Has any one a right to this name who is not an avowed disciple of Christ? Here is a man who lays no claim to having been "born again," but who deals justly, gives of his means to advance the kingdom of God, maintains a respectful if not a reverential attitude towards the church and its work. Every community knows such men. In not a few cases they are active helpers in what is called the secular side of church life. They may be found on boards of trustees, and building committees; they are members of men's clubs in our churches or act as ushers; not infrequently they perform most valuable service. How shall they be classified? Does the Christian spirit which they manifest entitle them to the name Christian? or do they lack somewhat that is essential?

Over against this class is another made up of those who have professed faith in the Son of God and are members of Christian churches. Does this constitute a right to the name Christian? Some of them are covetous, unforgiving, unjust, and exhibit little or nothing of the mind that was in Jesus. Almost every church has members who do little or nothing to promote the interests of the kingdom of God, either by contributions of money or personal work. They seem content with having "joined" the church, and
—14C

a few of them do not show enough interest in the church and its work to attend the services. Some of them have their membership in a church which they cannot attend because of the distance, and refuse to help the church near at hand because their membership is elsewhere. Every large city has hundreds of Baptists who are doing nothing in any way to aid in local or general Christian work. Where shall we catalogue such people? Are they entitled to the name Christian?

Still another class worthy of consideration is made up of those who claim to be Christians but reject much that is generally believed concerning the life and teaching of Jesus. They deny the deity of Jesus, reject the gospel accounts of the incarnation, declare that the belief of the early Christians in the resurrection of Jesus was due to hallucination. They are often men of altruistic spirit, strive to embody the golden rule, and are generally found engaged in reformatory and philanthropic enterprises. Individually they assume the name Christian, and when banded together in organized form they are classed as a Christian church. Are they justly entitled to the name they bear?

It seems ungracious to deny the right of any man to the name which he claims. There must always exist the presumption that those who assume to be Christians are really such. We know ourselves better than any one else can know us, and while, in the pursuit of selfish ends, some may pretend to that which they do not possess, the great majority of those professing to be disciples of Jesus Christ will be found to be perfectly sincere. Fortunately, the task of classifying humanity into Christian and non-Christian has not been laid upon us. We can safely leave the final judgment to one who knows men's hearts as we cannot, and whose verdict will be in perfect accord with the facts. It is not at all necessary that we should undertake to divide the sheep from the goats; that work is beyond our power and is not required of us.

While this is true, no one who gives serious thought to the teaching of Jesus and to the Christian life can fail to form opinions concerning that which constitutes one a Christian. Involuntarily we differentiate the Christian from the Jew or the Mahometan, the earnest disciples from the indifferent. If we think at all about Christianity we inevitably come to some conclusions as to its contents. If we are wise these conclusions will be based not so much upon our personal assumption as upon historical evidence. "The disciples were called Christians first in Antioch." What distinguished these men and women from their fellows? What did they believe that non-Christians did not believe? What moral qualities did they embody which others lacked? What constituted them Christians?

It cannot be doubted that the early Christians believed that Jesus was the Messiah foretold in Jewish prophecy. Jesus Himself had claimed this, and when Paul preached in the synagogues he set forth the declarations of the Jewish scriptures concerning the Messiah, following this with evidence to show that these predictions were fulfilled in Jesus Christ. This carried with it the divinity of Jesus. He was to them the Son of God; not one among many sons, but the "only begotten." These early Christians made the resurrection of Jesus central in their teaching. It was at the point where Paul declared that Jesus had been raised from the dead that the Athenians broke in upon his address with their mockings. It was no mere persistence of influence that Paul taught, but the resurrection of the body that had hung upon the cross and had been laid in the garden sepulcher. Jesus was the Savior; not one among many, His cross one among thousands, but the only Savior, His cross the hope of the world. In view of these undisputed facts, the question may arise why any one who rejects that which was such a vital part of primitive Christianity should seek to be known as a Christian. Do we understand Christianity better than Paul did? Can we improve upon the doctrinal teachings of those who established Christianity? If so, then we may have a right to throw out that which does not suit us and make over Christianity according to our greater knowledge. But if Christianity as a historical religion has had certain essential features from the beginning, then our inability to accept these organic factors simply reveals our unlikeness to the original Christian type. If we cannot believe that Jesus was the Son of God in an unique and peculiar sense, that He was raised from the dead, that He is the only Savior from sin, if we feel compelled to reject that which was fundamental in the belief of the early disciples of Jesus, to be consistent we should discard the name which stands for that belief. It is evident that belief in God is not enough to constitute a right to the name, else Mahometans might bear it. The word was originally descriptive of a certain attitude of heart and mind towards Jesus Christ, and it is difficult to see how we are to maintain an attitude radically different from that held by the primitive church, and at the same time preserve a right to the name.

The term as originally applied to the disciples of Jesus had its large ethical meaning. Jesus had taught moral truths the embodiment of which was essential to discipleship. This ethical teaching was summed up in the word "love." The Christian might not crave revenge nor give place in his heart to hatred. He must seek the highest good of all men, even his enemies. If he would find life he must lose it, and the way to the throne lay in the lowliest service. No one will question that this was the teaching of Jesus, or that the early disciples interpreted His words as demanding these moral qualities in His followers. They may have fallen short of the perfect keeping of the "royal law," but this was their ideal. Is the man who refuses to incarnate this spirit a Christian? Can we be real disciples and reject that which is fundamental in the lesson placed before us by our teacher? If we are unwilling to give love and ministry why not say so, and discard a name which does not represent our real attitude towards God or man?—Christian Work.

CHRISTIANITY AS A WORKING FORCE

BY THE REV. J. E. ADAMS

"Do men gather grapes of thorns or figs of thistles?"—Matthew 7:16.

Jesus Christ delighted in the concrete. He avoided all abstract teaching; all vague generalizations; all specious pleading. He spoke with authority and not as the scribes. His words combined love and logic. The logic was there. Behind His promises was the power of performance; behind His statements the indestructibility of eternal truth. Never man spake as this Man, because man's statements are limited by man's imperfect knowledge and well-developed prejudices. Jesus spoke out of the fullness of His knowledge and experience; in other words, out of His own fullness—He was the Truth.

In this simple question Christ repudiates the claims of every form of teaching which is not buttressed by results in life and character. This is the supreme test. By their fruits ye shall know them. It is a challenge to the world. He Himself, as a prophet, and His religion stand or fall by this test. We note how ready Christ was to afford the test. When John the Baptist, discouraged and imprisoned, sends to the Messiah that his doubts may be removed and asks, "Art Thou He that should come, or look we for another?" Christ offers precisely this proof. The things that are seen and heard, the fact that the blind see, the deaf hear, the lame walk and the lepers are cleansed—these are the practical proofs of Jesus' Messiahship. These grapes are not the offering of the thorn bush; these figs have not been begotten of the thistle down. When Thomas, by nature skeptical, demands such evidence of Christ's resurrection as would appeal to his senses—and a very natural demand it is, it seems to me—Jesus at once offers him the opportunity of putting the statement of the disciples to the test. "Reach hither thy finger, and behold My hands; and reach hither thy hand and thrust it into My side." And the writer goes on to say in this connection: "Many other signs truly did Jesus in the presence of His disciples * * * that ye might believe that Jesus is the Christ, the Son of God, and that believing, ye might have life through His name."

Let us, then, consider the character of the results achieved by Christ in several relations of life. And let us take the largest of all worlds, which dominates and directs, as does the sun the solar system. I refer to the world of thought. Call it by what name you will—literature, poetry, esthetics, philosophy, learning, and ask the question: Is there such evidence here of the reality of Christ's claims as to render Him not only useful, but indispensable to our life? I speak not of the life to come, though I believe that there we shall but continue what has been Christ inspired here, but of this present life. There is abroad today what is called the spirit of "religious restlessness," a spirit which demands more than ex-cathedra teachings, a spirit which is content not simply with examining the bark and branch and twig, but must analyze also the fruit, and judge thereby of the genuineness of the tree. And the question is, Is that spirit satisfied as it enters the higher branches of life, and seeks out therein some tangible, essential proofs of the reality and power of Christ? I believe we can answer this question with affirmation. I believe that never has there been so wide and profound a recognition of the indispensability of Christianity to cult and culture as at the present time.

But you may say, This is not true respecting the Oriental nations, for example. They, too, have their culture, some of it of a very high type. They have their philosophy and their art and their literature; and yet these are not derived from Christ or the Christian religion. True! And when the Christian enters India and Persia and Arabia and China he finds sacred books replete with noble teaching. What is his attitude toward them? If he be a wise man, certainly not of enmity or opposition. The missionary of the cross of Christ does not demand of these people that they cast aside as useless and worthless their literature; but he asks them to accept of the Christian revelation, because he can present in it One in Whom are hid all the treasures of wisdom and knowledge. Just as the morning hour the stars pale and die before the brightness of the sun, so in Christ all lesser intellectual lights are swallowed up and lose their luster. It has been said of Voltaire that if everything of his writings which was built upon the Christian idea should be taken from them the greater part of his ninety-seven volumes in Dalibon's edition would be disemboweled. Literature, science, philosophy, all are planets, their light borrowed from the great spiritual sun, the Sun of Righteousness. In the world's libraries, we are told by Frederick Harrison, there are now 2,000,000 volumes, and that every ten years the press issues enough new volumes to make a pyramid equal to St. Paul's Cathedral. William Ewart Gladstone, in his famous tilt with that great agnostic, asked him publicly, through the pages of the Fortnightly Review, if at least 1,000,000 of these 2,000,000 books were not directly traceable to the Christian concept. His question was never answered.

One of the most remarkable facts connected with music, in lands which are not essentially Christian, is that the minor keys predominate. There is a note of sadness, of despair, of misery running through it all. A fortnight hence the voice of song will be heard throughout this and every other Christian land. And the inspiration? Jesus Christ, risen from the dead; conqueror of the grave; bringing to light, life and immortality. Eliminate Jesus Christ and you destroy the masterpieces of music, put away His influence, and you destroy the inspiration which has moved the masters to prodigies of art and poetry. Well has it been said that Shakspeare borrowed much from Jesus. Milton was suckled at the breast of Bethlehem. The green pastures of the New Testament color Dante's blood. Tennyson's "In Memoriam" is an exposition of Christian hope. Wordsworth takes an excursion into the fields of nature and soaks himself in the New Testament he carries along. Similarly Coleridge and Browning; their brightness is derived from the great Sun that prevented them. They are interpreters, not revealers; satellites, not suns. The more they absorb of Christ, the more brilliant their creations, as pearls increase in value by exposure to the glare of day.

To Christ and His religion literature owes its existence. Christendom would be well nigh bereft of literature if all the books which directly or indirectly owe their existence to the Bible were destroyed. Literary merit, philosophic thought, poetic depth, all spring from the fountainhead of the Son of Man. The masterpieces in painting, sculpture, music, poetry and architecture are Christian in their concept and origin. The inspiration which produced Milton's "Paradise Lost," Handel's "Messiah," Powers' "Eve" and St. Peter's at Rome, has all come from Christ. The temples of the Greeks, their palaces, statues, vases, pictures, embroideries, all were of surpassing richness. In their poems, orations, dramas, philosophies and histories, they were unchallenged; even in their ruin they are treasured by the nations. But when Paul came to the Greeks with the message of the cross, he set before them a spiritual excellence which far transcended all physical, sensuous and intellectual perfection. As they admired loveliness, so he unveiled to them the reality of which hitherto they had seen only the shadow. We are told by Cicero that a prisoner who had spent his entire life in a dark dungeon knew the light of day only from a single beam which filtered through a crack in the prison wall. Great was his distress when he understood that the wall was to be pulled down, because he feared it would rob him of his gleam of light. He did not realize that the destruction of the wall would bathe him in noontide splendor, and gladden him with the infinite glory of the wide world. When Christ came He pulled down the walls of prejudice. He rent the veil in the midst thereof and opened men's eyes to the illimitable splendors of truth.

Let us take up another phase of this subject and speak of Jesus in the realm of philanthropy. Here again, we may safely challenge the skeptic and say: Christ has proven the reality of His claims in the lives of thousands and tens of thousands who, inspired by His own spirit, have gone about and are going about, doing good. Today, more than ever before, the second commandment of Christ: Thou shalt love thy neighbor as thyself, is being emphasized and enforced. More and more are men embracing the healthy philosophy of altruism. They are hearing the voice of Him who said: "A new commandment give I unto you, that ye love one another; so shall ye be My disciples." Perhaps one of the greatest and most influential men of letters is Count Tolstoi. He declares that for thirty-five years of his life he was a nihilist. Then his life underwent a complete transformation, and in the preface of one of his books he writes: "All I have done, all I am doing and all I hope to do are owing to Jesus Christ." Born to a luxurious life, with splendid wealth at his disposal and endowed with a literary genius of the highest order, he has been living side by side with his fellow men in the utmost simplicity, working for their betterment and uplift, only through the inspiration and for the sake of Jesus Christ. How easy the task to multiply illustrations, and recount the splendid lives which have been actuated by the spirit of Him who came not to be ministered unto, but to minister. There is a beautiful legend of St. Francis of Assisi. The blood which came from his way-wounded feet, as he went about doing good, transformed thorn bushes into flowering shrubs; the spots where he knelt to pray became gardens. The wells at which he quenched his thirst were ever afterward medicinal springs.

There are many who pass life's pathway; perhaps unknown and unnoted; whose touch is a benediction, whose words live like sweet forget-me-nots in the memories of those who have been helped on the upward way by their Christ sympathy and unselfish service. Standing among hopeless, wretched men, whose lives have been seared and scarred by sin, last Thursday night in the Bowery mission, a young woman, touched with a feeling of human infirmities, spoke out of the fullness of a loving, sympathetic heart. She said but few words, but they were the precious words of the Word. "For God so loved the world that He gave His only begotten Son, that whosoever believeth in Him should not perish, but have everlasting life." Of Miss Helen Gould's ministries, what need that I speak this morning? What hope, and happiness, and healthfulness, has she not brought into the lives of countless of God's children through her benevolences and sympathetic ministries. And this because she has chosen the philosophy of the Man of Nazareth as the philosophy of her life, and found her greatest joy in the services of others. And such joy is not evanescent; nor is it superficial; it is real and deep and permanent.

Professor Huxley was great in the scientific world. He saw more truly and more deeply in many regards than most of his fellow men. But toward the end of his life he confessed that beyond all honors that had come to him for successful research was the knowledge that he had helped some people to carry life's load with less strain and fret and care. And so it was with Michael Faraday. John Tyndall said of him: "He prized the love and sympathy of men almost more than the renown which science had brought him." He said: "The sweetest reward of my work is the sympathy and good will which it has caused to flow in upon me from all parts of the world." Men loved him, not because he was great, but because they saw that all his greatness was consecrated to helpfulness. His discoveries flashed light, both material and moral. He never allowed a discovery to be announced with any interpretation lessening faith in God; never let it fall as a cold ray which a pessimist could use to chill human aspiration and hope, but always saw to it that, like the sunshine, it was charged with warmth as well as with light. It was Agassiz who said: "I haven't time to make money," and many a man of wealth today is realizing and acting upon the realization that true joy and true honor consist, not in making, but in the use of money, in the spirit of the Master. We know God best when we know Him as a Father, Who is love; and we best serve Him as, with Abou Ben Adam, we "serve our fellow men." Modern Christian philanthropy is a living illustration and proof of the vital, essential power of Christ in the world today.

And again, let us look at the power of Christ, as exhibited in personal life. Here, again, the tree is known by its fruit. When Christ healed the blind man and both physician and patient were at once confronted by a skeptical world, he who had been healed, responding to the insinuation that Christ was beside Himself, replied: "Whether He be a sinner or no, I know not; one thing I know, that whereas I was blind, now I see!" The answer was unanswerable. The logic was invincible. The tree was known by its fruits. Again we throw out the challenge; and dare to maintain it in the face of Christ's inquisitors. Christ is a living power in the world today; just because the spiritually blind are made to see; the lepers are cleansed and the poor have the gospel preached to them. More and more magnificent is it becoming to be a Christian. It is joining the great army that is enriching knowledge, abolishing slavery, ameliorating war, unshackling fetters and elevating humanity. It is standing in with the majority. It is being on the winning side. There is no development of human character apart from the cross of Jesus Christ that can change the son of a poor, ignorant, savage heathen woman into the Bishop of the Niger. There is no vision save the vision of Him who filled the sky with His risen glory, that can change the proud Pharisee, pupil of Gamaliel, into the tender, earnest, consecrated apostle to the Gentiles. That is a miracle of personal life that you can account for only on the supposition that our Lord has fulfilled His promise and is here, with us, in His almighty delivering power, aye, even unto the end of the world. When this old world can produce any power that can change lust into purity, lawlessness into rectitude, drunkenness into sobriety, despair into hope, malevolence into love, impurity into chastity, and godlessness, riot and confusion into godliness, order and harmony, then, and not till then, may we give it even a hearing. Before such a task, art, philosophy, science, evolution, are all self confessed failures. There is only one power that can do it; and that is the power of the cross. We are told of some subtle chemical compound that can change the dull carbon into the semblance of the diamond; but there is only one fountain that can cleanse the guilt and pollution of a soul, and that is the

Fountain filled with blood, drawn from Immanuel's veins.
—Brooklyn Daily Eagle.

THE RELIGION OF JESUS

BY THE REV. WM. S. RAINSFORD

I want to make some suggestions on two passages in St. Paul's writings: 2 Corinthians 5:19: ''God was in Christ reconciling the world unto Himself, not imputing their trespasses unto them,'' and Galatians 1:15,16. But when it pleased God, who separated me from my mother's womb, and called me by His grace to reveal His Son to me, that I might preach Him among the heathen, immediately I conferred not with flesh and blood.''

The one tremendous and new message which the gospel of Jesus Christ brought to men, and Paul was never weary of insisting on it, taught men to look for God in a new place. First, as man's dawning sense grows upon him he will naturally look for God in the things around him, and we know this happens. The primary, barbaric religionists associated God with what is called nature worship. The God that men worshiped in a crude sort of way was the God of the forces of the physical universe, of which forces they were afraid, and religion first took the form of fear. The lightning flash that pursued them, the God of battle which they never seemed to escape. In other words, the Strong God was the first object of man's worship, and it was the best worship of which they were capable, and therefore it was good. You find traces of this in the early part of the Bible. The Bible is a literature, not a book; it is the literature of a great people, and as such it gives us an insight into the beginnings of the religion of a great people. Gradually men formed another conception, a more complex and ample idea of God conveyed by the immediate forces of nature. The next really striking development of religion takes the form of a Covenant God; that is, a God who is especially favorable to a few, who fights for them and against their enemies—the God that goes with the Jewish hosts and destroys their enemies, the God who cares for some men and curses others. This is an advance on the others, because God is already commingling with human affairs, and God is thought of as a man. It may be startling to say it, but a great many have a sort of muddled idea of God still, saying: "God is for America , or for England. against the rest of the world," or "God is for the man who goes to church or subscribes to charities or accepts certain religious convictions." This form of religion forms a large part of the Old Testament and comes up occasionally in the New. I am not saying anything against it. It was the highest form of religion men were capable of for a long time and represents a truth as far as men were able to see it.

But when you come to the teaching of Jesus you find something totally different. His was not a religion of time or tribal relations, but one world-wide religion. Jesus came to reveal "God like Me." He said: "He that hath seen Me, hath seen the Father." In other words, see the best man that ever lived (and no man, morally sane, doubts that Jesus was the best.) I know of no man with any learning who wishes that Jesus had spoken or acted other than He did in any recorded instance, and He stands before the world today and men bow to Him in absolute adoration as great; yes, greater than the world has ever seen. I believe there is more learning, strength, intelligence, profundity of thought, humility exhibited at the name of Jesus than ever before. Why? Because men believe today that God stands for all that is conceivably good and great in man. Jesus' gospel is this: Looking at man for God. That is the power of the gospel. Jesus says: "Look at the biggest man you have ever dreamed of and you look most near to God." Is not that a great gospel? We have not grasped it yet. One step further: Jesus did not simply say: "Look at Me and see God." Jesus' revelation was not simply the revelation of one man. I am saying something which is true absolutely. If

Jesus' revelation had been the revelation of one man, it is absolutely essential that the whole facts of His life should be known, not merely something from the more or less distorted memory of many men, because when that one man steps off the world the light of the glory of God is gone. Jesus took no such step. He never wrote or caused anything to be written down and never employed a man capable of keeping a diary. All the records we have differ largely in detail, in many things more than detail. And why? Every effort to maintain that the New Testament is an accurate, definite, verbally inspired story of what Jesus did and said ends in absolute ludicrous. No serious scholarship attempts to defend such a position today. Why? Because that was not Jesus' way. What was His way? He had an idea how His gospel and His life were to go through the world. He said, "I am the light." Yes, and you are the light. I am the salt. Yes, and you are the salt. More than that, I am the first of a big family. It is expedient that I go away. Why? "Because after I go the Comforter will come and do greater things. You will address multitudes that won't hear me. The life that I live, ye shall live also." It is the gospel revealed in a million men, not having its expression in one man, one skin, one color, but in the race of men, wherever they live, giving expression to the everlasting truth of God in its fullness in Jesus Christ. That is Christianity. Christ's spirit living on and on and on in you—God in man.

Do you not see the practical duty this implies? A Christian community cannot do God's will unless it is really Christian. Only one way can we go out into this new nation and claim it for God, and that is to honestly and reverently remember that God has given us a religion which simply amounts to this: That Jesus Christ has got to live in our own lives. Men say that is all right in theory, but it is just a little bit too high for human nature; it is too much to ask. They turn away, not because they cannot believe this doctrine or creed, but because they think the whole thing too high for them. That arises not from lack of but from increase of spirituality. Forty years ago men joined the church more readily; they were thicker skinned and less spiritual than now. It behooves us to teach the world that God is not unreasonable and will not ask too much of men. Did Jesus make excessive demands? You must not take the Bible literally. For instance, take the lesson of the woman who cast her two mites, all she had into the treasury.   There Jesus set down the principle that if we are going to serve God we must give something that costs something.   If a man has two dollars or $2,000 and you say the right thing for him to do is to give that $2,000 to the church, then you are a fool, and you are making the man a fool.   He ought not to do anything of the sort.   He has a wife and child or some obligation.   Jesus was speaking as a poet, a parable maker after the method of one of His day.   "Let the dead bury its dead, and come, follow Me," He said, but does anybody in his senses suppose that the great, loving, gentle Jesus wanted a man to leave his father unburied?

The point I want to make is this: That God is revealed (I say it reverently) in the person of weak Peter, of Paul, of John, and so on, from day to day, a never ending stream of good men and women trying to do the best they can.   There you have a tangible, good religion that commends itself to human reason: "God reconciled to us," is a mistaken idea.   God's attitude to me needs no change.   He says: "I want you just to come into My life just as you are, but I do not need to change.   Men all down the ages have been talking of changing the mind of God.   Man's mind and attitude needs to be changed, not God's.   How do I know it? Look at Jesus.   Did any man ever want Him changed?   The unchanging Jesus represented God.—Brooklyn Daily Eagle.

CHRISTIANITY'S POWER

BY THE REV. DR. P. S. HENSON

"When the Son of Man cometh shall He find faith on the earth?"—Luke 18:8.

Grave problems confront us as we sweep through the portals of the twentieth century. Momentous questions agitate the public mind and demand a speedy answer—financial, political, educational, sociological—questions touching the relations of capital and labor, of trusts and combines, of expansion and imperialism, and I know not how many more. But all of them are puerile and contemptible in comparison with the one whch today will be the theme of our thoughts.

Undoubtedly for twenty centuries Christianity has been a mighty factor in this world's affairs. Many have professed it who never possessed it, and many who were genuine disciples of it have so utterly misunderstood the genius of it that in its name they have perpetrated the most abominable atrocities. But take it all in all, its beneficent restraints have contributed more than all other agencies to hold in leash man's brutal passions and to awaken within him the noblest ambitions. It has been the banner bearer in the march of human progress and has laid the foundations and reared the walls of all the noblest structures of modern civilization. In education and in politics, in literature and in law, in reformation and emancipation, it has been the all pervasive and determinative element.

Pre-eminently is this true of our American republic. Here, indeed, as nowhere else in all the world, is there utter divorcement of church and state. Lord Baltimore of Maryland and Roger Williams of Rhode Island—the one a Roman Catholic and the other a Baptist—shook hands on this. If there be anything ineradicably written in our fundamental law, it is that in America no priest or politician shall lay his hand upon the individual conscience to coerce or constrain it in matters of religion. But religious freedom in the state is one thing and an atheistic state is another thing, and a very monstrous and hateful thing at that, so hateful that heaven's judgments may be expected to overtake it. "The wicked," it is said, "shall be turned into hell with all the nations that forget God. But as there is no future for nations in the other world, it must be that their hell is here. France found it so in the reign of terror. God grant that such a reign may never curse our beloved land.

Whatever may be said of the trend of today, the fathers of the republic were God-fearing men. The Pilgrims in the cabin of the Mayflower before their feet touched the soil of this western world, where they were to help found a new nationality, drew up a declaration of principles, whose beginning was, "In the name of God, amen.' The sessions of the Continental Congress were opened with prayer, and in that immortal Declaration of Independence, which for a hundred and twenty-five years has gone ringing round the world shaking thrones and striking off shackles, the stalwart signers made reverent appeal to Almighty God for the rectitude of their motives and trusted their cause to Him who was throned above the national ensigns beneath which the fathers were neither atheists nor agnostics, but Bible loving, Sabbath keeping, God-fearing men. And if today our starry banner floats the highest of any that is kissed by the sun under the whole heavens, it is because of the inspiration that Christianity has given us. And if today the sturdy Anglo-Saxon race practically dominates the globe, it is because above the national ensign beneath which they march floats the blood stained banner of the cross.

And in a word it may be said that what the sun is to the solar system that Christianity is to all the magnificent enginery of our modern civilization. What a pall of despair would fall upon all the world if it were solidly certified that the sun were dying out? More dreadfully appalling yet would be the fact—if fact it could be proved to be—that, after all these years of magnificent achievement Christianity were losing its grip and was destined presently to pass away, leaving only broken monuments and a fading memory. And yet not a few whose very being has been warmed into life under the beneficent rays of the sun of Christian civilization, hail with a sort of ghoulish glee any apparent indication of its waning power. And such apparent indications are not wanting. The very prevalence of this manifest malevolence toward the whole Christian system is itself one of the most sadly significant signs of the times. Men have nothing better to propose in its place, but in growing numbers they are evidently anxious to have done with this. ''The kings of the earth and the rulers in the realm of thought, take counsel together against the Lord and against His anointed, saying, Let us break their bands asunder, and let us cast away their cords from us.''

The spirit has always been at work in the world, but the virus was never more malignant than now. It finds expression in the treatment accorded to the ministers of God. It goes without the saying that they are not paid the deference that was formerly accorded them. Perhaps they do not deserve it, but the fact remains that they do not get it, and it is quite the fashion to denounce them as the pocket curates of purse-proud plutocrats, or as hypocritical hirelings thundering theological dogmas which they themselves have long since ceased to believe. And if one of them is overcome in a fault and comes to grief, there is exultant shout as if an enemy had fallen, and he is dragged about like another sect around the walls of Troy. And as to the Day of God, never was there so determined an effort to break down every safeguard that has heretofore hedged it about as a day of rest and religious worship. The Sabbath was made for man, not for the few, but for the race, and while it is for humanity a necessity it is also the salute that the nations give to the King of Kings as the earth whirls round before His throne, and just because of its recognition of Him there is a constantly growing disposition to degrade it. And what with so called social functions and wide-open saloons and theatrical attractions, and a ''merry-go-round'' of ungodly amusements, there is danger that by and by there will be nothing left of the ancient Sabbath but a melancholy memory. And that the house of God in many quarters—of course excluding Brooklyn—is not frequented by such throngs of worshipers as used to crowd its courts is a fact that is only too palpably apparent.

The evening service especially is apt to present only a beggarly account of empty pews and as the poor preacher looks around upon the emptiness, only relieved by the presence here and there of a few discouraged worshipers, he is tempted plaintively to cry to these, 'Will ye also go away?' And in sheer despair he is sometimes driven to the adoption of sensational expedients—to so

—15C

called sacred concerts and stereopticon exhibitions and anything else that supposedly will prove more attractive than the gospel.

And the Word of God, though more widely circulated than ever before, we have reason to fear is very widely neglected by the very people that are supposed to prize it. It is snowed under by the blanket sheet papers and is buried out of sight beneath the tons of compost that under the name of light literature are dumped upon a long suffering public. Nor can it be denied that the reverence for its authority has suffered large abatement from the widely prevalent impression only too frequently fostered by theological professors occupying chairs in nominally Christian institutions, that the book we call the Bible is not so much a revelation from God as a record of the evolution of the religious thinking of the Semitic race. And the simple fact of the business is that evolution, which confessedly is only a plausible hypothesis, is very commonly accepted even by thoughtful Christian people as an established scientific fact, and accordingly we have evolution instead of creation, evolution instead of revelation, evolution instead of regeneration, and so, little by little, the very foundations of faith in the Christian system are insidiously undermined, and if the foundations be destroyed what shall the righteous do?' Anthropology has been largely substituted for theology, sociology for soteriology, and the powers of nature for a personal God. Is it any wonder that there is no wide sweep of religious revival as in the days when faith had a firmer footing and hope a clearer sky?

And in the midst of the fog a multitude of will o' the wisps are dancing, and multitudes are following them only to be mired in the bottomless bogs of so-called modern thought. Innumerable fads like the frogs of Egpyt are all abroad, only unlike those ancient frogs they find hospitable welcome even in the homes of refined and elegant Christian people. With more than Athenian eagerness we stand agape in the "agora" to gulp down "the newest thing out"—anything, no matter how monstrous, only so it be different from "the everlasting gospel" that has come sounding down the ages.

The causes of this revulsion are not far to seek. Pride of intellect inflated by the splendid achievements of this last half century is utterly unwilling to bow its haughty head to a religion whose keynote was sounded by its divine Author when He said: "I thank Thee, O Father, Lord of heaven and earth, that Thou hast hid these things from the wise and prudent and hast revealed them unto babes." And never was there an age more hot-footed in the pursuit of money or that bowed with a baser idolatry before the calf of gold, or one so madly intoxicated with the wine of pleasure. Is it any wonder there should be intolerance of the heroic exactions demanded by Him Who said, "If any man will be My disciple let him deny himself and take up his cross and follow Me."

This sterner aspect of the Christian life has not been greatly dwelt upon in these modern, "piping times of peace," and the very ministers of religion in their anxiety to swell the muster roll of their retainers have only too seldom appealed to the heroic element in human nature, and accordingly our churches are filled with light hearted picnickers instead of self-sacrificing soldiers, who are willing to endure hardship and in the shock of battle to stand and do and die, if need be, for God and the right.

An unfaithful church will always make an infidel world, and if the church itself be filled with gay revelers is it any wonder if it loses its grip. The church so-called may lose its grip, but Christianity never. Is not the pulpit losing its power? some sneering skeptic asks. We have only to answer that many a pulpit never had any power, simply because the preachers have toyed with a lute instead of blowing the trumpet of the gospel. Spurgeon's pulpit never lost its power, nor Moody's. Jesus, our Master, said, "I, if I be lifted up, will draw all men unto Me." This is the mightiest magnet that this world has ever known, and it will never lose its power to the latest syllable of recorded time. I have faith in the gospel and faith in God and faith in the future, in spite of all the sad omens in the trend of the times.

I do not say that all the world will ever be converted, for I find no warrant for such an optimistic declaration in the Book of books. But I do say that Jesus shall reign till He hath put all enemies under His feet, and that they who follow His all conquering banner shall reign with Him in glory. I do say that the fight is on and that we are in it, and that the last great epoch of human history shall witness such shock of battle between the powers of light and darkness as has never made earth tremble or sounded up to heaven. And, instructed by the Word of God, I do believe that in that last tremendous fight there shall stand forth such monsters of depravity as never before disgraced the world, and such heroes of faith as never before won the plaudits of a watching universe. But the issue of the conflict is not doubtful. The sacramental host of God's elect with the banner of the cross floating over it and the Captain of salvation riding at its head, shall triumph over all the powers of darkness, and all round the globe and up to the gates of glory shall ring the loud acclaim, "Alleluia! Alleulia! for the Lord God omnipotent reigneth!"

THE BLIND MAN'S LANTERN

Out West, a friend of mine was walking along one of the streets, one dark night, and saw approaching him a man with a lantern. As he came up close to him he noticed by the bright light that the man seemed as if he had no eyes.

He went past, but the thought struck him, "Surely that man is blind."

He turned round and said, "My friend, are you not blind?"

"Yes."

"Then what have you got the lantern for?"

"I carry the lantern that people may not stumble over me, of course," said the blind man.

Let us take a lesson from that blind man, and hold up our light, burning with the clear radiance of heaven, that men may not stumble over us.—D. L. Moody.

COST OF NOT LIVING THE CHRISTIAN LIFE

BY THE REV. DR. NEWELL DWIGHT HILLIS

(By permission of the Brooklyn Daily Eagle.)

"Which of you intending to build a tower sitteth not down and counteth the cost."—Luke 14:28.

This parable seems to have grown out of the spectacle of a half-built house. A certain youth fell heir to much gold on his father's estate. He was ambitious to live in the best house in the town. Scarcely, therefore, was his father dead than he razed the old homestead to the ground. Soon, on the side of his childhood's home, he began to build a mansion with a tower. But, because he had not earned the money he was spending, he did not know how to use it. Before the building was half done his funds ran out. In his ignorance and folly he had neglected to count the cost. Soon his workmen discovered that he had no money and they threw down their tools in disgust. At first he was startled, then humiliated; discredited, he fled from the community and quite disappeared. Years came and went, and the elements slowly turned the house into ruin. One day, Jesus stayed His steps before the half-finished house. The rain had fallen through the roof, the storms had driven through the open windows, the floors were rotten, the garden a tangle of thorns and weeds. The world holds few sadder spectacles than a deserted house. Pointing to the structure that represented vanity and folly, Jesus warned the multitude against building a house of passion and pleasure without first of all considering the cost thereof. The scene gave Him His favorite figure of the soul as a house; the good man built his house on a rock of truth; the wicked man built on the sand. In that hour, the theme that Jesus discussed was the price a man pays for building the house of pleasure, and the losses man suffers when he does not build the house of righteousness and character.

Every man who refuses the Christian life should carefully estimate the losses incident to a life of self-will and personal pleasure. At the very outset let us confess that the Christian life represents a large, a hazardous and a very difficult enterprise. It means intelligence for the intellect, resolution for the will and vast reserves of conviction. Unless a man has oak and granite in him, the struggle is not for him. The Temple of Fame does, indeed keep its doors open day and night for each adventurous youth, but unless the aspirant can eat crusts, wear rags, bear up against fierce winds, there is no room for him in these niches that are open only to the greatest. And the youth who is soft and flabby, without resolution and inflexible purpose, will not heed the call of Christ. Jesus' appeal is always to the heroic note. When you think of what it is to be a Christian, you must think of a plan as vast as a military campaign, as marvelous as the settlement of a new province, or the building of a new city. God is abroad, slowly bringing the vast machinery of nature, invention, science, industry and government under the control of law and the spirit of good will. The Christian is one who seeks to do God's will and forward Christ's plans, in Christ's way and in company with Christ's disciples. Upon each eager disciple, therefore, He imposes the yoke of law. By divers restraints the Christian spirit curbs the appetites, the motives, where the youth is overstrong. By divers stimulants it leads forth to a fuller strength those powers that are too weak, and the entire career of the disciple represents a series of sacrifices. The Christian life is a life of battle, where the weapons are thoughts, passions, and the enemies are invisible and spiritual. But once the victory is won, strange rewards appear.

In the life of the English scholar and preacher, Champness, there is a striking page. One day the boy of fourteen made his plan to see the football game between two rival teams. The month was August, the day was hot; but by ten o'clock the youth completed the Saturday's task. Going to his father, he made the report and asked permission and money for the football game. The father said quietly that he had planned for the youth to take a package in to a merchant at Manchester. In a moment the boy's hopes fell. In that household the rule was instant obedience. A half hour later the size of the package staggered the boy. It was almost as big as himself. Every moment it grew heavier and the day hotter. By easy stages the boy went slowly on, until the tramcar put him down at the other end of Manchester. Going into the store, he threw the bundle down on the papermaker's counter, and, hot and tired, turned away, with quivering chin and dim eyes; for his disappointment was very very sore. A little later he started toward the door to take the tramcar back home. Then the merchant called after him that there was an answer. He weighed the bundle, saying, "We will get some good linen paper out of this package," and then counted out the money for him. "Your father's letter says I am to give you this money to spend at the football game." With a bound the boy was back at the counter, with eyes shining like stars. Now how light the bundle seemed. "Oh, my!" he said. "I wish it had been four times as big!" At last he understood, for the football field was at this end of Manchester. But his father had tested his obedience and concealed the great reward. But this is what God is always doing when He lays any duty upon Christ's disciples. Christ imposes a yoke—yes, but the dry wood in that yoke ripens clusters for strength. He does impose a burden, but all of Christ's weights soon turn to wings. Obedience to God is its own exceeding great reward. What if that boy had disobeyed and then estimated the losses incident to non-obedience? You have refused to obey Jesus Christ; you have declined the Christian life, but at what cost will you estimate your losses in happiness and peace?

Others there are who suffer heavy loss in happiness and character by refusing to complete the house of character. They emphasize the foundation qualities called moralities, in themselves indispensable, fundamental and praiseworthy. Multitudes there are who insist they believe in patriotism, in honesty, in meeting their bills, in moderation. But they do not believe in the mystical element, and are not interested in worship or prayer, or self-sacrifice, or love to God, or a profession of faith in Jesus Christ. They say, I am trying to average up pretty well as a good citizen, and beyond paying my debts and living well I never expect to go and I'll run my risks as to the future life. Now, in a mechanical universe, without God, without any presiding will or intellect, that would be well enough. But if it should chance that this so-called good citizen is living in his heavenly Father's world, is being supported by his Father's bounty, if he is a son, squandering his Father's treasures and estates, it might be important to consider his Father's attitude and ask: "Am I giving pain to my heavenly Father through neglect, utter indifference and quiet contempt? Am I humiliating Him and injuring His divine government?'' If it should chance that there is a God standing behind the veil, then these fundamental moralities must be carried up to affection, loyal obedience and loving trust.

For example, here is a strong man, who founds a home, and has wife and children. He has built the house, put coal in the cellar, food in the pantry, and regularly pays all the bills. But the day comes when he turns upon his wife and children and says: ''I believe in the fundamental moralities, I believe in clothing you people, in feeding you with roots and grains and meats; I stand for a full pantry and a full coal-bin, but you must remember that I do not believe in these mystical relations of love. You must not expect any bosom-pressure from me. All the so-called sentimentalities make no appeal to my nature. Those invisible relations of the soul with exchange of affection, the asking and the giving of gifts which go on between a father and child, and husband and wife, who stand for the mysticism of love—well, I am a practical man, and I never expect to profess these things. I will look after the fundamental moralities and take my chance of your love, when I come to die and leave you.'' Now what kind of a man is that? Little chance he has of keeping the love of a good woman and rightly disposed children. These would prefer to starve rather than accept a cent from such a husband or father. And if you are in your Father's world, if God's providence has guided you, if His benignant hand has ripened these harvests at the Thanksgiving time, if His mercy has redeemed you from your sins, and you still say that you will ignore Him on the side of love, and prayer and trust, that you never expect to make any profession of your love for Him, or swear fidelity to His laws, that you intend to ignore God, but be a good citizen and run your risks for the next life—well, I have nothing to say about your getting into heaven, but if I had charge of hell, one thing is certain, I would not let as mean a man as you are hang around hell. Such a one is blacker than the pitch that burns under the devil's feet.

Out in the orchard the other day I heard a tree break into speech. It turned moralist, and began to boast. In its soliloquy it said, ''I believe in black clods. I believe in good fertilizers; I believe in roots and a stout trunk. I believe in boughs, and if necessary, in turning them into clubs. I believe in branches that serve for hoe handles and ax helves; but I am not a sentimentalist. If things were looked into it would be found that I am just as good as these other apple trees that make such pretentions. I am not interested in all this talk about apple blossoms and perfume, about ripe fruit and the aroma thereof. How silly it is to talk about birds building their nests in the branches and cattle finding shade from the heat of the fierce sun. These mystical, invisible spiritual elements of color and odor and food for the hungry do not appeal to me. "Why, I never heard a moralist explaining why he was not religious talk more learnedly than this apple tree. But after a while I looked up at it, and there it stood, without a leaf, without a single blossom on a May morning. No child played beneath its gaunt, dead boughs. It was an old, starved, shunned trunk, with naked branches, looking like a skeleton of bones, without flesh or life. The only sign of a living thing that came near the tree was a woodpecker boring for a worm. Great are the root and the bough and the trunk! But the test of an apple tree is the fruit on the branch. Important the moralities that make up a good citizen! But if there is a God in the world the test of manhood is in a pure heart, a surrendered will and an obedient life. The proofs are in prayer, in loving confidence, in short—in morality that blooms into religion, with all the fruits of the spirit named love and joy and peace. God is too large a fact to be ignored. When blades of grass can ignore the sun and summer, a man by emphasizing his moralities, can ignore God, and His goodness that leads the moralist unto repentance.

It is a proverb that the better is the worst enemy of the best. Man is so constituted that he is perpetually seeking for a compromise between his worst self and his ideals. In the nature of the case a living thing can be happy only by fulfilling its highest faculty. A worm can be happy in crawling, but not a turtle; a turtle can be happy in walking, but not a deer; a deer must run. The deer can be happy in running, but not a bee; the honey bee must fly toward the sweet clover field. A savage can be happy in fishing or hunting but not a man. A man must think, invent, sing, pray, love. Once you know what your highest faculty is, that moment you must use that faculty and subordinate all else to it, so you will be in constant collision with yourself. Paul could make tents, but his life is not in industry; Paul, in an hour of shipwreck has the power of a captain and a general, but his life is not there; Paul can write the ode on immortality, but his life is not in literature. Paul can assault evil, serve the slave and gladiator, in a passion of love send the evangel pulsating through the world, and there lies his real life, because it is his supreme gift.

It is possible, therefore, for a man to be entirely mistaken about himself. In living for the good, the secondary thing, he misses the best, and the ideal, the Christlikeness. It is easier, therefore, to call a bad man away from the worst things to the ideal ones than it is to induce a good man to go up to the ideal things. When Christ said the publicans and sinners shall go into the kingdom before the Pharisees and Scribes, and that Sodom should be saved before Jerusalem or Capernaum, what He meant was this. It is easier to reach a drunkard or a glutton than to reach a hypocritical Pharisee and Scribe. In Alaska I found two kinds of mines, the placer mine and the quartz mine. The gold in the placer mine is buried in the sand and mud. The gold is very filthy, and yet all you have to do to get the gold out is to have a spade, a shaking pan and a stream of water. When I washed gold out of the mud in Alaska I learned how easy it was to save Sodom. But there is another kind of gold up in Alaska, and that is the patrician gold imbedded in layers of quartz. Every atom shines like a hypocritical Pharisee, blazes like a theological Scribe, and is hard as the creedal points in a system of theology. To get this gold out of the quartz you bore in with a diamond drill, as hard as a sermon point, and then you put in dynamite and have an explosion, like a climax in a preacher's appeal, and then the stamp mills go to work, and every stamp weighs ten tons, and stamps, and pounds, and pounds, and thunders, until the quartz is ground to dust, and then the dust is passed through an acid bath, and finally the gold comes out of the quartz; and this stamp mill, with the infinite exertion necessary for getting gold out of granite, makes me think of the way some Gypsy Smith, with an army of helpers, has to pound away on cultured sinners for five weeks, when one hour's appeal will bring a prodigal boy back to his father's house. You can play the prodigal through your body, and recovery is simple; you can play the prodigal through your intellect, through selfishness, and recovery is difficult.

The thoughtful man also will estimate the losses of self-respect incident to having no place among those who have fought for God and His cause. Jesus Christ is the leader of a world-wide campaign. He is fighting to overthrow evil and selfishness intrenched in a thousand strongholds. Darkness must go down before His Day. Hate must surrender to love. Bats, things that creep and crawl, and tear, must be driven back into the night. Love, peace, prosperity, happiness, must fill all the earth, until God is all in all. Toward that consummation Christ wrought suffered and died. Then His apostles took up the flag and plunged it deeper into the ranks of the enemy. The martyrs made a new onslaught, and with their blood made Christ's banners crimson. Our own fathers forgot their tossings on the sea, their sufferings in the wilderness, to win their victory. The time has come when we must launch our Mayflower, sail our seas of difficulty, brave our enemies, and slay our foes. And once the true apostle and disciple of Christ appears, he is the one best man of his time, and the second best man in a thousand leagues behind him. No matter what the weakness of the Christian church, you cannot afford to die without having joined the ranks of His weakest disciples who are fighting His battle. It is not enough for you to say that you will fight a guerrilla warfare. It is an unworthy thing for you to add: "I sympathize with His church and His cause." Can you afford not to be found with the old guard?

When Richard Cobden died, and all England had but one heart, and that heart was very sore, it is said that an Englishman claimed that he spoke for the free corn laws with Cobden, and was the first of those who became his disciple; this man offered a large reward for some one who had heard him make that brief plea. He was ambitious to stand in that little inner circle and help bear the remains of that hero to their final resting place. But if you fight none of Christ's battles, if you have never marched under His leadership, if you have never suffered unto blood, striving against sin, the time will come when you will go up and down the streets of a lost universe, advertising that you will give everything you have save life itself, if only you can find some one who will say that some time, somewhere, under cover of night, you did make a confession of your faith in God and His loving providence, and in Christ your Savior. And when that hour comes, and the great assize draws nigh, and the heroes and the martyrs, the patriots and the poets, and your own fathers and mothers are assembled, and the all searching eye of God and conscience pass in review the events of your career, the very thought that you did not join Christ's old guard, and lead His hosts, and die at the front of the ranks will bring to you such immeasurable shame that you will call on the mountains and the rocks to fall upon you, to conceal your loss and your humiliation.

This it is to gain the world and lose one's soul. This is building the house of vanity and pleasure and power which will never be completed. In his reminiscences of the Lincoln and Douglas debate, Joseph Medill, editor of the Chicago Tribune, tells of the night when he heard a gifted orator, a noble patriot, and an old friend, plead with Douglas not to compromise, and not to make his speech. I have always believed that this man was the eloquent and glorious figure Colonel Edward Baker, who uttered that sentence, "I see Liberty, God's dear child, unsheathing her sword, red with insufferable wrath." But Douglas would not be persuaded. He built a highway of compromise that sloped one way toward the prejudices of the South, and the other way toward the convictions of the North. At the other end, he thought, stood the White House. Putting away all entreaties and arguments, Douglas betrayed his deeper convictions of liberty and eternal justice. He gained the first prize, the Senate, and lost what he was struggling for, the Presidency. Then one day he found that rebellion was sweeping North with waves crested with fire. In that hour he knew that he had no place in the history of liberty. Shame came in like the tide of the sea. Grief overwhelmed him. Sickness followed. In his fever his biographer says that he heard Douglas whispering, "I missed it! I missed it I missed it!" Oh, all ye young hearts, at what price will ye estimate the losses incident to refusing the Christian life, in the hour when you exclaim, "I gained pleasure and the world, but I missed it! I missed it! I missed it!"

THE SUPREME TEST OF EVERY RELIGION

BY THE REV. JOHN CLIFFORD, D.D.

The history of man is the history of religion. In some form or other, religion is the soul of history. The world's most cherished heroes are the founders and reformers of religions. Abraham and Moses, Isaiah and Jeremiah, Confucius and Buddha, Savonarola and Martin Luther, Wycliffe and Wesley, stand out distinctively in the annals of our race as men remembered for their contributions to the religious life of mankind. The world's great books are books about religion. The Old Testament of the Jews, the Koran of the Islamites, the New Testament of the Christians, the Zend Avesta of the Persions, the Shastras of the Hindus—these stand out in literature as head and chief of all.

The world's most costly and precious buildings are dedicated to religion—its temples, cathedrals, and conventicles, and some of these last are infinitely more precious to some of us than even the finest temple or the grandest cathedral, because they are associated with deep spiritual experiences, in which we have met with God and seen His face, and gone forth strengthened for life's duty, or prepared for life's sorrow.

The history of religions is the history of man's reading or misreading of life, the aspirations he has felt for the highest and the best, the efforts in which he has striven to find the key to the universe, and the struggles and battles in which he has engaged on behalf of right and truth. That history constitutes in itself a prophecy—for as man has been in quest of religion in the past, so will he be in the future, and the story of his struggle for a pure religion is the brightest and most inspiring part of humanity's record. Out of religions, hard and cruel and rugged, he has toiled to religions of greater generosity, magnanimity and sweetness, of larger power of uplift, of greater force for expanding and enriching human life.

Therefore, the two questions we will consider are—(1) What is the task of religion? (2) What is the supreme test for every religion?

The task of religion is fivefold.

Here I am, not by my own choice, placed on a planet of which I know little, and in the midst of circumstances which hold me in their grip and threaten to determine my destiny apart from any choice of my own; and I ask myself, What can a religion that is really worth my acceptance do for me? What is the task which it should set itself ? And if I were to answer in one great word, I should say that its supreme business is that of reconciliation; its chief task is that of reconciling me first to my place— to the position in which God Himself has put me, to the circumstances which I describe as being my especial environment, so that I may get a footing, solid and sure, amidst the shifting sands of time; may find some rock upon which I can put my feet, and feel that, howsoever the waves may rise against me and break over me, still, still I shall be able to secure myself upon this piece of granite.

I want a religion that shall give to me such an interpretation of the trend of all human life, not simply of my own, but of the universe, that shall bring to me some measure of intellectual contentment and satisfaction. I want a religion that shall give unity and order to the whole universe of things, and show that there is not simply a plan which is being worked out, and a process which is being executed, but that there is also a purpose unifying the whole life, creating cosmos out of chaos, and bringing beauty and charm out of that which seems to be ugly and repulsive. I want a religion which will not leave me like Jeremiah, saying, "I hate the day on which I was born,' 'or like the prophet Elijah, exclaiming when some particular difficulty is in front of me, and despondency has seized me, "Would that I could die, for I am not one whit better than my fathers!" I want a religion that shall keep me from cursing the day of my birth on the one hand, or from falling into sudden despair when some particular calamity overtakes me.

Again, I want a religion which, besides satisfying my intellect by giving a true conception of the scheme of things, and of the ultimate issue of the whole administration of God's providence, will also secure for me the mastery of life, put me in a position to use it, to turn its opportunities to advantage for myself and others—a religion that, in other words, may be fitly described in the language of Jesus Christ, when, speaking concerning His own mission to this earth, He said, "I am come to give life"—that men may have it, the intensification of life as love intensifies it, the quickening of life as love quickens it, the expansion of life as love expands it—"I am come that ye may have life, and have it more abundantly." The task of religion is to make me more effective personally, to endow me with such force and energy that I shall be able, instead of being "cribbed, cabined and confined" under the tyranny of the gaoler circumstance, I shall move forward as a free man, stand on God's earth as one possessed of freedom in God, mastery over myself, victory over my circumstances. That is the kind of religion I want. My misery comes to me in consequence of being a slave to the world, to its customs, to its maxims, to its traditions. My blessedness comes from being master of myself, capable of directing my own steps, able to use wisely and effectively and to the full measure of their advantage, whatsoever God brings within the sweep of my vision or puts within the grasp of my hand. I want a religion which will execute for me this most difficult of things—namely, that of enabling me not simply to see the right but to do it, not merely to know the truth but to speak it, not only to comprehend what I ought to be but to attain to what I ought to be. That is the task of religion.

Nay, more; the religion that is to do its full work for the sons of men must put each man in a position where he can establish God's rule—make him capable of extending, consolidating, widening it. In other words, it must help to the realization of that dream of the prophets and philosophers, of the coming of the kingdom of God, the rule of the Eternal over the fleeting, transitory life of man; in which man shall find his joy, not in living to himself, but in sweeping out of the corners of his being all his egotism and selfishness, and introducing instead thereof a genuine altruism by means of which he shall be impelled forward in acts of real self-sacrifice, not for the benefit of this or of that section, but of the whole of humanity.

And that carries me to my fifth and last point—the religion that is to accomplish for the sons of men all that religion is really capable of doing must reconcile me to God. Not to the God of the distant heavens simply, but to the God of my everyday life, the God of the circumstances through which I am getting my education, by which I am being disciplined from day to day, prepared and equipped for the doing of life's work; must reconcile me to His ways of thinking of, and interpreting the actual facts of human existence; reconcile me to His way of feeling, brotherly, lovingly, helpfully, towards men who hate me and despitefully use me; reconcile me to His willing, so that my will and His shall never cut across one another, but shall always be one with the other in perfect and complete harmony; reconcile me to doing at all costs, and in spite of all risks, whatsoever God Himself determines should be done by the creature whom He has formed after His likeness, and whom He is developing and fashioning according to His own ideals. That is the task of religion. It has to do these five things for us if it is to be a religion worthy of the acceptance of the whole man; and I say that the religion that can stand that test is the true, the eternal religion. This, then, is the supreme test; you may bring others, but you cannot bring one that is more comprehensive, more central, more fundamental; it underlies every other you may use—tests philosophic or historical, and tests scientific; the one great final, supreme test is the effectiveness of the religion in accomplishing these five results, or this fivefold result, summed up once more, in the great word reconciliation. I am not going to say that the Christian religion is the only religion that has reconciling force in it. Were I to utter that, I should be misreading the entire story of the ages, and treating humanity as though it had only been dealt with in fragments by the Father of us all. I should be pushing Him out of certain wide realms of human life, and saying that He had no share or interest outside Judaism and the Christian religion. No, there have been reconciling forces in Buddhism, in Confucianism, in Hinduism, forces that have gone some distance towards bringing man into harmony with life; but they have done it with so much imperfection, both as to outlook and immediate impulse, as to make it necessary for those who have received the fuller and completer revelation of God in Christ Jesus to go to these peoples, with their partial, with their half-developed religion, and offer them the gospel which will be the crowning and consummation of them

all. Evermore has God been at work in the life of the ages for
this one purpose of reconciliation. If you ask me what God has
been attempting to do since first of all He made man, my answer
is simply: He has been seeking to reconcile man to Himself, to
draw him over by His own divine magnetism, by His infinite
attractiveness, into accord with Himself, to make him one with
Himself. Christianity is God's chiefest way of getting back to
Himself, and Christ is Christianity. "God was in Christ reconciling the world unto Himself, not imputing unto men their trespasses." Harmonizing, reconciling energies have gone to work
through the great religious leaders of the world's history, but they
have not gone to work with anything like the effectiveness and
completeness, with the promise of final and universal victory, such
as that which is presented to us in Jesus Christ our Lord.

In a few sentences I should like to establish this proposition,
and I do it by reminding you of this, that the task of religion is
presented to us as completed in the personality of the founder of
the Christian religion. Whatever I have said that the religion
for men should do, you will find abundantly achieved in Christ
Jesus. Turn your attention to His consciousness; for the interest
today is not so much in the nature of Jesus Christ, and how it was
compounded, and what were the elements that entered into it, as
to what was the consciousness of Jesus Christ? Our students are
all seeking to analyze that, to interpret it, and to get at the springs
and characteristics of the true religion by that analysis and interpretation. Well, if you follow your gospels, and read the consciousness of Jesus Christ as it is presented to you in His ideas,
as it is seen in the impression which He makes upon His immediate disciples, you will see that there is no discord in the nature
of Jesus. There is not the slightest confusion in His mind, no
breach of His moral order. He is always at one—at one with the
Father. He could say to the men who were challenging His authority, and say it concerning His purposes and spirit, "I and My
Father are one." He knew it. His life was lived in the light of
the Father's countenance; He came out of the Father's bosom
out of the infinite intimacies of communion with Him. He knew
what was in God, and that self-same was in Him, and so, looking
upon a disordered and disturbed world, He Himself was filled

—16C

with an unutterable peace, and out of His own fathomless peace-
fulness was able to distribute to others; "My peace I give unto
you." Jesus Christ's personality is the unique witness to the
ability of Christianity—that is to say, to the ability of Christ
Jesus Himself, to accomplish the end—the true end of religion.
The task can be done; it has been done, and what has been done
may be repeated. It is presented to us in Christ Jesus, not as
something attempted, but as something done, and as we gaze upon
Him, we see the pattern of what each one of us may be. We have
an example set before us of the capability of Christianity for
making manhood, for helping a man to master his own place in
life, and determine his attitude towards it, and so fit himself into
it, that instead of its being a prison for him, it shall be a mansion
of glorious freedom. It shows itself in Him as He possesses the
true conception of what is life's drift, towards what all God's
work is going, the ultimate issue, even the brotherhood of man
participant in the life of God, brotherhood in its full experience,
in its richest achievements. It presents itself in Him as a mastery
of life such as has never been surpassed, and never shall be beaten.
The devils attacked Him, but He mastered them. The Pharisees
attacked Him, and they went with the devils; the Sadduces came
along, and they had to go to the same place, Scribes, Herodians—
they all came up against Him, but He was always Master. He
died Master, put to death on the cross, yet He was triumphant.
Mastery of life is the great revelation of the Christ. Was it not
He who spake in parables of "linked sweetness long drawn out,"
of the kingdom, how it comes by the little ferment which is put
into humanity, how that ferment spreads from man to man, from
life to life, until at length it fills the whole of humanity with its
energy? Was it not He who not only spoke of the kingdom, but
laid the basis for it, and thus introduced that rule of God which
is man's abiding blessedness? He and the Father were one.

The reconciliation of humanity to all it ought to be, if I may
so speak in regard to Christ Jesus, presents itself in its finished
and perfected result in Jesus Christ, the Creator, the founder of
Christianity.

Again, Christianity being an historical religion, the distinctive
convictions of the Christians who have made up the Christian

race show themselves as demonstrations and proofs of the capability of the religion of Jesus Christ to repeat in man what is in the founder. Men have walked even as He walked, men have suffered even as He suffered, men have died to themselves even as He died to Himself. Christ Jesus has been repeated, not only in the experience of a solitary individual here and there, but of communities. Were it only in a single case, like that of the Apostle Paul's for example, you might question it, attribute it to hallucination, or to some figment rather than to a force, but when you find these effects spreading themselves over mass after mass, some in Ephesus, some in Corinth, some in Rome, some in Jerusalem, community after community, you have an accumulation of facts demonstrating the historic distinctive convictions created by Christianity, in their triumphant inworking in the lives of men, and outworking in the life of the world. I say, then, that you have proofs to which you may make appeal, that there is in Christianity the capacity to discharge the task of religion.

Contrasting for one moment, and only a moment, another religion with the one I have just described to you, I find, in a book which has recently appeared, by Prof. J. C. Oman, on the subject of "The Brahmans, Theists and Moslems of India," a description of the Kali Ghat at Calcutta. From that particular deity Calcutta gets its name. Of that image Mr. Oman says it is: "A form to be remembered for its grotesque and startling ugliness—a hideous black woman, with four well-developed arms, and a huge blood-red tongue hanging out of her mouth. In one hand she holds a drawn sword, in another the severed head of a mighty giant, while the other two hands are supposed to be engaged in welcoming and blessing her votaries. Thus in her visible manifestations does the goddess unite her attributes of avenger and protector of her people. Such, then, in outward semblance is the goddess Kali of the Bengalis." The conclusion to which Mr. Oman comes is this: "In Bengal, assuredly, religion would seem to be a morbid abnormal affection, whether sacred or not, but which in some form or other every man and woman is subject, and today, as in past generations, this morbid emotional affection tends to sap the manhood of the people, and effeminate the race." It does not accomplish the end of a religion, but goes right in the opposite direction. That is one illustration of the defects of the religions of the earth, one that perhaps could not be paralleled from many other religions, but it presents in an extreme form the antithesis of the religion of Jesus Christ. There you have a conception of God, and of the reconciliation of the worshipers to the god, which produces effeminacy, destroys manhood. In Christ Jesus you have a representation of God, and of the reconciliation of the worshiper, of the believer with the God thus manifested, which produces manhood, strength, purity, peace; develops power, expands the whole nature, makes a man capable of being what he ought to be, and of achieving what he ought to achieve.

I do not say that every difficulty which the world presents is removed by the revelation which is in Christ Jesus—far from it. There are tragedies in life for which we have no explanation; there are mysteries which it is impossible for us to fathom. We contemplate them, and we are filled with awe, if not with horror, but I do say that on the principle of probabilities, which is our guide in life, there is no interpretation of life itself and of its contents that brings so much intellectual satisfaction, or so much power to the will, or illumination and quickening to the conscience and love to the heart as the revelation of God in Christ Jesus our Lord. The task of religion is accomplished in the gospel of the Grace of God.

Here, then, dear friends, is a test for you and me. I am a disciple of Jesus Christ. What has that Christianity done for me? Has it made me a better man? When I see a lie, and am tempted to utter it, do I say: "That is a lie, I will not utter it, although all the kingdoms of this world and the glory of them were given to me?" When a falsehood comes along the line of my business, and there are cheques at the end of it of considerable value—money to go into my purse—do I say: "This is a falsehood, and I will have nothing to do with it, though I go into the workhouse?" When I find myself confronted with peril and trouble, do I cast myself upon the infinite care of the God who has promised to be my Leader and my Deliverer, and has shown what He can do in the resurrection of Jesus Christ the Crucified One from the grave? Or am I cowardly, and shrink from the trouble and peril, taking care of myself: a certain sort of graceful selfishness, a cultivated egotism being my principal characteristic?

What is religion doing for you? You claim to be on the side of Jesus Christ: what is the testimony you are bearing day by day to the people who are close to you? Brothers, the effectiveness of a religion is itself the best apologetic for the religion. There is no argument in favor of Christianity that carries so much weight with it as the Christianity that has embodied itself in sweetness and power, in a hallowed and hallowing life.

Now, I should like to say four things to my young friends especially, and the first is this. These things being so, the ground of our appeal to the intelligence and judgment of men for the acceptance of Christianity rests upon experience, but not upon the experience of an individual, though he be one of the elect of the earth; not upon the church simply, nor a group of churches who have themselves arranged that some one of their number shall be put at the head of the church or churches and described as infallible; not on a book, though that book be the Bible, but on the accumulated experiences of Christian men throughout nineteen centuries. The sifting of that experience, and the scientific treatment of it, offer a basis upon which we can make our appeal to men to accept the gospel of the grace of God. We do not say, with our fathers of fifty years ago, "Here is the Bible; you must accept it, must believe it word for word." No. We do not say with the High Churchman, or with the Roman Catholic, "Here is the church, you must be obedient unto it." We say this: "Here are these three moral, spiritual facts, accumulated through successive ages, and presenting themselves in great communities. The Bible has gone into the life of men, has won its way into their hearts, has helped them to Christ Jesus. Christ Jesus has brought them into fellowship with the Father. They have come from that fellowship to fellowship with men, and thus they have borne their witness to the effectiveness of the religion of Jesus Christ. That is the position upon which we stand when we appeal to the judgment of men to accept Christianity. The evidences concerning dogmas will carry you some distance. It is a great advantage for you to know this, that a re-examination of the New Testament now taking place under the guidance of the best scholarship of the time, gives us every confidence that the record is true. That carries you some distance, but not all the way. The appeal is really to the massed experience of Christian men throughout the centuries.

But, never forget, you can only test the Christian religion by trying it. If I may quote a very homely parable, "The proof of the pudding is in the eating." There is a man who says that an oratoria was rendered very badly. You find after you have talked with him that he could not hear, and you give no attention to his criticism. There are certain things you must try before you can judge. The Christian religion is one of them. You must try it, put it into practice, make it part and parcel of your life to be a Christian before you can judge it. Life is the greatest laboratory of all, and experience is a succession of experiments; we all must make them, and the experiment that you young men ought to make is the experiment of finding out whether Christianity is really the religion that is capable of doing this or not, whether it can keep your hand out of the till, keep you from being false, from living an untrue and an ungodly life. Do not judge it by mere critical examination and book evidence, come and test it for yourself, see whether it can help you to harmonize yourself with God, to get that mastery over yourself by which you shall do the things you ought to do, and in any situation in which you are placed. Till you have tried it yourself do not pass sentence upon it.

That means, then, does it not, in the next place, that the final appeal is always to the will, not to the intellect, not to the judgment, but always to the will. "Ye will not come unto me that ye might have life." "We have received the ministry of reconciliation whereby we beseech you, be ye reconciled unto God." God is reconciling. He has no force at work that does not end in reconciliation. There is no energy in His universe that is not directed specifically to bringing you over into harmony with Himself. The will, the will, the will!—that is the spinal column of our personality. And if you will to do the doctrine, you shall understand what it means, find its truthfulness, develop it into life.

And that means this, that if you will not win, the whole responsibility is on your own shoulders; you must not blame anybody else, but take it, with all that it means of impoverished life. I know you fellows who, for want of the will to be Christian, who have seen that they ought to be Christians, that it was their privilege and duty so to be, but have turned aside, they have become pleasure-seekers, and have cared not for God or for God's rule. Mind and heart are impoverished to the uttermost, and as for usefulness they have not any. I have seen it again and again. Young men, I beg of you, if you want to live a life that has really something in it that shall be of value to yourself, and of value to your fellows, well, be Christ's disciples. Say, "Master, Thou art mine. A better leader I cannot have, a truer friend I never can know, a gentler spirit never can lead me. Master, I am Thine."

And in the end, the intellectual and the moral are one. Man is a unit, and at last heart and brain move together in blessed harmony. If we treat ourselves fragmentarily, we always have to pay for it. If we cultivate the moral at the expense of the intellectual the moral becomes enfeebled, effeminate—perhaps it may decay. If we cultivate the intellectual at the expense of the moral we shall have to pay a heavier price. You can suffer in intellect more advantageously, if I may so speak, than you can suffer in morals. The ethical is supreme, and consequently a man who strives to be morally right though it be with confused thinking, is a man who will be likelier to get to the genuine manhood, than a man who strives always to be intelligently right and will not devote himself to ethical rectitude because he is not intellectually right. Do you see? Begin with the ethical, start with the will, and the intellect will come into line, and the whole man will by-and-by be reconciled to God.

Wherefore, once more I beseech you, in the name of Christ, "Be ye reconciled to God."—Christian World Pulpit.

HOW PATTI IDENTIFIED HERSELF

On her marriage to Baron de Cederstrom, Patti left orders at her home that her mail should all be forwarded to the Cannes postoffice. On her arrival there she went to the postoffice and asked if there were any letters for Baroness Adelina de Cederstrom Patti.

"Lots of them."

"Then give them to me."

"Have you any old letters by which I can identify you?"

"No, I have nothing but my visiting card. Here it is."

"O, that's not enough, madam; any one can get visiting cards of other people. If you want your mail, you will have to give me a better proof of your identity than that."

A brilliant idea then struck Madame Patti. She began to sing. A touching song she chose, the one beginning, "A voice loving and tender," and never did she put more heart into the melody. And marvelous was the change as the brilliant music broke through the intense silence. In a few minutes the quiet postoffice was filled with people, and hardly had the singer concluded the first few lines of the ballad when an old clerk came forward and said, trembling with excitement: "It's Patti, Patti! There's no one but Adelina Patti who could sing like that."

"Well, are you satisfied now?" asked the singer of the officer who had doubted her identity. The only reply which he made was to go to the drawer and hand her the pile of letters.

WHAT IT IS TO BE A CHRISTIAN

BY THE REV. ROBERT MACDONALD, D.D.

What constitutes a Christian? Is it to be a communicant of any church? Is it to subscribe to any creed? A hundred times no! All trustworthy sources make it to be a believer in Christ. But what do you mean by belief in Christ? Well, what do you mean when you tell a person you believe in him, that you believe he is a good citizen, a faithful husband, a loving father? You may believe in him as all that, yet not be willing to trust him with a dollar out of your sight, or open your home to him as a friend. You honor him not most unless willing to trust him with money uncounted, your good name, the very secrets of your heart. A belief that does not express itself in confidence does not count for much. All else is cold, impersonal opinion. You must not offer Christ less than you would your friend. A belief in the historic Christ only never saved a soul, any more than a belief in Cæsar or Luther or Washington, even though you believe Him as more than a Teacher sent from God, more than a prophet, even the very Savior of the world. Just as friendship is more than an intellectual opinion, even a possession of a life, just as love, that divine essential in all true living, without which society is a self-centered, self-circumferenced conglomeration, and the home a den, denying its own existence, is virtue of the heart instead of a secretion of the brain; so religion has its abiding place in the heart, else nowhere in the life at all.

To be a believer in Christ then is no different than to be a believer in man. Tell him whom you profess to call your friend you believe in him. When you will not confide in him, when in perplexity you seek another's counsel, and in sorrow another's sympathy, and you have insulted faith, and friendship has become in your hand an empty name. If you believe in a man trust him as all men demand you should. You say you love? Show it by loving and manifesting the self-denial love demands, else your profession is a sounding brass, an empty name, a dastardly affair.

Do you believe in Christ? Show it by a loving trust. Otherwise, you believe ony intellectually, and that means you do not want to have much to do with Him. It means self first and always. And if perchance you start to follow Him from so superficial a motive be not surprised if the first time His demands conflict with your plans you turn traitor and swear you never knew the man. The test is, My sheep hear My voice and I know them and they follow Me. That is the test—to hear His voice and follow Him.

Now, what is the purpose of a church, and in how far does church membership constitute a Christian? Church membership constitutes a Christian just so far as a Christian constitutes a church member. No church, whatever its name and influence, has of itself power to make a man a Christian, unless the Roman church, and that is only in its own estimation. We fall into one or the other of two errors: Either of thinking of Christianity as an abstraction, or as a fact identical with an organization of earth, when it is grander than both. There is no Christianity apart from the life of its founder. It is not to be born in a Christian community. It is not to be swayed by religious excitement. It is not, under the uplift of fine music, nor the tender sentiment of a keen sorrow to catch some celestial glimpse of truth, and conclude you are henceforth a religious man. To be a Christian is nothing other than Christ within you the hope of glory.

Then there is the other mistake of making the visible church identical with the reality, instead of the symbol of the reality. Indeed, symbols are important. We can never tell how much satisfaction the religious devotee receives from the picture of the Virgin or the image of the Christ. The line between the symbol and the spirit may be less attenuated than we think. More symbols may lead to more realities than we dream of. An object of sense may, however, oftener hinder access to the spirit than be a viaduct thereto. Many a person joins a church for the sake of being a church member rather than to be a better Christian. Many a person worships their church and minister rather than the Christ the church represents and the minister preaches. Being a good denominationalist is not necessarily being a good Christian, although if we are good Christians we ought to be denominationalists, and better denominationalists than we are. Denominations give form and content to Christianity which some souls would never otherwise perceive. But on the other hand, denominationalism should have no content to boast of except what the gospel imparts.

Don't think that to be a Methodist, Presbyterian or Baptist is equal to being a Christian. It may be so. It depends whether your denomination intensifies or materializes Christianity. You may have the form of godliness, but your very devotion to the form is a denial of the power thereof. I have in mind a member of a former church who would sooner give up Christ than his immersion and communion. His unspiritual life shows he has done that very thing. He has permitted those two sacred rites to steal away his Lord, and he knows not where they have laid Him. Scriptural warrant for ecclesiastical forms is good. But no ecclesiastical form should take the place of the pure heart, the Christ spirit. Christianity is a Christ-imparted divine state of life. All within the charmed circle, whether of my church or yours, or of neither mine nor yours, are my brothers because also of Christ. "Other sheep I have not of this fold." Don't forget that. Christ said it. Therefore, it must be true. There shall be one flock and one shepherd. Not one fold, as it is translated. There may be many flocks in one fold. But one flock.

By and by boundary lines will fade away. We think then they will all be Baptists. The Congregationalist expects they will all be Congregationalists. And the Methodist is sure they will all be Methodists. Ah, brother, better still, they will all be Christians. And as some saint in glory 10,000 years asks, Who are these? as they all come trooping home like tired children after the toils of the day are over, so some John will answer: "These are they who believe on the Lamb of God which taketh away the sins of the world." Who knows, Jesus Himself may say: "These are they for whom I died." These? These? These are they who come up through great tribulation and have washed their robes and made them white in the blood of the Lamb!—Examiner.

THE APPEAL OF CHRISTIANITY TO PRUDENCE

BY THE REV. L. L. TAYLOR

"What shall it profit a man if he shall gain the whole world and lose his own soul?"—Mark 8:36.

In the opening chapter of Bunyan's "Pilgrim's Progress," being admitted to the wondrous dreamland into which the walls of Bedford jail dissolved more than 200 years ago, we see a very wide field, on the borders of which two men are in earnest conversation. Suddenly one of them begins to run. He has not run far from his own door when his wife and children begin to cry after him to return. But the man puts his fingers in his ears and runs on, crying, "Life, life, eternal life!" The man he had been talking with was Evangelist, who had found him wandering solitary in the fields, reading in his book and greatly distressed in mind. Evangelist, having inquired into the cause of his misery, the man made answer: "Sir, I perceive by the book in my hand that I am condemned to die and after that to come to judgment; and I find that I am not willing to do the first nor able to do the second." Then said Evangelist, "Why not willing to die since this life is attended with so many evils?" The man answered, "Because I fear that this burden that is upon my back will sink me lower than the grave and that I shall fall into Tophet." Then said Evangelist, "If this be thy condition why standest thou still?" He answered, "Because I know not whither to go." Then he gave him a parchment roll and there was written within: "Flee from the wrath to come." The man, asking whither he should flee, Evangelist pointed out with his finger over the field toward the wicket gate and the shining light above it. It was then that the man began to run. Before meeting with Evangelist he had said to his wife and children, "I am certainly informed that this, our city, will be burned with fire from heaven, in which fearful overthrow both myself, with thee, my wife, and you, my sweet babes, shall miserably come to ruin, except (the which I see not) some way of escape can be found whereby we may be delivered." Failing to interest his family in these forebodings of his and having had the way pointed out to him, he enters upon it, fleeing with frantic haste, his fingers in his ears to shut out all other considerations and crying in his flight, "Eternal life! Eternal life." You know the rest of the story. It is all of a piece. It represents the progress of a soul, resolved on making sure of its own salvation, from the City of Destruction to the Celestial City, and the fellowship of the shining ones.

Now, the "Pilgrim's Progress" represents one aspect of the appeal of Christianity to the principle of prudence. The principle of prudence is concerned in all matters of danger and safety, loss and gain. When the gospel speaks of being lost and saved, it is addressing itself to the principle of prudence. When it says, as no one can deny that it says, "A due regard for your personal welfare should lead you to repent of your sins and turn to God," it is appealing, and appealing legitimately, to the principle of prudence. The whole representation of the gospel as a way of salvation is an appeal to the principle of prudence. As a manifestation of divine love and grace, it appeals to the sentiment of gratitude, and those who ignore it prove themselves ungrateful. As a manifestation of divine righteousness and as an offer to make things right, it appeals to the conscience and leaves us the alternative of remaining in the wrong and under condemnation, or being set right with God. As a way of salvation, Christianity appeals to the principle of prudence, and leaves us the alternative of being, in its own terms, "lost or saved." This is the aspect of Christianity which is set forth in such an inimitable way by John Bunyan. This is the gospel as it was presented in the preaching of our fathers. And this is the view of the gospel which prevails most widely today, both among believers and among unbelievers. It is thought of by many as being, first and last, a way of personal escape, a way of personal salvation, this, and nothing more.

No one can fail to see that a general reaction away from these views of the gospel has set in. The gospel is not preached today as it used to be. Other aspects of Christianity have come into prominence and men are more open to approach at other points. The same emphasis is no longer placed upon the fact of future retribution, nor are the same explanations of its nature given. Not only is this true, but the same place of supreme importance is no longer given to the duty of seeking salvation, each for his own soul. It is even asserted that in this aspect Christianity is, or may become, an appeal to the most dreadful form of selfishness, and that a man may become so absorbed in seeking the salvation of his own soul as to forget the very things which Christ lived and died to make us remember. The whole view of Christianity as represented in the "Pilgrim's Progress" is held up for repudiation by the enlightened. We are told that Bunyan's pilgrim might better have remained in the City of Destruction and worked for clean streets and better dwellings for the poor. The true Christian is not a fugitive, but a reformer.

To a considerable extent I am in sympathy with this reaction. The half hath not been told when the gospel is presented as nothing but a plan of salvation for the individual sinner. Some of the noblest sentiments to which Christ Himself appeals are neglected by those who confine themselves to the appeal to men's fears and hopes, to the calculations of their prudence. Then, too, the love light of the gospel is bound to be obscured by giving undue prominence to the retribution from which it would save us. The spirit of the gospel has a poor chance to manifest itself in the preaching of a man who dwells with undue predilection upon the more vindictive aspects of truth. All truth has its vindictive aspects. All truth has in it the seeds of vengeance for those who disregard it. But there is so much of the vindictive in us by nature that it is safer to dwell for the most part on the more genial bearings of the truth. We sympathize with Whittier when he says:

> "I want no pulpit hammered by the fist
> Of loud asserting dogmatist,
> Who borrows for the hand of love
> The smoking thunderbolts of Jove."

There are very few men who can be trusted with "the smoking thunderbolts of Jove." Let Jonathan Edwards be our witness. Here are a few sentences in which he made what he conceived to be the appeal of Christianity to the principle of prudence: "The God that holds you over the pit of hell, much as one holds a spider or some loathsome insect over the fire, abhors you. You are 10,000 times as abominable in His eyes as the most hateful and venomous serpent." Do we read in the parable of the prodigal son that his father ever dreamed that he had been turned into a serpent? Was the love that never let him go a slender, flame threatened thread?

But, says Edwards: "You hang by a slender thread, with the flames of divine wrath flashing about it and ready every moment to singe it and burn it asunder. There is no other reason to be given why you do not this very moment drop down into hell. Do but consider what it is to suffer extreme torment forever and ever; to suffer it day and night, and from one day to another, from one year to another, from one age to another, from 10,000 ages to another, and so, adding age to age, and thousands to thousands, in pain, in wailing and lamenting, groaning and shrieking and gnashing your teeth; with your souls full of dreadful grief and amazement, with your bodies in every member full of racking torture, without any possibility of getting ease; without any possibility of moving God to pity by your cries; without any possibility of hiding yourself from Him; without any possibility of diverting your thoughts from your pain; without any possibility of obtaining any measure of mitigation or help or change for the better any way. Your bodies which shall have been roasting and burning all this while in glowing flames, yet shall not have been consumed, but will remain to roast through an eternity, yet which will not have been shortened by what shall have been past.

Can we wonder that there should be reaction from that sort of thing? If anything like that is true I do not want to look upon the stars above or upon the flowers below—I do not want to look upon the cross of Christ.

We should remember that this was not the whole gospel of Jonathan Edwards. We should not forget that there must be an awful reality in sin so to inflame a mind whose clearness and whose power have been the marvel of succeeding generations. We should not forget that other great minds have had orbits which have carried them through Infernos of this sort. Jonathan Edwards came in some respects, nearer than Milton, to being the Puritan Dante. Nor can the real tragedy of life and destiny, veiled in their words, be gainsaid. But, thank God, the appeal to prudence no longer relies upon the pictorial embellishment of retribution, but upon the ethical interpretation of its nature and its processes. I believe that we know better today than ever before what it is to be saved or lost. We may not be able so to terrify sinners by proclaiming them irrevocably lost, but we are in a position to show them the irreparable loss of living apart from God as He has revealed Himself in Jesus Christ. We need have no fear that Christianity will lose its power of appeal to the principle of prudence. We were never in a better position to press that appeal. I know that altruistic hands are raised in horror at the dreadful selfishness of a man who can be induced to reflect upon the personal consequences of his sin and his personal interest in the salvation which is offered to him. But shall prudence be debarred from matters spiritual and shut up to things material? Shall prudence be consulted in questions of time and ignored in questions of eternity? What shall it profit a man if with prudence in things temporal, he shall gain the whole world, and, with improvidence in things eternal, lose his own soul? What do these words of Jesus mean if not that any degree of prudence which stops short of taking into account the fortunes and destiny of a man's own soul, is recklessness itself?

Nor is the appeal of Christianity to the principle of prudence as it bears upon eternal destiny, a character for willful folly in the affairs of this life. Christianity is not a scheme of worldly wisdom, but it presents one. There are many paradoxes in it. We are taught, as Faber puts it, how "to lose with God," and so to make our richest gains. And yet Paul surely does not misrepresent the claim of the gospel when he says that the "godliness" to which it calls us "is profitable unto all things, having promise of the life that now is, and of that which is to come."

WHY BE A CHRISTIAN?

BY DR. CHARLES S. WING

"Come thou with us and we will do thee good, for the Lord hath spoken good concerning Israel. * * * And thou mayest be to us instead of eyes."—Numbers 10:29-31.

The Israelites were about to leave the mount of God. The law had been received, the ark of the covenant completed, the tabernacle and its furniture prepared and directions given for the march through the wilderness. It was time to move. Hobab, Moses' brother-in-law, came to visit him, with a part of his clan, who belonged to the tribe of the Midianites. These children of the desert were evidently in sympathy with the Israelites. Descendants from Abraham, they knew something of the claims of Jehovah and were ready to accept, in a measure, His leadership. They had doubtless been greatly influenced, also, by Moses, for this remarkable man had lived among them forty years and had married the daughter of their priest. It is impossible to doubt that his culture, his unusual ability and splendid character, would give him great weight among these people, and his marriage seems to indicate that they were impressed by his religious belief. They would be naturally rather proud to have him appear now in the desert as the chief man in so large an enterprise. Then their Arab life developed an instinctive love of freedom which made them take sides with a movement which liberated millions from Egyptian bondage, and they were doubtless fascinated by the greatness of the project which Moses had in hand; its lofty aim, sublime faith and divine leadership.

They stood just where many stand today, accepting, in a general way, the doctrines of the church, believing in its purposes, admiring its faith, but withholding from it their allegiance. All such people ought to be in the church. Moses appealed to these Kenites to unite with God's people. "Come thou with us and we will do thee good." We have what you need. The life you follow has no future, no progressiveness. You are like your fathers and your children will be like you, and so on from generation to generation, hardship, poverty, freedom, death—that is all your Arab life

—17C

has to offer. To preserve the traditions, cherish the revenges and inherit the heirlooms of your tribe is all you can hope for. Man needs something larger than that for the development of his best nature; some higher aim, some wider and worthier purpose. Here is a great movement. We are going to Palestine to plant a nation and develop institutions and practice the law of God. The plan is His. It is so important that He is directing it in person. He gave us our liberty, our courage, our statutes and our worship. His presence will go with us to guide us, protect us and lead us to achievement. "He has spoken good concerning Israel." We are to be lifted up for the help, the happiness and the salvation of the world; our influence for good is to be as wide and continuous as human destiny. You should come with us. It is a great privilege to become allied to God's people and be partakers of their inheritances.

Thousands of years have passed since Moses made this plea, and history shows how truly he spoke. The Arab is still what he was in every respect; he follows the same habits, wears the same dress, eats the same scanty food, and repeats the deeds of his fathers. He is as changeless as the desert in which he lives and the mountains in whose presence this invitation was given. But Israel became the religious teacher of the world and made a history so marvelous that men call it divine. From a weak and feeble people they became the genius of civilization and are still able to furnish statesmen and financiers for all nations. The Christian church, inheriting Israel's hope and led by Israel's God, is pressing forward to complete the undertaking Moses had in hand, and she invites all you who believe in her mission, who accept her teachings as a revelation of the divine will, who recognize the purity of her ideals, the sincerity of her purpose and the beneficence of her influence, to join the ranks of her followers. We will do you good, for God hath spoken good concerning us. The life we are trying to lead is of His direction and under His blessing. We bring to you Jehovah's message and invitation. The truth we preach will cure the ills and heal the woes of mankind. It is worth while to live in connection with such an enterprise. It appeals to the best there is in you, and offers an opportunity that is sure to result in the ripening of your faculties and the elevation of your character, and will crown you with everlasting life.

Now, for some reason this plea did not avail to persuade Hobab and his clan. I wonder why. The argument ought to have been effective—ought still to be effective. Perhaps their old life, narrow and without prospect, appealed to them. They loved the desert and felt bound to tribal loyalty; they loved their wild freedom, and religion means restriction; but it is a restriction which removes limitation and leads to liberty. So possibly the old ways and habits bind you, and you are loath to surrender to the restriction co-operation with God's people would impose, even though you recognize some of the advantages which would result from church fellowship.

Again, I suspect that Hobab and his followers were not greatly impressed with the Israelites. Centuries of slavery had not developed an attractive manhood, and the superior qualities which would appear under divine culture had not yet become common among them. They were not very good examples of what God can do for men, and these Kenites very likely felt superior to them. They should have looked at Moses and Aaron and Joshua and Caleb. Why is it that we pick out the worst and measure ourselves by them? I was once trying to persuade a man to accept Christ. He was at the head of a large factory and had many men in his employ. He met my plea by calling my attention to the poor character of several members of my church. After trying in vain to defend them I, in sheer desperation, said, "My friend, is there not some one in whose religious character you have confidence? Did you never see a man whom you believed had been truly converted?" "Oh, yes," he replied, "there is Eddy. Before he professed religion he was the hardest man to manage I ever saw, and now he is the best man in the shop. I believe in Eddy's religion." "Well," said I, "what God did for him He can do for you. Why not try Eddy's religion?" What makes the world admire the character of William McKinley? His praise is on every lip, and every commended trait in this admirable man is Christian. He is simply the perfect fruitage of a Christian faith. Why should men look at defective church members and stumble over their faults? Why not give Christianity credit for its best results and measure it by them?

But if this argument fails Moses had another, and so have I. "Come thou with us, and thou mayest be to us instead of eyes." You need us and we also need you. We were brought up in Egypt and are unaccustomed to the desert, but it is your home. You know its wells and fountains, and fuel supply and camping places. You know how to avoid the hurricanes and protect yourselves against enemies. Your alert trained vision sees everything that moves and knows its meaning. You are wise where we are ignorant, and safe where we would be in danger; you can be of vast use to us. We have Jehovah, but He expects us also to employ human sagacity. We have a great future which you cannot only share, but help us to secure. You can do us good. Dear friend, do you not know that your life will count for more in the church of God than any- where else? The very defects you criticize we need your help to remedy. Some of you have culture which will enable you to intel- ligently lead those who have been less favored. Your love of art and music will improve the taste and elevate the service, while your self-control will steady other lives and make them more con- sistent. Your business skill will show the way to proper methods in the management of God's house. We need you all with your varied talents, and many of the defects of the church would quick- ly disappear if we had your help. We are trying to do a great work. It is God's own project, and we are workers together with Him. The laborers are few, and we want your aid. You can help us see our way and do our work. Nowhere else can you so richly invest your life and influence. We shall succeed at last in bring- ing the world under the power of the gospel, ''for God hath spoken good concerning Israel;'' but you can help to hasten the time. We shall go on without you if you will not come. But we need your wisdom to make our way more rapid and prosperous. It is a great thing to be on the right side, the winning side. ''Come thou with us.''

This argument prevailed, and the Kenites went with Moses, probably acting as scouts and rendering invaluable service. The rich reward of the kingdom had not been able to persuade them out of their old life, but the prospect of usefulness was an attraction they could not resist. They endured all the trials of the wilderness and at last entered the promised land, receiving an inheritance in the southern portion of Palestine. They were noted to the end of the history of Judah, and it was they who, in the great siege of Jerusalem, furnished the Rechabites, who pitched their tents in the streets of the ctiy, and rather than drink wine endured patiently the parching thirst of famine. So in God's name I appeal to you. The Christian religion can do great things for you, and without its aid your life will be a desolate failure. If you could do nothing for the church we should still plead with you to accept its gracious benefits, but if these will not allure you from the world, perhaps, like the Kenites, you will hear our cry for help and come to our aid.— Brooklyn Daily Eagle.

IF THIS WERE TWENTY CENTURIES AGO

If this were twenty centuries ago,
   And three wise men should seek my house and say:
   "We bring glad tidings! Christ is born today;
Arise and follow yonder star, whose glow
   Will lead you to the Child?" would I obey
If this were twenty centuries ago?

From out my urn of precious hoarded things,
   Would I make haste to pour the richest share
   For him? The sweetest of my perfumes spare
To bathe the feet of the young King of kings?
   Or break the costliest ointment on his hair,
From out my urn of precious hoarded things?

Alas! I dare not say this would I do,
   Since I have slighted many another guest
   That came from God, have stayed from many a quest
That would have led me to the good and true,
   To slumber on with head upon my breast;
Nay, nay! I dare not say this would I do.

My best resolves like shifting shadows are;
   Each day some holy light shines on unsought,
   And while my silly, fluttering wings are caught
By the world's rosy candle, Christ's own star—
   How can I tell?—might beckon me for naught;
My best resolves like shifting shadows are.

And when Christ comes again—as come He will—
   And wise ones hasten forth with rapt delight
   To welcome Him and own His kingly right,
Will men be questioning and doubting still,
   As when upon that first, far Christmas night—
When Christ shall come again, as come He will?

CHRISTIANITY, A NEW LIFE FELLOWSHIP

Luke 5:10.

Here we have Luke's version of the calling of Peter and Andrew, James and John. The account is more complete and detailed than that of Matthew and Mark but the main facts are the same in all. The essential point in all three accounts is that Jesus called these men to a life of fellowship in service and they immediately responded to His call. The service they were to render was significantly described when He declared that they were to be "fishers of men." The fellowship in service was promised when He asked them to follow Him.

The story clearly reveals what Christianity meant to these men. Jesus did not ask them to adopt a new creed, a new ethical ideal. He did not ask them to identify themselves with a religious organization. He did not prescribe for them a round of religious observances. He asked them to follow Him in the work of human redemption. He offered them identification with Himself in the great work of saving men. That is what Christianity meant to these men and that is what it means today. There are people who imagine that Christianity is synonymous with membership in a Christian organization. It is not true. No man is a Christian simply because he may belong to a Christian church. Generally speaking such a man is a Christian but his membership in the church does not make him such. Occasionally the officers of a church are deceived and men are received who are anything but Christians. Belonging to a church is not Christianity.

Nor is a man a Christian simply because he accepts the principles of Christian morality. Many a man has the very highest ethical ideals and principles who is not a Christian. Adopting a new creed does not constitute a man a Christian.

Nor is Christianity synonymous with religious observance. A man may go to church regularly, twice a Sunday, even go to prayer meeting and to other services and still not be a Christian.

What is Christianity in its essence? It is a new life fellowship, a fellowship in service. It is not identification with an organization but with a person. In a word, Christianity means following

Christ. A man is a Christian who has accepted Christ as his Savior and leader and who is trying to follow Him. In that life there will come some element of renunciation and sacrifice. For fellowship with Christ means that we share with Him the cross, and with Him we work for the salvation of men. It is not a profession, it is a passion.

There are Christians whose lives are unsatisfactory because their fellowship is spasmodic. There are periods when they are in close fellowship with the Savior and periods when they follow afar off. Such Christians are only enjoying a part of their privilege, and are only accomplishing a part of what they are capable. Jesus calls us today to a life of continuing fellowship, a life of abiding power and ever-increasing usefulness. He calls us to this life, and by His power makes it possible for us to live it.

WHY SHE WAS A CHRISTIAN

A little girl had a great desire to join the church. Consequently she went to the minister, asking to be received into the church. He inquired if she had experienced a change of heart, and she answered "Yes." The minister inquired further.

"Were you a sinner before?"

"Yes."

"Are you a sinner now?"

Again she answered, "Yes."

"Where, then, is the difference between your former and present condition?"

After some moments' meditation she said: "Before I was converted to Christ I was a sinner that runs after sin. Now I am a sinner that runs away from sin."

CHRISTIANITY AND LIFE

Matthew 25.

The real test of Christianity today lies in its power of application to the conditions and problems of human life. Of course evidence for its authenticity and authority is not to be confined here. Its historical documents and its historical facts and its formulated doctrine still have their place. And yet in the final end of it the abiding of Christianity and the question of its acceptance by men as a whole will depend upon as we have said, its complete application to the demands of human life.

Now then, is it not true that however Christianity may be tested in this direction, it proves itself able to withstand and meet all requirements? Is it not true that taken into the human heart and enthroned as a controlling principle in human life it makes the individual better and truer and nobler and of greater service to his kind? Is it not true that embodied in the home it promotes harmony and fidelity to family relations and helps to cultivate mutual thoughtfulness and helpfulness, and makes of that home what it ought to be? Is it not true that in proportion as it obtains in society it makes that observant of the principles of business integrity and social purity and political honor, and national sanity? Is it not true that enthroned in a nation it would make that nation careful as to the rights of others; more solicitous for blessing than conquering and more helpful than hurtful in all the relationships into which it might come with its fellows? Is it not true that brought in its fullness into this old world of ours it would redeem it from evil and cause it to be filled with the Spirit of God and of universal brotherhood among all its inhabitants?

We believe that the answers to these questions must all be in the affirmative. We believe, moreover, that as the preacher of Christianity may be emphatic in showing its applicability to human life in all its different manifestations he will command a hearing and be successful in winning men to its support. It is right here where the recreancy of those who fail to support the Christian system comes in. They are enjoying its light; they are in possession of its privileges; they are sheltered by a civilization of which it is the chiefest force, and yet they withhold their hands from its advancement and contribute little or nothing to its support. Perhaps the condemnation of those who thus fail to aid in enthroning Jesus Christ in the hearts and lives of men will lie just here. It may not be so much what they did as what they failed to do that shall cause the sentence "depart." That is the lesson of the 25th of Matthew, and that may be the verdict of life.

GROWTH OF CHRISTIANITY BY CENTURIES

Close of first century............................... 500,000
Close of second century.............................. 2,000,000
Close of third century............................... 5,000,000
Close of fourth century.............................. 10,000,000
Close of fifth century............................... 15,000,000
Close of sixth century............................... 20,000,000
Close of seventh century............................. 25,000,000
Close of eighth century.............................. 30,000,000
Close of ninth century............................... 40,000,000
Close of tenth century............................... 50,000,000
Close of eleventh century............................ 70,000,000
Close of twelfth century............................. 80,000,000
Close of thirteenth century.......................... 75,000,000
Close of fourteenth century.......................... 80,000,000
Close of fifteenth century...........................100,000,000
Close of sixteenth century...........................125,000,000
Close of seventeenth century.........................155,000,000
Close of eighteenth century..........................200,000,000
Present time...400,000,000

—Presbyterian Year Book.

IS THE IDEAL OF CHRISTIANITY FEMININE?

Mr. Lecky, the English historian, declares in one of his works that the ideal of Paganism was essentially masculine, while the ideal introduced by Jesus and embodied in Christianity was essentially feminine. Paganism, he says, laid stress upon strength, courage and self assertion and these are essentially masculine characteristics —Jesus, on the other hand, in the ideal outlined, emphasized gentleness, humility and love, characteristics, says Mr. Lecky, essentially feminine. This, he says, accounts for the position and influence of women in the early church. Now, if Mr. Lecky is right, we have the solution of one of the problems of modern Christianity, the problem of interesting the men. If the ideal of Christianity is a feminine ideal, we can understand why there are more women than men in our churches and why men of strength, force and masculine energy are not attracted to it. Is the statement true? A thousand times —no. Brilliant historian though he is, Mr. Lecky has missed the truth here. We cannot dispute that gentleness, humility and love are essentially feminine characteristics, nor question that Jesus emphasized them. But why did He emphasize them? Because Paganism never recognized them at all. Love, gentleness and humility were unknown to the Pagan ideal. It was a harsh, cruel and un-sympathetic ideal and Jesus recognized its weakness and limitations. Hence, He emphasized those virtues that Paganism had neglected. But side by side with them He put the virtues of Paganism, the masculine virtues of strength, courage and self assertion.

Is it not true? We look at Jesus Himself, the most perfect embodiment of His own ideals that the world has ever seen and we find gentleness, humility and love very strongly developed and clearly shown. But do we not also see the great masculine characteristics of strength, courage and self assertion? Certainly we see the last. He was the meek and humble Jesus, but He was also the One who said, "I am the light of the world;" "I am the Way, the Truth and the Life." "Behold a greater than Solomon is here." Surely the conscious virtue of the old Pagan philosophers finds its parallel in the man who said, "Which of you convinceth me of sin?" "I do always those things that please Him."

And in what life are courage and strength more beautifully revealed than in the life of the One who without human friend to understand or sympathize, bore in His own great heart the burdens of human sin and went of His own accord to the suffering of the cross?

Jesus was the incarnation of the masculine virtues. And if He lived them, He also emphasized them in His teaching. Did He not call upon men to count the cost, and insist that fellowship with Himself meant the cross? It was always to the heroic that He appealed. He did not ask men to follow Him to please their relatives or to be happy—He called them to help Him save a world. And that demanded courage, strength and assertiveness.

Christianity today still emphasizes humility, gentleness and love, but it also lays the finger of peculiar emphasis upon strength, courage and self assertion, virtues that are essentially masculine.

MOUSTACHES AS A SIGN OF CHRISTIANITY

Few people are aware of the origin of the custom of growing moustaches; but hundreds of years ago this adornment of the face was a sign that the owner was a Christian. The custom first originated in Spain, when the Moors were in possession of that country, prior to their being driven out by the Christians. The Moors were Mohammedans, and it was very difficult to tell the difference between a Mohammedan and a Christian.

The Christians, wishing to let their "light shine before men," decided to let the hair grow upon the upper lip and on the chin in the form of what is known as the imperial, thus producing the rough form of a cross. In this way the Christians were able to recognize one another at all times, and flock together when in trouble to make a combined defense.

CHRISTIAN RESPONSIBILITY FOR THE GENERAL IN-
TEGRITY

The psalmist once said, "in his haste," "All men are liars." Some one has responded, "He might have said it at his leisure." Good old-fashioned integrity! Has it gone out? George Washington "could not tell a lie." It would be hard to think of Abraham Lincoln as deliberately lying, or of General Grant treating a promise lightly, or William McKinley going back on his word, or Theodore Roosevelt juggling with a compact. Keeping one's word, accurate statement of fact, stanch keeping faith with your promise, professing only the genuine, sedulously showing only what really is in you, not what ought to be, might be or is expected of you—the real in experience, purpose, aspiration—these things make character. O! for real, not sham, things, verities, not show! All that glitters like true gold, let it be true gold. Let the polishes be of solid oak, not veneer. Character, not clanging cymbals; quality, not bluffs. Alack, the unreality of life! Business that is not honest, society that is not sincere, politics that are tricky, diplomacy that is craft, civilization that is full of sham, philanthropy that is self-seeking, religion that is hollow and irreligion that is transparent humbug!

I sit often wondering how much our failure of profound sincerity in religious expression and experience may have to do with general insincerity. Here, if anywhere, we ought to exhibit solid, reliable verity and nothing else. These Christian souls ought to be of the best human fiber. In their religion they are supposed to be dealing at first hand with the most searching powers of the universe, with the all-seeing One. From Him no most inner truth is veiled. By His awful intelligence every sham is shot through and through with instant and explosive indignation as insult to His majesty. Mere seeming is of no avail, pretense has no ghost of a chance and false claims no shadow of a show.

In these things pretenses before men are to be exploded, masks torn off, veils rent from top to bottom. We are promised that the secrets of the heart are to be revealed, the covered laid open, the secret like a herald's cry, and the hidden stand out like a snap-shot photograph. The substantial religious experience ought, therefore, to be the most solid and veritable of all things. Repentance, faith, the divine righting of the heart from the center out, the new creation in righteousness and true holiness, and the subsequent companionship with Christ—these things must be genuine or the most accursed of falsehoods. These inward experiences are confessed and avowed in church membership under the most solemn of conceivable circumstances, ratified by the sacred right of baptism and the yet more solemn use of the broken body and the blood of our Great Redeemer as a sacramental oath and seal. Besides, the genuineness of these experiences is the ground, and the only ground, of the most precious hopes for the eternal life of the soul itself. Every conceivable motive, therefore, exists why this experience, in every phase of it, should be profoundly genuine. Every ungenuine thing in it is sacrilege—fruitless sacrilege.

Now this genuine type of Christian life emphasizing itself in all the homes, societies, businesses, pleasures—in all the walks of life, civic and religious—would make mightily for like lives in whose communities, providing for them their practical standard— their working type. With such living standards, fairly enacted, all life and performance would compare or contrast itself and be shamed by contrast. All standards of morals are inevitably set by the highest in sight. The very best that can be done for man is to set him the loftiest ethical ideal realized in life. Toughest demoralization is such a standard bedragged to depraved practice.

Here, then, we have in the face of all communities these pure and lofty standards of the Christian faith. What must be the effect on the general integrity, if those who commit themselves to such standards and put themselves on their regimen, under these mightiest forces that can make for righteousness, are seen to be in sad contrast with all that they ought to have attained? If men see them obviously careless of loyalty to their own ideals and laws of holy living, reckless of their covenants and sacred pledges, negligent of privilege and obligation alike, must not the conscience of all be dulled? If these transcendent ideals and most strenuous motives to a solid integrity, with supernatural powers to inspire and uplift them, with many elaborate and costly institutions to concentrate and conserve their energy and zeal, with the most magnificent hopes to stir their enthusiasm and allure their imagination, and with the solemn covenants with God and man, sealed with so awe-inspiring sacramental ceremonial—I say, if with all these things making for absolute genuineness in the Christian character and experience, these Christians are but as other men, we have no right to expect a high tone of integrity in the great world outside the experience of such special redeeming powers. Such well-noted inconsistencies must perforce pull down general ethical standards and impulses and speed the general conscience to degeneracy. Demoralizations are epidemic, contagious. If the Christian be no more honest, public-spirited, clean in politics, pure in social and domestic life, no more gentle, generous, charitable and lovely, no truer to his word nor more stanch to his pledge nor strenuous to his compacts than another, he lets down the whole tone of the public life.

Come now to the peculiar and intimate things of the Christian covenant itself. The Christian walks in the midst of a very observant world. It knows well his pledges to his great Master and to his fellows, knows his vast beliefs and the express compacts of Eternal Life. It knows exactly what he has promised to Christ and His church, as to public worship and the means of grace—attendance upon and support of them. He notes how consistently or faithlessly he walks; whether he takes these faiths and pledges seriously or not. The world knows whether he is honest or not. This world is relatively trifling and transient. Real treasures are in heaven. Does the Christian really believe that? The world knows. The care and love and power of God make all things work together for good to him. Is he, then, in unbroken peace, unworried in the midst of the "accidents' 'of life? Men know. He, this son and heir of God, does he get bitter in adversity, rebellious in affliction, despondent and forlorn in defeat and present ill, when all the glories of the universe are just ahead? The chief concern for himself and his children and his fellows is the soul's immortal welfare. Men know whether he really holds to that! The gospel is the glory and hope of mankind; its institutions and ordinances are the way of the world's redemption. The world sees whether his zeal and enthusiasm and glad sacrifice bear out that faith. The supreme delight, good and joy in life are in the fellowship, love and service of Jesus. Are they? The world notes keenly the irregular, perfunctory, unexpected routine of a listless formalism. The "High Calling of the Christian," his "Great Commission," everybody knows that—the salvation of men, the glory of the Christ, the establishment of His kingdom in our souls. Is that the actual fact of Christian business? The whole world sees.

Now the effect of all this on the public mind and heart? The impression must be of wide, deep, general insincerity, unreality, even in these most sacred realms of Christian faith and experience. The reaction must be toward breaking down the general moral integrity—toward hollowness and insincerity in all life. When the hearts of Christ's professed followers have gone untrustworthy and their lives deny their sublime faiths, the very foundations of characters are upturned. We may well expect frauds, vices, hypocrisies and crimes to corrupt all grades of personal, domestic, social and civic life.

We are 28,000,000 of church members in this country, and of the richest, best cultivated and most influential classes, quite sufficient to leaven the whole lump of our time with our principles. And we do it! Alas, not for the best! Brooding on these things and lamenting, one must say, "Judgment must begin at the House of God!" (1) No man may say, "I dedicate myself, body, soul and estate to Christ" unless he does it. Who says that and does not do it lies to the Holy Ghost—makes himself the world's supreme sham, is depraved by it, and the world knows it. (2) None must say, "I love the Lord Jesus supremely," unless he does that. He must make every testimony of his love and loyalty true to the fact of his spiritual experience. He must make no claim to joy, peace and blessedness in Christ, which, indeed, he ought to have, but does not possess, which he hopes to have, but has not found, which somebody else claims, and so he may profess without starting cavil. (3) I often shudder when I hear a crowd singing lustily, "I will go where You want me to go," and think of the jungles of Africa, where the Master wants Christian feet, and guess whether these reckless singers would go there! Or "I will say what You want me to say," and think of this, that and other in their circles who need, for very life, a Christian word, and have not heard it. Or "I will do what You want me to do," and think of the thronging opportunities they let slip. Or, "I will be what You want me to be," and ponder the sweet, strong and lovely beauties of holiness into which He would fain have transfigured these vocalists. (4) None may take these sacred vows of the Christian church and endeavor without solemn care and profound purpose to fulfill them to the letter and in the spirit.

Friends, our prevailing sin is to take covenants lightly and break them recklessly. We enter sacred vows, under most awful seals of the Sacraments, and then live as if they were empty of real meaning, vacant of binding force. We hold immense faiths as if they were vagaries. We contradict our professions by a thousand inconsistencies. We walk 18,000,000 of evangelical church members, servants and exemplars of Jesus, exponents of the highest known type of faith and morals, beside keen-eyed fellows, who know our professions, and know us! They mark well the contrasts, settle their convictions as to moral integrity, and their standards will not be loftier than our own.

How far, then, are we, of the Christ's part, answerable for the hollowness, sham, pretense and broken integrity of our time? Who shall dare to judge, lest he be himself condemned? But this may at least be said: The larger, outer world will come to no standing of solid, all-around integrity of character, of grounded and solid virtue before God and man, until the church of Christ shall have demonstrated for itself the mastery of its mighty faiths upon its character, the command of its standards upon its conduct, and shall have come actually to control its life in accord with its holy pledges and covenants with God and man. Christian integrity must redeem the full sweep of its sacramental vows. If souls regenerate, under the sanctifying power of the Spirit of God, in all the play of Christian grace, cannot keep their integrity unchallenged, can we wonder at the deadly collapses that imperil and bedevil the outer world? "Ye are the light of the world!" "If the light that is in you be darkness," what then? "Ye are the salt of the earth!" "If the salt has lost its savor," what then? How far, then, are we—the 28,000,000 of professed followers of Christ—we the 18,000,000 members of the evangelical churches of this Republic, answerable for the low estate of morals and the frailty of the integrity of our times?—Christian Work.

DESCRIPTION OF A CHRISTIAN GENTLEMAN

1 Corinthians 13.

Over the thirteenth chapter of First Corinthians might be written the heading: "Description of a Christian gentleman." True politeness is only kindness of heart made manifest in every action. It cannot be secured by reading books of etiquette. It cannot be learned of a dancing master. It does not consist in bowing gracefully to a friend on the street, or in bandying compliments with a belle at an evening party. It can be learned only by finding the way in which true kindness of heart would lead one to act in one's intercourse with others. Every rule of true etiquette is based upon the Golden Rule, and all codes of behavior that have not directly or indirectly some such basis are not worth a rush. "The Spirit of Christ," says a high authority, "does really what high breeding does outwardly." A high-bred man never forgets himself, controls his temper, does nothing in excess, is unbane and dignified, and that even to persons whom he is anathematizing in his heart and wishing far away. But a Christian is what the world seems to be. Love gives him a delicate tact which does not offend because it is full of sympathy. It discerns far off what would hurt fastidious sensibilities, feels with others, and is ever on the watch to anticipate their thoughts.

And hence the only true, deep politeness, that which lies not on the surface, but goes deep down into the character, comes from Christian love. Here is a portion of the description of this Christian gentleman: Love suffereth long, and is kind; love envieth not; love vaunteth not itself, is not puffed up, doth not behave itself unseemly, seeketh not her own, is not easily provoked, thinketh no evil; rejoiceth not in iniquity, but rejoiceth in the truth; beareth all things, believeth all things, hopeth all things, endureth all things!

CHRISTIANITY AND MODERN SOCIALISM

BY THE REV. DR. J. G. BACCHUS

"And all that believed were together, and had all things common; and sold their possessions and goods, and parted them to all men, as every man had need."—Acts 2:44, 45.

In portions of the second and fourth chapters of his graphic book of the Acts of the Apostles, St. Luke gives us a glimpse of the religious and social life of the church at Jerusalem. Its religious life, as portrayed by him, found expression in a steadfast oneness of faith in the risen Lord as the present and abiding head of the church, in an unbroken Christian fellowship characterized by oneness of mind and heart, in a weekly observance of the Lord's Supper, and assemblages for prayer, from day to day, in the temple and from house to house.

A very sweet, simple, contented, idyllic life on its religious side is thus presented—a life to which many souls that "were being saved" were daily added. After giving us this picture of the religious life of the church at Jerusalem, St. Luke proceeds to depict a profoundly interesting feature of its social life. "And all that believed," he says, "were together and had all things common; and sold their possessions and goods, and parted them to all men, as every man had need." Neither said any of them that aught of the things which he possessed was his own, but they had all things common, neither was there any that lacked, for as many as were possessors of lands or houses sold them and brought the prices of the things that were sold, and laid them down at the apostle's feet; and distribution was made unto every man according as he had need. A study of this social-economic feature of the church's life in that early time is well worth while in view of the fact that "here all our Socialists," as the author of "Epochs in Church History" remarks, "from the earlier Cenobite to the later St. Simon, have sought the exact pattern of their systems."

Further, it is well to know exactly what this social-economic phase of the church's life was and how it worked, in view of the claim made by a large and growing group of people that Christianity and modern Socialism are essentially one in aim, and that the aim of each is to establish the social and economic equality of all men. The group of people who hold to this view stoutly maintain that the community of goods which obtained in the social life of the early church strongly makes for the theory that Christianity and modern Socialism are substantially one in setting up a social program which embraces the social and economic equality of all men. In order to see what grounds, if any, exist for such a claim, we must try to get a clear notion as to what modern Socialism really is. Proudhon defined Socialism as "an aspiration toward the improvement of society," and a large number of persons, as Kidd says, regard it as an aspiration toward the improvement of society by society. Manifestly these are not true definitions of modern Socialism, for there may be aspirations toward the improvement of society by individuals who are in no true sense Socialists, and there may be endeavor to improve society by society without adopting the methods of Socialism. The philanthropist may aspire to improve society without adopting the methods of modern Socialism. The city and the state may aspire to improve society by maintaining hospitals, common schools, retreats for the needy, a water supply, lighting plants, and even public transit without availing themselves of the methods of modern Socialism. This is seen to be true when we get at the true differential of Socialism. John Stuart Mill says: "What is characteristic of Socialism in the joint ownership by all the members of the community of the instruments and means of production; which carries with it the consequence that the division of the produce among the body of owners must be a public act performed according to rules laid down by the community." Here we have the differential of Socialism. It is public ownership of the instruments and means of production and a division of the produce, which flows out of their communal use, among all the industries of the community by the community according to the rules laid down by the community. In other words. it is the abolishment of private ownership of the means and instruments of production, or, as we may say, the doing away with private ownership of property.

The purpose in view of this substitution of public for private ownership of property is to do away, as Kidd well says: "With that personal struggle for existence which has been waged, not only from the beginning of society, but, in one form or another, from the beginning of life." The gist then of modern Socialism is the substitution of public for private ownership of both the raw material and the instruments of production, and this substitution is to be made for the purpose of suspending that personal rivalry and competitive struggle of life which now prevail.

It claims that the present competitive struggle of life is pitiless and drives, sooner or later, to the wall the weak, and selects as its favorites only the gifted and strong. The only thing to do is to suspend its baleful working by the introduction of the principle of common ownership of everything in place of the principle of individual ownership of everything. Here, as I understand it, is the marrow of today's Socialism. That I am not mistaken as to the pith of Socialism appears from Mr. Bellamy's definition of it as "a community in which even children are to become entitled to an equal share of the national wealth in virtue of being born." If such, then, be the significance of modern Socialism, we can readily see that much endeavor by the individual and society for the improvement of society, which is described as socialistic, is not really so in the sense in which modern Socialism employs the word. There are those, both at home and abroad, who advocate co-operative associations, both productive and distributive, where all might work together as brothers. There are guilds and settlement clubs working for the betterment of the hand-laboring class in respect of securing for them better dwellings, more playgrounds, shorter hours of labor, and a juster wage. There are thousands of benevolent institutions throughout our land which work for the uplift of the less favored in the world of human life. All these are doing a noble social service, but they are not socialistic in the true sense of that word—for that word denotes the advocacy of the tenets and methods of modern Socialism, the gist of which, as we have seen, is common ownership of all the instruments and means of production and a common sharing of the produce of their communal use.

Having got our definition of modern Socialism we must go on to ask if Christianity, as voiced by the church of Jerusalem, favored and employed a social and economic program substantially identical with that of modern Socialism? This is no mere academic question, for the Socialists of today are loud in insisting that our Lord was a Socialist, and that the Christian church in its earliest days was a socialistic organization, and as proof of this assertion they point to the community of goods that obtained in the church at Jerusalem. It is then no mere academic question we are considering, for there are today nearly 9,000,000 Socialist voters throughout the world. In our own country the gain by this party during the past four years is estimated as sevenfold, and it has been pointed out that an increase during the next eight years in the same ratio would enable the Socialists to elect a president of the United States.

Let us try to find out what that community of goods was, how it worked, how long it lasted, and what lessons are to be drawn from it.

There is little room to doubt that this social-economic feature of the life of the church at Jerusalem was a downright bit of communism, for as many as were possessors of lands and houses, so runs the narrative, sold them and brought the prices of the things that were sold and laid them down at the apostles' feet, and distribution was made unto every man according as he had need.

It was not simply a common fund provided by the beneficent, well-to-do, to meet the wants of the many poor among the 3,000 converts to the Christian faith. It was without doubt a surrender of the right of private ownership and the turning into a community goods the prices of their lands and houses. It cannot be explained away by saying that it was a community of use and not a community of goods. The narrative unmistakably indicates a social-economic condition in which all had all things in common. It is important, however, to observe that this social-economic phase of the church's life was not enforced on all the members of the Jerusalem church by rule. It was commended as the best way of ministering to the common welfare, but it was at the same time voluntary, not compulsory. Converts might or might not enter into it. This is shown in the case of Ananias and Sapphira. The reprobation meted out to them by Peter found its justification not in their refusal to surrender the right of private ownership of property, but in the fact that they lied, in that they professed to put all the price of their land into the common stock, while in fact they withheld from it a part. It was not their refusal to embrace the communistic idea which called down dire and condign punishment upon their heads, for the apostle tells them that the bit of land was theirs, to do as they liked with it—either to put its price into the community of goods or not; but, professing to put all the price into the common stock while keeping part of it back, they were lying, trifling with conscience, mocking the church and sinning against the Holy Spirit of God. The community of goods was voluntary, not compulsory. It is evident there were Christians at Jerusalem who did not take to this scheme of a community of goods at all. At any rate, it is pretty clear that they still held title to property after this communistic plan had been set on foot. It seems reasonably certain that the mother of John and Mark owned and occupied a house in Jerusalem subsequent to the inauguration of the social-economic feature we are considering. So we make the point that the community of goods was an act of free will, not enforced by rule; an understood custom, perhaps, but it was within the power of any individual not to comply with it.

It ought to be noted again that this community of goods is only found in the church at Jerusalem. No trace of it is discoverable anywhere else throughout the early Christian church. In proof of this we find St. Paul, in writing to Timothy, mentioning both the rich and poor. If this community of goods had been commensurate with the whole church St. Paul's exhortation to the rich that they be not high minded, nor trust in uncertain riches, but in the living God, that they do good, that they be rich in good works, ready to distribute, would be quite unintelligible. There would have been neither rich nor poor where distribution was made to every man according to his need.

Or take again St. Paul's directions to the church at Corinth. "Now, concerning the collection for the saints," he says, "as I have given order to the churches of Galatia, even so do ye. Upon the first day of the week let every one of you lay by him in store, as God hath prospered him, that there be no gatherings when I come." What relevancy would there be in the apostle's urging a collection for the poor saints if this community of goods prevailed throughout the whole church. There would be on that supposition no poor, no rich, but every man would have his several needs met. St. James, too, exhorts his brother Christian to hold not the faith of our Lord Jesus Christ with respect of persons. The man bejeweled and clad in goodly apparel must not be treated better than the poor man in coarse raiment. Now our point is that if this **community of goods prevailed throughout the entire church this** exhortation would have been quite superfluous, for its members would have lived out of a common stock, which would have furnished each with jewels and goodly apparel, or, what is more likely, covered them all with the vilest kind of clothing. It would not be difficult to multiply proofs that this community of goods did not exist outside of the Jerusalem church, that no trace of it is to be found elsewhere and that the church at large had no thought of adopting it.

We remark further that this social-economic feature of the church at Jerusalem did not continue for long in the Holy City, and for the reason that it did not work well. We read in the Acts of the Apostles: "And in those days when the number of the disciples was multiplied there arose a murmuring of the Grecian-Greek-Jewish Christian against Hebrew-Christian because their widows were neglected in the daily ministration, i. e., in the daily distribution of the necessaries of life. Complaint and dissatisfaction, observe, even among those who had agreed to surrender individual ownership of property to live out of a community of goods! Seven deacons were appointed to take oversight of this business, to right the wrongs of the widows, to see that they received their due share of the community of goods. How well or ill they succeeded in this matter we are not informed, but one can fancy, if impecunious human nature was as cross-grained in that early time as it is in a modern city parish, those poor deacons must have found their hands full of trouble! And we may well ask just here if the surrender of private ownership of property is to bring in a millennial period of peace, plenty and happiness, why did it not in this church at Jerusalem? Instead of economic content there was unrest and attrition from the very start. The scheme did not work well. Nor should it pass unnoticed that of all the Christian churches, in that early day, the Jerusalem church seems to have been the poorest. It lived in a state of chronic poverty. St. Paul devoted a good deal of his precious time to begging for the "poor saints" at Jerusalem. Perhaps this after all was the much disputed "thorn in the flesh" of which we hear so much in the apostle's life. "Now I go," he says, "unto Jerusalem to minister unto the saints, for it hath pleased them of Macedonia and Achaia to make a contribution for the poor saints which are at Jerusalem."

That is, he is going to the Holy City with money given by the churches in Greece to relieve the wants of this ever needy church at Jerusalem. The community of goods seems not to have abolished the poverty there after all. To the Corinthians the apostle writes, "And when I come, whomsoever ye shall approve by your letters, them will I send to bring your liberality unto Jerusalem." Another contribution for the poor saints at Jerusalem! The truth is the community of goods in the Jerusalem church neither wrought satisfactorily, nor in any sense adequately met the wants of its members and for this reason soon ceased to be.

That it was an honest, loving, self-denying effort to meet an economic exigency by a temporary surrender of the right of private ownership of property and a merging of that property into one common stock, in order to remove the fiscal inequalities of the life of the Jerusalem church, there can be no doubt. Its motive was pure, lofty and aflame with Christian fervor, but its practical working was attended by unrest and discontent, persistent and ineradicable poverty and issued at last, in a discontinuance of the whole scheme.

What then are the lessons to be gathered from our study of this social-economic feature of the church at Jerusalem?

Is one of these lessons that our Lord was a Socialist, and that His church in its best days committed itself to Socialism? No, it teaches no such lesson. If it teaches anything it is that this bit of fleeting communism was an outright, downright failure, and that the Christian church so profited by the lesson of its failure that she never tried it again. And as to the notion that our Lord was a Socialist it ought to be said that if there is anything perfectly clear in respect of His social teachings, it is that He never in anywise committed Himself to any social program whatsoever. With economical conditions and contemporary circumstances, as Harnack says, He did not interfere; had He become entangled in them; had He given laws which were ever so salutary for Palestine, what would have been gained by it? They would have served the needs of a day and tomorrow would have been a burden and a source of confusion. And yet while he was no Socialist, no teacher ever proclaimed such an energetic social message and so strongly identified Himself with that message. His message was, "Love thy neighbor as thyself,' 'and that message really taken into the heart sheds a light upon all the concrete relations of life, upon the world of hunger, poverty and misery. Our Lord proclaimed the solidarity and brotherhood of all men, but laws or ordinances or injunctions bidding us forcibly alter the conditions of the age in which we may happen to be living are not to be found in His gospel.

What positive lesson, then, may we gather from our study of the temporary community of goods in the church at Jerusalem? Is it not this—that the spirit of subordinating private interest to the common happiness, which found exaggerated and unwholesome expression in an unworkable communism in the Jerusalem church, that this spirit, I say, is still a true spirit and is needed to temper the harsher features of the competitive struggle of our modern life? Its spirit of love and brotherhood should work more and more zealously to secure and preserve free and fair competition between men in their common struggle for livelihood. Such a spirit makes for fair play and energizes to remove all artificial and unjust restriction in the path of the full right of every man to complete ownership of himself. But to assert that this spirit can only realize itself by adopting the tenets and methods of modern Socialism is entirely gratuitous. The spirit of Christ may utter itself in manifold ways and work in and through the most diverse social methods, and its one superlative aim is, as a great thinker puts it, "to transform the Socialism which rests on the basis of conflicting interests into the Socialism which rests on the consciousness of a spiritual unity."—Brooklyn Daily Eagle.

PALM TREE CHRISTIANS

"The righteous shall flourish like the palm tree."—Psalm 92:12.

When the Psalmist uses the palm tree to put forth the life of the righteous, he uses a very strong, impressive and instructive illustration. There are some features of the Christian life that would be aptly portrayed by any living tree, which firmly planted in the soil from which its roots take the nourishment that gives to the tree life, and growth, and vigor to withstand the fierce elements that may at times assail it, lifts its head up towards the heavens, and stretches out its limbs, offering shelter to all who may seek beneath them protection from the heat of day or the damp of the night.

Any tree thus growing very fittingly illustrates the Christian, united to Christ, and drawing from Him that spiritual nourishment that shall fit him to withstand all bitter opposition that may be arrayed against him by the world, the flesh and the devil, and in the midst of it all to grow.

But while any tree may be used to represent the general characteristics of the Christian, the palm tree possesses some special features which are adapted to strongly emphasize particular traits in the Christian life.

Some of the special features of the palm tree are these:

It grows in pure soil. It abhors the dunghill. It does not flourish in filthy soil. The Christian cannot grow if fed only with that which is untrue and wicked, or if fed only with the husks that the swine eat.

The palm tree is tall and graceful, lifting its head high above its surroundings; and its limbs all look upward, too. Heavy weights cannot prevent this upward growth, nor turn them from their straight course. The heavier the burden the higher will be the upward advance.

In this upward tendency, in a straight course, how the palm tree illustrates the true life of the Christian, which should ever be upward, turned aside by nothing, and by the burdens and trials and cares of life, only made to grow the faster, the stronger, the higher, getting constantly nearer and nearer to the great sun of righteousness who is the source of all his growth.

The palm tree when young is very tender and weak. When planted they are placed in groups, and as they grow up together, they are mutual supports to each other; thus illustrating how Christians, who in their early Christian experiences may be weak and tender, may by joining together become mutual helps.

The palm tree is always green, showing a constant life and vigor; bears a very pleasant and delicious fruit.

So the Christian life should bear a constant freshness and vigor, and one that produces abundant and delicious fruit.

Then in the palm tree the Psalmist gives to us a very beautiful and impressive picture of what the true Christian life should be. Such are the Christians that shall flourish. Those who have their roots deep in the rich soil of divine truth from which they are drawing nourishing food. Trusting in Jesus Christ as their Savior, and drawing their strength and vigor from Him, they stand beautifully conspicuous for their spiritual height, uprightness, freshness, and abundant fruitfulness.

OWNERSHIP WITHOUT POSSESSION

"What man of you having an hundred sheep, if you lose one of them?" A man can own what he does not possess, as he can possess what he does not own. Mr. II. M. Moore came into the noon meeting at Tremont Temple with a good hat and overcoat and he put them down, thinking that all Boston was honest. He still owns that overcoat, but another fellow possesses and wears it. There has been no breaking of the right of ownership. He owns it, but the thief has it. So God owns us, but the devil may possess us. God owns, but we may be lost. "What man of you having an hundred sheep, if he lose one of them?"

CHRIST'S IDEA OF THE CHRISTIAN LIFE

BY THE REV. DR. NEWELL DWIGHT HILLIS

(By permission of The Brooklyn Daily Eagle.)

"Take up thy cross and follow Me."—Matthew 16:24.

A recent mail brought a letter from a young collegian. He has been reading books about the church, creeds and the Christian life. Unfortunately, the more he reads, the more confused he becomes. His intellectual difficulties are many and grave. He is troubled about the Bible. Is it a book of exact science and accurate history? If not, how can it be trustworthy in morals? He is troubled about the churches. They are many, but one, he thinks, must be the true church. He has read a book on theology, and he asks which creed is correct? All the astronomers say one thing, that the earth goes round the sun. Why do the theologians say many things and oppugnant? For him, the clouds hang low, life is shadowed because the sun is hidden. He walks forward in the solemnity of a great darkness. He asks if I can light for him a torch by which he may find his way through the City of Dreadful Night. And because this youth represents a multitude and his dark mood often represents itself in our questioning moods, I am going to ask you to think about Christ's idea of the Christian life, with its simplicity, as opposed to the complex notions of the scholastics.

Let us begin our reflections with the thought that the court of final appeal is Jesus Christ Himself. Not the theologian, not the scholastic, but Christ has the right to say what makes the man a Christian. Does a man ask what is gravitation? Isaac Newton has earned the right to answer. Does a man ask what is the nature of the X-ray? Let Professor Roentgen reply. Does some one question the nature and uses of this new electric mechanism that makes the deaf hear? The man who had the genius to invent it earned the right to give the answer. Plainly, we do Jesus Christ a great injustice when we go to creeds and catechisms for statements how to become a Christian. The scholastic may have the best intentions, but they have been berubbished, begrimed, and obscured the simplicity of Christ. Indeed, my young friend's state of mind reminds me of the condition of the Venetian church in 1840. The government sent a minister to consider the condition of the noble building. Standing upon the threshold, he found the church in a sad state of disrepair. The roof had been neglected, and the rain was slowly sinking through the frescoes of Tintoretto. The vast nave was damp, full of decay, and therefore deserted. The windows were covered with cobwebs, dust and smoke that had accumulated through a score of years. Slowly the work of renovation proceeded. But the faraway end of the church was an enigma, whitewashed as it was with a whiteness that had become black during two centuries of neglect. Strangely enough, also, there was no window in the end. Believing, however, that there was some beauty to be discovered, the artist set his workmen to the task of removing the whitewash, when lo! they uncovered a row of frescoes portraying the founders of the faith, from Abraham and Isaac to Moses. Cleansing another section, higher up, they uncovered a series of kings, judges and patriots—noble enough to have been painted by an archangel standing off and drawing free hand. Above came the prophets and poets; higher still, the apostles. Then at the point where the roof began to narrow they found a group of the disciples who were closest to Jesus. There, too, they found that two small windows had been stoned up, in deference to the eyes of some reader who had been forgotten for two hundred years. When the plaster was removed, lo, two tiny, exquisite rose windows. Then it was that the artist realized that between them was room for a portrait that should be the climax of the ascending frescoer. So agitated was the discoverer that he could not trust his hands to remove the thick grime, so assistants were called in, when, lo, they uncovered the face of the Master! For the wall was built for one vast canvas, and every hero and judge and king and prophet and poet and apostle converged toward the central Master, Whose majesty and beauty shed a soft radiance upon all the scene. That central figure made all the other figures plain, and fully revealed their meaning. And so the mind of many a youth has been clouded and disturbed by the dust of controversy, the grime of old books and perished systems. Christ is a sun whose beams of light are self-explanatory. His light is its own message and needs no explanation.

If you ask me, then, how to become a Christian, I answer, Let us go back to Christ. One day Jesus met several young men and bade them rise up and follow Him, and they became Christians. John, the beloved disciple, was one of that glorious company. But John, who stood nearest to his Master, had none of the troubles about the Bible, or the church, or the creeds. John was not a Christian because he believed in the Bible, for the New Testament, with its books about Christ, had not been written. John was not a Christian because he had joined a certain church, for Jesus Christ never organized a church. John was not a Christian because he believed a certain creed, for even the "Apostles' Creed" was not written until a century after Christ's death. What made John a Christian, therefore? He was a Christian because he was trying to do Christ's work in Christ's way. John had seen Christ's manner of life, its purity, its self-sacrifice, its magnanimity, His devotion to duty; he wanted to imitate that life. John had heard the blessings that Christ called down upon the peacemaker, the meek, the poor in spirit and those who hunger and thirst for righteousness; John wanted to do what Christ said. Just as the name of Lincoln stands for patriotism, and John Wilkes Booth for treason, so the name of Judas stood for wrongdoing and the name of Jesus suggested for John the ideal Christian. To be Christian was to be Christlike. All of which simplifies religion. Sabaher calls religion "the life of God in the soul of man." With his definition in mind, we discern that life is one thing and the description of life another thing. Put life in the physical body and you have a man. Describe that life and you have a physiology. Put the life into the soul of man and you have religion. Describe that life and you have a theology. The life in the man needs certain forms of exercise to promote health and growth. One exercises by running, and one by walking; and the life of God in the soul of man needs exercise, and one obtains it by written prayers, and one by extempore prayers, and another by secret thoughts and hidden vows. The physiologist is alive when he writes his book. But though he is in perfect health physically, he may make many mistakes in his written physiology. Moses had the life of God in his soul, but he may have made mistakes in his wars, in his ideas of slavery, in his science. You may be a Christian, because you have Christ's life in your soul, and are doing Christ's work in Christ's way. But you will do well to read this book, the Bible, that contains the experiences of other men, who have experienced the life of God in the soul of man. You may try to nurture this inner life, some of you by being baptized with much water, some of you with little water, some of you like the Quakers with no water, but the form and value of the ordinance depends upon the temperament of the Christian. One man may describe his religious experience in terms of John Calvin, and another in terms of Arminius, and still another in terms of radual growth, like Professor Drummond. But this divergency and variety need work no mental disturbance. There are many books on mental philosophy, but the intellect and the memory and the judgment are the same in all the writers. Away, therefore, with all doubts, troubles based upon conflicting views as to Bible, church or creed. To be a Christian is to have the life of God in the soul of man, and to do Christ's work in Christ's way. Christ's idea of the Christian is one who has followed his Master, in thought, and prayer and life. The simplicity of the gospel is in two words of Christ, "Follow Me."

From all this, therefore, it follows that the church is a school and the Christian a scholar. The church is not an assembly of perfect people, but of those who want to be perfect. The disciple is the learner. Slowly the scholar goes toward full wisdom, moving step by step. With earnest purpose he casts off all amusements that would hinder his work as student. But years lie between the day when the boy enters college and the time when he graduates. I know many good men, who stand hesitant and undecided before the church. They are conscious of imperfection in daily life, and not until they have fulfilled their highest ideals are they willing to unite with the church. But no student declines to enter the academy until he is conscious of full wisdom. Suppose a youth should ask for entrance to some college like Yale. "What have you done in the way of preparation?" "Well," answers the boy, "I read Latin at sight. I think, also, in Greek. French and German are like my native tongue. I have passed one hundred in all the mental and political sciences." Do you think the faculty would admit so ripe a scholar? Would not the inevitable answer be, "This is no place for you?" Colleges are founded, not for perfect students, but for ignorant boys who want to become students. And the church is for imperfect people, conscious of selfishness, greed, pride, and sometimes envy and hate, and all those sins of the upper faculties that work like dry rot in the soul. Therefore, with full confidence, I urge every youth who stands for the culture of his intellect to take his stand with those forces that strengthen the church, as the school of Christ for the training of the affections, the conscience, faith and hope and love. Begin now your career in Christ's school.

Consider also that no man increases his obligations by joining a church, and swearing fidelity to Christ, and no man evades any responsibility by refusing the Christian life. Duty is embedded in the nature of things. The obligation to right living does not depend upon our recognition thereof. Steam will scald you, even if you do say, "I never promised to obey the law of steam." The fire burns, the water drowns, the rock crushes, gluttony weakens, drunkenness wastes, untruth dishonors, selfishness corrodes. Why? Because it is their nature to do so. Recently, a friend told me that he felt that he was freer outside of the church, and escaped certain obligations that might fetter his happiness. Here is a boy who plays truant, and will not go to school, and refuses books. At eighteen he secures a position, and writes his first letter. An hour later his employer calls him up and exclaims, "Why, you misspelled this word very." And the youth makes answer, "Well, I know it ought to have two rs, but I am always forgetting and using only one. Still, I never promised to obey the law of spelling. I never joined a school. I want liberty to spell just as I please. I never joined a class in arithmetic. I never pledged myself to say that eight times eight are sixty-four." Do you think any youth escapes the obligation to obey the laws of rhetoric and the law of the multiplication table by refusing to join a college? The Ten Commandments are based on the nature of things. The obligation to the Christian life began when you were placed in the cradle by your parents. You do not add one duty to your life by recognizing these pre-existing obligations. You do not escape one duty by declining them. Nature and God took vows for you, when you were born. Therefore, it is the part of wisdom and prudence to discover the Christian laws, and to practice them, with as much earnestness and resolution as the artist discovers and practices the laws of beauty, as a musician practices the laws of melody, as an orator studies the laws of eloquence, as a writer studies the laws of logic and literature. Every motive of self-interest, not less than of gratitude and a sense of generosity toward the all loving God and the all helpful Christ, impels the noble nature to recognize the soul's obligation to follow Christ, as the pupil follows a great master.

Because that Christ, Who said He was the Way and the Truth, adds that He is also the Life, it follows that the Christian life is a growth and a development. Religion is not a gift, altogether. In the fields, for the grain of wheat, the sun and the rain are gifts, but the sheaf comes only through growth. If the root refuses to grow, then no matter how kindly the sun, or how fruitful the rains, the root remains dead and dormant to the end. The sun can do much for black soil; but the sun falling on sand and dust, leaves sand and dust. Not otherwise it is with the soul. It begins with nothing, and must grow. God's graces fall on the good heart as on good soil, and on the evil mind as on stony ground. The soul is a seed. It is born a long way from the full grandeur of the Son of God. The distance between the babe in the cradle and the statesman of seventy is as nothing compared to the distance between that John the fisherman who heard Christ's invitation to follow Him, and John the beloved disciple, writing his visions and dreams of a golden age, on the Island of Patmos. Slowly man drills the body and masters it. Slowly he unfolds the intellect. Slowly vanity and selfishness and greed are expelled. Slowly the will is subdued. By long processes the emigrant changes the wilderness into a garden, draining swamps, clearing out the forest, developing the pasture, and the vineyard. Oh, if religion could only be achieved quickly, how would the aspirants multiply into an eager multitude. If men could only uncover character as they uncover gold mines, or buy integrity like a bale of goods! That boy in Oregon came down from the mountain side with $2,800 worth of gold nuggets. But men cannot go out and uncover a rich ledge of goodness, with outcroppings of piety, and carry graces back in a sack.

It seems, therefore, that the Christian life is at once the happiest life, the fullest and the freest in the world. There is no more

—19C

comprehensive definition of Christianity than Paul's. What avenues are open to the Christian? Whatsoever things are true, whatsoever things are pure, whatsoever things are lovely, whatsoever things are of good report—if there be anything that makes for virtue or for praise, all these things are yours. It is God's world. Whatsoever is sweet in the singing of birds, the beauty of flowers, the splendor of the sunset, the strength of man, the beauty of woman, the wisdom of books, the power of gold, whatsoever is glorious in progress or service—all these are God's, and all, therefore, ours. The Christian life is not the repressed life. Away with your cave, your haircloth and your ascetiscish. The soul is a harp of forty strings. Bernard cuts the string of wit and humor and beauty; Peter the Hermit cuts all the strings of wisdom and culture, one by one the other partialists cuts each his string. They look all about them in God's nature and they say: "The vineyards belong to the devil; beauty belongs to the devil; and when they have given the largest part of God's world over to the devil they shut the Creator up in a corner and say these few things belong to God. But this is a perversion of reason, a mutilation of nature, and it maligns God. This world is God's world. He who obeys the law of truth, or beauty, or invention, or purity, or prayer and trust, will at least discover for himself the happiness of Jesus Christ, Who lived victorious in the world as in his Fathers' house. Oh, if Christians would live like Christ! Would that a company of disciples might rise up here, who would lead the happiest and fullest and freest life, that is clothed with beauty! Against a Christlike Christian there is no argument. Orators can indeed declaim against ascerbity, superstition, bigotry and intolerance. But to talk against a beautiful and Christ-like soul, a character that must be likened to some moving garden, glorious in its spiritual fruits and flowers, is as impotent as to declaim against roses and hyacinths and lilies and orange blossoms. Is there any one who can dislike joy? Or rebel against peace and long-suffering and beautiful service? Immeasurable the influence of one Christ-like Christian.

How erroneous, therefore, the idea that the thought of being a Christian to avoid penalty, here or hereafter. Ignoble that conception of religion as a kind of insurance against punishment, and a guarantee against risks. The Christian life has nothing for those who do not want to be Christians here and now, but will be if they must. Some there are who come cringingly, because they are afraid they will be damned hereafter; they do not want to keep the commandments, but rather than be damned they will do so. But no man ever developed a great enterprise, and achieved a great thing, under the scourge of fear. The inventor must love his tool, the reformer must love his task, the patriot pursues his law with a passionate devotion that cannot be changed. And blessed is the Christian who can say "the love of Christ constraineth me." The fear of the Lord is the beginning of wisdom! Yes, but the "fear" is only "the beginning" and the root; the bough and the blossom thereof are love and hope. It is utterly ignoble to do as you please here, and then hereafter claim that you did otherwise. The cheat is always unworthy. And how shall a man rob God, and be ungenerous toward the great-hearted and open-handed Father? Be not deceived! God is not mocked; whatsoever a man soweth that shall he reap. Every motive of prudence, therefore, and honor, asks you to begin now. Do not wait for any mysterious change. Enter upon the Christian life, with the resolution with which you enter upon any important enterprise. The way to begin is—to begin. Today, if ye will hear His voice, harden not your heart, but rise up and follow Him.

SOCIAL CHRISTIANITY

Mr. Roosevelt had been saying that our republic is rooted in the rightmindedness of the average man. "Back of the law, back of the administration, back of our system of government lies the average manhood of our people. In the long run we are going to go up or go down according as the average standard of citizenship does or does not wax in growth and grace." The fact here enunciated must be self-evident to him who brings thought to the subject; the principle which it involves may not be quite as obvious, but it is equally compelling to him who penetrates the full meaning of these words.

For if the words mean anything they mean that it is the concern of all society to see that "the average man" has his opportunity "to wax in growth and grace," and that this obligation becomes the more imperative in proportion as the outward circumstances and personal equipment of any individual lift him above the plane of "the average man." In other words they mean that society is one, and that we being all members one of another it is in the nature of things and not by an arbitrary dictum or a counsel of perfection that he who is greatest must be the minister of the others. He who is most deeply implicated in the existing order must become the servant of this order. And by the same test it becomes evident that it is an organic law of society and not a mere pious analogy that those parts of the body politic which seem to be more feeble are necessary. Hence it comes about that every social institution or condition which thwarts the normal development of any considerable number of people is a menace to the state, and in the nature of things impossible of toleration.

This is the social doctrine of Jesus, and it is a happy thing for the future of civilization that an increasing number of individuals in this and other countries are profoundly realizing that it is the inevitable social doctrine of the future. Consciously or unconsciously—and most happily for our country—the President of the United States belongs to this group of people, some of whom do and a larger number of whom do not call themselves Christian Socialists, but all of whom perceive that the hope of society lies in adopting and carrying out in industrial and political as well as in private life the social principles of Jesus Christ.

When Jesus lived in this world society was comparatively simple while now it is exceedingly complex. The question, ''What would Jesus do?'' in any given case may therefore be an utterly inopportune question and incapable of an answer. But the question, ''What would Jesus think?'' in any given case is always in order, for His principles were of no limited application, but of universal scope, being rooted—as we are more and more coming to perceive as we study them more profoundly—in eternal laws and the essential nature of things. Fundamental to all His social teachings is His doctrine of the brotherhood of men and the ''neighbor'' character of whomsoever one may have opportunity to serve. And this being the case it is not a matter of choice but a question of political life or death, as the President perceives, that every man shall enjoy the fullest opportunity to ''wax in growth and grace.'' Or to quote a formula of that little group of Christian Socialists, the Brotherhood of the Kingdom, that every man shall have ''the most ample opportunity to realize his sonship to God and his brotherhood with men.''

It is profoundly true that, as Dr. Josiah Strong has of late powerfully taught, ''the next great awakening'' will be the awakening of the social conscience. And the time is at hand. Already in many places does it show signs of arising from sleep. Such men as President Roosevelt are its prophets not less than the preachers and poets who announce it; and it matters not whether such men, practical and sagacious men of affairs, remain or do not remain in positions of obvious leadership; the social consciousness of such men being awake, the general awakening will not be slow to follow. A few days after the Boston utterance already quoted President Roosevelt said at Bangor: ''The worth of a civilization is the worth of the man at the center. When this man lacks moral rectitude material progress only makes bad worse, and social problems still darker and more dark.'' Happy the nation who has a ''man at the center'' who recognizes this important fact!

For ''the man at the center'' is distinctly not ''the average man,'' but the man in trust—the man of whom every member of the community is "neighbor" because he is in a position to serve every one; it is he who has his hands upon the springs of social life. The time is at hand when "men at the center" will take their trust more seriously than does that man of enormous influence and social power who lately said that the conduct of a great business is the private affair of those who control it, and that with the management of business neither religion or philanthropy has anything to do. This potentate is representative of a considerable but rapidly vanishing group. A few years hence—a very few, we believe, so rapid is public enlightenment when once the sun has risen upon the mountain tops—such a state of mind will be as impossible as it now is for an American to look upon any man as a chattel, though two generations ago there were many enlightened Christians who did so in all sincerity. This view of things will vanish, not as did the other in a great contest and awful social upheaval, but by the quiet and imperative working of an eternal social principle—the social principle of Jesus. The time is at hand when men holding views uttered by the railway magnate above referred to will no more hold places of industrial leadership than a blind man would be entrusted with the decoration of a magnificent public building—not because government, or the people, will interfere to prevent, but because the social conscience will forbid.—Christian Work.

WHY SHOULD I BE A CHRISTIAN?

BY THE REV. MALTBIE D. BABCOCK, D.D.

There is no reason why I should not be a Christian, and every reason why I should be a Christian. I live in certain relations to God, to people, and to myself. Some of the time I may get away from people; but I can never escape from God; I can never escape from myself. Then the most natural and imperial demand of my conscience is that I should be in right relations and on the best terms with people, with God and with myself.

But how am I to know what are the right relations, what kind of life is best? Take the best you know till you find a better. The only failure in life is not to be true to the best you know.

Then I must be a Christian. There is no one better than Jesus Christ. There is no standard higher than His. Men not in sympathy with Jesus have yet been obliged to confess that He stands alone, supreme, incomparable. They said long ago, "I find no fault in Him;" "Never man spake like this man;" "Truly this man is the Son of God." In our day men have said, "Higher than Jesus human thought has never gone;" "Whatever the surprises of the future may be, Jesus Christ will never be surpassed." Richard Watson Gilder has shown us that there is no dilemma even for the man who has doubts of the divinity of Jesus Christ. If he is honest and earnest, he must follow Him anyway.

> "If Jesus Christ is a man
>   And only a man, I say
> That of all mankind I will cleave to Him,
>   And to Him I will cleave alway.
>
> "If Jesus Christ is God,
>   And the only God, I swear
> I will follow Him through heaven and hell,
>   The earth, the sea, and the air."

Peter's question, "Lord, to whom shall we go?" is unanswered and unanswerable. Every now and then some one sings the praises of Buddhism or Zoroastrianism or Stoicism, but does any one think it would be a step forward to take up a religion of no God, or two gods, or many gods. Christianity has the gentleness of the

Buddhist, the virtue of the Zoroastrian, the love of beauty of the Greek, but without the defects which have carried two of the systems to the grave, and will bury the third also.

As a philosophy, a teaching of truth concerning God and man, life, providence, character, death, Christianity is matchless. The best modern movements of thought and action, like altruism and ethical culture, are children of Christianity, and cannot live far from home. One of the most acute of modern philosophers, no particular friend of Christianity, said that the best way to turn religion from the abstract to the concrete was to live so that Jesus Christ would approve our life.

Am I a Christian if I believe this? Not necessarily. I may know what is right and not do it; I may see the truth and not live by it; I may recognize Christ and yet refuse Him. But that is moral degradation; that is spiritual suicide. There is no peril so great as his who has light and turns his back upon it, who sees Jesus Christ and chooses Barabbas. To live in a Christian land, to go to a Christian church, to come of a Christian family, and not be a Christian, is to be in the worst kind of danger. Jesus said it would be better in the day of judgment for Sodom and Gomorrah than for the men of Capernaum, who knew Him, but would not obey Him. Do not put yourself in such condemnation!

Look out into the world. What does it need so much for its sin and trouble and strife, misunderstanding and hopelessness, as the spirit of Christ's brotherhood? The light and hope of the world is the kind of life Jesus led. Be one of His brothers. See Him in little children, in the sick and discouraged, in the prisoner, in the poor, in the overworked and underpaid, in any one you can help. The world needs some one like you to show right where you live how to be loyal to duty, victorious in temptations, brave in trial, loving in every human relation. You owe it to the society in which you live, and which has given you your opportunities, that it should have your best life in Christ for its upbuilding and purifying. "Ye are the light of the world;" "ye are the salt of the earth." You owe it to your fellow men to live Christ's life among them and for them.

Look into your own heart. You know you must be yourself forever. Can you save your self-respect, your conscience, your character, yourself, when you know that you are untrue to the best, when you are living a life of unbelief and disobedience and self-indulgence? Tendencies petrify; character crystallizes. Every choice away from God hardens your heart.

> "Forever round the mercy-seat
>   The guiding lights of love may burn;
> But what if, habit-bound, thy feet
>   Should lack the will to turn?"

You have Christ's word for it that, if you are not for Him, you are against Him. Can you let another day steal away its share of what interest you have today, what protest of conscience, what sense of sin, what longing to be better, what prodigal's homesickness? Turn your face to your Savior now. Give yourself to Him now and forever. Let nothing prevent you.

Matthew did not know much about Jesus, but he heard the words, "Follow Me," and he began to follow. Peter was impulsive and over-confident; Thomas was a natural born doubter; James and John had fiery tempers; but they followed Jesus, and gradually knew Him better, and through Him got the victory over themselves. You owe it to yourself to be your best self in Christ's name, to be Israel, not Jacob; Peter, not Simon; Paul, not Saul. Jesus Christ by His Spirit today can give you victory over your besetting sins, can make self-development and self-devotion follow self-mastery, and at last give you a new name as a gift and secret of love to Him that overcometh.

Do you say now, "I give myself to Thee, my Savior?" Hear His words: "And him that cometh to Me I will in no wise cast out."

> And didst Thou leave Thy home above
> To tell me of my Father's love,
> To give eternal life to me,—
> And can my heart say, "No" to Thee?
>
> And didst Thou go to Calvary,
> And suffer there, O Lord, for me,
> Dying that Thou mightst set me free,—
> And can I turn away from Thee?
>
> And dost Thou wait with hands outstretched
> To me, with endless doubtings vexed,
> With sins and fears and cares oppressed,—
> And can I spurn Thy promised rest?

And dost thou say, if I neglect
If I Thy dying love reject,
That I Thy glory shall not see,—
And dare I turn my back on Thee?

I cannot, dare not, thus refuse;
Thee for my Savior now I choose;
And since, Lord, Thou hast died for me.
Help me in love to live for Thee.

             —Christian Endeavor World.

THE CHRISTIAN RELIGION IN ITS LAST ANALYSIS

BY THE REV. DR. DONALD C. MAC LOUD

"Simon, son of Jonas, lovest thou Me? Yea, Lord, thou knowest that I love Thee."—John 21:17.

There is an inference so strongly suggested by the text as to come to us with all the force of positive teaching, viz.: The permanence of Jesus' humanity. This appearance of Jesus to His disciples was after His resurrection. All through His ministry Jesus manifested His true humanity in no way more striking than in His craving for human sympathy, devotion and affection. He repeatedly came to His disciples and made known to them His troubles and sorrows, yearning for their sympathy, although they were so slow to understand Him and so ready to rebuke Him; and, on various occasions, especially when the world would forsake and persecute Him, would He ask questions that would lead His disciples to make a personal profession of their faith in Him and devotion to Him. It is quite evident this was an element in our Savior's motive in asking the questions of the text. Truly, he had finished His work. He had led captivity captive. He had risen victoriously from the grave. He was about to ascend into heaven to sit upon the throne of universal power and dominion. But, notwithstanding these facts of His triumph, glory and power, He was still a man in every particular, "Very man of very man." He was still, as much as ever, bound to the race of men in indissoluble bonds of common dependence and sympathy. He still craved for marks of devotion from His disciples. His heart would still rejoice to hear Peter confess his love for Him.

Jesus propounds His questions. What do you suppose He asks him? Does He say, Peter, do you know the Ten Commandments? Have you made a careful study of the Old Testament? Do you believe Moses wrote the Pentateuch? Do you believe the description of creation in Genesis is historical or allegorical? What about Job and Jonah; are these myths or historical facts? Did Isaiah write the last twenty-five chapters of the book ascribed to him? What do you believe in regard to the genuineness of the book of Daniel? Do you believe in the plenary inspiration and inerrancy of the Bible? (Define your doctrine of God, the Trinty and the Person of Christ.) What do you believe in regard to fore-ordination, election, the immortality of the soul, and the endless questions that are agitating the minds of the Pharisees, Sadducees and the Essenes? It is a remarkable fact that none of these entered into Christ's examination of Peter's qualifications for the great work of his ministry. These are the questions we ask. Such are questions that have been burdening the heart of the church all through the ages. Such are the questions that have brought together ecumenical councils and caused enmities, schisms, persecutions and atrocities in the life of the church, the very mention of which causes us to blush with shame and makes our very blood turn cold in the channels of its flow. Such are the questions that still cause divisions in the body of Christ and are occupying the time and energy of the church at the sacrifice of the salvation of men and the upbuilding of the church purchased by the precious blood of Jesus.

One characteristic of great men is that they are able to see below the complexity and confusion lying upon the surface of things and perceive the fundamental principles that are the essence and life of things. The less a man knows about a given subject the more questions he must ask in order to discover what you know. If a man is master of a subject, he can with a few fundamental questions search the center and circumference of your knowledge in a moment of time. Jesus, with His divine insight, reaches the very essence of His religion with the fundamental and searching question of the text. All those other questions I suggested, and as many more as human ingenuity could devise, I venture to say, could be answered by Judas Iscariot without a moment's consideration. That he was a good churchman and an expert theologian appears upon the surface of his criticism of Mary's use of the alabaster box of ointment. He knew well the law of the Jewish church, demanded the ointment should be sold for the benefit of the poor. Yet this expert theologian betrayed his Lord with a kiss. Do you not see the wisdom of our Savior's questions?

* * *

Christianity has creeds innumerable. Christianity has doctrines and institutions. But the power of Christianity is not in these. That energy which made it move, and by which it has been moving the world, is the Living, Personal God-man, Christ Jesus, who gives vitality to its organizations and life to its doctrines. How long will it take the world to learn the forces of this universe are centered in personalities? All the great achievements of history were conceived and carried into execution by persons. Wherein lies the power of the present day? In persons, law, literature, painting—all these are only instruments constructed and wielded by personality in the realization of intelligent purpose. You cannot love a principle nor a creed, nor can you be moved to action by them only as they preserve the life and image of the person who gave them birth. This is the great truth of the text. The essence and power of the Christian religion is Christ. He says: ''I am the energizing life that gives power to the church. If you love Me; if you have faith in Me, you can become possessed with My power. You can stand in Me and in the power of My might.'' Men are engaged in strifes and controversies over creeds and philosophies, while Christ is crying to the world, forget your creeds and systems, and look at Me and you will find unity, peace and power. Creeds and confessions have played their part in the history of the church. They have been a blessing to many, but when they hide Christ and become the occasion of controversy they become a hindrance and a curse. Creeds, confessions and systems should be kept subordinate to the Christ. You cannot love creeds. Your devotion cannot be inspired by philosophic principles. Your life cannot be changed by the speculation of philosophy—only contact with a person, Christ Jesus, can effect these wonderful transformations. The cry of the age is for a Christocentric theology. Go back to Christ. Brush away the cobwebs that scholasticism has woven over your vision; with unveiled face behold your Savior. Love Him, and you will become a living and powerful disciple of Christ. The question of the text becomes a personal question to all of us in view of our relation to Jesus. His question to us as individuals is: 'Lovest thou Me?' Do you love Christ? Is His presence to you so real and superlatively beautiful that the supreme devotion of your life springs up spontaneously in response to His perfections, so that your confession to the world, with all the sincerity and enthusiasm of a Peter is, "Yea, Lord, Thou knowest that I love Thee."

THE CHRISTIAN'S EQUIPMENT

BY THE REV. DANIEL H. OVERTON

"Stand therefore, having your loins girt about with truth."—Ephesians 6:14.

Paul is fond of martial figures. They occur often in his writings. To him life was a warfare, and the Christian a soldier. So he loved to use the language of the battlefield, and to exhort all Christians to be good soldiers under their great captain, Christ.

This was what Paul does in this letter to the church of Ephesus. It was troublous times for those early churches. A crisis of extreme danger was approaching. The days were evil days. The times were degenerate. Nero, the profligate ruler of Rome and of the Mediterranean world, had laid upon the Christians of Rome that which his own wicked hands had done, the burning of the city; and, not content with burning the city, was now burning the Christians.

Paul is writing the letter from his prison-house in Rome, and he sees the situation as no other had the power to see it. The days soon to come were to be days of severe conflict, and desperate struggle for the Christian church and for every Christian in the world. Knowing this, Paul mentions the foes that the Christians must meet and fight. They are as follows:

The devil—the spirit of evil; evil principalities and powers, world-rulers of darkness—the whole kingdom of darkness and ignorance and spiritual wickedness in high and in low places, in their own hearts and in the hearts and lives of others.

These are their foes, and in order that they may not be disheartened, he appeals to them as a general would to his men. He calls to them: "Be strong in the Lord, and in the strength of His might. Stand firm! Hold your ground! Maintain your honor! Defend the dearest interests and the highest, holiest hopes of human life! And then, that ye may stand, and withstand, and win the victory, be equipped—take up and put on the whole armor of God." This armor of God is the Christian's equipment for the great battle of life.

We have need of this equipment, as had those Ephesian Christians, for we have foes to fight as did they. We must fight the spirit of evil, and all the evil spirits of the world. We must fight the kingdom of darkness and of ignorance, as did they. We have to battle against wickedness in high places and in low places. We must meet and withstand sin in our own hearts and lives and in the hearts and lives of our fellow men. The days are not as bad as were the Roman days; the times not as degenerate; but the foes of the better life are still many and strong, and many there are who fall before them. We need to be equipped with the whole armor of God if we would win the victory over them and live the higher life and attain the greatest usefulness.

There is nothing like a full equipment for any great and good task. Time spent in preparation for any great work is rarely if ever wasted. Many fall and fail in life because they are so poorly prepared. So is it in the Christian life. The Christian art is the highest art in the world—the art of right living. To live aright, to make the most of life—to make this life the fittest beginning of the endless life, the Christian needs the best preparation, the fullest equipment. Many fall and fail in the Christian life because they do not make use of the infinite resources that a divine Master and a loving Father wait and wish to give them. They do not take on the whole armor of God, but only some little part of it, and so the powers of evil pierce them through.

It ought to be of profound interest to us, therefore, to learn just what equipment is necessary in order to win the victory in the great battle of life. Nothing else should concern us quite so much as to know what that equipment is, and then to get it. Paul tells us here in this letter and chapter what it is, and how to get it. It is the girdle of truth, the breastplate of righteousness, the sandals of readiness for proclaiming the gospel of peace, the shield of faith, the helmet of salvation, the sword of the Spirit, which is the Word of God, and with it all, persevering and prevailing prayer. These are the equipment of the Christian. These possessed give strength to character, and victory to life.

It is of the first of these that I would speak today, "The girdle of truth." Wearing loose garments as they do in the warm Eastern countries the girdle becomes a very necessary part of the costume, especially when any great action is required. Into it the under garments are tucked and bound, and to it the sheath for the dagger or the sword is fastened. In it also the traveler carries his money, and his jewels. It is fitted to brace up and fasten and support the body in action. Without it the soldier would become entangled in his garments, would stumble and fall, and would be able to fight but little. The girdle, therefore, stands foremost in the soldier's equipment. It stands for constancy and firmness, for strength and readiness.

It is not without reason, therefore, that Paul gives truth the first place in the armor of God, and in the Christian's equipment. What the girdle is to the soldier in the East that, and more than that, truth is to the Christian soldier. Truth gives constancy and firmness to character and conduct. Truth binds a man to reality, and makes the soul sincere. A man who has no clear views of truth is an easy prey to evil. Character that has not truth for its basis is lax, and loose, and little. Truth is the unifying and sustaining principle of life and character. Any man whose life is false can be no soldier of Christ's. Without the girdle of truth he cannot fight the great battle of life and win the victory. Without the girdle of truth he will fall and fail in the conflict. The foes of life are too fierce for any life to win the victory over them if that life is founded in falsehood or ungirdled with truth.

Especially is it important that the Christian should have and live "the truth as it is in Jesus Christ." This is what constitutes man a Christian, and makes him a Christian soldier. A man must love and live the truth of Christ if he is to be a good soldier in the cause of Christ. This is self-evident, and I need not dwell upon it, but hasten on to say that we as Christians are witnesses of the truth. Truth is on trial for her life out in the great world-field of battle, and every man is a witness for or against her. Christian truth is on trial in this world, and in our lives as Christians. Christ Himself, Who taught the truth, and Who said, "I am the Truth," is on trial still in the great world-court, and we are witnesses for or against Him. We are either saying, "Even so, come Lord Jesus, occupy and possess our lives," or we are crying, "Away with Him! away with Him! we will not have this Man to rule over us. We will not give Him the leadership in our lives."

The girdle is the thing seen by all who see the soldier who is girdled with it. Wherever the soldier went in the battle he bore witness to the fact he was equipped with the girdle. Its bright and striking color was everywhere seen.

So the Christian is a witness for the bright and striking truth of Christ. Some men are trying to live the truth. We must make it easier for them to live it. We are to so live the truth that they will see the truth in us, and love it and live it, because they see it in us.

We are also to bear witness for the truth even before those who love it not—before the very foes we fight. If our foes are flesh and blood, they are lost brothers for whom Christ died, and we are to win them back to Him. If our foes are the powers of evil we must meet them with the powers of truth and righteousness. They are the intruders in God's fair world, and one day they must be cast out, and put down. We must bear witness to the truth with such valor that they will hide from the conflict and no longer oppose.

Then let us remember that we as Christians are, also, messengers of the truth of Christ. Truth, the gospel of Christ, is a message that we have to bear, and we are messengers of that truth. If men will only love the message, and take it, and act upon it, and live it, it does not matter so much if they forget the messenger who brought it. Yet we must never forget that the message is enhanced and enforced by personality, and that when men love the personality of the messenger they are more likely to accept as true the message. The message that we bear out to the great battle-field of life is the message of the love of God as made known in Jesus Christ. The message is from God, the great loving Father, through Christ, and then through Christians, to all men.

The great utterance of great truths, and, better, the great living of great truths, and the humble doing of daily duties, is the great work of the soldier of Jesus Christ. There are great truths that run like rivers through every life. Christ found these truths, and uttered them. So must we as Christians. Our lives must be open to the truth of God, and to the needs of men, and as faithful messengers we must bring the truth of God to the needs of men. We must know the wants and woes of men, the problems and dangers of men, and apply God's truth to these. Nothing can finally or fully satisfy the soul of man except God's truth. Of this satisfying truth of God we as Christians are messengers to the souls of men.

It is our duty to fight the evil, but it is our privilege to make the good shine. Let us make it shine so that men will love it and live it. We are responsible for the defense of the truth of Christ in the world, but let us know that we defend it best by living it, and by proclaiming it. "Truth crushed to earth will rise again," we say. But it will not. Truth of itself is powerless to rise or to shine. It is only as truth is caught up and made vital in life that it has power to bless the world. Let us put on the girdle of truth and wear it everywhere.—Brooklyn Daily Eagle.

CROSS BEARING, CROWN WEARING

The message of the gospel is not an order of repression—but of development. It looks to the fullest culture of every man and all there is in man. Every faculty is to be developed; every power shall be enlarged; every joy increased; every true emotion developed to its fullest possibility. Self-control is not self-crucifixion; it is the power of restraint in order to larger enjoyment, greater capabilities—a larger measure every way, unto the stature of the Son of God. What a wrong notion is that of many young people—that the gospel is a constant call to "give up." In truth it is a call to drop the brass and take the gold; to throw away the tinsel and get the genuine metal. It is a call from a lower life to a higher life—from character to character, from glory to glory. It is cross bearing—but that is only a preparation for crown bearing.

—20C

CHRISTIANITY IS REVOLUTIONARY

BY DR. T. DEWITT TALMAGE

"These that have turned the world upside down are come hither also."
—Acts 17:6.

There is a wild, bellowing mob around the house of Jason in Thessalonica. What has the man done so greatly to offend the people? He has been entertaining Paul and his comrades. The mob surround the house and cry: "Bring out those turbulent preachers! They are interfering with our business! They are ruining our religion! They are actually turning the world upside down!"

The charge is true, for there is nothing that so interferes with sin, there is nothing so ruinous to every form of established ininquity, there is nothing that has such tendency to turn the world upside down as our glorious Christianity. The fact is that the world now is wrong side up, and it needs to be turned upside down in order that it may be right side up. The time was when men wrote books entitling them "Apologies for Christianity." I hope that day has passed. We want no more apologies for Christianity. Let the apologies be on the part of those who do not believe in our religion. We do not mean to make any compromise in the matter. We do not wish to hide the fact that Christianity is revolutionary and that its tendency is to turn the world upside down.

Our religion has often been misrepresented as a principle of tears and mildness and fastidiousness, afraid of crossing people's prejudices, afraid of making somebody mad, with silken gloves lifting the people up from the church pew into glory, as though they were Bohemian glass, so very delicate that with one touch it may be demolished forever. Men speak of religion as though it were a refined imbecility, as though it were a spiritual chloroform, that the people were to take until the sharp cutting of life were over. The Bible, so far from this, represents the religion of Christ as robust and brawny—ransacking and upsetting 10,000 things that now seem to be settled on firm foundations. I hear some man in the house say, "I thought religion was peace." That is the final result. A man's arm is out of place. Two men come, and with great effort put it back to the socket. It goes back with great pain. Then it gets well. Our world is horribly disordered and out of joint. It must come under an omnipotent surgery, beneath which there will be pain and anguish before there can come perfect health and quiet. I proclaim, therefore, in the name of my Lord Jesus Christ—revolution!

The religion of the Bible will make a revolution in the family. Those things that are wrong in the family circle will be overthrown by it, while justice and harmony will take the place. The husband will be the head of the household only when he is fit to be. I know a man who spends all the money he makes in drink as well as all the money that his wife makes, and sometimes sells the children's clothes for rum. Do you tell me that he is to be the head of that household? If the wife have more nobility, more courage, more consistency, more of all that is right, she shall have the supremacy. You say that the Bible says that the wife is to be subject to the husband. I know it, but that is a husband, not a masculine caricature. There is no human or divine law that makes a woman subordinate to a man unworthy of her. When Christianity comes into a domestic circle, it will give the dominancy to that one who is the most worthy of it.

As religion comes in at the front door, mirth and laughter will not go out of the back door. It will not hopple the children's feet. John will laugh just as loud, and George will jump higher than he ever did before. It will steal from the little ones neither ball nor bat nor hoop nor kite. It will establish a family altar. Angels will hover over it. Ladders of light will reach down to it. The glory of heaven will stream upon it. The books of remembrance will record it, and tides of everlasting blessedness will pour from it. Not such a family altar as you may have seen where the prayer is long and a long chapter is read, with tedious explanation, and the exercise keeps on until the children's knees are sore, and their backs ache, and their patience is lost, and for the seventh time they have counted all the rungs in the chair, but I mean a family altar such as may have been seen in your father's house. You may have wandered far off in the paths of sin and darkness, but you have never forgotten that family altar where father and mother knelt importuning God for your soul. That is a memory that a man never gets over. There will be a hearty, joyful family altar in

every family circle. You will not have to go far to find Hannah
rearing her Samuel for the temple or a grandmother Lois instruct-
ing her young Timothy in the knowledge of Christ, or a Mary and
Martha and Lazarus gathered in fraternal and sisterly affection, or
a table at which Jesus sits, as at that of Zaccheus or a home in
which Jesus dwells, as in the house of Simon the tanner.
The religion of Jesus Christ, coming into the domestic circle, will
overthrow all jealousies, all janglings, and peace and order and
holiness will take possession of the home.

Again, Christianity will produce a revolution in commercial
circles. Find me fifty merchants, and you find that they have
fifty standards of what is right and wrong. You say to some one
about a merchant, "Is he honest?" "Oh, yes," the man says,
"he is honest, but he grinds the faces of his clerks! He is honest,
but he exaggerates the value of his goods. He is honest, but he
loans money on bond and mortgage with the understanding that
the mortgage can lie quiet for ten years, but as soon as he gets the
mortgage he records it and begins a foreclosure suit, and the sher-
iff's writ comes down, and the day of sale arrives, and away goes
the homestead, and the creditor buys it in at half price." Honest?
When he loaned the money he knew he would get the homestead at
half price. Honest? But he goes to the insurance office to get a
policy on his life and tells the doctor that he is well when he knows
that for ten years he has had but one lung. Honest? Though he
sells property by the map, forgetting to tell the purchaser that the
ground is all under water, but it is generous in him to do that, for
he throws the water into the bargain.

Ah, my friends, there is but one standard of the everlasting
right and of the everlasting wrong, and that is the Bible, and when
that principle shall get its pry under our commercial houses I believe that one-half of them will go over! The ruin will begin at
one end of the street, and it will be crash! crash! crash! all the way
down to the docks. "What is the matter? Has there been a fall
in gold?" "Oh, no." "Has there been a new tariff?" "No."
"Has there been a failure in crops?" "No." "Has there
been an unaccountable panic?" "No." This is the secret:
The Lord God has set up His throne of judgment in the
exchange. He has summoned the righteous and the wicked to come
before Him. What was 1837? A day of judgment! What was

1857? A day of judgment! What was the extreme depression of two years ago? A day of judgment! Do you think that God is going to wait until He has burned the world up before He rights these wrongs? I tell you nay! Every day is a day of judgment.

The fraudulent man piles up his gains, bond above bond, United States security above United States security, emolument above emolument, until his property has become a great pyramid, and as he stands looking at it he thinks it can never be destroyed, but the Lord God comes and with His little finger pushes it all over.

You build a house, and you put into it a rotten beam. A mechanic standing by says: "It will never do to put that beam in. It will ruin your whole building." But you put it in. The house is completed. Soon it begins to rock. You call in the mechanic and ask: "What is the matter with this door? What is the matter with this wall? Everything seems to be giving out." Says the mechanic: "You put a rotten beam into that structure, and the whole thing has got to come down." Here is an estate that seems to be all right now. It has been building a great many years. But fifteen years ago there was a dishonest transaction in that commercial house. That one dishonest transaction will keep on working ruin in the whole structure, until down the estate will come in wreck and ruin about the possessor's ears—one dishonest dollar in the estate demolishing all his possessions. I have seen it again and again, and so have you.

Here is your money safe. The manufacturer and yourself only know how it can be opened. You have the key. You touch the lock, and the ponderous door swings back. But let me tell you that, however firmly barred and bolted your money safe may be, you cannot keep God out. He will come some day into your counting room and He will demand: "Where did that note of hand come from? How do you account for this security? Where did you get that mortgage from? What does this mean?" If it is all right, God will say: "Well done, good and faithful servant. Be prospered in this world. Be happy in the world to come." If it is all wrong, He will say: "Depart, ye cursed. Be miserable for your iniquities in this life, and then go down and spend your eternity with thieves and horse jockeys and pickpockets."

You have an old photograph of the signs on your street. Why have those signs nearly all changed within the last twenty years? Does the passing away of a generation account for it? Oh, no. Does the fact that there are hundreds of honest men who go down every year account for it? Oh, no. This is the secret: The Lord God has been walking through the commercial streets of our great cities, and He has been adjusting things according to the principles of eternal rectitude.

The time will come when, through the revolutionary power of the gospel, a falsehood, instead of being called exaggeration, equivocation or evasion, will be branded a lie, and stealings that now sometimes go under the head of percentages and commissions and bonuses will be put into the catalogue of state prison offenses! Society will be turned inside out and upside down and ransacked of God's truth until business dishonesties shall come to an end, and all double dealing, and God will overturn and overturn and overturn, and commercial men in all cities will throw up their hands, crying out, "These that have turned the world upside down are come hither."

The religion of Jesus Christ will produce a revolution in our churches. The noncommittal, do nothing policy of the church of God will give way to a spirit of bravest conquest. Piety in this day seems to me to be salted down just so as to keep. It seems as if the church were chiefly anxious to take care of itself, and if we hear of want and squalor and heathenism outside we say, "What a pity!" and we put our hands in our pockets, and we feel around for a two-cent piece, and with a great flourish we put it upon the plate and are amazed that the world is not converted in six weeks. Suppose there were a great war, and there were 300,000 soldiers, but all of those 300,000 soldiers, excepting ten men, were in their tents or scouring their muskets or cooking rations. You would say, "Of course defeat must come in that case." It is worse than that in the church. Millions of the professed soldiers of Jesus Christ are cooking rations or asleep in their tents, while only one man here and there goes out to do battle for the Lord.

"But," says some one, "we are establishing a great many missions, and I think they will save the masses." No; they will not. Five hundred thousand of them will not do it. They are doing a magnificent work, but every mission chapel is a confession of the disease and weakness of the church. It is making a dividing line between the classes. It is saying to the rich and to the well conditioned, "If you can pay your pew rents, come to the main audience room." It is saying to the poor man: "Your coat is too bad and your shoes are not good enough. If you want to get to heaven, you will have to go by the way of the mission chapel.' The mission chapel has become the kitchen, where the church does its sloppy work. There are hundreds and thousands of churches in this country—gorgeously built and supported—that even on bright and sunshiny days are not half full of worshipers, and yet they are building mission chapels, because by some expressed or implied regulation the great masses of the people are kept out of the main audience room.

Now, I say that any place of worship which is appropriate for one class is appropriate for all classes. Let the rich and the poor meet together, the Lord the Maker of them all. Mind you that I say that mission chapels are a necessity, the way churches are now conducted, but may God speed the time when they shall cease to be a necessity. God will rise up and break down the gates of the church that have kept back the masses, and woe be to those who stand in the way! They will be trampled under foot by the vast populations making a stampede for heaven.

I saw in some paper an account of a church in Boston in which, it is said, there were a great many plain people. The next week the trustees of that church came out in the paper and said it was not so at all; "they were elegant people and highly conditioned people that went there." Then I laughed outright, and when I laugh I laugh very loudly. "Those people," I said, "are afraid of the sickly sentimentality of the churches." Now, my ambition is not to preach to you so much. It seems to me that you must be faring sumptuously every day, and the marks of comfort are all about you. You do not need the gospel half as much as do some who never come here. Rather than be priding myself on a church in front of which there shall halt fifty splendid equipages on the Sabbath day I would have a church up to whose gates there should come a long procession of the suffering, and the stricken, and the dying, begging for admittance. You do not need the gospel so much as they. You have good things in this life. Whatever may be your future destiny, you have had a pleasant time here. But those dying populations of which I speak, by reason of their want and suffering, whatever may be their future destiny, are in perdition now, and if there be any comfort in Christ's gospel for God's sake give it to them!

Revolution! The pride of the church must come down. The exclusiveness of the church must come down! The financial boastings of the church must come down! If monetary success were the chief idea in the church, then I say that the present mode of conducting finances is the best. If it is to see how many dollars you can gain, then the present mode is the best. But if it is the saving of souls from sin and death and bringing the mighty populations of our cities to the knowledge of God, then I cry revolution! It is coming fast. I feel it in the air. I hear the rumbling of an earthquake that shall shake down in one terrific crash the arrogance of our modern Christianity.

The sea is covered with wrecks, and multitudes are drowning. We come out with the church lifeboat, and the people begin to clamber in, and we shout: "Stop! stop! You must think it costs nothing to keep a lifeboat. Those seats at the prow are one dollar apiece, these in the middle fifty cents and those seats in the stern two shillings. Please to pay up or else flounder on a little longer till the mission boat whose work it is to save you penniless wretches shall come along and pick you up. We save only first class sinners in this boat."

The talk is whether Protestant churches or Roman Catholic churches are coming out ahead. I tell you, Protestants, this truth plainly—that until your churches are as free as are the Roman Catholic cathedrals they will beat you. In their cathedrals the millionaire and the beggar kneel side by side. And until that time comes in our churches we cannot expect the favor of God or permanent spiritual prosperity.

Revolution! It may be that before the church learns its duty to the masses God will scourge it and come with the whip of omnipotent indignation and drive out the money changers. It may be that there is to be a great day of upsetting before that time shall come. If it must come, O Lord God, let it come now!

In that future day of the reconstructed church of Christ the church building will be the most cheerful of all buildings. Instead of the light of the sun strained through painted glass until an intelligent auditory looks green and blue and yellow and copper colored, we will have no such things. The pure atmosphere of heaven will sweep out the fetid atmosphere that has been kept in many of our churches boxed up from Sunday to Sunday.

The day of which I speak will be a day of great revivals. There will be such a time as there was in the parish of Shotts, where 500 souls were born to God in one day—such times as were seen in this country when Edwards gave the alarm, when Tennent preached, and Whitefield thundered, and Edward Payson prayed; such times as some of you remember in 1857, when the voice of prayer and praise was heard in theater and warehouse and black-shop and factory and engine house, and the auctioneer's cry of "a half, and a half, and a half," was drowned out by the adjoining prayer meeting, in which the people cried out, "Men and brethren, what shall we do?"

In those days of which I am speaking the services of the church of God will be more spirited. The ministers of Christ, instead of being anxious about whether they are going to lose their place in their notes, will get on fire with the theme and pour the living truth of God upon an aroused auditory, crying out to the righteous, "It shall be well with you," and to the wicked, "Woe! It shall be ill with you." In those days the singing will be very different from what it is now. The music will weep and wail and chant and triumph. People then will not be afraid to open their mouths when they sing. The man with a cracked voice will risk it on "Windham" and "Ortonville" and "Old Hundred." Grandfather will find the place for his grandchild in the hymn book, or the little child will be spectacles for the grandfather. Hosanna will meet hosanna and together go climbing to the throne, and the angels will hear, and God will listen, and the gates of heaven will hoist, and it will be as when two seas meet—the wave of earthly song mingling with the surging anthems of the free.

Oh, my God, let me live to see that day! Let there be no power in disease or accident or wave of the sea to disappoint my expectations. Let all other sight fail my eyes rather than that I should miss that vision. Let all other sounds fail my ears rather than that I should fail to hear that sound. I want to stand on the mountain top to catch the first ray of the dawn and with flying feet bring the news. And, oh, when we hear the clattering hoofs that bring on the King's chariot may we all be ready, with arches sprung and with hand on the rope of the bell that is to sound the victory, and with wreaths all twisted for the way, and when Jesus dismounts let it be amid the huzza! huzza! of a world redeemed!

Where and when will that revolution begin? Here and now. In your heart and mine. Sin must go down, our pride must go down, our worldliness must go down, that Christ may come up. Revolution! "Except man be born again, he cannot see the kingdom of God." Why not now let the revolution begin? Not next Sabbath, but now. Not tomorrow, when you go out into commercial circles, but now.

Archias, the magistrate of Thebes, was sitting with many mighty men, drinking wine. A messenger came in, bringing a letter informing him of a conspiracy to end his life and warning him to flee. Archias took the letter; but, instead of opening it, put it into his pocket and said to the messenger who brought it: "Business tomorrow." The next day he died. Before he opened the letter the government was captured. When he read the letter, it was too late. Today I put into the hand of every man and woman who hears or reads these words a message of life. It says: "Today, if ye will hear His voice, harden not your heart." Do not put away the message and say, "This business tomorrow." This night thy soul may be required of thee!

CHRISTIANITY AN EDUCATIONAL FORCE

BY THE REV. HENRY M. KING, D.D.

The ultimate aim of education is confessedly personal character. All educators are agreed on this point. Education that is worthy of the name, covers the entire spiritual nature. Not only the intellect, but judgment and conscience, will and affection are included within the scope of its active influence. Prof. J. L. Diman, in his Phi Beta Kappa oration at Harvard University, justly said, "Admirable culture of whatever kind must have its roots in the moral sentiment." Man is more than cold intellect. The perfect man would be more than an intellectual giant. Even John Stuart Mill said, "Education has for its object, besides calling forth the greatest possible quantity of intellectual power, the intensest love of truth." The affectional and moral nature can not be overlooked in any educational system that has regard to the whole nature of man, and its symmetrical development. Revealed religion presents to man the sublime thought of God with reference to Him, and the sublime possibilities of growth that are shut up with Him. The claim of Christianity as the highest educational force is established in three ways, or rather by three facts.

First, it furnishes the highest, the absolutely perfect model of character. Reference is not had now to its moral teachings, which are acknowledged to be the most perfect that the world has ever seen, and have been made the basis of all respectable ethical systems, but to the person and character of Christ, Who was pre-eminently the Son of Man, the typical, the ideal man. Christ not only died for us, but He lived for us. He was born in the flesh that He might show us how to live in the flesh. What the world needed was not a new decalogue but a new life. So Christ took up life and lived it as it ought to be lived, free from humiliating weaknesses and debasing sins, and became the absolutely perfect character and example for all ages and for all men. He was God manifest in the flesh, and He was man manifest in the flesh. He revealed to us the perfect Godhood, and at the same time the perfect manhood. He was the wisest, truest, noblest, most godlike, manliest of men. This is the verdict of His age, and of all ages, of friend and foe alike. The inspired writer declared Him to be "holy, harmless, undefiled and separate from sinners." Prof. Leslie Stephen pronounces Christ "the ideal man, therefore king of men." Edwin Arnold calls Him:

> "First-born of heaven, first soul of human souls,
>   That touched the top of manhood, and from height
>   Of Godlike, pure humanity, reached God."

Tennyson says:
> "Thou seemest human and divine,
>   The highest, holiest manhood thou."

Every young man should read Thomas Hughes' monograph on "The Manliness of Christ," that he may get a conception of what Christ was, and of what he ought to be, that he may learn that the Christian life is the truly manly life, that to be Christlike is to be manly, and to be un-Christlike is to be unmanly. Christ is the one model for us all. He towered above not only His own time, but all times. He is not yet outgrown or superseded. Indeed, after eighteen centuries of boasted progress He is not yet overtaken. He still leads the human race, and by no inconsiderable distance. All evolution of character is still backward toward the Galilean peasant of 2,000 years ago. Every man who desires to attain unto genuine manliness of character and life, will find his model in Jesus Christ.

Secondly, Christianity furnishes not only the perfect model of character, but the adequate motive for securing it. Here is where all other religious systems utterly fail. They have their ideal of life, their code of ethical teachings of a grade more or less perfect, but they have no motive power to make the attainment of their ideal possible. The highest moral teachings, the most perfect ethical standard, would be unavailing unless there was some mighty force, some controlling motive, some indwelling and impelling affection to push us on towards it. That motive is found in the love of Jesus Christ, who is the world's Savior as well as the world's example. The entrance of that love into the soul is the beginning of a new life, the generation of a new spiritual force which impels a man toward the lofty goal which before he may have admired, but had no power to reach. All spiritual life, all moral changes, all best growth have their origin in this. It purifies and exalts the affections, it stimulates the intellectual life, it exerts its most potent influence upon that mighty factor in our being which we call the will, controlling its choices, rectifying its decisions, and bringing it into beautiful and cheerful subjection to the all-wise, all-holy and supreme will of the universe. As the divine Architect is allowed to work in us, "to will and to do of His good pleasure," we shall become fully and rightly developed men after the original plan and according to the Christ standard.

And thereby Christianity furnishes not only the perfect model of character, and the sufficient motive to secure it, but also, the necessary means for its development; viz., its own inspired and inspiring truth, personal communion with God, and personal service for God and men. The Bible should be the king of books in the libraries of men. Its wisdom is divine, and is deposited nowhere else. Prayer is the divine artist who dips his brush in the fadeless tints of immortality and transfers them to human characters. He who would mount the scala santa that leads to true manhood, must do it on bended knees. Moreover, the strength of Christ's manliness was His helpfulness, His usefulness, His unwearied and unselfish activity. The movement of His feet, the labor of His hands, the utterance of His lips, the outgoing of His spirit—these were the evidences of His true divinity and of His perfect humanity. The highest life is reached in service, rendered to Christ and for Christ. He who would be greatest among you, let him be the servant of all.

"Unheard, because our ears are dull,
Unseen, because our eyes are dim,
He walks on earth, the Wonderful,
And all great deeds are done for Him."

If therefore, the ultimate aim of education is personal character, Christianity must be a necessary element in it. Christianity has created and multiplied educational facilities, and has kindled a desire for knowledge and mental discipline and growth. It has been the mother of schools and has founded academies and universities. It has stimulated thought and inquiry. It has pushed on investigation and discovery. It has widened the boundaries of knowledge. It has given birth to scholars and libraries and literatures. But its supreme value as an educational force is seen in the completeness of its conception of the education which man needs as a moral and spiritual as well as intellectual being, and in the fact that it furnishes in itself the only perfect model, the only adequate motive, and the only sufficient means for the attainment of the highest nobility, perfection and manliness of character, of which we have any knowledge.—Standard.

THE GOSPEL OF LOVE

BY PRESIDENT HYDE

The spirit that was in Jesus was one of love to God and the humblest of God's children. That spirit is at once the spirit of the Father and of every Christian man. Whoever has that spirit is a Christian; whoever lacks it is none of Christ's. Christianity, which is the reproduction of Christ's spirit of universal love in the hearts of His followers, includes the truth in Epicureanism without its error. It has a logical bond, a moral dynamic, a spiritual motive to altruistic conduct which no Epicurean logician or prophet could evolve. This dynamic is love to the Christ who loves every one. Christianity, then, has the Epicurean gladness without its exclusiveness; its joy without its selfishness; its naturality without its baseness; its geniality without its heartlessness.

Christianity likewise includes the truth and excludes the error in Platonism. It gives us the Platonic aristocracy of virtue without its narrowness of sympathy; its supremacy of reason without the suppression of the lowly. Likewise Christianity gives us the Aristotelian intensity without its inconsiderateness; its sanity without its self-centered calculation; its friendship without its exclusiveness. Christianity is the gospel of love; the love of the alien to the enemy, as well as of the fellow citizen to the friend; of the unthankful and the evil, as well as the gracious and the good. Christianity, therefore, is the final type of personality. All modern thinking is saturated with it. All our great modern thinkers put this principle to the front. Kant's "Treat humanity, whether in thyself or in another, ever as an end, never as a means;" Hegel's "Be a person and respect others as persons." Royce's "In so far as in thee lies, act as if thou were at once thy neighbor and thyself.

Treat these two lives as one,'' are all different translations of Jesus' Golden Rule; so many different ways of stating the supreme law of love which is the heart and core of Christianity. Personality in a world of persons lovingly sensitive to the claims of all upon the thoughts and feelings, words and deeds of each, is the distinctive Christian principle. Towards this all other systems, in so far as they were true, have tended; this Christian principle is the climax and consummation of them all.

MACHINE RELIGION

There is a limit to inventions. The preacher may print his ideas on a typewriter at the rate of sixty words a minute, but he must think them out in the old way. The young man may telephone his sweetheart to meet him by moonlight, but he must win her in the old, old fashion. And there is no patent way of bringing religion and people together. Religion must get incarnate, put on hats and boots, and go to the people one at a time. This is the way Jesus did. He loves mankind. But when we look for the proof of that generalization we find it in the fact that He went home with Zaccheus, and put His hand on Bartimeus, and said to Matthew, ''Follow Me.''—The Interior.

THE TIE THAT BINDS

I have heard of two Christian men who met in the waiting room of a railway station in a foreign land. They were all alone, and they would willingly have beguiled a weary hour with conversation, for each of them felt instinctively that they had something in common. But they belonged to different nations and neither of them understood the other's tongue. At last one of them looked pleasantly at the other, and said in a reverent voice, ''Immanuel,'' and the other gladly answered, ''Hallelujah.''

SACRIFICE OF SELF

At Northfield, Dr. H. C. Mabie related this instance of self-denial: In Sherman's campaign it became necessary, in the opinion of the leader, to change commanders. O. O. Howard was promoted to lead a division which had been under the command of another general. Howard went through the campaign at the head of the division, and on to Washington to take part in the review. The night before the veterans were to march down Pennsylvania avenue General Sherman sent for General Howard and said to him: "Howard, the politicians and the friends of the man whom you succeeded are bound that he shall ride at the head of his old corps, and I want you to help me out." "But it is my command," said Howard, "and I am entitled to ride at its head." "Of course you are," said Sherman. "You led them through Georgia and the Carolinas, but, Howard, you are a Christian." "What do you mean?" replied Howard. "If you put it on that ground it changes the whole business. What do you mean, General Sherman?" "I mean that you can stand the disappointment. You are a Christian." "Putting it on that ground there is but one answer. Let him ride at the head of the corps." "Yes, let him have the honor," added Sherman, "But, Howard, you will report to me at nine o'clock, and ride by my side at the head of the whole army." In vain Howard protested, but Sherman said gently but authoritatively, "You are under my orders." When the bugle sounded the next morning, Howard was found trembling like a leaf, and it required another order from General Sherman before he was willing to take the place assigned him. He had, as a Christian, yielded the place to another which rightly belonged to him, and in the grand review found himself not at the head of the corps, but at the head of the army.

THE CHRISTIAN IDEAL OF LIFE

BY THE REV. HUGH MACMILLAN, D.D., LL.D.

Of all places in the Holy Land, Banias, near Cæsarea Philippi is, by common consent, the fairest. It received its name from the worship of the god Pan, which was introduced there by the first Greek emigrants. Niches, with Greek inscriptions in his honor, are carved in the great ruddy amphitheatre of rock that shuts in the Pagan sanctuary from the world; and the whole scene seems to be conscious of the presence of this sunny god of nature, and to be musical with the sweet melody of his pipings. The traveler, oppressed by the long aridity of the stony hillsides over which he has passed, feels the refreshment of the vivid and beautiful life of the place; the rustling green foliage and laughing waters, and the cool flickering shadows, into which the snows of Hermon have been transformed. The whole landscape looks like a bit of Greece transported to this northernmost corner of the alien land; and the worship of the leafy god is here brought into strange association with the lofty, austere faith of the Jewish people.

In striking contrast with the joyful nature of the place, it was here that our Lord for the first time gave the revelation of Himself as the suffering Messiah. Here He first displayed the cross, and showed that His life was to be one long avenue of sorrow, ascending up to the cross in Jerusalem at the end. Peter had just made the noble confession of his faith, "Thou art the Christ, the Son of the living God." Flesh and blood had not revealed to him this great truth, but the Father in heaven. And yet what a different revelation of God, a God stooping, suffering, dying, did Jesus give, from that which human imagination had pictured of its divinities in that spot. The god worshiped at Banias was the impersonation of all that was loveliest and happiest in the world. He was placed there as the presiding genius of the place, the representative of all the gods of Olympus. And we know how these gods were regarded by their votaries. The Greeks conceived their divinities to be placid beings, sunk in immortal repose, beyond the deep blue sky. They were always pictured by the poets as free from sorrow, leading lives unruffled by any care, satisfied with their own glory, "haunt-

—21C

ing that lucid interspace of world and world,'' where no sound of human sorrow could mount up to mar their everlasting calm. Or if they did occasionally visit our woe-stricken world, they came down to it only as visitors, bent upon selfish amusement, or agreeable adventure; undertaking, but only in sport, our human tasks, and altogether untouched by the burden of our woe. The beautiful Pantheism of the Greek religion, worshiped at Banias, seemed altogether aloof from the deeper and sadder experiences of human life. It had nothing akin to sympathy with sorrow. It was a selfish enjoyment, an æsthetic charm. And like the gods were their votaries. They lived in the age of nature, in a climate divinely fair. They loved all beautiful things, and strove to give them an immortal permanence in their art and poetry. Enjoyment of the senses, of the intellect, of the imagination, was their highest conception of life.

How entirely different from this Greek ideal was the revelation of sorrow and self-sacrifice which our Lord gave at Banias, such a revelation, as I have said, seemed altogether alien from the associations of the spot. No wonder that Peter's mind could not take in such a contradictory idea as that of a suffering God. All that he had been told of this great being, whom the world expected, was concerned only with glory and triumph and joy. The idea which the Jews had of their Messiah was that He would restore the kingdom to Israel; that He would bring back the glories of Solomon's reign. Carried away by the popular conceptions the disciples themselves were actually dreaming dreams, and cherishing hopes regarding the high positions they expected to occupy when their Master should come into possession of His kingdom. And therefore, if Jesus was truly, as Peter was beginning in a dim way to recognize, the Son of the living God, it was not possible that He could be subjected to such indignities and sufferings as He foretold. In his forward impulsive way he gave expression to the deep revulsion of feeling which took place in his mind, ''Be it far from Thee Lord: this shall not happen unto Thee.'' But Jesus put aside the personality of Peter altogether, and addressed Himself to the evil power that was making Peter its instrument and mouthpiece—''Get thee behind me Satan; for thou savorest not the things that be of God, but those that be of man.''

The incident vividly recalls the first temptation of our Lord. How different were the two scenes; the arid, leafless wilderness of Judea, the most desolate, forsaken spot on the Lord's earth, where all the circumstances were in perfect harmony with the gloom and misery of the Satanic kingdom unveiled in it, and created a hunger, not only of the body, but also of the soul; and this lovely spot at Herman's Ford, where the soul drained a full goblet of sensuous delight, and only suggestions of human happiness could come to the mind. But the nature of the temptation to our Lord in both cases was the same. It was to choose a life of ease and self-indulgence; to use His divine power for selfish purpose, instead of choosing a life of self-sacrifice and suffering for the good of others. In the one case Satan employed all the terrors of the wilderness to compel Christ, and the force of repulsion and contrast, to choose the easy indulgent life. In the other case Satan employed all the charms and blandishments of nature at his loveliest, and human friendship at its sweetest, to allure Him, so that on this Delilah's lap He might be shorn of the locks of His strength, and abandon His career of voluntary sacrifice.

But Jesus had as resolute a sense in the first temptation as in the second that the Messiah from heaven was to win His kingdom only by patient endurance and patient suffering. He was to conquer not by wielding the sword of power, but by drinking the cup of sorrow. His glory was to be displayed in bearing the shame of the cross. He was to save others through His inability to save Himself. The Creator could not become the Redeemer by a mere word of power, costing him nothing. Only through the fellowship of human woes, could he heal these woes. Only through being made sin, could He make an end of sin. "It behooved the Christ to suffer," was the divine truth, of which He had the clearest recognition, and this conviction He strove to impart to His disciples. Jesus was to go before bearing His cross; but they were to follow Him bearing theirs which was also His. They were to know the fellowship of His sufferings and to be made conformable to His death. Their life was not to be a life of ease and enjoyment and selfish ambition; but a life of ministering to others, and giving themselves up even to death for this purpose. They had to go up to Jerusalem, to leave the beautiful scenes of Banias, and take the straight and narrow way of hardship and toil and self-denial where the cross of martyrdom awaited them. It is seldom that the narrators of the gospel story tell their own feelings; but on this occasion they were moved to indicate them. And what a picture do they give us! Jesus went before them, and "they were amazed, and as they followed, they were afraid." They had for a moment spiritual vision. They saw over our Lord the shadow of the cross; and that while He was shrinking with a natural human shrinking from it, He was bracing Himself for the strain. There was on His face the light of unconquerable resolve; and the sight filled the disciples with a nameless awe and fear. But they followed Him nevertheless, drawn by the spell of His presence; in their fear and awe clinging only the more closely to Him, and as they followed Him up the steep and arduous mountain path to the cross that crowned it, they found in their after experience that it was a path that led to life and glory everlasting. Putting behind them the things that be of men, which were Satan's temptations, so natural and pleasing to the self-indulgence of the human heart, they set their faces steadfastly to the place of their trial desolate and painful to flesh and blood, although the prospect and reality might be. And so they were companions in the kingdom and patience of Jesus Christ. They suffered with Him and they reigned with Him.—Christian Work.

WHAT CHRISTIANITY HAS DONE FOR EDUCATION

BY PRESIDENT CHARLES F. THWING, D.D., LL.D.

The purpose of Christianity is identical with the purpose of education. The purpose of Christianity is to establish the kingdom of God among men; the purpose of education is to create the highest type of a human being. The purpose of Christianity is to cause men to know the truth, to love the good, to do the right; the purpose of education is to increase knowledge, to persuade men to prefer the better course, and to make conditions righteous. The purpose of Christianity is to incarnate divinity in humanity; the purpose of education is to cause men to curb passion, to regulate desire, to purify affection and to exercise proper self-control. In securing its purposes Christianity makes use, among other means, of a Book; in securing its purposes, education makes use among other means, of books. Christianity employs the greatest of motives, love; education also employs the same motive, and employs it the more constantly and the more potently as its success is the greater. Christianity does not neglect the personal force in securing the finest type of personality; education also employs personality as a means, as well as embodying an ultimate aim. Christianity in its founder has a Teacher, and those who came into the most intimate association with Him were called disciples; education finds its center of influence in the teacher, and about the teacher are clustered learners and students. In Christianity the two words, Christ and Disciple, are primary in point of time and of importance; in education the two words, teacher and scholar, are also primary in point of time and of intellectual and ethical value. Therefore it should at once be said that Christianity and education are in many respects identical. Yet in other respects they are to be differentiated, for education, as we usually use the word, applies to a movement or an institution of human origin and destiny; Christianity, as we usually use the word, applies to a movement or an institution of divine origin.

In this necessarily brief discussion of the influence of Christianity upon education, I shall limit myself to its influence upon the higher education. Yet this limitation is not by any means to be received as an acknowledgment that Christianity does not have an influence upon education of every form and degree. For in this most important field of public education Christianity does have a tremendous influence. Even if the influence is rather atmospheric than institutional, rather general than organic, it may perhaps be all the stronger. For Christianity belongs to the very nature of public education. It underlies the purposes of the public school; it supplies the motives for work in the public school; it aids the public school in the training of its teachers, of its students. Christianity is more vitally related to the public schools than it is to any other department of this great body, political and civil.

But upon the institutions and methods of the higher education the influence of Christianity is yet more clearly manifest and distinct.

The colleges of Oxford and Cambridge are essentially ecclesiastic foundations. It was the religious spirit which moved their founders. The glory of God and the increase of knowledge respecting Him was the purpose that prevailed in their establishment. The relation of the college to the church was and is constant and intimate. Scholarships were especially founded for students of divinity; masters and teachers were not infrequently required to be clergymen. Christ College, founded in 1532, at Oxford, is essentially a cathedral foundation; its head is a dean, and five of its canons are professors of divinity. Many of the conditions respecting the students indicated the religious relationship. The requirements as to divine worship, and the reading of the Bible and its public explanation, the provisions made for holding theological disputations, the giving of divinity lectures—those and other similar details indicate the specifically religious character of the colleges of our oldest universities. Not only in their foundation, but also in their continued work, the same religious relationship is made conspicuous. The English church has, since their foundation, found in Oxford and Cambridge its worthiest and most constant support. The schools on the banks of the Cam and the Isis have proved to be sources from which the church has drawn sustenance. They have been arsenals for weapons defensive and offensive. One of the greatest works of the English church in the last 200 years and more has been in its ministry to and through the higher education. If Oxford and Cambridge or similar agencies had not existed, this ministry of the church could not have been made. Whatever is largest and strongest, of highest privilege, and of greatest dignity, which the English church today possesses, it has drawn and still continues to draw from these ancient ecclesiastical foundations.

The American college was and is molded after the English examples. We have adopted rather the collegiate than the university system. Our American colleges are to a large extent religious, and even denominational foundations. At the present time, according to a personal letter sent to me by Dr. Harris, the United States Commissioner of Education, there are in this country 695 institutions conferring collegiate degrees. This number includes 163 colleges for women only, and also fifty-one schools of technology. Of the 481 institutions which are for men only or are co-educational, 109 only are non-sectarian. The remaining 372 are controlled by religious denominations, as follows:

Roman Catholic, 58; Methodist Episcopal, 57; Baptist, 50; Presbyterian, 39; Methodist Episcopal South, 25; Congregational, 25; Lutheran, 23; Christian, 20; United Brethren, 13; Reformed, 8; Friends, 7; Cumberland Presbyterian, 7; United Presbyterian, 6; Protestant Episcopal, 5; African Methodist Episcopal, 4; Evangelical, 4; Universalist, 4; Seventh Day Adventist, 3; Methodist Protestant, 2; Free Will Baptist, 2; Reformed Presbyterian, 2; Southern Presbyterian, 1; Christian Union, 1; Seventh Day Baptist, 1; African Methodist Episcopal Zion, 1; Church of God, 1; New Church, 1; Latter Day Saints, 1; Unknown, 1.

Of the 163 colleges for women fifty-four are non-sectarian, and the remaining 109 are controlled by religious denominations, as follows:

Baptist, 27; Presbyterian, 22; Methodist Episcopal, 20; Methodist Episcopal South, 18; Protestant Episcopal, 5; Lutheran, 5; Moravian, 3; Cumberland Presbyterian, 2; Reformed, 2; Christian, 2; Roman Catholic, 2; Universalist, 1.

The bare record of these facts is proof of the degree to which Christianity, as embodied in various churches, is controlling the higher education in the United States. We must not forget, also, that in not a few of the colleges that are described as non-sectarian the Christian influence is quite as strong as it is found to be in colleges that are called sectarian.

Let us also bear in mind that in certain of the state universities the Christian influence is pervasive. The state university has the right to be—as also I may say it has the duty of being—as Christian as is the state itself. Although the influences of certain state universities may on the whole be anti-Christian, yet the influences of the far greater number are in favor of Christianity, both as a system of theology, and as embodying rules and principles of conduct. I may be allowed to say, at this point, that it was the intense sectarianism of certain churches in the newer states in the first half of the present century which contributed to the foundation of universities under the control of the state. It was the rivalry of the churches which prevented the religious part of the community from acquiring that influence which it ought to have acquired in the promotion of the higher education. It was only when the most intelligent and patriotic men of certain of our states came to perceive that the churches would not unite in the establishment of great universities that they at last felt compelled to turn toward the state as their hope for founding and equipping worthy seats of scholarship and of the higher training.

It is ever to be remembered that a religious, and not infrequently a denominational, or even a clerical, purpose obtained in the founding of many of our colleges. Our oldest college was founded not only for the general purpose of promoting piety and learning, but also for the specific purpose of training a ministry for the church. The second college founded in this country, William and Mary, in 1693, grew out of a desire to give Virginia a well-equipped body of Episcopal clergymen. Yale, beginning its work in the first year of the last century, embodied in its establishment the aim of promoting a more orthodox type of piety than prevailed elsewhere. Princeton, although not originally connected with the Presbyterian church, was, through the first efforts made for the erection of a college in New Jersey, associated with the first schism in that church, and he who was chosen its first president was selected largely on account of his being a great preacher and a great scholar in divinity. The earliest intimation that has been discovered of any design of founding a college in the state of New York is found in the records of Trinity church, and the charter of the college named as one of its governors the Archbishop of Canterbury.

The influence of Christianity in founding colleges is quite as constant, as pervasive and as conspicuous in the nineteenth century as it was in the seventeenth century and the first half of the eighteenth. As population has moved westward, the church has moved westward, and, with the church, the college has also moved westward. Christianity as an aggressive force has organized and constituted itself into denominations, and these denominations, embodying aggressive Christianity, have founded the colleges in the states that lie between the Alleghanies and the Pacific. The primary purpose of the church in laying and cherishing these foundations has been manifold. The church has desired to promote the highest interests of humanity, broadly interpreted; it has perceived and felt that the public schools system was necessary for the advancing of the best interests of humanity; it has known that no system of public schools can be properly administered without receiving that aid and inspiration which come from the presence of learned men in the community. In order to create men of learning the church founded the college. The college has perceived, also, that its own growth depended upon the presence of worthy leadership in its pastorate. Such leadership, it has known, must be constituted by men of learning and of culture. It has, therefore, founded the college. When one reads such a record as Hamilton College, founded in 1812, Kenyon in 1824, Western Reserve in 1826, Dennison in 1832, Oberlin in 1833, Marietta in 1835, Wabash in 1834, Illinois in 1835, Knox in 1837, Iowa in 1847, Ohio Wesleyan in 1844, Beloit in 1846, Northwestern in 1851, Lake Forest in 1856, Hillsdale in 1855, Olivet in 1859, Hamlin in 1854, Wheaton in 1861, Berea in 1865, Carleton in 1866, Hiram in 1867, Wooster in 1866, Colorado in 1874, Doane in 1872, Drury in 1873, one has evidence sufficient, through the bare mention of these names, and the names of scores of other colleges, to prove the proposition that Christianity has founded and has cherished institutions of higher education. These institutions have sprung up in the wake of the westward-moving population, and have sprung up because of the activity and zeal of Christian people. Whatever the state may do—and it has done much, and will continue to do much—this great people of ours cannot be too often told, or too strongly impressed with the great truth that Christianity has done more for the higher education than all other agencies.

The history of the higher education that is thus suggested as one of the results of Christianity, is a history that, in its self-sacrifice, brave daring, and triumphant faith, is one with the noble annals of the eleventh chapter of Hebrews.—Examiner.

POSSESSION NOT ENJOYMENT

Here is a story of a miser told by the Roumanian papers. A Greek died in the small town of Caracal, having always lived on the alms of his compatriots. Before dying he made his wife swear that she would bury him in the dirty old overcoat which he wore every day. The poor woman had to ask the Greeks of Caracal to help her to provide the costs of the funeral. A kind-hearted Greek went to see her in her affliction, and, pointing to the body, said he would give her a better coat to bury the man in. Then she told him of the dead man's last wish. The Greek, whose suspicions were awakened, told her that she should certainly not part with the body before she had well examined the coat, for there must be some particular reason for the request. The widow unpicked the lining of the overcoat and found 35,000 franc bank notes which the miser wished to take into the grave with him. So are there those to whom by the grace of God are given the treasures of divine goodness, yet they live as spiritual paupers. There are misers in eternal things as well as in temporal.

THE CHRISTIANITY OF TODAY

BY THE REV. P. S. HENSON, D.D.

My subject is the *Christianity* of today, and I propose to consider it under four distinct heads—that is, more or less distinct: its peculiarities, its power, its perils, and its prospects.

First, as to its peculiarities. The thing that perhaps more than anything else distinguishes it is the fact that it is pre-eminently liberal; liberal in respect to differences of religious belief among Christians, who are regarded as evangelical. Time was when professed followers of Him Who was meek and lowly of heart, Who gave us the sermon on the mount, and Who was love incarnate, burnt each other at the stake for Jesus' sake. And this intolerance was exhibited not only by Papists, but even by the Puritian fathers, who were a queer lot, and who while they sought "freedom to worship God according to the dictates of their own conscience," were not always careful to concede that freedom to others, as Roger Williams, if he took the witness stand, could testify. And so they subjected our Baptist fathers to all sorts of pains and penalties for being disturbers of the public peace. And the Episcopalians, at least in my own old state of Virginia, were not far behind them in the matter of intolerance. And even Baptists, if the whole truth must be told, were not slow to pronounce anathemas against those who differed with them as to the ordinances of the gospel, and they did not feel that they properly expounded the word unless they properly pounded those whom they regarded as perverters of that word. They did not content themselves with speaking the truth in love, but gnashed their teeth and clenched their fists and pawed the earth and clawed the air, and were inclined to believe that no man could hold a contrary view unless he were willfully blind, and a child of the devil beside.

Now, there are not only interchanges of ordinary courtesies among Christians of different denominations, but exchange of pulpits and hearty co-operation in evangelistic and philanthropic work, and a cordial concession of mutual sincerity in the things wherein we denominationally differ. And accordingly, whatever may be

said of open or close communion, interdenominational love feasts
have become so common as scarcely to excite remark; and our favorite scriptural motto today is, "Whereunto we have already attained, let us walk by the same rule, let us mind the same things."
And even as to the Catholics the fierce antagonism that once raged
seems to have subsided, and it is no uncommon sight to find papal
prelates and Protestant ministers on the very same platform, engaged in the same religious services—and this was notably true
during the World's Fair. And Jews and Christians, that used to
stand so far apart, have come so close together that even in the
same house of worship, and that a Baptist house, in this city, the
Jews worship one day and the Baptists the next, and there seems to
be no antagonism or disturbance of the peace. And in our great
Baptist University of Chicago a distinguished Jewish rabbi is
counted as among the foremost members of its faculty.

Not only so; but as to the faiths that were once accounted
heathen it used to be supposed that they were all of them fabricated
by the devil, conceived in sin and shapen in iniquity, and that all
of their adherents were simply given over to be damned. They
were supposed to be rude barbarians, nude, or nearly so, and intellectually about as scantily furnished as they were physically,
and morally as being scarcely above the brutes that perish. It has
latterly been discovered that in their so-called sacred books there
are many things that are beautiful and true, lofty sentiments and
salutary precepts, and that among these so-called heathen there are
many very admirable things, things that have quite carried away
even such an accomplished and erudite scholar as Edwin Arnold,
carried him away so far that he has been carried away bodily, becoming enamored of a dark-eyed oriental maid and turning his
back upon "the little tight bound isle" to revel in the "Light of
Asia." The Parliament of Religions was an eye-opener to many.
We discovered that these heathen could talk. You remember the
picture of the child and the dog, and underneath the legend, "Can
you talk?" We not only discovered that they could talk, but could
talk so fluently and forcefully and suavely as quite to overpower
many susceptible and unsophisticated souls, and to raise the question whether Christendom has not heretofore been befooled by
peripatetic missionary agents who have made men believe that the
heathen were only degraded and miserable reprobates. And we

have come to consider whether instead of seeking a *casus belli* we ought not rather to find some *modus vivendi,* and adjust some compromise, making mutual concessions, and by securing universal consensus agree upon some sort of world religion, a kind of religious Volapuk, that would make an end of all this Babel of theological confusion. In any event we have come to have a higher respect for the so-called heathen, and to understand that they are not to be belabored, but to be affectionately labored with, and that we need to send as our representatives to them not the men who by reason of their incapacity and illiteracy and mental feebleness are unable to obtain occupation in Christian lands, but to send instead our foremost scholars and astutest thinkers.

And as to the future state of those who are not avowed and consistent Christians there has been an unmistakable softening in the tone of public teaching and of private thinking. It is very noticeable that hell and damnation are words that are under the censor's ban, and may scarcely be uttered in a fashionable pulpit, and that in our revised version in most cases the former is softened into hades and the latter into condemnation. You remember the story of the two ministers who met by the roadside on Monday morning, and one of them asked the other what he preached about the previous day. "I gave 'em hell," he replied, as if he loved the taste of brimstone. That man is dead, and so far as I know he has no successor. There is nobody that now believes what they used to believe, that there are infants in hell not a span long. Nobody now believes that there are infants in hell, no matter how long. Nobody now, so far as I know or have reason to believe, insists that there is material fire—if fire can be called material—in hell, or a real worm, or real chains, any more than we believe that there are harps such as we are used to, and crowns such as we think of, and pearls such as earth knows of, in heaven. We have come to believe and teach that hell is a state; and there are many who have come to doubt whether it be a place at all. I am not now speaking in this particular about my own opinion, and yet I am willing to have all men know that I believe that these forms of speech to which we are accustomed, the worm, the chain, the fire, are simply figurative representations of things infinitely dreadful and for which no words of which we are masters can give us any conception. The tendency is to teach that it is not a place but a state, and that the punishment is not so much in the nature of physical infliction as psychical suffering. ''The mind is its own place, and of itself can make a hell of heaven, a heaven of hell.'' It is beginning even to be questioned whether there is either such a state or place for those who, like the heathen, have not had a chance, or what may be supposed a fair chance in this world. And the question is also raised as to whether for those that are not heathen but live in Christian lands, and yet have been the victims of unfortunate heredity or unfavorable environment, there will not be another chance, in a state of future probation. Nay, more, the question is very widely discussed whether for anybody, heathen or other, there is any such state of utter and eternal misery. There is cultivated a larger hope, a broader humanitarianism, a sensitive shrinking from the thought of eternal suffering for any of God's creatures. There is a deeply felt difficulty in the minds of many in reconciling such a condition with man's conception of God's goodness, to say nothing of His justice. And along with this there is raised a question as to whether sin is not rather a disease to be pitied than criminality to be punished. And there is an intensity of sympathy with unfortunate conditions for which we make allowance and for which we are disposed to think that God ought to make allowance. I am stating simply the trend of our time.

As to manner of life: Time was when asceticism marred the sweetness of Christian character, and made men shrink from it as utterly unnatural and unlovely. Men and women thought that the world was essentially evil, and therefore they must flee from it and hide themselves in convents and cloisters, in dens and caves, in forests and mountain fastnesses. They thought that the body was evil, and therefore was to be macerated and flagellated and subjected to untold torture. These heathenish notions very largely prevailed even in some branches of the Christian church. And some of our Protestant American ancestors were of that persuasion, and the Pilgrim Fathers well deserved the name ''Pill Grim.'' Whether as the result of the infusion of European elements or of a broader and juster view of the uses of the Sabbath, we have bravely got over at least our Sabbath scruples. And as to diversions and indulgences that were once accounted worldly and from which professed Christians were debarred, we have certainly attained unto a broader view and allow ourselves a larger latitude. And while this relaxation has its attendant perils, concerning which a word by and by, there cannot be a question that the Christianity of today has in it more of sweetness and of light, more of sunshine and of song, more of winsomeness and therefore more of wisdom than the joyless and apparently loveless type that it has happily superseded.

Second, The Christianity of today is rational. I do not mean to say that rational Christianity was just born today, but there is a widespread revolt against mere superstition, and there has been a great deal of it, even adhering to Christianity, the outgrowth of ignorance and the ready resource of ecclesiastical tyrants. And the revolt has spread to tradition. The fact that a thing has been believed time whereof the memory of man runneth not to the contrary may raise a sort of presumption in its favor, but presumption is not proof, and time and again a presumption has been overthrown by the loosened avalanche of truth. The fact that the fathers taught it or that councils decreed it is not so conclusive as it used to be. Men want to know, and they properly want to know, for what reason they taught it and on what ground they decreed it. The fact that a man has been dead a thousand years gives no overpowering weight to his dictum, but rather raises a presumption against him, as having been dead so long as to be behind the times. Men want new and live things rather than fossiliferous remains, no matter how saintly.

And men depreciate dogma as they never did before, and have come to hate it as intensely as a notorious faith healing fakir in Chicago hates drugs and doctors and professes to hate the devil. Dogma means formulated doctrine that is to be received upon authority; and modern Christianity is not predisposed to be especially deferential to authority, but insists that the teaching shall commend itself to the reason and the conscience. And as a consequence there has been a re-examination of the tenets of theology and a restatement of many of them in terms that are more apprehensible by rational human beings and worthier of God Almighty. The iron molds and the Procustean beds which were fashioned by some of the elder theologians have been broken up and sent to the junk shop, while elastic forms, elastic because instinct with life, have been adopted by the church instead.

In dealing with the Bible the place of reason has been recognized more largely than ever before. In the examination of its credentials and method of construction, Christians have come to be aware of the existence of other so-called sacred books, and have felt that it was not amiss to bring the Book we call the Bible to the bar of reason and demonstrate its transcendent superiority to all other books; for the Lord does not require of us a blind credulity, for He says, "Come now, let us reason together." And realizing that the Bible was not let down from heaven like the sheet that Peter saw, or dug out of the earth as the Book of Mormon professes to have been, and that it was not spoken out of a phonograph, but was written by mortal men providentially raised up for the purpose, Christianity today recognizes the legitimacy of inquiries as to the human authors and the contemporary circumstances of these compositions, and even as to the use by Scripture writers of pre-existing materials. Nor does it regard it as an invalidation of the authority of the Book if such use should be demonstrated beyond all peradventure; any more than there is raised a presumption against the Calvary Baptist Church edifice, because it was constructed out of materials that once composed the main building of the old University of Chicago. If some one passing that way should recognize a door or a window that had once done service on the campus of that now long dead institution, and would say, "I have seen that before somewhere; you have stolen that from the old university,"—no matter for that. No matter though these materials were pre-existent, no matter though this is the very same window of the very same door, the only question is as to whether this house is adapted to the purposes of worship, whether it meets the end that was contemplated in its construction. In all this and out of all this critical inquiry there is destined to come a clearer understanding of the Word of God, a removal of difficulties that have painfully perplexed many thoughtful minds, and a firmer faith in God and His Word. For let us be assured of this, that the foundation of God standeth sure, and that digging down to the foundations will not undermine the foundations, and though ever and anon something may fall away and a cloud of dust be thrown in the eyes and a shout of exultation be raised by the enemy, it will presently be discovered that what fell away was only some stucco plastered on the walls by impertinent human hands, but that in the wall itself not one of the living stones has ever been jostled out of place; for though heaven and earth pass away, not one jot or tittle of God's Word shall fail.

In the third place the Christianity of today is intensely practical. The transcendental type of piety,

"Whose lifted eyes salute the skies,
Whose bended knees the ground"—

has had its day and gone its way.

"Ye men of Galilee, why stand ye gazing up into heaven?" said the angels to the transfixed disciples, the meaning evidently being that there was a world of work to be done between Christ's coming and His going, and they needed to be "up and at it." This is realized in our time as never before in all time.

Mr. Gough used to tell of a beautiful woman, who, withdrawing her glove from her hand, on the sidewalk, dropped a beautiful diamond ring, which bounded into a gutter brimming with slush, and seemed for a time to be hopelessly lost, but, drawing back the lace from her white arm, she thrust her hand and arm into the slush and felt until she found the treasure she had lost.

The like of this, Christianity is doing today. Time was when the church was characterized by such daintiness as found expression in the Song of Solomon, "I have washed my feet, and how shall I defile them?" Now she boldly wades into the slums and is heroically striving to clean them out. The Christianity of today not only believes in attending the prayer-meeting but the primaries; not only in preaching the gospel but in purifying politics; not only in opening the Sunday-school but in closing the saloon; not only in preparing for a heaven above but in doing what we can to make a heaven below.

And as to power, never has it had such swing and sweep as today. The world's whole literature is saturated with it. Every publishing house in civilized nations is sending forth countless tons of books and periodicals dealing with religion, for it or against it. It is hardly possible to publish a successful novel unless it deals with religious questions, as witness that novel with a Latin title by an author with an unpronounceable name. Morally and politically—I put these together because only on moral grounds should the church deal with political questions—it has swept slavery

—22C

from the face of the earth, at least in civilized lands. It inaugurated the irrepressible conflict that ended with the emancipation proclamation. It has blotted out Mormonism, and will never let up on the saloon. It has damned indecent politics. The man from Kentucky would have lifted his brazen front unblushingly in congress immediately after the uncovering of his infamy in any time but this, and now he is damned beyond redemption. And that once famous member of the United States Senate that presided after a fashion over that intractable body and prodded the Confederates with the spear of Ithuriel, spoke once on a time to the effect that the moral law had no place in politics and that the purification of politics was an iridescent dream; and ever since he has himself been nothing but a dream, only anything but iridescent. And Christian conscience is making an impression even in Chicago, and damning the doctrine that to the victors belong the spoils. And today it holds in leash the dogs of war and covers with contempt the dancing jingo thirsting for blood. It demands in the name of God Almighty that Cuba shall be free, but it stands by the patient and patriotic president who is resolved to exhaust every resource under heaven before the bloody carnage shall begin. God grant that his labors may be crowned with success and that in this last decade of the nineteenth century Christianity may have its proudest triumph not in letting loose the dogs of war, but holding them in leash as long as possible, and, let us hope, giving us freedom for Cuba with honor for America.

And yet there are perils that seriously threaten Christianity today. One of them arises from that very liberality in which we have been wont to glory. There is danger of its degenerating into a culpable indifference even with reference to the very fundamentals of religion. We ought never to forget that it does make a difference what a man believes. We ought not only to love our brethren well enough not to suffer sin upon them, but well enough not to suffer them, even in doctrine, to go wrong to their detriment. Paul was not lacking in love to Peter when he withstood him to the face. And Peter afterward did not love Paul any the less because he had so fearlessly and faithfully dealt with him.

We do not come to see eye to eye by shutting our eyes. I think we have reached a stage in history where we can speak the truth in love, and discuss without bitterness with other Christians the things wherein we differ, and we shall never attain to the unity of the faith and the knowledge of the Son of God until we do.

And as to the great ethnic faiths, there is danger that as the result of the rose-colored representations of them, many professed Christians that are only too ready to husband their resources, may be soothed into somnolence by the comforting persuasion that the heathen are in no particular distress or peril. Let the heathen alone, they are tempted to say, for while Christianity may be well enough for the occidentals, the venerable ethnic faiths are just the thing for the orientals. And so there is likelihood of the loss of such might of motive as was once roused by Jonah Warren, when, in a great missionary mass-meeting, he said, ''Oh! brethren, I cannot sleep at night for listening to the tramp of the hundreds of millions of heathen that are marching to perdition.''

When men believed and felt that way they were ready, if real Christians, to give their last dollar to the treasury, and to send their sons and daughters, or to go themselves to rescue the perishing. And may it not be that our altered and mischievously exaggerated liberal view may have more to do with our depleted missionary treasury than the hard times of which we have heretofore been accustomed to complain.

And as to sin in general, there is danger of our losing sight in our excessive liberalism of the deep and damning significance of a word that God has written in letters of blood and fire, so silencing the thunders of Sinai, and robbing of its glory the cross of Calvary.

And as to liberalism in life, there is imminent danger that liberty will degenerate into license, and that ''O, be joyful,'' will be rendered into ''O, be jolly!'' In our anxiety to popularize religion and to crowd our churches, we are letting down the bars and lowering the conditions of church membership until there is danger of utterly eliminating the heroic element.

When the Lord would enlist Saul of Tarsus under the banner of the cross, he did not invite him to a picnic, but he rather said: ''I will show him how great things he must suffer for my sake.'' And that put him on his mettle by appealing to all that was noblest in his manhood.

And there is danger arising from the rationalizing tendency of our time—danger of eliminating the supernatural element, and substituting the laws of nature for the God of nature—and fixing our thoughts upon mere processes instead of on Him from Whom all things proceed. Danger of substituting evolution for creation, evolution for revelation, and evolution for regeneration. Danger that in our pride of intellect we be tempted to reject as incredible whatsoever is incomprehensible by our microscopic faculties, and that instead of setting our watches by the stars, we shall insist upon setting the stars by our watches. There is danger that we shall be tempted to minimize the miracles in the Bible as if they were a heavy load to carry, of which, if we could only be happily rid, "the sweet reasonableness" of the remainder would win for the Bible a wider acceptance, and so we ingloriously fall into line with those "scoffers" of whom Peter prophesied long time ago, as arising in the last days, and hooting at miracles upon the ground that "all things continue as they were from the beginning."

And there is danger in the very practicality of our Christianity. There is danger of mistaking the means for the end—of putting sociology in the place of soteriology, man in the place of God, and earth in the place of heaven. There is danger of our putting Leigh Hunt's Ben Adhem at the head of the procession as the banner-bearer of the Christianity of today. The angel who might be supposed to know, could not conscientiously enroll him as a lover of the Lord, but Ben Adhem insisted that he was at least a lover of men, and thereupon we are assured that the good angel revised his book and put Ben Adhem's name at the head of the list, as though he had said, "No matter about loving and serving the Creator only so you love and serve the creature." There is danger of this, and danger of substituting care for the promotion of what we have come to call the solidarity of society for solicitude in behalf of the salvation of the individual soul, and of supposing that the world is to be lifted by jackscrews working from below, instead of by supernal agencies drawing from above. There is danger, as the sage of Upland has forcefully said, of diverting our thoughts from the salvation of souls to the mere improvement of material conditions. Humanitarian efforts have their uses, but these uses ought to have reference not so much to the seen and temporal as to the unseen and eternal. "The time is short" and it makes comparatively little matter whether it be spent in abject poverty or in palatial splendor. Humanitarian efforts are chiefly valuable as credentials of Christianity and as giving poor, oppressed and ignorant and sin-sodden mortals a better chance to get a glimpse of heaven, and to attain to glory and honor and immortality and a world beyond the stars.

As to the prospects of Christianity today I have not space to speak; nor need I do more than to say that I believe its grandest triumphs are to come. And while evil men and seducers shall wax worse and worse, the hosts of God shall go from strength to strength, from victory to victory, until Satan's last stronghold shall be demolished, and He Whose right it is to reign shall come, and before Him every knee shall bow, and every tongue confess that He is Lord above to the glory of God the Father.—Standard.

IS MODERN CHRISTIANITY THAT OF CHRIST?

BY THE REV. GEORGE BODDIS

If we compare modern Christianity with that which is recorded in the New Testament, we cannot fail to see that the one presents a strong contrast to the other. The New Testament church was in the world, but not of it; but if we look at the modern church and its purposes, we see little or no difference between them and the world. This leads us to ask, "Is modern Christianity the Christianity of Christ? It has the same name, but is it the same thing?" Every candid student of the Apostolic age will be compelled to answer, "No, it is not." I do not mean by this that there are no professors who can be considered Christians in the Christ-sense. In every age men have lived of whom the world is not worthy. And this age is not an exception. But in general, the Christianity which now presents itself to men is not the Christianity of Christ.

Our conception of Christianity is not that of Christ. The most of us have some conception of what Christianity is. To some it is a church which stands as a monument to one, Jesus, and composed of those who profess to believe in and follow Him. Others look far above and beyond that. To them it is a philosophy emanating from Christ, and through which the world is going to be saved. There is a certain measure of truth in both these ideas; but Christianity is more than either or both of them combined. The Bible leaves no sincere student in doubt as to what Christianity is. It is union with a person, even Christ. John 5:15; John 15:1-6; Galatians 2:20. Without this there can be no Christianity. The Christian life springs from Christ, and is sustained by Him. He lives in Christians, thinks in them and acts through them. Thus Christianity is the introduction into our lives and conduct of the Christ-spirit. Every Christian is to be a living epistle of Christ, known and read of all men. Christianity is the power of God for conquering and regenerating the world. It was for this Christ died and rose again. For this purpose the Holy Spirit breathes His silent influence within the church. For this end the church was instituted. And unless this is done the church has no right to exist. Such, I believe, is the Bible conception of Christianity; can we say it is ours? It may be in theory; but theory is nothing unless it be put into practice. Many of us lack that vital union with Christ. Otherwise, the fruits of the Spirit—love, joy, peace, long-suffering, gentleness, goodness, faith, meekness and temperance— would manifest themselves in our lives. We have not introduced into our lives the Christ-spirit. The things that concern this present life are just in our thoughts, and our conduct even in our church-life is prompted by a spirit the very reverse of our Master's. Neither can we say we aim to win the world for Christ. Instead of going into the highways and hedges in order to bring in the lost, we are content to invite them to our churches.

The conduct of modern Christians is not based upon the examples and teachings of Christ. Christ requires that the mainspring of our actions shall be love. But with us it is just the reverse—the love of praise, the love of pleasure; in short, selfishness. Is it not time for us to pause? We cannot serve Christ without love, for He puts love prior to obedience. If our actions were impelled by love, the world would soon declare for Christ. Again, Jesus requires that our lives shall be a protest against the recognized usages of the world. His life was a protest of this kind. His Apostles were called the men who turned the world upside down. But could the same be said of us? On the contrary, the world has so crept into the church that, except by profession, it is hard to distinguish the one from the other. Christ says, "Renounce the world." He bids us sell all we have and give to the poor. He commands us when we make a feast to invite thereto the poor, the maimed, the lame and the blind. But the modern Christian says, "I shall do no such thing. Such a sacrifice as the surrender of wealth is not required in these days. As to calling the poor to the feast, I cannot do anything so absurd. I must keep up my social rank, and therefore can invite only my friends and equals." We do as the world does, and the world is perfectly content to have it so. We adopt the world's pleasures and customs. We carry on business after the world's methods. We say in deeds, if not in words, "The methods of Christ will not work, and if carried out literally no one could succeed." Jesus requires that we shall spend and be spent in the service of others. Is not this what He did? And has He not said, "If any man will be My disciple, let him deny himself, and take up his cross daily and follow Me?" But we have utterly ignored this. "Every man for himself" is our motto. Gold is our god. We thirst for it, and our attempts to get it know no laws but success. How many are driven to the wall by the methods pursued by so-called Christian merchants? And has the Christianity of today no protest against this? Has it no remedy for this state of things? The Christianity of Christ had. If ours has not, if it does not touch the needs of the present day, it is dead.

The power of modern Christianity is not that which Christ gave to His church. He established His church to save the world, and endowed it with the power to accomplish this mission. What was this power? Was it money? The earth is the Lord's and the fullness thereof, and He can supply us with all we need. Was it intellectuality? That, too, is necessary, and so it is written, "If any man lack wisdom, let him ask of God." But the promised power was not in these. "Ye shall receive power," said Jesus, "after that the Holy Spirit is come upon you." This was the power through which Jesus accomplished His work. Though He was God, yet He accepted our human conditions of service, and wrought only in the power of the Holy Ghost. The Spirit transformed Jesus, and guided Him in the accomplishment of His work. This proves He promised it to the church. It was for this the Apostles waited; it was this which they received and which transformed them and gave them success. This power has never been removed. Yet the church today does not possess it. It is a sad thing, but true, that we have put other things in the place of the Spirit. Money has largely superceded the Holy Ghost. This is a great mistake. Money never did, and never will, hire men to do the work of God. The hireling can never be a shepherd of Christ. This office can be filled only by him who has received the Holy Ghost. Intellectuality has taken the place of the Spirit. Mental power is not to be despised; but it can do nothing without the Spirit. It may fill our houses of worship, but it has no Spiritual uplifting power. It is the gospel applied and enforced by the Holy Ghost which alone saves men. "But," it is objected, "we do have the power." Yes; some few like Moody, Gordon, Spurgeon and others, but it is not true of the church as a whole. If it were true, the world would feel the power more. We cannot for one moment think that these things were for the early church only. God gives his best wine at the last.

The zeal of Modern Christians is not that of Christ. How zealous Christ was! How zealous the Apostles were! But how indifferent are we! If we really believe the gospel, we should be more abundant in labors. Can we believe in the future punishment of the wicked as it is set forth in the New Testament, and continue to lie at our selfish ease? We are up in arms if any one denies there is a hell. But our actions give the lie to our profession of belief in that doctrine. If we were Christians in the Christ-sense, we should all labor for souls. The Apostolic church was abundant in labors. Every one engaged in the work. They that were scattered abroad went everywhere, preaching the Word. Oh, that this were true of us. Our work is not personal. We try to do it by proxy. If we contribute to the support of the gospel at home and the extension of missions abroad, we imagine that our work is done. Christ wants not our money as much as ourselves. If we are His, our money will be His, too. The command to work is personal, and those who neglect personal work are living in disobedience to Christ.

IS CHRISTIANITY PLAYED OUT?

BY THE REV. JOHN CLIFFORD, D.D.

The question is, "Is Christianity Played Out?" The answer I give tonight derives its materials from the Victorian era. For during these five-and-fifty years, as during so many more, Christianity has been in the fiercely-heated laboratory of our manifold life and the results are sufficiently before us to enable us to pronounce a verdict as to whether Christianity ought at this moment to be dispensed with in the service of man, or whether it is worth our while to try to retain its presence a little longer.

Now, in giving answer, I do not close my eyes to certain antagonistic elements which have been powerfully at work during this Victorian era. I can almost shudder now as I think of priests uttering their benedictions upon armies going to war for the destruction of one another. My spirit is grieved exceedingly as I remember the way in which divines went to their Bibles for the purpose of holding up American slavery. As I contemplate the injustice which still enters into the very heart of the conditions of labor I am appalled at the lazy way in which Christian men apply the principles of the gospel to the conditions of our times. I do not forget these enormously antagonistic forces. Forget them? We can't; we wouldn't if we could. Forget them! I am anxious to remember them; for if I find, as I shall do before I have done, that Christianity is alive, and that it is doing the best work that is being done upon this planet at this very moment, then it proves far more completely the strength, the tremendous strength, that there is in the Christian fact, in the Christian idea, and in the Christian spirit. If its victories are being won in the presence of these gigantic foes, treachery within and enmity without, then I claim your confidence for the Christianity that marches on with such consciousness of final victory—unhesitating and unresting— assured that the goal shall be won and that man shall be placed in the full enjoyment of the justice of God.

Sir Humphrey Davy, being congratulated on one occasion because of the brilliance and splendor of some of his chemical discoveries, replied: "My greatest discovery was a man." He found Faraday. Jesus Christ came to seek and to save what was lost. He found, He redeemed, He renewed; He called men from the toll booth and the boat, from sitting at the receipt of custom, and from pursuing their ordinary avocation on the lake. He made those men His friends; He transformed them in character by the penetrating influence of His Spirit; He transfigured them with His own grace and beauty of nature; He fashioned them with His own likeness; He sent them out into the world to make men in the same way that He had made them; and they went, and they made the men, and the men wrought on, and the new race came, and some of it is here tonight. Emerson tells us: "A personal ascendency—that is the only fact much worth considering." All good enters into the world through good men. The better the man, the purer his spirit, the clearer his conceptions of truth and of justice, the larger and the richer his contribution to the life of the world. He, therefore, who makes the best men, he who makes good men, better men, and best men, he is the real leader of mankind. A personal ascendancy is the only fact much worth considering; Jesus Christ made the men who were possessed of the spirit of personal ascendency, who won the triumph over the various forces that were against them, and who wrought righteousness and subdued kingdoms and built up the kingdom of our Lord and Savior Jesus Christ.

The question is whether Christ Jesus is doing anything like that today. Professor Huxley takes a crawfish, and with it he introduces the student of biology to the whole field of investigation; I will take a man that I knew in Christ about forty years ago, skeptical in thought, not pure in life; eager to be just and to be true, but swayed by the influence of bad companions toward injustice and toward untruth. He is captured by the hand of Christ and taken into the school of Christ, and so trained there that his skepticism concerning God and the progress of the human race passes away, and a strong faith in God and in man takes its place. His life is completely changed—changed at the center, changed right to the circumference. Fortunately for him the circumference was a good way off the center. Some men have their circumference so near the center that it is not a hand-stretch to get to it;

but the Christ Who had seized him took him forward and gave him a passion for the salvation of his fellows; and he wrought at it, and wrought until within four years ago, when it pleased the Lord to remove him from his sphere of work; but not before he had been the means of making a number of young fellows disciples of the Lord Jesus Christ, and training them in blessed crusadership against the evils that afflict humanity, and that prevent the progress of the race.

That's my one case. I ask you to go out toward the study of like facts as they present themselves in the history of these fifty-five years. A little while ago, owing to a correspondence that I had with somebody in the Times, it was necessary that I should go and investigate a number of the converts of the Salvation Army that I should see them for myself in their homes, see other people about them, and get reports of their behavior. For it had been asserted by one who claimed to know, that these converts did not stand. I went, I inquired, I gave three days to the investigation, and the result of my inquiry was this: That I discovered these men had been converted from the love of wrong to the love of right, from dissolute habits to virtuous habits, from being the dread and the terror of wife and child, to being comforter and the helper of both. And these facts were so indubitably proved to me that I could not help coming to the conclusion these men were sincere; they gave evidence, we have a right to ask for, of the genuineness of their repentance and the thoroughness of their conversion to God; and I wrote in the spirit and according to the tenor of that statement.

Now I want to know what new force had been at work producing this effect. Here we have a set of facts. You notice their character; here comes a new effect, altering the character of the previous effects. What is the new force that has been injected? What fresh energy has been brought to play? You can't have a result without a cause. The only thing that I could discover was this—and I say it as confidently as if I were talking about an experiment that had been conducted in a chemical laboratory—the only cause that I could discover was this; that some men who thought they knew Jesus Christ had power in Him for making bad men good, went to these men, told them so, and these men believed it, and they themselves became new men, and lived the new life. I am not going to say that there are no hypocrites in connection with the Salvation Army, or in connection with Christian churches. I am afraid there are. If you know any society anywhere without hypocrites, tell me of it; I should like to belong to it. But I pray you recognize this fact, that the presence of a few hypocrites cannot invalidate the testimony which I bring up from the case that goes back forty years, and from these other cases that I have personally investigated within the last three years. That testimony is as reliable as any that a chemist can present to you concerning any compound result which had been produced by the fusing of two or three elements. Don't let us make the mistake that the world of literature is the whole world. These people give no sign by voice; they rarely write to the papers. Literature is only a fragment of the life of humanity; and although the press was never so ubiquitous and never so powerful as it is today, still it is true to say of it that it is only a fragment, and the life of the world doesn't get its full utterance in the press of today.

> "The healing of the world
> Is in its nameless saints;
> Each separate star
> Seems nothing, but a myriad stars
> Break up the night and make it beautiful."

There are 4,000,000 Baptists who sign no creeds, who hate all priestism, who battle against the organized ecclesiasticisms that fetter human progress and imperil human justice; but I imagine there are not more than 400 out of 4,000,000 who write. Let us note, then, that we cannot reach a conclusion concerning the forces that are at work in our day, simply by sitting and looking at humanity through some metropolitan club window and judging of it by what passes, or by what is contained in the newspapers. No; the best life of the world never speaks. The truest life, that which is the very salt and saving of the nations, is scarcely ever vocal. It suffers, it fights, it obeys, it prays, it yearns, it loves, it lives, and by living makes the world anew from day to day. For the only fact worth considering is the fact of personal ascendency, and Christ Jesus today is making such men, sending them out into the world, and so keeping society sweet, and giving to it an infallible pledge of its onward march toward final victory.

I say, then, that Christianity is not played out, because today within a half century, there have been presented to this and to other countries the splendid results of the operation of the ideas and of the spirit and of facts of Christianity in men and women, renewed in the spirit of their mind and living lives of righteousness and of consecration to human service.

Besides personal ascendency there is a force at work in the life of the world that I must describe as the ascendency of ideas. Conceptions rule men, shape their action, determine their attitude toward movements and measures, the speed and safety with which they do their work as helpers of mankind. False ideas work mischief of humanity. Every true idea is a seed which being sown is productive; and my question tonight is whether there are any orchards rich in human fruitfulness which unquestionably had Jesus Christ as their Husbandman, and concerning which it is possible for me to affirm, he is the Creator of this fruit; all that may be gathered here is gathered because He Himself is at work and has been at work. Christianity is a body of ideas concerning God, man, life, duty, destiny; man and man, man and woman; man, woman and child; weak men, suffering men. These are hints of the direction in which I might travel had I time. I simply seize one of the ideas which we owe to Jesus Christ. When He stood in the world as a Teacher, He found as the prevalent conception concerning God that He was the Eternal, the All Holy, and that that meant the infinite aloofness of deity from the life of man; and could only be translated when looked at in the light of His claims for worship as presenting an exacting demand for a splendid ritual, for a beautiful ceremonial. Jesus displaced that idea, He abolished it and brought it to nought, and in the stead of it He put the kindly, genial, inspiring, helpful, renewing thought of Father. "He that hath seen Me hath seen the Father"—God is like Me. It was a revelation in a word, because there was a revelation in the Person. God is like Me; as accessible as I am to My disciples, as friendly toward the poor and the wretched, as merciful toward the harlot, and as compasionate toward the sinful. God is like Me; if you want to know what God is, look at Me—"He that hath seen Me hath seen the Father." And so men were quickened by this conception of God until they felt that the slave who was also a robber in the streets of Rome was worthy the love of God; and the great, cultured, saintly Paul would baptize that slave, Onesimus, with all the affection of his heart, because he felt that the slave was none other than his redeemed brother.

Science has given to us within the last fifty years a boon of incomputable value. It has restored to the Christian church something of ancient Hebrew awe; for it has made us to understand that God is order, God is law, and that throughout His realm, from east to west, from north to south, is the sway of law. This conception has penetrated into history; it has compelled us to read over again the records of the past, and to turn over the story of our experience with an open-eyedness and a freedom of thought such as our predecessors could not reach. And, therefore, we know Jesus Christ today better than the men of the second century did; we have a clearer conception of Jesus Christ than had the thinkers and writers and Christians of the second and third centuries; for we have gone back to Jesus Christ. And the sign and proof of that return is that we have got back the great and blessed truth: "He that hath seen Me hath seen the Father." That thought of God is the one that is now operative, creating a new social conscience, inspiring fresh social enthusiasms, getting into Parliament even and altering its legislation, so that our treatment of subject peoples shall be on the basis of brotherhood, and not on the basis of subjection in fact, it is revolutionizing the world. Christianity played out in its ideas! They are more regal today than at any moment in the world's past history.

Christianity is a spirit. Like a lane of light through the gospels runs the spirit of self-sacrifice in the service of man. Vicarious self-sacrifice—I hear it from yon cross. Vicarious self-sacrifice—I hear it from yon tomb. The essence of Jesus Christ's life is the giving of Himself up to work, to service, to life, to death—for the welfare of others. Isn't that the spirit of the gospel? Have you not in that one expression of Jesus Christ's, "I am come that men may have life, and that they may have it abundantly," the key to his career, and the interpretation of His influence? And will you not bear me witness that within the last fifty years the spirit of self-sacrifice has been winning upon the heart of man, expelling even from the church of the Lord Jesus Christ the old and cherished idea that it is

"A garden walled around
Chosen and made peculiar ground."

That's gone, and the church understands now that it is a soldier fighting the evils that oppress the hearts of men; a friend assuring men of the infinite love; a comforter of those that mourn. And so you have throughout the ranges of Christendom the accession of immense power to the churches in consequence of the ascent of the spirit of self-sacrifice, if not to supremacy, yet to greater power than it has had in the century preceding.

And if you ask me whether I can bring before you proofs convincing and conclusive concerning the sway of this spirit, I remind you that men who were anxious to serve Jesus Christ according to the dictates of their conscience left this country, as the Pilgrim Fathers for the United States, built up what we call the New Republic— a republic which within the last fifty years, mark you, has cast out from itself the viper of slavery, which it had so long cherished and out of whose presence it seemed to extract so much profit. Whose voice is it that wrings aloud today crying for a different treatment of the criminal, asking that we shall not be content to hang our murderers and imprison our burglars and then turn them out upon the world, but shall really seek to save the criminal? It is the voice of the leader of the Salvation Army. Whose cry is it that has stirred the hearts of the maidens of this country on behalf of their fallen sisters? As it comes from a woman in Liverpool it is scarcely heard at first, but it goes on, and still on, until, at length it effects such a revolution in the conscience of England as to alter its statutes in this respect, and such a revolution in the heart of England as to make us take a sympathetic attitude toward those whom we have been in the habit of calling our fallen sisters. The woman whose voice is thus heard by us is Mrs. Josephine Butler, who would say that every breath she draws she would use in the service of Jesus Christ, and every power she possesses to influence others she derives from Jesus Christ. Who is it, again, that has made us understand the teaching of Jesus Christ concerning childhood? Who has lifted the veil that hid from England's view the cruelties that had been inflicted on little children by brutal parents? It is my friend, Mr. Benjamin Waugh, himself instinct with the pities of the Christ, and urged forward in all his activity by his sense of obligation to Him and to them for whom Christ lived. Who are they that have gone into Africa and lived by the side of miasmatic lakes? Mackay, of Uganda, the great Livingstone, the immortal Moffat. These are the men who have gone, not in quest of diamonds, not for the purpose of filling their own pockets, but that they might reach out the hand of help to the most lost, and become the friends of men in actual need. All these are indications that the vicarious spirit of Jesus Christ is yet operating in men's minds, producing some of the greatest changes that are taking place in our midst today.

Now, if I wanted to discover a parallel to the fifty-five years through which we have passed, and to which I am especially referring, I should have to go to the fifty-five years beginning with the ministry of Jesus Christ and ending, say, about the year eighty for my first and best parallel, and then I should have for the next to start with 1517, and run on through some fifty-five years through that century for my second parallel, and what should I discover? In both I see the new thought of God. Jesus reveals it in the first period; it is preached by apostle and by prophet; it is witnessed to be. martyr and confessor. Martin Luther discovers it in the second period and breaks down the barriers that men have built up, the barriers of sacerdotalism and priestism, in the way of access to God, and secures for men freedom of approach, spirit to spirit, to the very heart of the Father. And if it be true that out of that first fifty-five years you got the regeneration of the old world, and out of this second fifty-five years there comes the regeneration of modern Europe, then I venture to say out of the fifty-five years through which we have passed we may expect to have a new manhood, a more glorious future for the sons of men. The signs and prophecies are all around us telling us to look onward with a mighty hope, assured that Christ Himself is really at work amongst us, and that His toil will proceed even unto final victory.

Are we content, then, with the forces that are proved to be at work in our era? Content! It is the function of Christianity to breed discontent so long as there is an injustice to be driven off the face of the earth, and wrong riots through the coveteousness of men or oppression through the indolence of men. Christianity puts within us the spirit which exclaims, "Not as though I had already attained, or were already perfect, but I follow after, if that I may apprehend that for which I am apprehended by Jesus Christ." The power of Christianity has been displayed in the way in which it has made it impossible for those who have received it to sit still in the presence of enormous wrongs. Our God calls out and says, Who will go up for Me against the workers of iniquity? Whom shall I send? May every man amongst us say, "Here am I, Lord, send me." Oh, thou fiend, Alcohol, who shall capture thee first and chain thee, so that thy destructive reign shall be ended? Oh Slavery accursed! thou art not yet banished from amongst the sons of men. Up, guards, and at it! up, guards, and strike it to the death! Oh Covetousness, that still riots over the inhumanities of man to man, and for the sake of filling its maw with greed ignores righteousness and justice and brotherhood, who will be ready to go with all energy, faith, hope, and consecration, to rid the earth of it, so that this world may become the habitation of goodness, of truth, of righteousness, and thus of God?

RELIGION PERSONAL

Though, in many ways, others may do much for my religious comfort and welfare, yet nothing that they may do can even modify, much less annul, my personal duty and accountability. Others may be anxiously concerned about me, they cannot be for me, that is, in my stead, so that what they say and feel and do may be placed to my credit, as though it had been said and felt and done by myself. For instance, another cannot believe for me, repent for me, confess for me, receive for me pardon and peace and joy through the blood of Christ. Another cannot, in my stead, so that the benefit shall redound to me, love and obey God. Among the great truths of Revelation frequently insisted on, is the one that religion is pre-eminently personal. The essential and best things of the Christian religion are only possible to the soul's experience through personal exertion and appropriation. Every soul must seek God for itself; have its own direct experience; its own act of submission; its own adoption as a child of God.—Intelligencer.

—23C

WHAT CHRISTIANITY HAS DONE FOR PHILANTHROPY

BY THE REV. DANIEL DORCHESTER, D.D.

Philanthropy is the child of Christianity, begotten by her, born in her fold, invested with her image, inspired with her spirit, and working towards the same beneficent end.

Before Christ came there was no background of benevolence in human life, no ideal of tenderness and compassion. Christ's life shows the love of God. From that time everything in the relation of man to his fellows, especially to the suffering and the needy, has changed. Woman, babes, the sick, the insane, the blind, have come into a new relation to humanity. Whatever of criticism may be expended on the Sacred Books of Christianity, nevertheless the fact remains that "in the limpid clearness of the gospels we see a new light, which brought a new spirit into the world"—a new ideal of duty between man and his fellowman.

Christianity came forth saying, "Whoever will do the will of My Father which is in heaven, the same is My brother, and sister, and mother." What a lesson it taught in the stories of the Good Samaritan and of the Prodigal Son—new fellowships unknown before. Germane to these examples were the words, "Bear ye one another's burdens, and so fulfill the law of Christ." The basis is, "Beloved, if God so loved us, we ought also to love one another." Hence, "a new commandment I give unto you, that ye love one another even as I have loved you." What power also in these words of Jesus, "I was sick and ye ministered unto Me."

Dean Stanley called philanthropy "the divine Eleventh Commandment." It was new, because human affection for the good of others was lifted into a paramount place, hitherto unknown; and because it presents the tender side of man's nature in loving sympathy with the infinite heart of love. The virtue was new, the example was new, and the benefits were new. The original commandments were written on the hard rock of Sinai; but this new commandment is written on human tablets, warmed and fused with divine love.

The new dispensation opened with a new illustration of Christian life. All that believed "had all things common, and they sold their possessions and goods, and parted them to all men, as every man had need'' (Acts 2:44; 4:32). Then followed an organization for philanthropic work—the first delegated humane association in all history. Seven men were selected for this work that all might be cared for.

It became, henceforth, a common remark, ''See how these Christians love one another.'' Minucius Felix said, ''They love one another before they know each other.'' And Lucien said, ''Their Law-giver has persuaded them that they are all brethren.'' St. Crysostom said, ''All the world sings with us,'' for there were no barriers to the new fellowship. The songs of the new religion echoed around the couches of dying saints, the burning stakes, martyrs, and even in the dungeons of prisoners—sights hitherto unknown.

The word philanthropy can be traced back into classic Greek, and was used by Plato and others. But no such idea of philanthropy as was taught by Christianity ever appears in the ancient Greek and Roman classics. Why? Because the conception did not exist among those people. Max Muller said, ''The word 'mankind' never passed the lips of Socrates, or Plato, or Aristotle. Where the Greeks saw barbarians we see brethren; * * * where the Greeks saw nations we see mankind.'' In short, heathen literature lacks that class of ideas which, in our day, are designated as humanitarian and philanthropic. It lacks, too, the idea of God's love for man, out of which philanthropy springs. Even the more intelligent Pagan nations, with interesting forms of civilization, fail to give evidence of either the principle or practice of philanthropy.

Dr. Packard, a life long professor of ancient languages in Bowdoin College, said, ''I have never met, in my reading, with the idea of an infirmary or a hospital among the ancients, except for sick cats (a sacred animal) among the Egyptians.'' Infanticide was common and uncondemned in the palmiest days of Greece and Rome. That eminent moralist, Seneca, said, ''Monstrous children we destroy, and the weak and illformed we drown, not in anger, but in reason, to separate the worthless from the sound.'' Even legitimate children were ''exposed'' at the Velabrum, in the age of Augustus, to be carried off by speculators and sold as slaves or reared as prostitutes. Gibbon (Vol. III., p. 170, Harper's edition) says, "The exposure of children was the prevailing and stubborn vice of antiquity; it was sometimes prescribed, often permitted, and almost always practiced with impunity, even by nations who never entertained the Roman idea of parental power."

Greece and Rome had their high culture, art and eloquence, but no humanity. They had shrines for numberless divinities, forty theaters for amusements, thousands of perfumery stores, but no shrine for brotherly love, no almshouse for the poor. Asylums and "homes" were unknown. The Latin "philanthropy" was first used in Justinian's code of laws, about the sixth century A. D. The stereotyped dictionary meaning was "benevolence." The word philadelphia, "love for one's brother," occurs much earlier.

The Encyclopædia Britannica says: "Although in ancient times there may have been places for the reception of strangers and travelers, it seems at least doubtful if there was anything of the nature of a charitable institution for the reception of the sick, such as existed after the introduction of Christianity. * * * Among the Greeks there seems little evidence of establishments for the sick." Among the earliest hospitals on record is one by Valens (baptized into the Christian faith by Eudoxius) in Cæsarea (379-380 A. D.), and one by Fabriola, a friend of St. Jerome. It was founded outside of the walls of Rome (A. D. 380). This noble Christian woman was a descendant of the Fabii family. She sold her goods and used the proceeds in founding a hospital for the poor, sick and infirm whom she had seen stretched on the public ways. She served the hospital in person, and carried the sick to their rooms on her back—her only ambulance. When she died her funeral procession was attended with rare demonstrations of public grief and esteem.

Modern paganism is no better. Neither the Chinese nor any other Pagan language has any word to express those fruits of the Spirit, "long-suffering, meekness, gentleness." The gospel of humanity is not in the Koran, nor in the Vedas or Shasters, nor in the Zend Avesta. "To this day monkeys are worshiped and provided with gorgeous temples, and $50,000 have been expended, in one day, on the marriage of two sacred apes." "Boa constrictors are maintained in state, but no provision is made for suffering humanity." Dr. Schneider, forty years a missionary in Turkey, said he knew of but one Mohammedan hospital in the Turkish

Empire, and that was in Constantinople, where the first Christian hospital was founded. With this solitary exception, we look in vain for philanthropical institutions among the 160,000,000 of Turks and Arabs, among the barbarians of Africa, the East Indies and the Pacific Islands, and among the 250,000,000 Hindus.

In China and Japan are a few institutions very slightly resembling Christian philanthropies. But they are endowed on the selfish principle of purchasing favor from their deities, not for the recovery of the vicious or to relieve the miseries of the unfortunate. Girls only are received in some of them, to be trained for lascivious purposes. Paupers who will beg for a part of their living are sometimes admitted. What miserable, shameful imitations of Christian philanthropies does paganism in its best conditions exhibit! Barbarous natives forsake their sick, and leave them to die alone. The Hindus are far more anxious to get their decrepit friends to the Ganges than to provide for their comfort at home.

Philanthropy, inaugurated by Christianity, declined during the Middle Ages. The mediæval period, and that which closely followed, was distinguished for art, for building and decorating grand cathedrals—an age of the most profound colorists and the most dramatic artists, whose profuse tropical genius flowed luxuriantly, but in which little philanthropy was seen. The groans and the anguish of suffering humanity were unalleviated. "Better," says Motley, "the sanguinary rites of Belgic Druids; better the yells of slaughtered victims from 'the wild wood without mercy,' of the Pagan forefathers of the nation, that this fantastic intermingling of divine music, glowing colors, and gorgeous ceremonies, with all the burning, beheading, strangling work which characterized the inquisitorial system of human sacrifice."

Philanthropy glorifies God by causing wealth to fertilize the lowest vales of humanity, rather than by rearing gorgeous temples in which cringing paupers may kneel. It clothes the naked, redeems the criminal, and feeds the hungry, less by alms and homilies, than by preventive institutions, and beneficent legislation and education. It lifts the race upon a level of culture hardly attained by any class in earlier times. This is a loftier task than to accumulate piles of ecclesiastical splendor. Ecclesiastical splendor was then at the maximum, and philanthropy at the minimum. Thus was the true task of Christianity misunderstood.

The aspiring pinnacles of magnificent temples pierced the mist that had long brooded over the world, and coldly looked down without sympathy upon the victims of vulgar violence and destructiveness, which despotism was crushing under its heel. Side by side were lofty cathedrals and the vaults of the inquisition, reeking with the blood of its victims. Even the spirit of the early reformers was often fierce and lacking in philanthropy. The age was waiting for the Sun of Righteousness, long hidden by the damps and clouds of the Middle Ages, to break through the obscured sky, and pour down his genial rays upon the earth.

The reformation, at first, could do but little specifically benevolent work, though its whole trend was to uplift and liberate humanity. It soon freed the gospel from its bondage, and sent it forth to bless the world with its beneficent ministrations. These took form slowly, during several centuries, for Christianity was still hampered and held back; but under the larger liberty and fuller spiritual baptism of the last 150 years, philanthropies without number have sprung up as out of the fertility of a new creation. But they have come forth in the radiance of the cross, and not where the cross has been ignored or denied.

Eloquently did Rev. T. Starr King say, speaking of philanthropy, "All the great enterprises of Christian history have been borne from the influence, immediate or remote, which this vicarious theory of redemption has exercised upon the mind and heart of humanity. * * * The man who has faith in it must be a maniac or a missionary. * * * It has linked itself with mighty energy to the long, deeply freighted train of human interests."

There was no conspicuous philanthropy during the Middle Ages, but there were some alleviations of poverty and distress, though overcast and blunted by the grossness and brutality of that period of wars and oppressions. The present hospital system, says the Britannica, grew out of monastic arrangements for the care of the sick, the indigent, the aged, the blind, etc., and they remained in the hands of the clergy until after the reformation. They were few in number, until the eighteenth century, but have more rapidly multiplied during the present century. Other philanthropies, great and small, exceedingly varied and manifold, like the leaves of the tree of life "for the healing of the nations," have gone forth on every hand to bless the world. Their name is legion. I need not cite them in detail, but they are all directly or indirectly traceable to Christianity.

In support of this view, I cite the testimonies of two distinguished writers, of free-thinking habits, but of great weight. Rousseau (Boyle Lectures, by Rev. William Harness, 1821, Vol. I., p. 165) said: "A purer faith has given greater gentleness to Christian manners. This improvement is not the work of literature; for, wherever literature has previously flourished, humanity has not been the more respected by its means, the cruelties of the Athenians, the Egyptians, the Roman emperors and the Chinese are examples of this truth."

Lecky (European Morals, II., p. 163) said: "As a matter of fact, Christianity has done more to quicken the affections of mankind, to promote piety, to create a pure and merciful idea, than any other influence that has ever acted upon the world."

Again, "The simple record of three short years of Christ's active life has done more to regenerate and soften mankind than all the disquisitions of philosophers and all the exhortations of moralists. It has been the well spring of whatever is best and purest in the Christian life."

Again, "The history of self sacrifice, during the last eighteen hundred years, has been mainly the history of the action of Christianity upon the world; the moral type and beauty of the Christian faith have chiefly called it (self-sacrifice) into being, and it is by their influence alone that it can be permanently sustained."

I cite one other testimony, which shows not only the Christian origin of philanthropics, but also accounts for the surprising increase of them in the last one hundred and fifty years. Professor Green (History of the English People, IV., p. 273) says: "A yet nobler result of the religious revival (the Wesleyan) was the steady attempt, which has never ceased from that day to this, to remedy the guilt, the ignorance, the physical suffering, the social degradation of the profligate and the poor. It was not until the Wesleyan impulse had done its work that this philanthropic impulse began. The Sunday schools established by Mr. Raikes, of Gloucester, at the close of the century, were the beginnings of popular education. By writings, and by her own personal example, Hannah Moore drew the sympathy of England to the poverty and crime of the agricultural laborers. A passionate impulse of human sympathy with the wronged and the afflicted raised hospitals, endowed charities, built churches, sent missionaries to the heathen, supported Burke in his plea for the Hindu, and Clarkson and Wilberforce in their crusade against the iniquity of the slave trade.''

Within this century Christianity has done more for humanity, in a single decade, than in long centuries before. An English poet sang:

"Better fifty years of Europe,
Than a cycle of Cathay."

—Examiner.

THE GOSPEL'S SWEET MUSIC

"And into whatsoever house ye shall enter, first say, Peace be to this house."—Luke 10:5.

A visitor to Amsterdam wished to hear the wonderful music of the chimes of St. Nicholas, and went up into the tower of the church to hear it. There he found a man with wooden gloves on his hands, pounding on a keyboard. All he could hear was the clanging of the keys when struck by the wooden gloves, and the harsh, deafening noise of the bells close over his head. He wondered why the people talked of the marvelous chimes of St. Nicholas. To his ear there was no music in them—nothing but a terrific clatter and clanging. Yet all the while there floated out over and beyond the city the most entrancing music. Men in the fields paused in their work to listen, and were made glad. People in their homes and travelers on the highway were thrilled by the marvelous bell tones which fell from the tower. So there are many hardworking Christian men and women whose lives are so burdened by toil and pressed by trial and struggle that many looking on suppose them to be very hard, and imagine that their lives make no music. They seem to be pouring out all their strength in hard toil, but all the time there is going out through the children that grow up in their homes, through their money and their influence which goes forth to support the gospel message to the ends of the world, sweet sounds, so that the weary and the broken-hearted hear comforting music because these toilers have struck the rude keys with their wooden gloves in faithful, patient service. Whatever the struggle of life to the Christian, it finally issues into peace.

CHRISTIANITY FOR ORDINARY MEN

BY THE REV. DR. T. DEWITT TALMAGE

"Salute Asyncritus, Phlegon, Hermas, Patrobas, Hermes, Philologus and Julia."—Romans 16:14, 15.

Matthew Henry, Albert Barnes, Adam Clark, Thomas Scott, and all the commentators pass by these verses without any especial remark. The other twenty people mentioned in the chapter were distinguished for something, and were therefore discussed by the illustrious expositors; but nothing is said about Asyncritus, Phlegon, Hermas, Patrobas, Hermes, Philologus and Julia. Where were they born? No one knows. Where did they die? There is no record of their decease. For what were they distinguished? Absolutely nothing, or the trait of character would have been brought out by the apostle. If they had been very intrepid, or opulent, or hirsute, or musical of cadence, or crass of style, or in any wise anomalous, that feature would have been caught by the apostolic camera. But they were good people, because Paul sends to them his high Christian regards. They were ordinary people moving in ordinary sphere, attending to ordinary duty and meeting ordinary responsibilities.

What the world wants is a religion for ordinary people. If there be in the United States 70,000,000 people, there are certainly not more than 1,000,000 extraordinary; and then there are 69,000,000 ordinary, and we do well to turn our backs for a little while upon the distinguished and conspicuous people of the Bible and consider in our text the seven ordinary. We spend too much of our time in twisting garlands for remarkables, and building thrones for magnates, and sculpturing warriors, and apotheosizing philanthropists. The rank and file of the Lord's soldiery need especial help.

The vast majority of people will never lead an army, will never write a state constitution, will never electrify a Senate, will never make an important invention, will never introduce a new philosophy, will never decide the fate of a nation. You do not expect to; you do not want to. You will not be a Moses to lead a nation out of bondage. You will not be a Joshua to prolong the daylight until you can shut five kings in a cavern. You will not be a St. John to unroll an Apocalypse. You will not be a Paul to preside over an apostolic college. You will not be a Mary to mother a Christ. You will more probably be Asyncritus, or Phlegon, or Hermas, or Patrobas, or Hermes, or Philologus, or Julia.

Many of you are women at the head of households. Every morning you plan for the day. The culinary department of the household is your dominion. You decide all questions of diet. All the sanitary regulations of your house are under your supervision. To regulate the food, and the apparel and the habits, and decide the thousand questions of home life is a tax upon brain and nerve and general health absolutely appalling, if there be no divine alleviation.

It does not help you much to be told that Elizabeth Fry did wonderful things amid the criminals at Newgate. It does not help you much to be told that Mrs. Judson was very brave among the Bornesian cannibals. It does not help you very much to be told that Florence Nightingale was very kind to the wounded in the Crimea. It would be better for me to tell you that the divine friend of Mary and Martha is your friend, and that He sees all the annoyances and disappointments and abrasions and exasperations of an ordinary housekeeper from morn till night, and from the first day of the year until the last day of the year, and at your call He is ready with help and re-enforcements.

They who provide the food of the world decide the health of the world. You have only to go on some errand amid the taverns and the hotels of the United States and Great Britain to appreciate the fact that a vast multitude of the human race are slaughtered by incompetent cookery. Though a young woman may have taken lessons in music, and may have taken lessons in painting, and lessos in astronomy, she is not well educated unless she has taken lessons in dough! They who decide the apparel of the world and the food of the world decide the endurance of the world.

An unthinking man may consider it a matter of little importance—the cares of the household and the economies of domestic life—but I tell you the earth is strewn with the martyrs of kitchen and nursery. The health-shattered womanhood of America cries out for a God Who can help ordinary women in the ordinary duties of housekeeping. The wearing, grinding, unappreciated work goes on, but the same Christ Who stood on the bank of Galilee in the early morning and kindled the fire and had the fish already cleaned and broiling when the sportsmen stepped ashore, chilled and hungry, will help every other woman to prepare breakfast, whether by her own hand or the hand of her hired help. The God Who made indestructible eulogy of Hannah, Who made a coat for Samuel, her son, and carried it to the temple every year, will help every woman in preparing the family wardrobe. The God Who opens the Bible with the story of Abraham's entertainment by the three angels on the plains of Mamre will help every woman to provide hospitality, however rare and embarrassing. It is high time that some of the attention we have been giving to the remarkable women of the Bible—remarkable for their virtue, or their want of it, or remarkable for their deeds—Deborah and Jezebel, and Herodias and Athalia, and Dorcas and the Marys, excellent and abandoned—it is high time some of the attention we have been giving to these conspicuous women of the Bible be given to Julia, an ordinary woman, amid ordinary circumstances, attending to ordinary duties, and meeting ordinary responsibilities.

Then there are all the ordinary business men. They need divine and Christian help. When we begin to talk about business life we shoot right off and talk about men who did business on a large scale, and who sold millions of dollars of goods a year; and the vast majority of business men do not sell a million dollars of goods, nor half a million, nor quarter of a million, nor the eighth part of a million. Put all the business men of our cities, towns villages, and neighborhoods side by side, and you will find that they sell less than a hundred thousand dollars worth of goods. All these men in ordinary business life want divine help. You see how the wrinkles are printing on the countenance the story of worriment and care. You cannot tell how old a business man is by looking at him. Gray hairs at thirty. A man at forty-five with the stoop of a nonogenarian. No time to attend to improved dentistry, the grinders cease because they are few. Actually dying of old age at forty or fifty, when they ought to be at the meridian. Many of these business men have bodies like a neglected clock, to which you come, and when you wind it up begins to buzz and roar, and then the hands start around very rapidly, and then the clock strikes five, or ten, or forty, and strikes without any sense, and then suddenly stops. So is the body of that worn-out business man. It is a neglected clock, and though by some summer recreation it may be wound up, still the machinery is all out of gear. The hands turn around with a velocity that excites the astonishment of the world. Men cannot understand the wonderful activity, and there is a roar, a buzz, a rattle about these disordered lives, and they strike twelve when they ought to strike six; and they strike forty when they ought to strike nothing, and suddenly they stop. Post-mortem examination reveals the fact that all the springs and pivots, and weights, and balance-wheels of health are completely derangea. The human clock is simply run down. And at the time when the steady hand ought to be pointing to the industrious hours on a clear and sunlit dial, the whole machinery of body, mind, and earthly capacity stops forever. Oak Hill and Greenwood have thousands of business men who died of old age at thirty, thirty-five, forty, forty-five.

Now, what is wanted is grace—divine grace for ordinary business men, men who are harnessed from morn till night and all the days of their life—harnessed in business. Not grace to lose $100,-000, but grace to lose ten dollars. Not grace to supervise 250 employes in a factory, but grace to supervise the bookkeeper, and two salesmen, and the small boy that sweeps out the store. Grace to invest not the $80,000 of net profit, but the $2,500 of clear gain. Grace not to endure the loss of a whole ship load of spices from the Indies, but grace to endure the loss of a paper of collars from the leakage of a displaced shingle on a poor roof. Grace not to endure the tardiness of the American Congress in passing a necessary law, but grace to endure the tardiness of an errand boy stopping to play marbles when he ought to deliver the goods. Such a grace as thousands of business men have today—keeping them tranquil, whether goods sell or do not sell, whether customers pay or do not pay, whether tariff is up or tariff is down, whether crops are luxuriant or a dead failure—calm in all circumstances, and amid all vicissitudes. That is the kind of grace we want.

Millions of men want it, and they may have it for the asking. Some hero or heroine comes to town, and as the procession passes through the street the business men come out, stand on tiptoe on their store step and look at some one who, in arctic clime, or in ocean storm, or in day of battle, or in hospital agonies, did the brave thing, not realizing that they, the enthusiastic spectators, have gone through trials in business life that are just as great before God. There are men who have gone through freezing arctics and burning torrids, and awful Marengoes of experiences without moving five miles from their own doorstep.

Now, what ordinary business men need is to realize that they have the friendship of that Christ Who looked after the religious interests of Matthew, the custom-house clerk, and helped Lydia, of Thyatira, to sell the dry goods, and Who opened a bakery and fish-market in the wilderness of Asia Minor to feed the 5,000 who had come out on a religious picnic, and Who counts the hairs of your head with as much particularity as though they were the plumes of a coronation, and Who took the trouble to stoop down with His finger writing on the ground, although the first shuffle of feet oblit-erated the divine caligraphy, and Who knows just how many lo-custs there were in the Egyptian plague, and knew just how many ravens were necessary to supply Elijah's pantry by the brook Che-rith, and Who, as floral commander, leads forth all the regiments of primroses, foxgloves, daffodils, hyacinths and lilies which pitch their tents of beauty and kindle their camp-fires of color around the hemisphere—that that Christ and that God knows the most mi-nute affairs of your business life and however inconsiderable, un-derstanding all the affairs of that woman who keeps a thread-and-needle store as well as all the affairs of a Rothschild and a Baring.

Then there are all the ordinary farmers. We talk about agri-cultural life, and we immediately shoot off to talk about Cincin-natus, the patrician, who went from the plow to a high position, and after he got through the dictatorship in twenty-one days went back again to the plow. What encouragement is that to ordinary farmers? The vast majority of them—none of them will be patric-ians. Perhaps none of them will be Senators. If any of them have dictatorships it will be over forty, fifty or 100 acres of the old home-stead. What these men want is grace, to keep their patience while plowing with balky oxen, and to keep cheerful amid the drouth that destroys the corn crop, and that enables them to restore the garden the day after the neighbor's cattle have broken in and trampled out the strawberry bed, and gone through the Lima-bean patch, and eaten up the sweet corn such large quantities that they must be kept from the water lest they swell up and die.

Grace in catching weather that enable them, without imprecation, to spread out the hay the third time, although again, and again, and again, it has been almost ready for the mow. A grace to doctor the cow with a hollow horn, and the sheep with the foot rot, and the horse with the distemper, and to compel the unwilling acres to yield a livelihood for the family, and schooling for the children, and little extras to help the older boy in business, and something for the daughter's wedding outfit, and a little surplus for the time when the ankles will get stiff with age, and the breath will be a little short, and the swinging of the cradle through the hot harvest field will bring on the old man's vertigo. Better close up about Cincinnatus. I know 500 farmers just as noble as he was. What they want is to know that they have the friendship of that Christ Who often drew His similes from the farmer's life, as when He said, "A sower went forth to sow," as when He built His best parable out of the scene of a farmer boy coming back from his wanderings, and the old farmhouse shook that night with the rural jubilee; and Who compared Himself to a lamb in the pasture field, and Who said that the enternal God is a farmer, declaring: "My Father is the husbandman."

Those stone masons do not want to hear about Christopher Wren, the architect, who built St. Paul's Cathedral. It would be better to tell them how to carry the hod of brick up the ladder without slipping, and how on a cold morning with the trowel to smooth off the mortar and keep cheerful, and how to be thankful to God for the plain food taken from the pail by the roadside. Carpenters standing amid the adze, and the bit, and the plane, and the broad ax, need to be told that Christ was a carpenter, with His own hand wielding saw and hammer. Oh, this is a tired world, and it is an overworked world, and it is an underfed world, and it is a wrung-out world, and men and women need to know that there is rest and recuperation in God and in that religion which was not so much intended for extraordinary people as for ordinary people, because there are more of them.

The healing profession has had its Abercrombies, and its Abernethys, and its Valentine Motts, and its Willard Parkers; but the ordinary physicians do the most of the world's medicining, and they need to understand that while taking diagnosis or prognosis, or writing prescription, or compounding medicament, or holding the delicate pulse of the dying child, they may have the presence and the dictation of the Almighty Doctor Who took the case of the madman, and, after he had torn off his garments in foaming dementia, clothed him again, body and mind, and Who lifted up the woman who for eighteen years had been bent almost double with the rheumatism into graceful stature, and Who turned the scabs of leprosy into rubicund complexion, and Who rubbed the numbness out of paralysis, and Who swung wide open the closed windows of hereditary or accidental blindness, until the morning light came streaming through the fleshly casements, and Who knows all the diseases, and all the remedies, and all the herbs, and all the catholicons, and is monarch of pharmacy and therapeutics, and Who has sent out 10,000 doctors of whom the world makes no record; but to prove that they are angels of mercy, I invoke the thousands of men whose ailments they have assuaged and the thousands of women to whom in cries of pain they have been next to God in benefaction.

Come, now, let us have a religion for ordinary people in professions, in occupations, in agriculture, in the household, in merchandise, in everything. I salute across the centuries Asyncritus, Phlegon, Hermas, Patrobas, Hermes, Philologus, and Julia.

First of all, if you feel that you are ordinary, thank God that you are not extraordinary. I am tired and sick and bored almost to death with extraordinary people. They take all their time to tell us how very extraordinary they really are. You know as well as I do, my brother and sister, that most of the useful work of the world is done by unpretentious people who toil right on—by people who do not get much approval, and no one seems to say, "That is well done." Phenomena are of but little use. Things that are exceptional cannot be depended on. Better trust the smallest planet that swings in its orbit than ten comets shooting this way and that, imperiling the longevity of worlds attending to their own business. For steady illumination better is a lamp than a rocket.

Then, if you feel that you are ordinary, remember that your position invites the less attack. Conspicuous people—how they have to take it! How they are misrepresented, and abused, and shot at! The higher the horns of a roebuck the easier to strike him down. What a delicious thing it must be to be a candidate for Governor of a State or President of the United States! It must be so soothing to the nerves! It must pour into the soul of a candidate such a sense of serenity when he reads the blessed newspapers!

I came into the possession of the abusive cartoons in the time of Napoleon I., printed while he was yet alive. The retreat of the army from Moscow, that army buried in the snows of Russia, one of the most awful tragedies of the centuries, represented under the figure of a monster called General Frost shaving the French Emperor with a razor of icicle. As Satyr and Beelzebub he is represented, page after page, page after page, England cursing him, Spain cursing him, Germany cursing him, Russia cursing him, Europe cursing him, North and South America cursing him. The most remarkable man of his day, and the most abused. All those men in history who now have a halo around their name, on earth wore a crown of thorns. Take the few extraordinary railroad men of our time, and see what abuse comes upon them, while thousands of stockholders escape. New York Central Railroad had 9,265 stockholders. If anything in that railroad affronted the people all the abuse came down on one man and the 9,264 escaped. All the world took after Thomas Scott, president of the Pennsylvania Railroad, abused him until he got under the ground. Over 17,000 stockholders in that company. All the blame on one man! The Central Pacific Railroad—two or three men get all the blame if anything goes wrong. There are 10,000 in that company.

I mention these things to prove it is extraordinary people who get abused, while the ordinary escape. The weather of life is not so severe on the plain as it is on the high peaks. The world never forgives a man who knows, or gains, or does more than it can know, or gain, or do. Parents sometimes give confectionery to their children as an inducement to take bitter medicine, and the world's sugar plum precedes the world's aqua-fortis. The mob cried in regard to Christ, "Crucify Him, crucify Him!" and they had to say it twice to be understood, for they were so hoarse, and they got their hoarseness by crying a little while before at the top of their voice, "Hosanna." The River Rhone is foul when it enters Lake Leman, but crystalline when it comes out on the other side. But there are men who have entered the bright lake of worldly prosperity crystalline and come out terribly soiled. If, therefore, you feel that you are ordinary, thank God for the defenses and the tranquility of your position.

Then remember, if you have only what is called an ordinary home, that the great deliverers of the world have all come from such a home. And there may be seated, reading at your evening stand, a child who shall be potent for the ages. Just unroll the scroll of men mighty in church and state, and you will find they nearly all came from log cabin or poor homes. Genius almost always runs out in the third or fourth generation. You cannot find in all history an instance where the fourth generation of extraordinary people amount to anything. In this country we had two great men, father and son, both Presidents of the United States; but from present prospects there never will be in that genealogical line another President for a thousand years. Columbus from a weaver's hut, Demosthenes from a cutler's cellar, Bloomfield and Missionary Carey from a shoemaker's bench, Arkwright from a barber's shop, and He Whose name is high over all in earth, and air, and sky, from a manger.

Let us all be content with such things as we have. God is just as good in what He keeps away from us as in what He gives us. Even a knot may be useful if it is at the end of a thread.

At an anniversary of a deaf and dumb asylum, one of the children wrote upon the blackboard words as sublime as the Iliad, the Odyssey, and the "Divina Commedia," all compressed in one paragraph. The examiner, in the signs of the mute language, asked her: "Who made the world?" The deaf and dumb girl wrote upon the blackboard: "In the beginning God created the heaven and the earth." The examiner asked her: "For what purpose did Christ come into the world?" The deaf and dumb girl wrote upon the blackboard: "This is a faithful saying, and worthy of all acceptation, that Christ Jesus came into the world to save sinners." The examiner said to her: "Why were you born

—24C

deaf and dumb, while I hear and speak?'' She wrote upon the blackboard: ''Even so, Father; for so it seemeth good in Thy sight.'' Oh, that we might be baptized with a contented spirit. The spider draws poison out of a flower, the bee gets honey out of a thistle; but happiness is a heavenly elixir, and the contented spirit extracts it, not from the rhododendron of the hills, but from the lily of the valley.

FIRST CENTURY CHRISTIANITY

BY THE REV. O. P. EACHES, D.D.

There is a tendency to put the nineteenth century under the flail by comparing it with the first century and asserting the vast inferiority of the nineteenth to the first in the conception and practice of the Christian life. There is always a clamor about the past, a tendency to venerate the distant, to underrate the present. The first century of the Christian era is regarded as a kind of millenium, a golden age in comparison with which our age is one of clay or iron. A popular book of recent years was Primitive Piety Revived, the expression of the desire to see the first age piety transplanted in the nineteenth century. It is asserted that for real piety, a burning zeal, an unquestioned orthodoxy, we must go back to the first of the fourth century. In all this there is a vast misconception of the facts of the case.

New Testament Christianity as organized and represented in Jesus Christ is a large and lofty thing. The personal Christian life as existing in outline and in ultimate realization is one in fellowship with God, is filled with the fullness of God, is a sonship, is dead to sin and raised with Christ to a present resurrection life, is a life led of the Spirit, is full of the fruits of the Spirit, is living an overcoming life, is a life whose citizenship is in heaven. The Christian life as realized among men, as exhibited in flesh and blood, has always been very far below this high standard. A heathen man said to a missionary, ''I have found you out, you do not live by your Book.'' Measured by Jesus Christ and His teachings the first century was a very poor representation of Christ.

It was Christian, but only in a limited way. The New Testament describes the personal and church life of the first century as one of narrowness of conception, of imperfect zeal, of imperfections in life, of errors in teaching that had wide sway. There was nobleness of life, a joy in service, a spirit of martyrdom, a love for the truth, an unquenchable enthusiasm for Christ and His work on the part of many. But the New Testament does not reveal a history that was a spotless white, it would be strange if that first century Christianity were one with which no fault could be found.

The apostles under the shadow of the cross, seated at the Holy Supper, were engaged in selfish contests for supremacy. They had not caught the spiritual teachings of Christ as to the nature of His kingdom, they were all lying in the domain of outward kings and kingdoms. After the ascension of Christ did they get the meaning of the great commission, did they straightway, set on fir² by His words, begin a conquest of the world? It required a vision to enable Peter, years afterward, to get into the meaning of Christ's plan. (Acts 10.) When Peter had preached Christ's gospel to persons outside the Jewish faith he was called to account for this utterly strange and revolutionary procedure. (Acts 11.) There were no foreign missions for twenty years after the ascension of Christ, and then the work was begun, not by the twelve, but by Paul and Barnabas. (Acts 15.) It is commonly asserted that the early church under the lead of the apostles were filled with a burning zeal for the spread of the Word. Measured by the Careys, the Judsons, the Patons of this century, the apostles of the first century did not far surpass them in large plans and effectiveness. Had it not been for the large-hearted and magnanimous Barnabas it seems, humanly speaking, as though the life of Paul had been suppressed and crushed at the first, by the misconceptions and narrowness of feeling with which he was regarded. (Acts 9:27.)

Peter at one time taught doctrines so utterly subversive of the meaning of the gospel that Christianity would have been only an adjunct of Judaism had not Paul given the open rebuke and the larger truth. (Galatians 2:11.)

As to the teachers of the first century, the leaders of the churches, we have this word of Paul concerning Timothy: ''I have no man like minded. All seek their own, not the things which are Jesus Christ's.'' (Philippians 2:20, 21.) Had the nineteenth century brought this charge against the Christians of the first century it would have been charged with a slander of that age. Paul, writing in a careful way, speaks of the cowardice, the moral indifference, the unspiritual life of large numbers of his day. They were good men, doubtless, but they were not pillars. Archippus was a pastor, the picture of many in that day, who was living only a part of a possible life. (Colossians 4:17.)

The churches naturally were imperfect both in their conceptions of Christian truth, in the conduct of the members and in discipline. The Cretan churches were made up of poor material. (Titus 1:12.) The Galatian churches were easily and speedily seduced from the truth; as a whole they were foolish Christians, deserving the severe words of Paul. (Galatians 3:1.),The Corinthian church was full of pride, of division, with unseemly assemblies, with unholy men in the membership, some of whom denied even the resurrection, but it was a veritable church of Christ, a church that shone for Christ and did a large work. In the Thessalonian church was much unworthy living. In the Colossian church was a gross corruption of doctrine concerning Christ Himself. In Hebrews (10:25) we have an exhortation concerning attendance at church. In Hebrews (5:12) is a reference to many Christians who were living a dwindling spiritual life. In the Philippian church was a rupture between the prominent women. The letters to the seven churches in Asia Minor (Revelation 3:9) reveal a sad state of things in bodies that bore the beautiful name of Christ. James in his letter speaks of abuses in a manner that savors of the style of pastors who find just fault with the abuses of today.

The nineteenth century ought not to gloat over the faults, imperfections and errors of the first century. There were good men who lived and died nobly for Christ, churches that held fast to the form of sound words. There was a faith, a holy living, an earnestness of work for Christ that was so far above that of the surrounding society that Christianity won its way into the hearts and thinking of men and, in time, overthrew organized heathenism. But it is a vast mistake to hold up that age as one of unmixed correctness in doctrine, of unspottedness in living, of earnestness in mission work, of a membership that was pure gold in character.

That the first century churches, made up of men who had come from the narrowness of Judaism and the corruptions of heathenism, could do so much is a marvel that can be accounted for only by the overruling providence of God and the indwelling influence of the Holy Spirit. But it is to misread the New Testament and to bring reproach on the Holy Spirit to maintain that Jesus Christ and the Holy Spirit did their best and the most efficient work in the first century of the era. The nineteenth century Christianity is very far below the standard given by Jesus Christ, it needs to be lifted up to Christ and transformed by Christ. In like manner the Christianity as revealed in the pages of the New Testament is a very imperfect presentation of what Christ taught and commanded and illustrated in His own life. We ought in our day to pattern, not after the first century or any past century, but after Him Who made all that was good both in the first and in all the centuries. Let us worship, not the first century with its first century blunders and mistakes, but Christ Himself.

Let us not make use of the first century as a club, with which to cudgel the nineteenth. The nineteenth century may well blush when measured by Christ and His teachings. It need not blush when contrasted with the first—Examiner.

THE SUPERNATURAL IN CHRISTIANITY

The claim that Christianity is a supernatural religion is repugnant to many who have sympathy with its practical objects. Apologists have too often tried to soften down its claims so as to make it acceptable to those who are without. But to empty Christianity of its supernaturalism is to take from it its distinguishing glory, and the source of its peculiar power.

Christianity is, first of all, a supernatural fact, and then a supernatural force. It centers in Christ; and Christ cannot be explained on the ground of mere naturalism. His divinity was no less real than His humanity. In His life miracles occupied a natural place. They harmonize with the rest of the picture. They reveal not His power only but also His love and grace. He went about doing good, and miracles were a part of His good works. They outdistanced all other works in their moral quality. They were works "that none other man ever did"—mighty and merciful; showing a hand of omnipotence and a heart of love. And because of their moral quality they constitute a distinctive proof on behalf of Christianity. They show how God works, and are part of His self-revelation to man.

Now Christianity stands ready to be judged by its works, just as Christ was. "If I do not the works of My Father," He said, "believe Me not. But if I do them, though ye believe not Me, believe the works; that ye may know and understand that the Father is in Me, and I in the Father." Those who stagger at the doctrines of Christianity can believe in its works; and believing in its works they will find it easier to believe in its doctrines. Its works are patent to all eyes. They constitute the "greater works" which Jesus said His disciples were to do after His return to the Father; greater works, namely, than healing the sick, giving sight to the blind, and raising the dead. Moral miracles demand the exercise of a greater kind of power than physical miracles, and hence they afford a higher kind of evidence on behalf of Christianity. And the words of Jesus clearly intimate that in the coming days the church was to depend upon these "greater works" for the body of its evidence touching the supernatural character of Christianity.

The moral ascent of man was contemporaneous with the advent of Christ. Explain it as we may, at the coming of Christ a new force entered the world which has been gradually recreating society. Compare home life before Christianity with home life today where true Christianity reigns; compare the condition of woman before Christianity found her and since; compare the position of children before Jesus said, "Suffer them to come unto Me and forbid them not," and since these words were spoken; compare the condition of the servile classes before Christianity proclaimed the brotherhood of man and since, in order to see what it has done for the elevation of the race. It has ever been a fountain of beneficent influence. Schools, colleges, hospitals, have followed in its wake. To all inquirers it can answer, "Go and tell the things which ye do hear and see; the blind receive their sight, the lame walk, the lepers are cleansed, and the deaf hear, and the dead are raised up, and the poor have the gospel preached unto them." Christianity is ever ready to be judged by its fruits.

The greatest argument in behalf of Christianity is a regenerated life. Men may attempt to confute the doctrines of Christianity, but they are silenced in the presence of its palpable results. When the people saw the man who had been healed beside the beautiful gate of the temple, through the agency of Peter and John, standing beside them, they could say nothing against it. The tree that bore such fruit was not to be traduced. But, alas, that so many, when they see the healed man and are unable to resist the evidence that Christ is a divine healer, are merely silent. They can say nothing against it. They ought to say something for it.

WHO IS THE CHRISTIAN?

He who dwells in the world as a son in his Father's house, sharing with his brothers the good things it contains.

He who is free because he makes the Father's will, and the laws that spring from it, his own.

He who finds everywhere that the chance to love is the best thing any station can afford, and welcomes the suffering which puts it to the test.

He who instinctively takes the point of view of the man with whom he deals, and finds social service as absorbing as his personal affairs.

He who prefers the sweet peace of obscurity, yet lets his example shine as far and wide as God's glory and man's good require.

He who, recognizing his own elemental tendencies in others' failings, is ever ready to forgive.

He who sees that doing wrong is a worse evil than the injury it inflicts, and would cut off his right hand rather than cause another needless pain, or loss, or degradation.

He who is so intent on doing good that he never doubts that all needed goods will come to him in return.

He who needs no oath to support his integrity, and whose kindness knows no bounds.

He who speaks his inmost thought, and acts out his noblest impulses.

He who does these things? No.

He who, finding them beyond his strength, confesses as Lord and Master, the Christ Who did and taught them; and cultivates the Spirit by Whose aid these and a thousand kindred graces may be progressively attained.—The Congregationalist.

CHRISTIANITY NOT GIVING BUT TAKING

Christ didn't come down to earth and say, give up this and this. He wants to fill our life with joy and happiness. I want to resent the idea that Christians must be gloomy and sad. Christ does not say, "Give this up," but "Here is something better; take that." My wife went one day to see an old schoolmate. She found that her little boy had been cutting a string with a pair of scissors, when the scissors slipped and one of his eyes was put out, and his mother feared that he would lose the other. My wife was very much affected by what she had heard, and she said that our little boy should never play with scissors and knives. And so a prohibition was put on these articles, but when she left the room for a moment one day, the little boy, but two years of age, found his mother's scissors and was bound to have them. His sister said, "Mother does not want you to have the scissors," and she tried to take them from him, but he clung to them. Just then she happened to think that he was very fond of oranges, and she said, "Willie, don't you want an orange?" The minute she handed him the orange down went the scissors on the floor. You see, that was something better. That is the way Christ treats us. He does not wrench the scissors away from us, but He gives us an orange. When we are walking in the new way, we see as it says in the Book of Proverbs: "Her ways are ways of pleasantness, and all her paths are peace."

A BRAVE COWARD

In an address at Chicago, Bishop Whipple related the following incident as an illustration of the moral courage of Christian Indians:

One day an Indian came to our missionary and said, "I know this religion is true. The men who have walked in this new trail are better and happier. But I have always been a warrior and my hands are full of blood. Could I be a Christian?

The missionary repeated the story of God's love. To test the man he said, "May I cut your hair?"

The Indian wears his scalp lock for his enemy. When it is cut it is a sign he will never go on the warpath again. The man said, "Yes, you may cut it. I shall throw my old life away."

It was cut. He started for home, and met some wild Indians who shouted with laughter, and with taunts said, "Yesterday you were a warrior; today you are a squaw."

It stung the man to madness, and he rushed to his home and threw himself on the floor and burst into tears. His wife was a Christian, and came and put her arms about his neck and said, "Yesterday there was not a man in the world who dared call you a coward. Can't you be as brave for Him who died for you as you were to kill the Sioux?"

He sprung to his feet and said, "I can, and will!"

I have known many brave, fearless servants of Christ, but I never knew one braver than this chief.

THE METHOD OF CHRISTIANITY

It is interesting and instructive to observe how science, patiently toiling after prophecy, proves by long-continued and oft-repeated experiments the truth which the seers have perceived, as in a vision, by intuition. The doctors, in dealing with the body, are coming to the conclusion that the great remedy for disease is the nourishment of life. They still sometimes attack disease directly, as when they prescribe an antidote for a poison. They sometimes save life by lessening life, as when they amputate a diseased limb and the cripple lives, though always a cripple. But for the most part hygiene is taking the place of drugs. Nature is nursed and cared for, and drugs are used, if at all, only to strengthen nature and add to her recuperative power. Formerly, for example, the consumptive was shut up in a warm room, kept away from draughts, guarded against the cold, and often, if not ordinarily, insufficiently nourished either on gruels by the doctor's counsel, or on insufficient food for want of sufficient appetite. Now the consumptive goes to the Adirondacks, wraps up in furs, sits upon the porch in all weathers with the thermometer at zero, takes prescribed exercise, sleeps, rests and eats heartily. No attempt is made by drugs directly to attack the bacilli which are eating away the patient's life. The doctor simply attempts to nourish Nature and make her strong, and Nature herself, as the microscope demonstrates, surrounds the bacilli with tissues of her own producing, imprisons them in solitary cells, and so makes the man "immune" from the enemy which assails his life. When the reader sees advertised in a paper a "microbe killer," he may be sure that it is a quack medicine. Science is not endeavoring to kill the microbes. It leaves them severely alone, and seeks to develop such stalwart health that the man who possesses it will enjoy immunity from the microbes.

This modern method of dealing with physical disease is borrowed from Christ's method of dealing with moral disease, and at once illustrates and enforces the wisdom of His therapeutics. He has come, it is true, to save men from sin; but He does it by giving them life and giving it more abundantly.

It is not the office of Christianity to destroy temptation, or remove men from it. There are doubtless times when this process is wise, as means to an end, but it is not the end. Whenever this method has been tried, as an end, it has invariably failed. This was the method of Puritanism. The cathedrals were leading to sensuous worship—they destroyed the cathedrals; the statues and the pictures were ministering to the baser passions of mankind— they destroyed the statues and the pictures; the novel and the drama were debasing the imagination—they drove the novel from the home and closed the doors of the theater; the dance had degenerated from an innocent frolic to an instrument of voluptuous vice, and they prohibited the dance. But all these which they shut out from society have come back again—dance, theater, novel, picture, stauary, cathedral. We believe that the Puritan was right in his time. Looking back at the life of England in the reign of Charles II, we cannot question that the Cavaliers would have corrupted and destroyed England, and that the Puritans saved it. But their expedients were only temporary expedients; the world's redemption will never be accomplished by such processes of prohibition. Why does not the church, cries out the prohibitionist, shut up the liquor shops and gambling hells? Because, we reply, it is engaged in more important business; it is engaged in making men and women so strong in their moral life that liquor shops and gambling hells can do them no harm. If it were to close the liquor shops and leave the appetite master of the man, it would render but little service. Mohammedanism prohibits all wine drinking, and the prohibition is measurably well enforced, certainly better than the Maine Law is enforced in Maine. Christianity does not prohibit wine drinking, and the use of wine is customary in all Christian countries. But there is far more of animalism, sensuality, bestiality, in Turkey, proportionately, without drinking or drunkenness, than there is in the United States with drinking and drunkenness. Already the Christian church has accomplished by moral hygiene substantial immunity from drunkenness among the men and women whom it influences. A drunken member of a Protestant Christian church, or even a Protestant Christian congregation, is rare.

As it is not the office of Christianity to remove men from temptation, nor temptation from men, so neither is it the office of

Christianity to rescue a few or many from the mastery of evil left dominant in the world. It does this rescue service, but its efficiency is not to be measured by the number of those it rescues, any more than the efficiency of an ocean steamer is to be measured by the number of its passengers who are saved from a watery grave by the life-belts which it carries. When the yellow fever breaks out in the South, we all admire the nurses and doctors who, at hazard of their life, go into the South to save such as they can from the epidemic. But science renders a higher service to humanity than this saving of a few from the ravages of disease. By clean streets, pure water, sunlighted apartments, it makes a city in which disease can find no lodgment because there is no soil in which its seed can grow. The heroism is less, but the beneficent result is greater. To give a city immunity from pestilence is a nobler service than to save some hundreds or even thousands from the pestilence which has been invited to the city.

Jesus Christ came, it is true, to seek and to save the lost; but He saves them, as we have said, by giving them life and giving it more abundantly. The rescue work of the church is not its chief work; and the church is not to be measured by the number of men who have experienced what is called conversion. Its chief work is hygienic—the creation of an atmosphere with moral ozone in it; the production of such a state of public sentiment that virtue will be easy and vice will be difficult; the presentation of an ideal before the community which leads it on, step by step, ever higher and yet higher; the re-enforcement of the conscience, the faith, the hope, the love; the making men strong as Christ was strong to live in the midst of temptation unsullied, able to be tempted and yet without sin.

The work of redemption is not an intercalatory process. It is not a net let down to the sea in which a few favored ones are caught to be snatched up into a higher life. It is the whole process of divine development, by which the water-grub becomes a winged creature, flying in another atmosphere. Its end is the kingdom of God by the creation of divine men. It is interpreted by Paul in the description of its final issue: "Till we all come in the unity of the faith and of the knowledge of the Son of God unto perfect manhood, unto the measure of the stature of the fullness of the Christ." This is the issue to be kept continually in

mind by preacher, teacher, parent. We may temporarily guard
the feeble from temptation too strong for them; we may occasionally rescue the fallen and set them on their feet again; but our
great work, the work to be kept constantly in view, the work
which animates us with an inspiring hope and an unfaltering
courage, is the work of making a world of men "immune" from
sin; the work of so developing, strengthening, equipping our congregations, our pupils, our children, that they shall fear no evil and
shall be able to say with the Master, "The prince of this world
cometh, and hath nothing in me."—Outlook.

A TRIBUTE TO CHRISTIANITY

P. T. Barnum, the great showman, traveled extensively, and
was a keen observer. He once delivered this testimony: "Show
me a place where there are not any churches, and where preachers
are never seen and I will show you a place where old hats are
stuffed into windows, where the gates have no hinges, where the
women are slipshod, and where maps of the devil's wild land are
printed on men's shirt bosoms with tobacco juice—that's what I
will show you. Let's consider what these things have done for us
before we lightly esteem them."

A PRACTICAL RELIGION

We want a religion that softens the step and tunes the voice to melody, that checks the impatient exclamation and harsh rebuke; a religion that is polite, deferential to superiors, courteous to inferiors, and considerate to friends; a religion that goes into the family, and keeps the husband from being cross when dinner is late, and keeps the wife from fretting when the husband tracks the newly-washed floor with his muddy boots, and makes husbands mindful of the scraper and the door mat; keeps the mother patient when the baby is cross, and amuses the children as well as instructs them; cares for the servants besides paying them promptly; projects the honeymoon into the harvest moon, and makes the happy home like the Eastern fig tree, bearing in its bosom at once the beauty of its tender blossoms and the glory of the ripened fruit. We want a religion that shall interpose between the ruts and gullies and rocks of the highway of life, and the sensitive souls that are traveling over them.

> If we knew whose feet were standing
> Close beside the silent stream,
> If we knew whose eyes were closing
> In the sleep that knows no dream,
> We should be so kind and tender.
> Lightly judge and gently speak!
> Let us act as if our vision
> Saw the links that swiftly break.

WHY BE A CHRISTIAN?

BY I. EDGAR JONES

Because man without God is a soul without guide. Because immortality makes of time, a fragment of eternity, a whole. Because pilgrims who must wander here want a home hereafter. Because every creed without Christ is cracked. Because the Bible with possible mistakes eliminated is the greatest of books, the richest mine for level minds. Because love is life. Because travelers on long journeys need beacons, and our Bible is the best. Because infidelity is destructive, not constructive; it pulls down, but cannot rebuild. Because life which progresses must look ahead. Because the universe proves the existence of God to eyes anointed with the gift of seeing. Because measureless deeps and unspanned spaces all denote a Creator of infinite power and magnificent purpose. Because the homes of true Christians most resemble the vestibules of Heaven. Because sinners need a Savior. Because absolute unbelief is impossible; doers cannot always doubt. Because every chrysalis conceals folded wings. Because a man mocking God is an exclamation point doubting the dictionary. Because souls are telescopic lenses and must reflect distant lights, stars and suns unseen by unaided eyes. Because a broad-gauge soul, wise and wide, needs two worlds, and plans for both.—Ram's Horn.

AUTHORS

—25C

TEXTS

TOPICS